SCIENCE, TECHNOLOGY, AND THE NUCLEAR ARMS RACE

SCIENCE, TECHNOLOGY, AND THE NUCLEAR ARMS RACE

DIETRICH SCHROEER
University of North Carolina

JOHN WILEY & SONS
New York   Chichester   Brisbane   Toronto   Singapore

Copyright © 1984, by John Wiley & Sons, Inc.

All rights reserved. Published simultaneously in Canada.

Reproduction or translation of any part of this work beyond that
permitted by Sections 107 and 108 of the 1976 United States
Copyright Act without the permission of the copyright owner is
unlawful. Requests for permission or further information should be
addressed to the Permissions Department, John Wiley & Sons.

Library of Congress Cataloging in Publication Data:

Schroeer, Dietrich.
  Science, technology, and the nuclear arms race.

  Includes indexes.
  1. Atomic weapons.   2. Atomic warfare.   3. Strategic
forces.   4. Military policy.   5. Deterrence (Strategy)
6. Ballistic missile defenses.   7. Atomic weapons and
disarmament.   I. Title.

U263.S37 1984   355'.0217   84-7379
ISBN 0-471-88141-4

Printed in the United States of America

10 9 8 7 6 5 4 3 2 1

Preface

This book examines the effects of modern scientific-technological developments on military strategy. The focus is on the nuclear arms race. This general interest survey is to provide some technical background, to explain the motivations behind the development of various nuclear arms technologies and their deployment, and to explore the effects of these technologies on military, political, and social strategies.

The goal of this book is technical literacy, not technical expertise. An understanding of the nuclear arms race does require a feeling for the magnitude of effects. Why can an A-bomb be weight-for-weight a million times more effective than TNT, and why can the explosive yield of an H-bomb be yet another factor of a thousand larger? What does the term "effective" mean? How may the nuclear power industry increase the danger of nuclear proliferation? What are likely to be the next developments in the nuclear arms race? The exposition of the science and technology of the nuclear arms race will consist of qualitative discussions, tables, graphs, and some order-of-magnitude arithmetic calculations.

Once a technology is understood, the question can be asked, Why did it develop when it did? Something causes advancements in science and technology to take place when they do and governs the directions **v** in which they progress. Why was the first A-bomb exploded in 1945? Why was the first artificial earth satellite launched in 1957? Why is one of the major new technical developments now the cruise missile? Both technical imperatives and social driving forces are involved in converting scientific possibilities into the reality of major new weapons systems. These conversion processes will be examined.

As each new technical development leads to new weapons, so do new weapons lead to new military, political, and social strategies. The American A-bomb initially offset the seemingly overwhelming Soviet conventional military power, and then the H-bomb led to deterrence. In time, satellites allowed verifiable determinations of the nuclear balance. Now the cruise missile is helping to resurrect the possibility of fighting a tactical nuclear war. The predictability and controllability of these strategies will be considered. These questions concerning technical aspects, motivation, and social consequences will be asked repeatedly about a wide range of nuclear arms race technologies.

Many books have been written in the past four decades about the nuclear arms race; why one more? The primary reason is that no book exists that comprehensively surveys the nuclear arms race from a technological perspective. There are two reasons for the lack of general survey books on such an important topic. Many authors who have written about the technologies of this issue are either directly involved in the arms race or are professional experts on some aspect of it. They have been secretaries of state or directors of research for the Department of Defense, or they are social scientists who have a deep expertise through original research. But overall considerations of the nuclear arms race involve more than expertise. A complete discussion of this topic requires a synthesis of technical understanding, an historical outlook, and an appreciation of political institutions. Expertise in some specific aspects of the arms race may make it difficult to place all the various aspects of the issue in proper perspective.

I have no direct professional expertise in any aspect of the arms race. Instead I combine a personal interest in the subject with some experience at synthesis. I was brought up (1938–1951) in Germany while it started a world war, lost it, and bore the consequences of strategic bombing—that precursor of nuclear war. Thereafter, I lived in the homeland of the first nuclear weapons and experienced the growth of the balance of terror. Thus, understanding strategic war is of personal importance to me. Professionally, I have worked on radiation therapy of cancer, received a Ph.D. in nuclear physics, and studied solid-state aspects of radiation-damage phenomena. This provides a peripheral technical interest in the nuclear arms race. As a teacher, I am interested in the relationship between science and public policy, having developed a course for nonscientists on the relationship between physics and society and having taught a political science course on science and public policy. In these courses I have had to transform expertise to make it understandable to a broad public and have had to go beyond the quantifiable facts to examine social motivations.

This book is an effort to synthesize the many aspects of the nuclear arms race into a comprehensive whole and to examine the significance of relevant facts. The synthesis comes in part through two questions that unite all aspects of this subject. "Is nuclear war different?" "Is the nuclear arms race inevitable?" War can be waged without the use of nuclear weapons, and human beings can readily be killed by other means. Is nuclear war more humane or could it destroy civilization or even *homo sapiens*? Can the science of the nuclear arms race, its application, or its deployment in weapons systems be controlled? These questions can be answered only by connecting the technologies with their social consequences.

This is not supposed to be a technical text. But one must understand why nuclear weapons are millions of times more effective and why they were developed at a particular time, in order to understand their social implications. The selection of specific topics from the repertoire of nuclear arms race issues was actually the easiest part of writing this book. There is a general consensus that nuclear weapons and their effects, delivery systems, the balance of terror, alternatives to deterrence, and arms control are critical topics. The comprehensive picture, and the translation into common sense, are to be the contribution of this book.

I am indebted to the Curriculum on Peace, War and Defense of the University of North Carolina for providing me with a Z. Smith Reynolds curriculum development grant to develop a course on the arms race. The National Endowment for the Humanities bears no direct responsibility for this work, but a fellowship I received from it in 1972 encouraged me to believe that I could translate technical expertise into more common terms. A variety of reviewers have shed much red ink over this manuscript. I would mention them by name to acknowledge the great help provided by their criticisms, except that such thanks might imply their agreement with all that is left. So I thank them all anonymously, except for David Hafemeister who has also been a supportive friend for a long time. I dedicate this book to my wife Bunny for her patience and her humanistic common sense.

Contents

PART 4 ARMS CONTROL AND DISARMAMENT 297

CHAPTER 13 Technological Imperatives 299

CHAPTER 14 Nuclear Proliferation: A Technological Imperative? 315

CHAPTER 15 Arms Control: Nuclear Test-Ban Treaties 346

SCIENCE, TECHNOLOGY, AND THE NUCLEAR ARMS RACE

Introduction

This book has been written to deal with the technologies of the nuclear arms race in qualitative and order-of-magnitude terms. The discussions will be tied together by two themes of magnitude and control.

The first theme of this book is related to the magnitude of the nuclear arms race and asks the question whether nuclear war is different from conventional warfare. People have killed each other in wars with great effect long before the discovery of nuclear weapons. It has been estimated that during the 30-year religious war in the first half of the seventeenth century, as many as three-fourths of the inhabitants of some German states were killed by one or the other of the combatant groups. The federal armies in the American Civil War had 279,600 fatalities. In World War I the British suffered 370,000 casualties in the battles at Ypres; from 1914 to 1918 France lost 1,400,000 men dead and 4,500,000 wounded out of a total population of 40 million. In World War II mass slaughter took place not only on the battlefield, but also in homes and in concentration camps. At least 20 million soldiers and civilians were killed, not counting the 6 million victims of the holocaust. Why then has the threatened nuclear war so far led to deterrence, where previous arms races have led to world wars?

There is a quantitative difference in the magnitude of the total nuclear war that is now considered by many to be the likely outcome of any major conflict between the United States and the Soviet Union. It has been estimated that the present world stockpile of nuclear weapons, including those immediately deliverable plus stores of old and new weapons, represents an explosive capability of more than 50,000 megatons (Mt) (equivalent in explosive power to 50,000,000,000 tons of TNT, trinitrotoluene), compared with the 2 Mt exploded during the bombing campaigns of World War II. This current nuclear stockpile represents the equivalent of 10 tons of TNT per man, woman, and child on this earth. Of course, these explosives would not be evenly distributed over the world's population in the event of a war; those in the large cities of the major nations might be subject to overkill, whereas underdeveloped countries might not be targeted. But 50,000 Mt is a large amount of explosive power, no matter how it is distributed.

While he was Secretary of State, Robert S. McNamara reported during the antiballistic missile debate in 1969 that the number of fatalities in an all-out strategic nuclear exchange in the mid-1970s might be 120 million each for the United States and the Soviet Union. That would be one-half the population of both nations. The proposed minimum requirement for deterrence is to have left, even after a Soviet all-out surprise attack (first strike), enough retaliatory weapons to kill at least one-fourth of the Russian population and to destroy at least one-half of Soviet industrial capacity. These numbers of fatalities are overwhelmingly larger than any experienced in previous wars.

There is also a qualitative difference between nuclear war and previous wars using high-energy chemical explosives. The immediate radiations and radioactive fallout produced by nuclear bombs are not felt during exposure to them, so that their impact is more insidious. Their effects are judged somehow to be more horrible than those of chemical explosives; they produce both prompt radiation sickness and long-term effects of genetic mutations and induced cancers that may appear 20 or more years later. The large-scale use of nuclear bombs also may produce psychological effects. Their use is most likely to occur without prior warning; the radius of total destruction of a typical nuclear bomb will be measured in kilometers rather than in meters. The resulting intensity of psychological shock may be very great, and the circle of total social collapse may be very large. In Hiroshima and Nagasaki, the A-bomb explosions led to a breakdown in personal discipline and social order; some of the A-bomb victims even after 30 years have not recovered completely from these psychological effects.

Finally, total nuclear war threatens civilization. Some studies, such as the 1975 report by the National Academy of Science, may sound mildly reassuring when their findings seem to show that in a future major nuclear war *homo sapiens* will survive. Others, such as the 1983 "nuclear winter" report of Turco et al., are much more pessimistic. When the effects of the radiation from the exploded bombs on the earth's ozone layer is taken into account, it appears likely that significantly increased ultraviolet radiation may reach the earth's surface, particularly in the northern hemisphere, leading to increases in skin cancers, injuries to plant life, and even sunburn blisters for relatively short exposure times. The soot from burning cities may block most of the sunlight, leading to the death of much plant life. A full-scale nuclear war at the very least threatens modern industrial civilization.

The second theme of this book is the question of whether or not the nuclear arms race can be controlled. I have a belief in a certain inevitability of scientific-technological progressions. Consider the following example of what one might call a technological imperative. The cruise missile is one of the most technologically sophisticated current military developments. It is an unmanned self-propelled bomb flying subsonically at low altitudes, derived from the V-1 of World War II and the Regulus and Snark of the 1950s. One reason that the present cruise missile is so revolutionary is its tremendous accuracy; the new cruise missile guides itself toward its target by comparing its observations of the terrain over which it flies with the preprogrammed path on a pre-recorded road map. The accuracy of such a missile may be measured in tens of meters. This improvement in the weapon was inevitable as map-reading computers could be made small enough to fit within the small volume of the missile warhead. Once the technology of the cruise missile became feasible, the pressure to develop and deploy the missile was irresistible.

The progress of much of the science and technology of the nuclear arms race appears inevitable. The rate of progress can to some extent be modified, but probably not its ultimate direction. It is hoped that the application of technology to strategy, the actual deployment of weapons systems, can be controlled. The history of the nuclear arms race may tell how society can exercise that control.

References

National Academy of Sciences, Committee to Study the Long-Term Worldwide Effects of Multiple Nuclear-Weapons Detonations. *Long-Term Worldwide Effects of Multiple Nuclear-Weapons Detonations.* Washington, D.C.: NAS, 1975.

Turco, R. P. et al. "Nuclear Winter: Global Consequences of Multiple Nuclear Explosions." *Science* Vol. 222 (1983), pp. 1283–1292.

NUCLEAR ARMS

The world has not been the same since the first nuclear device was exploded in 1945. Nuclear weapons have changed not only balances of power, but even the nature of these balances. Massive and assured destruction of populations and industry through nuclear weapons may have made full-scale nuclear war unthinkable, though unfortunately, not impossible.

The first part of this text tells how the capability for massive, assured destruction came about. It deals with the development of strategic bombing doctrines, the release of energy through nuclear fission and fusion, and the building of A-bombs and H-bombs. It describes the technical revolution producing nuclear weapons and the decisions made by people concerning their development and use.

Chemical explosives will be discussed. The concept of strategic bombing, that is, the recognition of the military usefulness of very large—even if inaccurate—explosives came from World War II. The first large-scale strategic attacks on civilian populations and their consequences will be discussed, to answer the question whether World War II can provide a guide to the efficacy of nuclear strategic bombing.

The nuclear fission A-bombs of World War II are discussed on several levels. First, the technology of nuclear fission devices is described, that is, how they work, how they are made, and what effects they have. Then, the nuclear physics and engineering of A-bombs are discussed on a order- **5** of-magnitude basis. The effects of nuclear weapons are analyzed using the information from their use at Hiroshima and Nagasaki. Important questions raised are whether the development of nuclear weapons was inevitable, whether their use was controllable. Nuclear weapons now exist; does this mean that their technological improvement and deployment will uncontrollably continue?

The nuclear fusion H-bomb multiplied the effects of the A-bomb by as much as a 1000-fold. The technology of fusion bombs is reviewed. Efforts were made to guide the development of this larger weapon and to submit it to political control from the beginning; why did these control efforts fail?

Finally, the possible large-scale destruction created by nuclear weapons will be explored. Targeting lists for nuclear warheads will be discussed; how many fatalities can be caused and how much industrial capacity can be destroyed by a given amount of nuclear explosives? These calculations shed light on the question of what level of threatened destruction is sufficient to deter an enemy from some undesired course of action, that is, "How much is enough?" Can humankind survive a full-scale nuclear war?

CHAPTER
1

Nonnuclear Strategic War

A complete breakdown of the social structure cannot but take place in a country subjected to this kind of merciless pounding from the air.

Guilio Douhet, Italian general, 1921

The nineteenth-century Prussian military analyst, Karl Maria von Clausewitz, said after the Napoleonic wars that war is a continuation of politics by other means. Does this statement hold for nuclear war? To answer that question, the effects of nuclear war must be compared with those of nonnuclear war. Nonnuclear wars have been fought with swords, bows and arrows, bullets, chemicals, and high-energy chemical explosives. A person can be killed by as little as one inhaled milligram of some biological toxins, by one ingested gram of some chemicals, by a few grams of lead that penetrate the body as a bullet, by a tenth of a kilogram of chemical explosives such as trinitrotoluene (TNT) that spreads the splinters from a handgrenade at a distance of a few meters, or by a ton of TNT that collapses a building.

The explosive yield of the smallest deployed nuclear weapon is equivalent to the explosive effects of about 100 tons of TNT. Strategic bombing during World War II is the closest analog to nuclear explosions: the high-energy chemical explosives carried by hundreds of aircraft provide a scale for nuclear energy release, and the extensive area bombing of cities gives some information about the possible "effectiveness" of nuclear weaponry.

7

CHEMICAL EXPLOSIVES

Chemical energy is atomic energy, released when electrons from one atom are transferred to another. In a highly simplified model, the atom can be pictured as a miniature solar system. In the center is a positively charged nucleus (analogous to the sun), surrounded by a number of electrons (analogous to planets). The chemical properties of an atom are determined by the electrons in orbit around the nucleus.

A typical chemical reaction is the union of one carbon atom with two oxygen atoms. The nuclei of the atoms are not involved in this reaction; the reaction proceeds by a sharing of electrons to make a molecule. The carbon atom shares four electrons with the two oxygen atoms; this sharing makes the CO_2 molecule more stable (lower in potential energy) than are the separate components of carbon and oxygen. Thus, the reaction releases energy in the process called burning. The energy released in burning carbon and oxygen is typical in magnitude for chemical processes.

This energy can be expressed in a variety of ways. On an atomic scale one talks in terms of electron volts (eV). A battery made out of carbon and oxygen will have an electrical potential of about 4 volts (V), nearly as much as three 1½-V flashlight batteries in series. The production of one molecule of carbon dioxide from carbon and oxygen, therefore, is said to release 4 eV of energy. The magnitude of this energy is typical of that released in many chemical reactions; for example, the burning of one hydrogen atom with two oxygen atoms to make one molecule of water releases 3 eV. The process of photosynthesis requires about 2 eV of energy, and particles (photons) of visible light each carry 2 eV to 3 eV of energy. In contrast, reactions involving the nucleus release typically millions of electron volts (MeV) of energy.

Trinitrotoluene (TNT) has the chemical formula $C_6H_2(CH_3)(NO_2)_3$. When it explodes, the carbon, hydrogen and nitrogen in it combine with the oxygen to produce various oxides. These are all gases, so that in the explosion, the volume of the TNT very rapidly increases 1000-fold, producing the blast effect. The burning of one molecule of TNT releases about 10 eV of energy. On a macroscopic scale in the explosion of 1 kilogram (kg) of TNT, about 1000 kilocalories (kcal) or $4.2 \cdot 10^6$ joules (J) are released. The typical energy consumption of an active person is about 4000 kcal, the energy released in exploding 1 kg of TNT would keep a human being active for 6 hours (hr). The 1000 kcal in 1 kg of TNT could raise 1 tonne (metric ton)[1] of mass by about 400 meters (m) or keep a 50-watt (W) light bulb burning for one day.

---

[1] One U.S. ton (2000 lb) ~0.9 metric tonne, since 1 kg = 2.2 lb.

STRATEGIC BOMBING

These energies provide a scale against which to compare nuclear energies. But the effectiveness of chemical weapons is determined not only by the amount of energy applied, but also by the method of application. Biological weapons are powerful in the sense that they are specifically targeted on people, so that very small quantities of the weapons can produce fatal effects. In contrast, high-energy explosive bombs are less effective, in the sense that they are not very specific and must be applied in much larger quantities to be fatal. This combination of low specificity and large required quantities makes the bombing effort of World War II somewhat analogous to nuclear war; strategic bombing can be used at least as an initial point of reference for estimating some of the effects of nuclear war.

In 1921 the Italian Brigadier General Guilio Douhet published *The Command of the Air*, in which he argued that aggressive large-scale aerial bombing would win future wars, particularly by city bombardment:

> the effect of such aerial offensives upon morale may well have more influence
> upon the conduct of the war than their material effects. (Douhet, 1942, pp. 57–58)

By the time World War II broke out, airplane technology had progressed enough to make possible large-scale bombing along the lines conceived by Douhet.

In World War II two types of aerial bombardment were carried out: precision bombing and area bombing. Precision bombing had as its objective the destruction of military installations and militarily important industry through the precise distribution of explosives on the target. Thus the Schweinfurt air raid of 1943 was intended to wipe out the German ball-bearing industry, to cripple thereby all other industries. Such precision bombing was called strategic at the time, but it is now generally referred to as tactical bombing. The word "tactical" will be used in this sense from now on. Later it will be related to terms such as counterforce strikes and battlefield weapons. Precision bombing in World War II was not as successful as had been anticipated. The accuracy of bombing was often low due to the high altitude of the bombing runs, and the 10-ton limit on the bombs that could be carried by the bombers limited the ability to destroy machinery in the industrial plants unless direct hits were scored.

Human habitations, however, were vulnerable to saturation area bombing of cities. When many bombs were dropped simultaneously on large "soft" housing complexes, the accuracy of the bombing was not so critical, particularly if incendiary bombs could be used to set buildings on fire. In several incendiary bombing raids, targeting as many as 2000 tons of firebombs on a single city, firestorms were started (Fig. 1.1). In these firestorms, the combustion in the center of the cities was so intense that the central updraft led to a rush of air along the ground toward the burning center. The resulting hurricane-force winds fanned the flames, producing central temperatures of thousands of degrees. These firestorms were very deadly, killing tens of thousands of inhabitants in these cities and totally burning the central districts. For example, 40 square kilometers (km^2) were razed in the fire raid on Tokyo in March of 1943. When firestorms did not get started, the incendiary bombs could still produce conflagrations in which separate fires would unite to burn cities section by section, as illustrated by Fig. 1.2.

Ultimately, much of the World War II bomber offensive became concentrated on area bombing, what is now generally called strategic bombing. In this book the term "strategic bombing" will be used to describe targeting civilian homes and nonmilitary industries. It will later be related to the term "countervalue targeting." The area bombing of cities became policy with the objective of destroying homes, thereby either killing the civilian work force or at least ruining the morale of the enemy population and, in particular, of the industrial worker by driving them out of the cities. Strategic bombing forces, made up of as

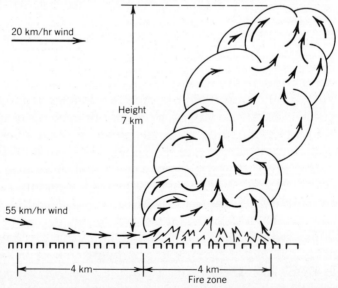

Figure 1.1 Firestorms occur when many individual fires in a city combine into one all-consuming fire, creating an updraft in the center of the fire and sucking air inward along the ground. In 1943 Hamburg was destroyed by the firestorm sketched here.

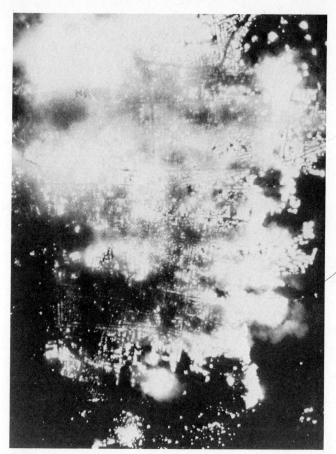

Figure 1.2 Night view of burning Toyama, Japan, after an incendiary attack on August 1, 1945. Ninety-five percent of the city was destroyed in one night, and 10,000 people were killed. (U.S. Air Force Photo.)

many as a thousand planes each carrying 5 or more tons of high explosives and incendiaries, bombarded the centers of many German and Japanese cities throughout the war. Altogether about 2 million tons of bombs (2 Mt) were dropped during World War II; the resulting fatalities were nearly one million persons, mostly civilians.

This experience with strategic bombing provides a scale against which future nuclear strategic (or countervalue) bombardment of civilian populations can be measured. Will nuclear weaponry present the same difficulty of precision targeting, making soft civilian targets attractive? Did the strategic area bombing of World War II have enough effect to give some indication that any strategic nuclear bombing might be effective? Some of the bombing raids of World War II were gruesomely effective in raising firestorms, as in Hamburg, Tokyo and

Dresden, where, respectively, about 40,000, 100,000 (Caidin, 1960), and 150,000 (Irving, 1963) people were killed.

The killing of civilians had no critical industrial effects in World War II. The total work forces in urban areas did not drop significantly, as shown in Fig. 1.3, although many nonessential dependents were evacuated out to the countryside. Compared with proposed production increases, some industrial outputs may have suffered up to 30% losses. However, industrial production of vital items such as friction bearings rose in Germany during the height of the bombing campaign, as shown in Fig. 1.4, dropping only when territories were lost. Morale among bombed civilians did drop, but it is doubtful that this drop significantly affected industrial output. In Japan the large-scale strategic bombing may have created a climate of fear that allowed the A-bombs to have maximum psychological impact, but the extent of that impact is unmeasurable. Strategic bombing inspired no revolt against the leadership in either Germany or Japan.

Area bombing of cities killed many civilians during World War II. However, it is difficult to prove by any cost-benefit calculations that such strategic bombing shortened the war by an amount worthy of the efforts that went into it. In Germany the 500,000 civilian fatalities cost the lives of 150,000 Allied airmen, although considerable military personnel was tied up in operating antiaircraft defenses. Bombers

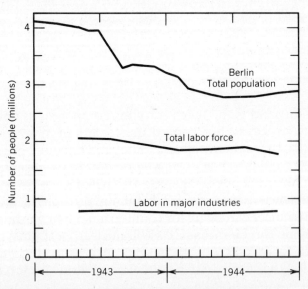

Figure 1.3 The population and work force in Berlin during World War II. The sudden decrease in 1943 was due to the evacuation of women and children. (After Iklé, 1958, Figure 10, p. 178.)

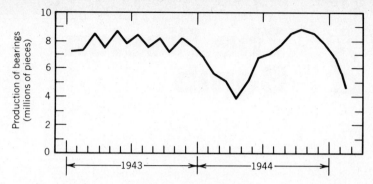

Figure 1.4 The production of friction bearings in Germany during World War II. (After U.S. Strategic Bombing Survey, 1945, Chart 14, p. 28.)

might have been used more profitably in tactical attacks on electric generating facilities. Alternatively, the Allied industrial production devoted to building bombers might have been better utilized in producing patrol planes to aid in antisubmarine warfare.

References

Caidin, M. *A Torch to the Enemy: The Fire Raid on Tokyo*. New York: Ballantine Books, 1960. A firestorm resembling the effects of a nuclear weapons explosion.

Douhet, G. *The Command of the Air*, trans. by D. Ferrari from the second Italian edition of 1927. New York: Coward-McCann, 1942.

Iklé, F. C. *The Social Impact of Bomb Destruction*. Norman: University of Oklahoma Press, 1958.

Irving, D. *The Destruction of Dresden*. New York: Ballantine Books, 1963. Irving's fatality figures for this firestorm are disputed in *Dresden im Luftkrieg* (Koeln: Boehlander Verlag, 1977), by G. Bergander, who places the number of fatalities nearer 35,000 on the basis of local German records.

U.S. Strategic Bombing Survey. *Strategic Bombing in World War II: Overall Report*. Washington, D.C.: Government Printing Office, 1945.

Verrier, A. *The Bomber Offensive*. New York: Macmillian, 1969 (1968).

Zinsser, H. *Rats, Lice and History*. Boston: Little, Brown, 1935. War has always been hell.

The Fission Bomb

Figure 2.1 The mushroom cloud of the nuclear bomb explosion over Hiroshima. (Photo courtesy Los Alamos Scientific Laboratory.)

On August 6, 1945 the first nuclear weapon was used in war; the fissioning of ^{235}U inside a 5-ton bomb, dropped by a high-altitude B-29 bomber, destroyed the Japanese city of Hiroshima (see Fig. 2.1). Nuclear explosives have not completely superseded chemical explosives in wartime bombing since that time. For example, the tonnage of high-energy chemical bombs dropped during the Vietnam War exceeded that of World War II. But nuclear weapons have raised the potential destructiveness of bombing to a new height, thereby introducing vast new military and political implications.

The nature of nuclear fission and the history of the fission bomb (the A-bomb) will be sketched in this chapter. Besides outlining the effects of nuclear explosions, the purpose will be to raise the questions whether the A-bomb represents an inevitable weapons development and whether the A-bomb is a qualitatively different weapon (and hence perhaps unusable in some kinds of war).

The history of the Manhattan District, the project of World War II that produced the first nuclear bombs, will then be briefly reviewed. That history will clarify whether the A-bomb was a scientific stroke of genius or a technological triumph. The effects of the A-bomb will be summarized in four parts, the physical destruction of structures and living things, the physiological damage to people, the psychological impact, and the political consequences. A review of the military situation in Japan in the summer of 1945, and of the Japanese response to the nuclear attacks, will focus on the question of whether the A-bomb is indeed a different weapon and whether its use was inevitable. Finally, the aftermath of World War II will show to what extent this new weapon could be placed under political control.

NUCLEAR FISSION

Isotopes

The energy released in the nuclear fission process comes from changes in the nuclei of atoms such as uranium and plutonium. The electrons in an atom control its chemical behavior. In contrast, the nuclear properties of an atom are determined by the number of protons and neutrons in its nucleus. The neutron is a nucleon carrying no charge, whereas the proton is a nucleon carrying a positive charge equal, but opposite in sign, to that of the electron. Both the proton and the neutron have masses about 1830 times that of the electron.

One can talk about the rest masses of these nucleons (their masses when they are not moving) in terms of an equivalent energy. Einstein's famous equation states that $E = mc^2$. This relationship says that if a mass is converted into energy, the released energy E is given by the mass m multiplied by c^2, the speed of light squared. The mass of one neutron is equivalent to an energy of 939.6 million electron volts (939.6 MeV); the proton's mass is equivalent to 938.8 MeV. In comparison, the electron's mass is equivalent to only 0.511 MeV. An element has different isotopes if several nuclei exist in which the number of protons (and hence the number of electrons) are the same, but the number of neutrons are different. The chemical properties of the various isotopes of a given element will be the same because they all have the same number of protons and hence of electrons. But the nuclear properties of the various isotopes of a given element will be different since they have different numbers of neutrons. An element X with Z protons and N neutrons is labeled by the symbol $^A_Z X$, where $A = N + Z$ is the atomic mass, the number of nucleons in the nucleus.

The element hydrogen can illustrate the concept of isotopes, as shown in Fig. 2.2. Ordinary hydrogen $^1_1 H$ makes up 99.985% of all naturally occurring hydrogen. The nucleus of this isotope is made up of a single proton. It is stable or nonradioactive; its nucleus does not change over the lifetime of the universe. The heavy hydrogen isotope $^2_1 H$, called deuterium ($^2 D$), makes up 0.014% of natural hydrogen. It has two nucleons in the nucleus: one proton and one neutron. It also is stable. A third isotope of hydrogen is superheavy hydrogen $^3_1 H$, called tritium ($^3 T$). It contains one proton and two neutrons in the nucleus.

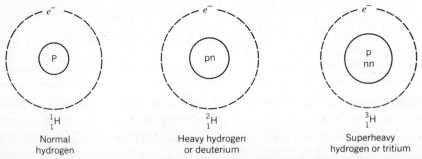

| Normal | Heavy hydrogen | Superheavy |
| hydrogen | or deuterium | hydrogen or tritium |

Figure 2.2 The isotopes of hydrogen are all characterized by $Z = 1$ since they each have one proton in the nucleus; their chemical characteristics are therefore essentially the same. However, they are characterized by different atomic masses $A = Z + N$ since they each have a different number N of neutrons in the nucleus; their nuclear properties are quite different.

Tritium is found in minute quantities in all water, where it is constantly being created by cosmic radiation. Tritium is radioactive, or unstable. During its radioactive decay process, a nucleus of ^{3}H emits an electron, converting to ^{3}He, as the *n-n-p* nucleus goes to *n-p-p*. The emitted electron has a maximum energy of 18.6 keV (18,600 eV). The decay process is characterized by a half-life of $T_{1/2}$ = 12.3 years. This means that the number of tritium nuclei decreases in the exponential manner shown in Fig. 2.3, being reduced by a factor of two every 12.3 years. If at some time there are some number N_0 of ^{3}H atoms, then after each successive 12.3 years, only half as many will be left; the remainder will have become atoms of ^{3}He. If in January 1985 A.D. there are 100,000 ^{3}H atoms, then by May 1997 A.D. 50,000 ^{3}H atoms remain and 50,000 ^{3}He atoms will have been produced. In September 2009 A.D. there will be 25,000 ^{3}H atoms and 75,000 ^{3}He atoms, in December 2021 A.D. 12,500 ^{3}H atoms and 87,500 ^{3}He atoms, and so on. The chemical properties of H, D, and T are essentially identical, so that they can form H_2O (normal water), D_2O (heavy water), and T_2O (superheavy water). But their nuclear properties are not the same; H and D are stable, whereas T is radioactive. Each radioactive isotope is characterized by a specific half-life, with the decay process following the curve of Fig. 2.3. Tritium has a half-life of 12.3 years. In fact, the only tritium to be found in nature is that which has been created recently (in the last decades) artificially in nuclear reactors and accelerators or in natural nuclear reactions induced by the cosmic rays that constantly bombard the earth.

The element strontium forms a more complex series of isotopes. All strontium (Sr) isotopes have Z = 38; that is, all have 38 protons in the nucleus, and hence all neutral Sr atoms have 38 electrons in orbit

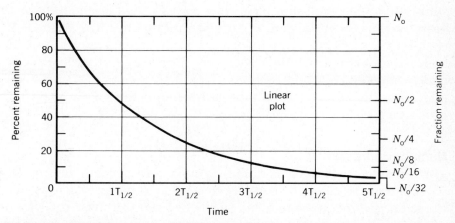

Figure 2.3 Plot of the exponential decay of an initial quantity N_0 of some parent isotope A with a half-life $T_{1/2}$.

Table 2.1 Isotopes relevant to the nuclear arms race, together with some of their more important properties.[a]

Isotope	Half-life	Emissions	Major Properties
^{2}H	Stable	None	Fuel for the H-bomb
^{3}H	12.3 years	β: 18.6 keV; γ: 550 keV	Fuel for the H-bomb
^{6}Li	Stable	None	Produce T by ^{6}Li + $n \rightarrow$ ^{3}H + ^{4}He
^{9}B	Stable	None	H-bomb tamper
^{14}C	5730 years	β: 156 kev	Produced from air by A-bombs
^{90}Sr	28 years	β: 546 keV; γ: 2.3 MeV	Fission product, bone seeker
^{131}I	8.05 days	β: 606 kev; γ: 364 keV	Fission product, thyroid seeker
^{137}Cs	30 years	β: 514 keV; γ: 662 keV	Fission product
^{233}U	165 kyrs	α: 5.3 MeV	Fissile material
^{235}U	710 Myrs	α: 4.4 MeV; γ: 185 keV	Fissile material, 0.7% of natural U
^{238}U	4500 Myrs	α: 4.2 MeV	"Contaminant" of ^{235}U
^{239}Pu	24.4 kyrs	α: 5.16 MeV	Fissile material
^{240}Pu	6580 yrs	α: 5.17 MeV	"Contaminant" of ^{239}Pu
^{242}Pu	380 kyrs	α: 4.9 MeV	"Contaminant" of ^{239}Pu

[a]The symbols kyrs and Myrs stand for 1000 and 1 million yr, respectively.

around the nucleus. But the number of neutrons in the strontium nucleus can range from less than 42 to more than 57, so that A can range from 80 to 95. $^{84}_{38}$Sr, $^{86}_{38}$Sr, and $^{88}_{38}$Sr are stable. The radioactive strontium isotope most relevant to the nuclear arms race is $^{90}_{38}$Sr. ^{90}Sr decays with a half-life of 28 years to $^{90}_{39}$Y by emitting an electron with up to 550 keV in energy; ^{90}Y in turn decays further with a half-life of 64 hours (hr) to $^{90}_{40}$Zr by emitting yet another high-energy electron. It is used in nuclear medicine; the electrons it emits are used to treat skin cancers. It is most significant because it is produced in nuclear fission reactions; it accumulates inside nuclear reactors and is a component of the fallout resulting from the explosion of nuclear devices. Its long half-life of 28 years (yr) makes it dangerous for a long time after it is formed. Its chemical similarity to calcium causes it to accumulate in growing bones; the electrons it emits have a very short range—they specifically damage the sensitive bone marrow. Table 2.1 presents a list of isotopes relevant to the nuclear arms race and some of their more important properties.

Nuclear Radiation

When a radioactive nucleus decays, it emits particles and energy. The particles can be charged, such as electrons, or neutral such as neutrons; the energy can be released as kinetic energy of these particles or as photons in the form of γ rays, x rays, or light. Depending on the decaying isotope, the most likely emissions from nuclear decay processes are alpha particles, beta particles, gamma rays, and x rays.

Alpha particles (α) are positively charged helium nuclei $^4\text{He}^{2+}$: they are emitted in the decay of some heavy nuclei such as plutonium. Their mass is about four times that of a proton.

Beta particles (β^-) are negatively charged electrons (e^-) emitted when a neutron in the nucleus decays into a proton (p^+) in the reaction $^1_0n \rightarrow {}^1_1p^+ + {}^0_{-1}\beta^-$. A neutral particle called a neutrino is released at the same time, but it has essentially no effect on physical material and hence has no relevance to the nuclear arms race.

Gamma rays (γ rays) are bits of energy released during nuclear decays; they are very energetic particles of light (photons) and carry energies up to several million electron volts (compared with the several electron volts for visible light).

X rays are also photons. They can be emitted in nuclear decays, but they can also be produced by bombarding materials with electrons. Their energy is generally in the kilo-electron-volt range. Protons are emitted in some very rare nuclear decays. Neutrons are emitted in nuclear fission reactions and very rarely through spontaneous fission of a few isotopes such as ^{240}Pu. Some radioactive decays involve the release of positrons (β^+) that have the mass of an electron but carry a single positive charge.

Besides the charges and the energy-mass relationships of these nuclear emissions, one important characteristic is their ability to penetrate various materials. Charged particles, including the alpha and the beta particles, have relatively short ranges; at the end of these ranges, they all come to a stop. A typical 4-MeV alpha particle travels a few thousandths of a centimeter (cm) in water or body tissue (the thickness of a sheet of paper), or about 2.5 cm in air, before it stops. Typical 500-keV electrons have a range of about 0.2 cm in water or body tissue and a range of about 3 meters (m) in air. Gamma rays and x rays do not have sharply defined ranges. Rather, they are absorbed exponentially by the material through which they pass. Thus their penetration can be characterized by a half-thickness, by the amount of material that is required to reduce the beam intensity by a factor of two. Typical 30-keV x rays and 1.5-MeV gamma rays, respectively, have half-thicknesses in air of about 15 m and 105 m; in water and body tissue of 0.9 cm and 12.5 cm; in concrete 0.25 cm and 6 cm; and in iron 0.01 cm and 1.8 cm. The neutrons from a fission bomb resemble fission gamma rays in absorption characteristics, except that their absorption half-thicknesses are about two-thirds as large and any hydrogen-containing material, such as water, absorbs them very well.

The Fission Process

The energies released in nuclear processes are about a million times as large as those from chemical processes; beta-particle and gamma-ray energies are on the order of approximately 1 MeV compared with the few electron volts released in chemical reactions. Releasing nuclear energies in a useful way however, is difficult. Chemical energy can often be readily extracted: a wood fire in which carbon is oxydized is easily started. In contrast, the extraction of energy on a very large scale from radioactive decays is not feasible. The rate of radioactive decay cannot be controlled (the half-life cannot be effectively changed), and it is difficult to gather enough radioactive atoms to make the spontaneously released energy useful. (Some space vehicles do use radioactive decay energies to produce small amounts of electric power.) The discovery, understanding, and control of fission ultimately made possible the large-scale release of nuclear energy.

Nuclear fission takes place when a nucleus splits (fissions) into two or more components. Fission reactions are most likely for nuclei with large Z and A. Neutron decay is a rare phenomenon; fission was not observed until it was artificially induced by neutron bombardment. Beginning in 1934, the Italian physicist Enrico Fermi bombarded all the elements he could obtain with neutrons and studied the end product of the reactions. Neutrons carry no charge, so they are not electrostatically repelled when aimed at a positively charged nucleus; therefore, they can readily penetrate into the nucleus. When Fermi bombarded uranium with neutrons, he observed some strange decay products, which he thought to be new superheavy transuranic elements.

In 1938 Otto Hahn and Fritz Strassman in Berlin finally correctly identified the products as lighter nuclei resulting from fission reactions. The neutrons caused uranium atoms to split into two smaller nuclei, as in the reaction

$$\,^{1}_{0}n \,+\, ^{235}_{92}U \rightarrow\, ^{102}_{42}Mo \,+\, ^{131}_{50}Sn \,+\, 3\,^{1}_{0}n \,+\, \text{energy}$$

One of the two product nuclei is generally slightly heavier than the other. The most typical fission reaction produces two isotopes with atomic mass 95 and 138. The products of the fission reaction generally are not stable. Because they are rich in neutrons, they quickly decay (typically by beta emission) to other isotopes, often in a sequence of decays, as does

$$^{131}_{50}Sn \xrightarrow{(\beta^-)} \,^{131}_{51}Sb \xrightarrow{(\beta^-)} \,^{131}_{52}Te \xrightarrow{(\beta^-)} \,^{131}_{53}I \xrightarrow{(\beta^-)} \,^{131}_{54}Xe$$

In the fission reaction just shown, a mass equal to that of 0.2 nucleons is lost, as it is converted into energy. The percentage of 0.2 nucleons out of 235 nucleons is $0.2/235 \simeq 0.1\%$. The mass of one nucleon corresponds to about 939 MeV, so the conversion of the mass of 0.2 nucleons into energy produces an energy release of about 0.2×939 MeV = 187 MeV. This energy release can be compared with that produced in the chemical production of water from hydrogen and oxygen. Correcting for the different masses of the reactants, and comparing the energy released per nucleon in the reactions, gives

$$\frac{E(\text{fission})}{E(\text{burning})} = \frac{188 \text{ MeV}/238 \text{ nucleons}}{3 \text{ eV}/18 \text{ nucleons}} = 4.7 \text{ million}$$

The nuclear fission process releases nearly 5 million times more energy per unit mass as does a chemical process. By definition (Glasstone and Dolon, 1977), the explosion of 1 kiloton (kt) of TNT is said to release as much energy as the complete fissioning of 0.056 kilogram (kg) of fissionable material (or $1.45 \cdot 10^{23}$ nuclei) and is equal to 10^{12} kcal, $4.2 \cdot 10^{12}$ joules (J), $1.15 \cdot 10^{6}$ kilowatt hours (kw h), or $3.97 \cdot 10^{9}$ British thermal units (Btu).

Not only is a large amount of energy released in fission reactions, but more neutrons are released than are absorbed. This makes possible a chain reaction to tap the nuclear energy. Some neutrons impinging on fissionable nuclei are absorbed to create some new isotope. But many neutrons captured by fissionable nuclei do lead to fission reactions. A given fissionable isotope can fission many ways, each yielding different numbers of product neutrons. The parameter of importance for sustaining a chain reaction is the average number η of neutrons released by a given isotope for each neutron that is absorbed.

Table 2.2 shows this average number η of neutrons released for various isotopes under bombardment with either slow or fast neutrons. For ^{239}Pu each fission actually releases 2.89 neutrons; but only 72% of all slow-neutron captures lead to fission. Hence, an average of η = 2.08 neutrons are released for each captured slow neutron. Table 2.2 shows, for example, when a fission event in natural uranium is initiated by a high-energy (fast) neutron coming from a nuclear explosion,

Table 2.2 The average number η of neutrons released by various isotopes per thermal (slow) and fast (high-energy) neutrons absorbed.

Isotope	η (n released per n captured)	
	Slow Neutrons	Fast Neutrons
U-233	2.29	2.45
U-235	2.07	2.3
U-238	0	0.97
Natural uranium	1.34	1.02
Pu-239	2.08	2.45

then the number of neutrons produced in an ideal case is hardly larger than the number that are absorbed: since $\eta = 1.02$ is only slightly larger than 1, an explosive chain reaction cannot be sustained. To maintain a chain reaction in natural uranium, the neutrons must be thermalized (reduced in velocity to that of room temperature thermal vibrations); then η is much larger than 1. Both ^{235}U and ^{239}Pu have η greater than 1 for bombardment with high-energy neutrons. Hence they can sustain explosive chain reactions. Since ^{239}Pu has an η larger than that of ^{235}U, it is easier to generate a chain reaction in a mass of ^{239}Pu.

Fission provides the means for releasing nuclear energy in a controlled way. Using the neutron amplification of the fission reaction, a sustained fission "burning" in a chain reaction becomes possible. Figure 2.4 sketches the process of a chain reaction. In each step of the chain, the number of nuclei fissioning increases by a factor called the

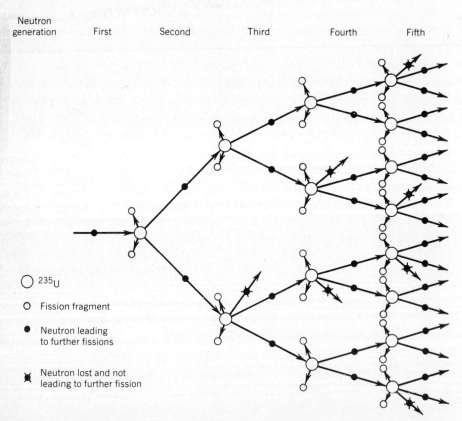

Figure 2.4 Sketch of a chain reaction in ^{235}U assuming an average of 2.5 neutrons released per fission event and a loss on the average of 1 out of 5 neutrons through absorption or escape from the fissioning mass.

neutron multiplication factor. If the chain reaction increases in size by a factor of two during every generation, then after about 80 generations 1 kg of fissionable material will have fissioned. This neutron multiplication factor is designed to be large, as close to η as possible. The design objective of a nuclear explosive is to fission the whole fissionable mass as quickly as possible, within a millionth of a second or so. In a nuclear reactor by design the neutron multiplication factor is maintained essentially at 1.

WAS THE KNOWLEDGE OF NUCLEAR WEAPONS INEVITABLE?

One major concern of the present nuclear arms race is the potential for nuclear proliferation. To build a nuclear bomb, certain scientific and technological knowledge concerning fission is required. How likely are the nonnuclear nations to acquire and understand this needed knowledge? The development of the first nuclear weapons provides a clue: to the extent that the discovery of the relevant knowledge was inevitable, one may judge that the requisite knowledge cannot be kept secret.

In a sense, the usefulness of nuclear fission is a fluke. It involves a very rare isotope of a rare element, since ^{235}U is only 0.7% of natural uranium and ^{239}Pu does not exist in nature. Yet it can be argued that the discovery of nuclear fission and its application to nuclear chain reactions was historically inevitable. Once physicists began to investigate the nucleus at the turn of the twentieth century, active intervention by some policymakers would have been required to halt the progression toward fission technology. Since fission yields two or more neutrons per reaction, physicists were bound to recognize the feasibility of a chain. The logic of nuclear physics, as developed through the natural curiosity of scientists, ensured that equivalent nuclear developments took place more or less simultaneously in research establishments in several countries. (The sociology of science teaches that multiple simultaneous discoveries of scientific facts and laws are the rule rather than the exception.) In 1938 the fissioning of uranium nuclei was reported for the first time by Hahn and Strassman. But various experimenters, including Fermi, had actually been fissioning nuclei since 1934. Only misidentification of the fission products had delayed the recognition of the process for four years.

The application of nuclear fission was also driven by forces internal to the scientific community. Several of the nuclear physicists had been committed from the beginning to tapping nuclear energy for useful purposes. Once the existence of fission processes was recognized, nuclear physicists everywhere knew that large amounts of energy would be released in them, suspected that some further neutrons would be released in the processes, and anticipated that a chain reaction would be possible if the number of neutrons released was large enough. In 1934 the Hungarian physicist Leo Szilard applied for a secret patent on the concept of a nuclear reactor before the fission of uranium was even discovered.

The exact timing of the various scientific and technological events was not predetermined. But for each discovery that came early through genius or serendipity, there were other discoveries that were delayed because of oversight or accident. Pioneering nuclear physicists were driven by the hope of exploiting the energy contained in the nucleus. The standard mythology claims that this nuclear research was pure and undirected. Indeed, as reported in *Nature* (September 16, 1933) Lord Rutherford issued a warning

> to those who look for sources of power in atomic transmutations—such expectations are the merest moonshine.

But this warning fooled no one; everyone was aware of, and was indeed looking for, the technical applications of nuclear energy. Back in 1903, Rutherford had talked about nuclear energy so convincingly that a listening engineering professor thought that scientists should put aside all their work to concentrate on research into nuclear phenomena. Many other physicists felt that the release of the energy in the nucleus would ultimately be achieved. The desire to extract nuclear energy not only motivated physicists after 1900, it affected the selection of research directions and inspired the performance of specific experiments.

The discovery of the nuclear chain reaction and its application was no accident; rather, it was a sought-after goal. Nuclear reactors and explosives were inevitable technical possibilities—a deliberate social effort would have been required to halt the building of nuclear reactors and nuclear weapons. Whether the use of nuclear weapons was equally inevitable will be discussed later in this chapter.

THE ATOMIC BOMB

By 1939 it was clear that a fission chain reaction was possible if sufficient fissionable material could be brought together—neutron multiplication had been observed. The science editor of *The New York Times*, William L. Laurence, published an article about the possibility of nuclear chain reactions on May 5, 1940. A Congressman, who was worried that nuclear power might lead to unemployment, read excerpts from this article to Congress, and all of it was reprinted in the *Congressional Record*. A follow-up article in the *Saturday Evening Post* was declared secret after publication. This scientific knowledge led to the building and the use of nuclear bombs within the short time span of World War II. Was this rapid application also inevitable?

The idea of building a nuclear weapon was not accepted easily by the military establishment. Neither the U.S. Army nor the U.S. Navy saw any obvious need for such weapons and showed little interest in exploring the principles involved. It took the sales ability of some foreign scientist refugees such as Szilard and Eugene P. Wigner (with the help of Einstein), and of some American science administrators such as James B. Conant of Harvard, Arthur H. Compton of the University of Chicago, and Vannevar Bush of the Office of Scientific Research and Development, plus the enormous administrative drive of General Leslie R. Groves, to obtain the initial approval and ultimately the $2 billion financing for the nuclear bomb project (known as the Manhattan Engineering District). The Manhattan project was successful not only because of the large funding but also because of the tremendous scientific and technical competence of scientists such as Fermi, Ernest O. Lawrence, and J. Robert Oppenheimer and the dedication of large industrial concerns such as the DuPont Company in turning scientific concepts into industrial production.

^{235}U

The production of the first atomic bombs presented very large technical problems. Table 2.2 shows that natural uranium has too small an η to be used in a fission bomb; the fast neutrons of the explosion are mostly absorbed by ^{238}U without causing further fissions. In contrast, either ^{235}U or ^{239}Pu can be used for a very rapid chain-reaction explosion with high-energy neutrons. Atomic bombs can be made of uranium heavily enriched in ^{235}U. The difficulty with such a design lies in obtaining the ^{235}U by separating it from the ^{238}U in natural uranium. These two isotopes are chemically identical; therefore, ordinary chemical separation techniques do not work. For the World War II project, it was well recognized the separation would instead have to rely on the small difference in mass between these two isotopes. Two approaches toward isotopic separation ultimately yielded significant amounts of enriched uranium in the Manhattan project.

The electromagnetic separation process helped to provide material for the first uranium nuclear bomb. This process uses combinations of magnetic and electric fields to separate the slightly lighter ^{235}U atoms from the dominant atoms of ^{238}U. This process was developed by Lawrence, based on his experience with cyclotrons; $444 million was spent on it. Electromagnetic separation did produce uranium enriched in ^{235}U; but only in relatively small amounts. Consequently, this process was ultimately completely replaced by the diffusion process.

The primary source of enriched ^{235}U for both military and civilian applications, in the United States and elsewhere, has been the gaseous diffusion process. When gases are forced through a porous barrier, as shown in Fig. 2.5, the rate of leakage (diffusion) depends inversely on the square root of the mass of the molecules. Thus ^{235}U diffuses more rapidly through such a barrier than does ^{238}U. Since uranium is a solid, the gaseous compound UF_6 is used in diffusion plants. It has an enrichment factor of only about 1.0043 per diffusion stage; that is, in each stage, the amount of ^{235}U relative to ^{238}U increases by a maximum of only 0.43% (say, from 0.7% enrichment to 0.703%). This enrichment factor is so small that enriching uranium up to 90% or more in ^{235}U requires about 4000 stages coupled together in a very complex manner to maximize the enrichment, as shown in Fig. 2.6.

The gaseous diffusion plant shown in Fig. 2.7 was built for the Manhattan project at Oak Ridge, Tennessee, at the cost of nearly a billion dollars. Some of this gigantic plant, nearly 1 kilometer (km) long and covering more than 60 acres, is still in operation. When producing ^{235}U, it draws up to 2000 megawatts (MW) of electric power out of the Tennessee Valley Authority network, about ½% of the average U.S. de-

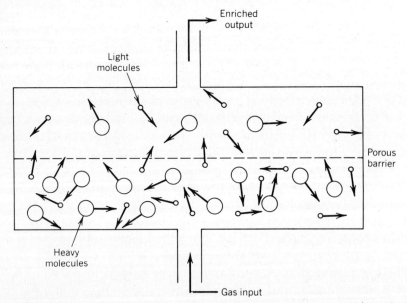

Figure 2.5 Light molecules diffuse more rapidly through a porous membrane than do heavy molecules.

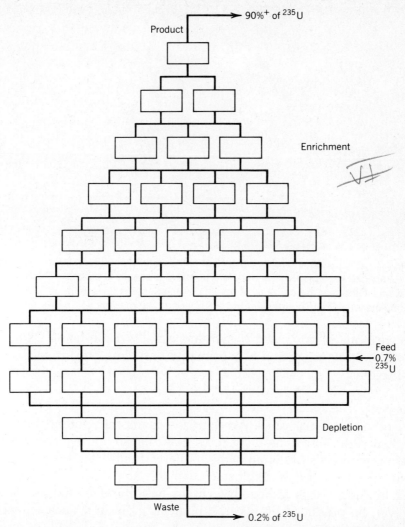

Figure 2.6 4000 diffusion stages can turn natural uranium with 0.7% ^{235}U into weapons-grade uranium enriched to 90% in ^{235}U while rejecting tailings containing uranium depleted to 0.2% in ^{235}U.

mand and enough to satisfy the electric needs of a typical city of over 1 million inhabitants. The three existing U.S. diffusion plants demand a maximum of 7000 MW of electricity.

The uranium hexafluoride gas used in gaseous diffusion plants is very corrosive. Consequently, the porous barriers are hard to make; that is, the diffusion technology requires considerable technological ability. This is the reason why all subsequent nuclear powers, except for China, preferred to make their first A-bombs using the somewhat less sophisticated method of producing ^{239}Pu in nuclear reactors. Nu-

Figure 2.7 The gaseous diffusion plants at Oak Ridge as they look today. The World War II U-shaped K-25 plant in the right foreground is presently in standby. The K-31 and K-33 plants in the rear are currently in operation, as are some units in the K-27 and K-29 plants on the left. (Photo courtesy of the U.S. Department of Energy.)

clear weapons of advanced design are usually made using ^{239}Pu; the present military usage of ^{235}U is primarily in fueling power reactors for naval vessels.

^{239}Pu

The isotope ^{239}Pu was quickly recognized as another potential fuel for a nuclear explosion. Table 2.2 shows that this isotope releases several neutrons when it is fissioned by high-energy neutrons. Hence it is well suited for sustaining an explosive chain reaction. But ^{239}Pu does not occur in nature; it is radioactive with a half-life of 24,400 yr. It can, however, be produced by neutron bombardment in a nuclear reactor when ^{238}U captures a neutron:

$$^{238}_{92}U + {}^{1}_{0}n \rightarrow {}^{239}_{92}U \xrightarrow{(24\ \text{min})} {}^{239}_{93}Np \xrightarrow{(2.4\ \text{d})} {}^{239}_{94}Pu \xrightarrow{(24\ \text{kyr})} {}^{235}_{92}U$$

The Manhattan project invested much effort to achieve a controlled chain reaction that would yield the neutrons for producing ^{239}Pu. Nuclear reactors were designed to use natural uranium as their fuel, where the ^{238}U is both a problem and a necessity. When absorbing neutrons, ^{238}U produces the desired ^{239}Pu, but this absorption also dampens the chain reaction. Table 2.2 shows that in natural uranium, η is much smaller for high-energy neutrons than it is for slow neutrons. Consequently, the early designs for nuclear reactors fueled with nonenriched uranium used a moderator to slow down the neutrons in the reactor.

This moderator is intermixed with the uranium fuel. It must be of low atomic mass, yet must not absorb neutrons. Light hydrogen, as in ordinary water, could be an excellent moderator. Because the mass of ^1H is essentially the same as that of the neutron—in a head-on collision with a neutron, most of the neutron's energy is transferred to it and the neutron slows down. Unfortunately, ^1H also can absorb neutrons. Considerable effort was invested by the Manhattan project to try out alternative moderators.

The nuclear reactor project of the French before World War II, and wartime efforts by the Germans and by a British-Canadian collaboration, focused on the most obvious alternative, developing a reactor using heavy water (D_2O) as a moderator. Heavy water is a good choice as moderator since the mass of deuterium is only twice that of the neutron; in a collision with deuterium a high-energy neutron will give a considerable fraction of its energy to the deuterium. Yet neither deuterium nor oxygen absorb neutrons to a great extent. The only problem was how to obtain heavy water in ton quantities. Until 1943 the Germans imported their D_2O from a Norwegian electric power plant at Vemork, where it was collected as a by-product of power generation. The difficulties of obtaining sufficient heavy water continually hindered the German nuclear project. This shortage was exacerbated by Allied bombing and Norwegian sabotage of that plant; consequently, there was never enough D_2O to produce a self-sustaining chain reaction. The British-Canadian effort to develop a heavy-water reactor at Chalk River in Canada was coordinated with the American Manhattan Project. It led to an operational reactor in 1946. The present successful Canadian CANDU commercial nuclear power reactors are fueled by natural uranium and moderated by heavy water.

The first self-sustaining nuclear reactor built in the United States used graphite as moderator. The ^{12}C nucleus in natural graphite is 12 times as heavy as the neutron; making it less than ideal for slowing down the neutrons. But pure carbon has a relatively low absorption cross section for neutrons.

On December 2, 1942 a team led by Fermi achieved the first controlled nuclear chain reaction at the University of Chicago. Cadmium readily absorbs neutrons, so control of the chain reaction was maintained by inserting and withdrawing control rods of cadmium to dampen or enhance the chain reaction. As soon as the Fermi reactor went critical (when the chain reaction became self-sustaining), several large nuclear reactors were built by the DuPont Company at Hanford, Washington, to produce the kilogram quantities of ^{239}Pu needed for a bomb. After irradiation of a natural uranium fuel element, chemical separation methods were used to separate the ^{239}Pu from the uranium and the fission-isotope mixture in the fuel element. (See the discussion of nuclear proliferation in Chapter 14 for more details.)

Bomb Design

As the ^{235}U and ^{239}Pu bomb material was being produced in the various industrial production plants at Oak Ridge and Hanford, the designs of the nuclear bombs were being developed under the direction of Oppenheimer in a laboratory at Los Alamos, New Mexico. A fission chain reaction, such as the one in Fig. 2.4, requires a positive neutron balance; more neutrons must be produced than are absorbed. Four things can happen to a neutron generated inside fissionable material. (1) It can produce a fission event leading to several further neutrons to sustain the reaction. (2) It can be absorbed, by ^{238}U or some impurity, without leading to the release of further neutrons. (3) It can escape from the fissionable mass, leading to no further neutron production. (4) It can escape into the material surrounding the fissionable mass, where it is either absorbed or reflected back inward.

When the production of neutrons by the fission events (1) exactly equals the loss of neutrons through absorption events (2) and escape events in (3) and (4), then a critical mass of fissionable material exists. The important parameter in making a mass critical is the ratio of its surface to its mass. Smaller masses have a relatively larger surface, so that a larger fraction of generated neutrons escape through the surface. An analogous situation to this neutron surface leakage is the fact that small animals must consume more food per unit body weight, because they radiate body heat more rapidly than do larger animals with a smaller relative surface area. If the mass of fissionable material exceeds the critical mass, then an explosive chain reaction can take place; if it is less, then a chain reaction, once started, will die out.

To decrease the neutron losses through the surface of the fissile mass, to reduce the amount of material required to form a critical mass, a nuclear explosive is usually surrounded by a tamper. A tamper consists of very heavy atoms such as uranium that readily reflect neutrons back into the fissionable mass or of a lighter element such as beryllium that does not absorb neutrons yet reflects them back reasonably well. The tamper may also be a partial neutron generator. When bombarded by high-energy neutrons, ^{238}U can fission; thus, a tamper of natural uranium does produce some additional fission neutrons to return back into the exploding mass. Beryllium also sometimes generates additional neutrons through the reaction:

$$\ _0^1 n + \ _3^9 Be \rightarrow 2\ _0^1 n + \ _3^8 Be$$

Table 2.3 lists critical masses of some fissionable isotopes for various combinations of enrichment and tampers.

The problem facing Oppenheimer's bomb design group at Los Alamos was to create a critical mass out of stable, smaller than critical (subcritical) masses by bringing them together quickly enough to avoid a prematurely ignited or a slow chain reaction. Premature ignition could be induced by the neutrons constantly released in spontaneous fission decays within the fissile material. If the chain reaction proceeds too slowly, the energy produced in the early portion of a premature weak chain reaction might physically blast the critical mass apart, producing a very small bomb explosion, an explosion in which only a small fraction of the fissionable material would actually fission. ^{238}U has a very low rate of spontaneous fission. Hence its bomb design configuration easily could avoid a premature, slow chain reaction.

The bomb design for ^{235}U could thus be a simple gun type, shown in Fig. 2.8. In this design two pieces of ^{235}U, both of slightly subcritical mass, are placed inside a gun barrel. An high-energy chemical explosive then drives these two masses together. As these two pieces became joined, those neutrons that previously might have escaped from each piece through the flat wall can lead to further fission reactions. The joined mass then goes beyond criticality, and an explosive chain reaction can take place. To start the chain reaction properly at the right moment, a source of neutrons is opened at the moment of conjunction in the center of the critical mass. The first uranium nuclear device was

Table 2.3   The critical mass for fission bombs utilizing ^{239}Pu or ^{235}U of various enrichment levels.
The bomb material may be made of metal or oxide, and various surrounding neutron reflectors (tampers) may be used. Adapted from A. de Volpi, 1979, p. 70 and pp. 203–211.

		Tamper	
Bomb Material	None	10 cm of Uranium	10 cm of Beryllium
^{239}Pu, α phase			
(0% ^{240}Pu)	10 kg	4.5 kg	4 kg
(20% ^{240}Pu)		5.4 kg	
(50% ^{240}Pu)		8.7 kg	
^{239}Pu, δ phase	16 kg	7.0 kg	
^{239}PuO$_2$	26 kg		
^{235}U (0% ^{238}U)	47 kg	16 kg	14 kg
^{235}U (50% ^{238}U)	68 kg		25 kg
^{235}U (80% ^{238}U)	160 kg		65 kg
^{235}UO$_2$ (0% ^{238}U)	100 kg		
^{233}U		5.5 kg	

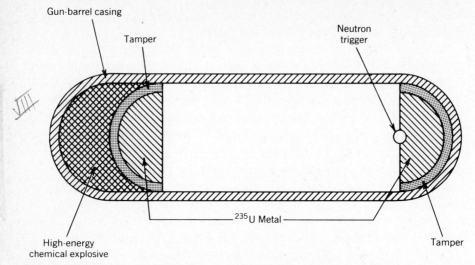

Figure 2.8 Gun-barrel design for a nuclear fission device using ^{235}U as the fissile material. The chemical explosive drives two subcritical masses together, creating a supercritical mass that can undergo a rapidly growing chain reaction.

exploded on August 6, 1945 over Hiroshima, Japan. It contained on the order of 50 kg of uranium enriched to about 70% in ^{235}U. The density of uranium metal is 18.7 gm/cm^3; hence, this mass was equivalent to a melon-sized sphere with a diameter of 17 cm.

The design of an atomic bomb containing ^{239}Pu had to be more complex than a gun barrel. As ^{239}Pu is produced in a nuclear reactor through neutron absorption by ^{238}U, there is a certain probability that it may in turn absorb another neutron to become ^{240}Pu (and further ^{241}Pu, etc.). Hence, some ^{240}Pu will be present in plutonium bomb material. (The extent of such ^{240}Pu production will be discussed in Chapter 14 in connection with nuclear proliferation problems.) ^{240}Pu is radioactive, and in a significant fraction of its decays, it spontaneously fissions, releasing neutrons. If two subcritical masses containing a mixture of ^{239}Pu and ^{240}Pu are brought together by a chemical explosion, they may preignite. As the masses approach closely, the decay-produced neutrons may initiate a premature chain reaction leading to the fizzle just described.

Because of this preignition problem, the plutonium bomb design was based on the implosion technique first conceived by Seth H. Neddermeyer, and shown in Fig. 2.9. In this technique a slightly subcritical mass of ^{239}Pu is surrounded by shaped, conventional high-energy chemical explosives. When these are exploded, their shapes focus the explosive force inward toward the central sphere of ^{239}Pu. The force squeezes the plutonium sphere until its volume is reduced to less than

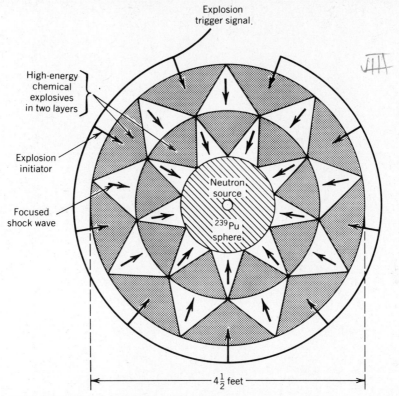

Figure 2.9 Design sketch of the first ^{239}Pu implosion nuclear bomb (not drawn to scale).

half. The plutonium atoms then are much closer together and the surface area is much reduced: fewer neutrons can escape the fissile mass before causing another fission; the subcritical mass is suddenly made supercritical. At the moment of maximum compression some neutrons are released in the center of the fissionable sphere; consequently, virtually complete fissioning of the whole mass may take place before the fission energy blows the plutonium sphere apart.

On July 16, 1945, at Alamogordo, New Mexico, such a ^{239}Pu implosion bomb became the first nuclear device ever exploded. Figure 2.10 shows the smallness of the fissionable core for this device. Because of the preignition problem, the bomb designers were not confident of their predictions about the size of the explosive power of the device; in the betting pool set up before this *Trinity* test, Oppenheimer put his money on 500 tons. The explosion in fact conformed to the detailed prediction made by the theoreticians that the bomb would have an energy yield equivalent to about 20,000 tons of TNT. The ^{239}Pu bomb exploded three weeks later over Nagasaki (see Fig. 2.11) had essentially the same explosive yield of 22 kt.

Figure 2.10 The core for the first ^{239}Pu nuclear device being hand carried by Sgt. Herbert Lehr inside a heavily shielded, shock-mounted container. (Photo courtesy Los Alamos Scientific Laboratory.)

Was the Development of Nuclear Weapons Inevitable?

The history of nuclear physics suggests that the discovery of fission and the understanding of chain reactions was more or less inevitable. It can be argued that this is also the case for the development of nuclear weapons. The timing of the start of development may have had some flexibility, but once a nuclear bomb project was started, the flow of developments displayed a certain logic.

The Manhattan project was triggered by the personal drive and fears of a few individuals. Because of the Nazis' anti-Jewish campaigns after 1933, many German, Italian, and Hungarian scientists fled to Great

Figure 2.11 A display of nuclear weapons on the patio of the Los Alamos Museum. At the extreme right is the "Fat Man" implosion bomb exploded over Nagasaki; at right center is the "Little Boy" gun-barrel bomb exploded over Hiroshima. The top and bottom horizontal bombs on the left are, respectively, a more modern tactical bomb equivalent in yield to the World War II weapons and a hydrogen bomb with a yield in the megaton range. In front of these on the left and right are a "Davy Crockett" mortar bomb and an 8-inch howitzer shell with kiloton yields. (Photo courtesy Los Alamos Scientific Laboratory.)

Britain and the United States. These scientists were very afraid of a possible Nazi victory in Europe; some of them knew a great deal about German progress in fission research. In 1939 Szilard became very concerned about the A-bomb programs that were then being initiated in Germany by the War Office, the Ministry of Education, and the Postal Ministry. Together with Wigner, he convinced Einstein to sign a letter to President Roosevelt pointing out the possibility of an A-bomb.

The immediate goal of the nuclear program need not to have been a nuclear weapon. Some nuclear scientists such as Fermi had their primary interest in building a nuclear reactor. Some German physicists, such as Werner Heisenberg, claimed that the focus of the German nuclear program during World War II was the development of a nuclear reactor. Indeed the German program never got beyond the reactor stage—perhaps because of technical mistakes and the low level of development effort (Irving, 1968). In the United States the fear of Hitler led the emigrés to persuade the American federal government and the Army to initiate the Manhattan nuclear bomb project.

Once the development of A-bombs was set as the goal of nuclear research, the technical progression was relatively straightforward, although the voluminous literature on the Manhattan project sometimes gives a contrary impression. One is often left with the impression that the A-bomb was the result of scientific genius (Davis, 1968). In fact, the great majority of A-bomb development funds went to industry (Hewlett and Anderson, 1962); it has been estimated that the cost of Fermi's first nuclear reactor was less than a million dollars. That reactor established the feasibility of ^{239}Pu production and led to immediate big industrial processes. The Manhattan project succeeded because of the willingness to commit $2 billion to it. The military situation combined with the scientists' fear to ensure that willingness. If World War II had come a few years earlier or later, nuclear weapons might not have been the first outcome of fission technology; but they would have come sooner or later. Any nation with equivalent resources and commitment can have nuclear weapons.

EFFECTS OF NUCLEAR WEAPONS

Nuclear devices release millions of times more energy per mass of bomb than do chemical explosives such as TNT. Do the resulting effects make nuclear bombs more terrible than conventional chemical explosives? The answer to that question depends not only on the physical and biological effects (Glasstone and Dolan, 1977; Committee for the Compilation of Materials on Damage, 1981; Peterson et al., 1982) of nuclear bombs, but on their psychological (Hershey, 1946; Hachiya, 1955; Lifton, 1968) and political (Fogelman, 1964) effects as well.

Physical Effects of A-bombs
Four basic physical effects are produced by a nuclear explosion. Typical fission bombs release 50% of their energy in a pressure (blast) wave, 35% in heat radiation (a flash of light), 5% in prompt (primary or immediate) radiation emissions (gamma rays, electrons, neutrons, etc.), and 10% in secondary radiation emissions from fission products. Fission bombs have been built with energy releases up to 500,000 tons (500 kt) of TNT equivalent. Tables 2.4 and 2.5 show the distances from the center of the explosion (the epicenter) over which these various energy releases have an effect dangerous to people. The damage created at Hiroshima and at Nagasaki can be used to evaluate the relative importance of the various effects in inflicting damage on a city.

Immediately upon explosion the bomb emits a short burst of radiation. Then the large amount of energy released in the explosion produces a fireball inside which the temperature is high enough to vaporize all solid materials. If the bomb is exploded at ground level, it produces a crater. (Figure 3.7 shows the crater produced by a large hydrogen bomb.) This fireball emits a very bright flash of light. The

Table 2.4 Expected damage distance for various effects from the center of a nuclear explosion, expressed in meters.
Cratering occurs only for a ground burst. The Fallout column assumes a ground burst in which 60% of the fallout reaches the ground within 24 hr and displays the areas over which a long-term exposure would reach 500 rem. Prompt and thermal radiation effects are calculated assuming an air burst at the height that maximizes blast effects and 12-mile visibility. Based on various equations and graphs in Glasstone and Dolan, 1977 and Peterson et al., 1982, p. 92.

Total Yield	Crater Radius Surface Blast	Immediate Radiation 500 rem	Fallout 500 rem Surface Blast	Thermal Burns (50% of Pop.)	
				2nd Degree 4–8 cal/cm²	3rd Degree 6–12 cal/cm²
1 t	2.9	120	2,000 m²	26	20
10 t	5.8	230	20,000 m²	82	64
0.1 kt	11.5	450	0.2 km²	260	200
1 kt	23	730	2 km²	800	630
10 kt	46	1280	20 km²	2,400	1,900
0.1 Mt	92	1800	200 km²	5,800	4,800
1 Mt	183	2400	2,000 km²	13,000	11,000
10 Mt	364	3800	20,000 km²	25,000	22,000

flash actually consists of two parts, as shown in Fig. 2.12: the ionized air at the edge of the fireball briefly becomes opaque to light. This flash of light can cause burns on the skin of exposed persons, as shown in Fig. 2.13, and can ignite fires. Second-degree burns result in blisters as in severe sunburn; third-degree burns mean that the full thickness of the skin is destroyed and are likely to be fatal if they occur over a sizable fraction of the body unless very extensive medical care is available. Walls and clothing provide shielding from this flash effect.

Table 2.5 Expected damage distances for blast effects, in meters from the center of a nuclear explosion.
Based on various graphs and equations in Glasstone and Dolan, 1977.

Total Yield	Blast			
	Lethal (50 psi)	Severe (10 psi)	Moderate (5 psi)	Light (3 psi)
1 t	15	33	50	71
10 t	32	71	110	150
100 t	67	150	230	330
1 kt	150	330	500	710
10 kt	320	710	1,080	1,500
100 kt	670	1500	2,320	3,300
1 Mt	1500	3250	5,035	7,100
10 Mt	3200	7100	10,800	15,000

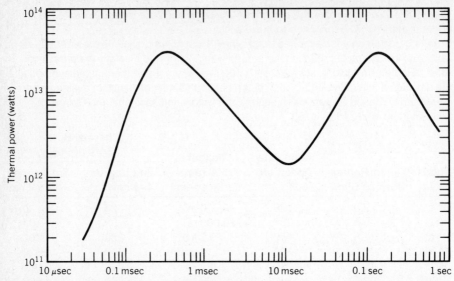

Figure 2.12 The double flash of radiant heat energy from the fireball of a nuclear explosion. The first peak is induced by the prompt radiation. The extinction occurs as the very hot ionized air at the edge of the fireball briefly becomes opaque to light. (After a drawing in *Science*, Vol. 209, 1980, p. 572.)

According to Glasstone and Dolan (1977, p. 566), at Hiroshima and Nagasaki,

> Unless protected by heavy clothing, thermal radiation burns, apart from other injuries, would have been fatal to nearly all persons in the open, without appreciable protection, at distances up to 6000 feet [1800 meters] or more from ground zero. Even as far out as 12,000 to 14,000 feet [3600–4200 m] there were instances of such burns which were bad enough to require treatment.

This observation agrees with the "Thermal column" in Table 2.5, where a 10-kt explosion is listed as giving a third-degree burn to at least 50% of the exposed population at a distance of 1900 m. That effect is expressed in terms of the energy deposited on a unit area of skin, in calories per centimeter squared.

The explosion of the A-bomb also leads to a shock wave, as the hot air in the fireball expands. This effect is similar to the primary destructive mechanism of a TNT explosion. A pressure wave moves out from the explosion with alternating compressions and expansions of the air as shown in Fig. 2.14. The magnitude of this effect is measured as an overpressure in units of pounds per square inch (psi) or atmospheres (atm, where 1 atm = 14.7 psi = $1.013 \cdot 10^5$ N/m²). An overpressure of 1 atm from such a shock front means that the body surface exposed to it has acting on it for a brief moment twice the usual force. For a typical

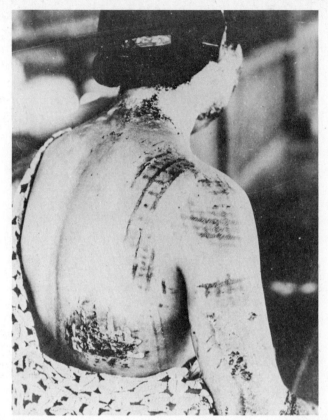

Figure 2.13 Flash burns on A-bomb victim in Hiroshima. The black pattern on the kimono absorbed the light from the fireball and caused burns wherever the dark cloth made contact with the skin. (Photo courtesy U.S. Department of Energy.)

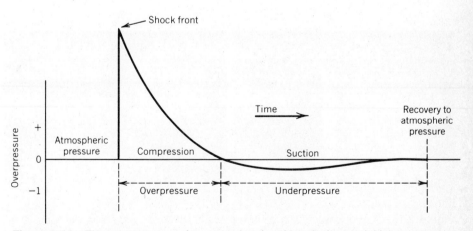

Figure 2.14 The pressure wave from a nuclear bomb explosion; an initial compression is followed by a decompression. The overpressure phase lasts on the order of a second.

person 1.65 m tall and 0.3 m wide (averaged over the body), 1 atm of overpressure would mean that the front of the body would experience an additional force of about 6 tonnes. A blast overpressure of 3 psi (⅕ atm) can be sufficient to destroy wooden houses, 10 psi (⅔ atm) to destroy concrete structures.

Figure 2.15 shows a two-story wooden home being torn apart by a 5-psi shock wave. Figure 2.16 shows the effect on a reinforced concrete building at Hiroshima ½ km from the epicenter (the point in space where the bomb exploded); it received an overpressure from almost directly overhead of about 20 psi. The effects of such shock waves on humans depend critically on geometrical arrangements. Inside a building, the overpressure can be either larger or smaller than in the open air, depending on how the inside walls reflect, absorb, or focus the pressure wave. The direct effect of the pressure on human beings is that

> The sudden compression of the body and the inward motion of the thoracic (chest) and abdominal walls cause rapid pressure oscillations to occur in the air-containing organs. These effects, together with the transmission of the shock wave through the body, produce damage which occurs mainly at the junctions of tissues with air-containing organs and at areas between tissues of different density, such as where cartilage and bone join soft tissue. The chief consequences are hemorrhage and occasional rupture of abdominal and thoracic walls. (Glasstone and Dolan, 1977, p. 548)

To be lethal, such direct effects on humans require overpressures of about 50 psi. Relatively few survivors of the A-bomb showed such direct effects. Rather, the injuries came indirectly, as through flying debris, which was largest inside some industrial buildings. Lacerations

Figure 2.15 A shock wave with an overpressure of 5 psi blows apart a home at a nuclear weapons test site. On the left, the house illuminated by the bomb flash; on the right the 5-psi overpressure has arrived. (Photo courtesy U.S. Department of Energy.)

Figure 2.16 The effects of 20 psi on a reinforced concrete building 160 m from ground zero (500 m from the center of the blast) at Hiroshima. (Taken from Glasstone and Dolan, 1977, Figure 5.22a, p. 161.)

from glass were received by A-bomb victims inside buildings as far away as 3 km from ground zero (the point on the ground directly below the bomb explosion).

If the objective of the bomb explosion is damage to buildings, then the bomb should be exploded above the ground. The pressure wave reflected from the ground adds to the direct pressure wave at the upper stories of the buildings to double the pressure, as shown in Fig. 2.17. Then the buildings are more likely to topple over, possibly burying the inhabitants. For bombs of 1 kt, 10 kt, 100 kt, and 1 Mt, respectively, the optimal explosion heights are 335 m, 750 m, 1550 m, and 3350 m.

The prompt nuclear radiations released at the instant of a nuclear weapon detonation, or within a fraction of a second later, include alpha

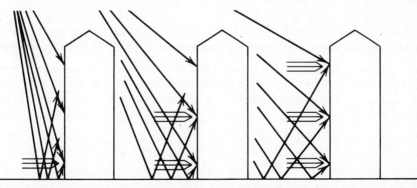

Figure 2.17 Air bursts of nuclear weapons are more effective for destroying buildings because the direct and reflected pressure waves add at the upper stories to topple tall buildings.

particles, electrons, gamma rays, x rays, and neutrons. Alpha and beta particles are absorbed by the air within the fireball before they can reach the target population. Gamma rays and neutrons can be absorbed exponentially by materials, as described on page 19. To reduce the intensity of A-bomb gamma radiation by a factor of two requires about 3 cm of steel, 9 cm of concrete, 14 cm of earth, 20 cm of water, or 38 cm of wood.

Inside body tissue, this radiation produces its effects through the ionization of molecules. The radical OH^- may be produced in water and hamper ordinary cell functions; ionization of DNA molecules may affect genes. These ionization processes consume energy; typically 30 eV of energy cause one ionization to take place. A 600-keV gamma ray may cause as many as 20,000 ionizations potentially damaging many cells. Radiation exposure is measured in terms of the roentgen (r), the radiation unit (rad), or the roentgen equivalent in man (rem). They all represent radiation doses in terms of an energy deposited per unit volume. The roentgen and radiation unit are defined in terms of energy release per kilogram of mass; the former is measured in air, the latter in tissue. The rad is that quantity of radiation that results in the release of 10^{-2} J per kilograms of tissue. The rem is that energy dissipation in tissue that is biologically equivalent in man to 1 r of gamma-ray or x-ray irradiation. This unit corrects for the fact that neutrons, for example, cause 2 to 40 times as much ionization in body tissue per roentgen as do gamma rays (Committee on the Biological Effects of Ionizing Radiations, 1980). The lower relative biological effectives (RBE) holds for high neutron doses, the larger RBE holds for small neutron doses. For most aspects of the nuclear arms race, these radiation units can be considered essentially interchangable, but the rem will be usually used in this text.

Humans are constantly exposed to radiation from internal and external sources. The typical American now receives over a lifetime a dose on the order of 10 rem from natural background radiation and medical exposures. In medicine, a chest x ray may give 0.05 rem, whereas a single mammogram may give 1 rem to the breast.

At Hiroshima and Nagasaki, the doses producing immediate biological effects were considerably larger. Table 2.6 shows the symptoms of radiation sickness experienced for various levels of radiation exposure, when these exposures are given in a single (acute) dose within a period of less than 24 hours. For a single 500-rem exposure of the whole body, 50% of the exposed population dies. That dose for 50% lethality is labeled LD50. This list of radiation symptoms does not include longer-range effects such as a shortening of life span due to cancer (occurring typically 20 years or more after exposure) or induced genetic defects.

Table 2.6   Symptoms of radiation sickness from observations made in Japan and on victims of nuclear accidents.
Based on Glasstone and Dolan, 1977, Table 12.108.

Symptoms	Dose			
	150 rem	500 rem	600 rem	1000 rem
Nausea and vomiting				
Incidence	Commonly	100%	100%	100%
Onset	A few hours	A few hours	A few hours	$\sim \frac{1}{2}$ hour
Duration	⩽ 1 day	1–2 days	⩽ 2 days	⩽ 1 day
Latent period				
(no symptoms)	2 weeks	2–3 weeks	⩽ 2 weeks	1 week
Final phase				
Duration	1 month	1 month	⩽ 1 month	1 week
Symptoms	Some loss of appetite; malaise; some depletion of leucocytes	Nausea; vomiting; malaise; diarrhea; hemorrhage under skin, from gums and intestines, and into organs; loss of hair; depletion of blood platelets; infection		
Survival	Essentially 100%	~50%	~10%	~0%

When the radiation dose is given over a long time period, the effects are considerably smaller. When one asks more specifically how radiation damage in human tissue is correlated to dosage, then one must consider which body organs are exposed, the type of radiation, and the rate at which the dosage is delivered. The sensitivity to radiation of human organs varies greatly. In general, radiation is most dangerous to actively dividing tissue as in a fetus or in the stomach lining; radiation damage to the latter leads to the diarrhea and loss of appetite observed in A-bomb victims. When the radiation dose is given over a long time period, the effects may be reduced by as much as a factor of 10.

For dosages below the lethal level, there still remain potential long-term harmful effects, such as the increased chances of having cancer. Such effects are difficult to demonstrate for very low dosages; hence, their magnitude is generally estimated by extrapolating from the effects observed at high radiation doses. Three general models have been used to estimate the magnitude such low-level effects.

The threshold model in Fig. 2.18 assumes that the damage caused by very small radiation doses is essentially repaired by the body; thus, the radiation must exceed a certain threshold before any permanent damage is caused. This threshold is sometimes assumed to be comparable to the radiation dosage received from natural background radiation deriving from cosmic rays, radioactive isotopes leaking from bricks, and radioactive atoms such as ^{14}C that are incorporated into the body, assuming that the human body, through constant exposure

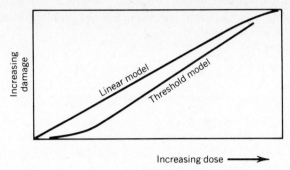

Figure 2.18 A sketch of the linear and threshold models for the effects of low levels of radiation exposure. In the threshold model, radiation is assumed to have effects only above the toe of the curve.

throughout its evolution, has learned to heal some of the effects from the average annual dose of 0.13 rem (10 rem/70 yr) from background radiation.

The linear and the linear quadratic models, in contrast, assume that no dosage of radiation is harmless, no matter how small it may be. In the linear model the exposure of 10,000 people to 1 rem of radiation is as harmful as the exposure of 1000 person to 10 rem (i.e., the total number of "person-rems" determines the total number of excess cancers induced). The linear model is controversial. Some contributors to the most recent edition of the BEIR-III report on radiation effects (Committee on Biological Effects, 1980) feel that a more complicated linear quadratic model is more correct for low-level doses.

For low-level, long-time exposures, the present estimates are that if 10,000 people each receive a dose of 100 rem (representing a dose of 1 million person-rems), this will produce about 200 excess deaths due to cancer and genetic effects. This is equivalent to saying that 5000 rem spread over a large population will produce on the average one delayed fatality. The proof that any of these models hold for very-low-dosage levels is very difficult, requiring experiments with millions of test subjects. The linear model holds at fairly large exposures and is generally used for calculations down to exposure levels of 20 to 50 rems. The debate about the linear versus the quadratic model becomes important for very-low-radiation exposures on the level of rems.

The effects of low-level exposures become particularly important in considering the consequences from the fallout produced by nuclear weapons. Fallout results when the fission products from nuclear weapon explosions are blown into the air by the explosion and subsequently fall to earth. At Hiroshima and Nagasaki, fallout effects were overshadowed by blast effects; only some cases of thyroid cancer many years later hint at the danger. Fallout problems become significant locally for nuclear explosions at ground level, where the fission products are quickly distributed along with the dirt picked up in the explosion; or globally for very powerful high-altitude nuclear explosions that inject fission products high into the stratosphere. Hence, fallout will be dealt with in detail when discussing the hydrogen bomb in Chapter 3.

It is interesting to note how these various effects vary with bomb size. The radius of destruction due to blast pressure of a nuclear weapon is approximately proportional to the cube root of the yield. The blast energy of the bomb is contained in a shell surrounding the explosion; the thickness of the shock wave increases as the radius of the blast front increases. As the yield increases by a factor of eight, the energy released can fill a volume 8 times as large. The radius of such an 8-fold more voluminous shell is only twice as large, since it must have twice the thickness as well as twice the radius. The damage radius in Table 2.5 for the blast effects increases by $10^{1/3} = 2.13$ for every 10-fold increase in yield, or by a factor of 10 for a 1000-fold increase in yield. The damage radius for the immediate radiation for the large bombs goes up even more slowly, since the gamma rays and neutrons are absorbed by the air surrounding the explosion. The amount of radioactive fission products is directly proportional to the fission yield of the bombs. For a given wind condition, this fallout is spread over an area that is also proportional to the yield. Hence the fallout column of Table 2.5 has a 10-fold increase in yield leading to a 10-fold increase in the area covered by fallout.

Which of these damage radii most accurately describes the lethal effects of a nuclear explosion? Experience at Hiroshima and Nagasaki indicates that all the different damage effects (excluding fallout) contributed to the fatalities. It has been estimated that 50% of the fatalities were due to burns of one kind or another. About 30% had received lethal doses of radiation, although this was not necessarily the immediate cause of death. Table 2.7 shows that injured survivors tended to bear injuries from each of these causes. Blast and burn injuries seem to have predominated. Table 2.8 shows the casualty rates at Hiroshima as a function of the distance from ground zero. Within

Table 2.7   Distribution of types of injuries among A-bomb survivors who were injured.
After Glasstone and Dolan, 1977, Table 12.18, p. 546.

Injury	% of Injured Survivors
Blast	70%
Burns (mostly flash)	65
Nuclear radiation (prompt)	30

Table 2.8   Casualty rates at Hiroshima and Nagasaki depending on distance from ground zero.
The fatality numbers include those who died from radiation effects within a few month after the explosions. (After Glasstone and Dolan, 1977, Table 11.09, p. 544.)

Distance from Epicenter	Population	% Killed	% Injured
Hiroshima			
0–1.0 km	31,200	86%	10%
1–2.5 km	144,800	27	37
2.5–5.0 km	80,300	2	25
Total	256,300	27	30
Nagasaki			
0–1.0 km	30,900	88%	6%
1–2.5 km	27,700	34	29
2.5–5.0 km	115,200	11	10
Total	173,800	22	12

1 km the great majority of the population was killed; outside 1.6 km nearly the whole population survived.

The data in Table 2.9 suggest that 1.4 km is the lethal distance from the epicenter at which 50% of the population died within three weeks after the A-bomb explosion at Hiroshima. That A-bomb had an explosive yield of 12.5 kt. Extrapolating Tables 2.4 and 2.5 for that size bomb, respective lethal damage radii of 1320 m, 2700 m, 2100 m, 345 m, 764 m, 1160 m, and 1620 m would be predicted for prompt radiation, second- and third-degree burns, and for 50 psi, 10 psi, 5 psi, and 3 psi blast overpressures. The fallout area and the crater radius are not relevant since the bomb was exploded at such high altitude that the fireball never touched the ground. The actual lethal radius of 1380 m corresponds to that predicted for a blast pressure of about 4 psi or a 500-rem prompt radiation dose. It is less than that predicted for either second- or third-degree burns. The fact that not all the injured survi-

Table 2.9   Average distance for a 50% chance of survival beyond 20 days in Hiroshima.[a]
After Glasstone and Dolan, 1977, Table 12.17, p. 546.

Conditions	Approximate Distance for a 50% Survival Rate	
	From Ground Zero	From Explosion Center
Overall	1280 m (0.8 mi)	1380 m
Concrete buildings	190 m (0.12 mi)	540 m
School personnel		
indoors	720 m (0.45 mi)	880 m
outdoors	2080 m (1.3 mi)	2140 m

[a]That A-bomb was exploded at an altitude of 576 m.

vors received thermal burns indicates that many inhabitants must have been shielded from the thermal flash.

A major fraction of all the fatalities at Hiroshima seems to have been produced by the collapse of buildings. Therefore, in line with the usual practice, throughout the remainder of this text the radius of destruction of a nuclear weapon in a city will be taken as being equal to the distance at which an overpressure of 5 psi is induced. Inside the area defined by that radius some would survive. On the other hand, outside that lethal area some fatalities would occur. The number of survivors inside the lethal distance would be approximately equal to the number of fatalities outside the lethal distance. For calculational purposes in estimating the total fatalities from a nuclear bomb explosion, to a first approximation one can act as if everyone inside the 5-psi area is killed and all outside survive. In an actual nuclear bomb attack, survivors and fatalities will be mixed over a large area.

Figure 2.19 summarizes the relationship between yield and lethal radius for 500 rem, 5 psi, and third-degree burns. At very low yields, the effects of prompt radiation predominate; at very large yields, the thermal effects have the largest potential damage radii. The nuclear fallout presents problems for ground blasts and for very-large-scale nuclear warfare. Everyone of these damage radii actually depends on the circumstances surrounding the nuclear bomb explosion. In Hiroshima and Nagasaki, if the season had not been summer, if everyone had worn more and heavier clothes, then the thermal heat flash might have had less impact. Table 2.9 shows that the lethal radius for

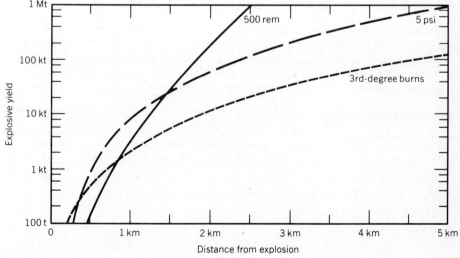

Figure 2.19 Damage radii for various effects from nuclear weapons, based on Tables 2.4 and 2.5.

people inside concrete buildings was half that for the average person. Therefore, if the population had sought shelter in concrete buildings, the survival rate would have been higher.

Psychological Effects of the A-bomb

Nuclear weapons may have an effect beyond the destructive nature expressed in the tonnage of TNT to which they are equivalent. Robert J. Lifton in his *Death in Life: Survivors of Hiroshima* (1968) suggests that the effects of the A-bombs dropped on Hiroshima went beyond physical destruction. One objective of the strategic bombing campaign in Germany had been the destruction of morale; but more than 1½ million tons of chemical explosives did not depress the morale sufficiently to affect the outcome of the war. Lifton argues that for the A-bombs in Japan, however, the unexpectedness of the destruction, the smallness of the attacks (a single bomb), and the mystery of the effects combined with the sheer magnitude of the catastrophe to create a social collapse of a kind previously unknown. John Hershey in *Hiroshima* (1946) and Dr. Michihiko Hachiya in *Hiroshima Diary* (1955) have described the terrible experiences of individual A-bomb survivors. Lifton argues that these individual sufferings were more than additive, that they combined to produce a collapse of the social structure in these cities. This collapse caused both temporary and long-term psychological damage to people beyond their immediate suffering.

Each atomic bomb erased a whole city in an instant. The totality of the damage was an inexpressible shock for the survivors. That shock led to deadening of the human spirit:

> Indeed one thing was common to everyone I saw, complete silence . . . no one spoke . . . (Hachiya, 1955, p. 4)
> Those who were able walked silently toward the suburbs in the distant hills, their spirits broken, their initiative gone. . . . They were so broken and confused that they moved and behaved like automatons. (Lifton, 1968, p. 4)

Social responsibilities were abrogated. This was particularly terrible in Japanese society where social relations are very much emphasized. Neighbors ignored their friends to save themselves. Teachers did not watch over their students; they themselves were suffering pain and shock and were trying to survive. Even within families there were social lapses; some relatives ignored each other's cries for help. It is terrible to think that, as Takashi Nagai, a physician of Nagasaki, put it,

> those who survived the bomb were, if not merely lucky, in a greater or lesser degree selfish, self-centered, guided by instinct and not civilization . . . and we

know it, we who have survived. Knowing it is a dull ache without surcease.
(Lifton, 1968, p. 48)

The survivors of these atomic bombs still carry with them psychological scars from that experience. They are more likely to be hypochondriacs, as any mild physiological disorder they experience will in their mind be associated with possible radiation effects, with cancer and death. These fears have sometimes led to inability to work, problems in finding a marriage partner and marital difficulties, and even suicides. These survivors of the A-bombs, the *hibakusha*, feel and are made to feel that they are an inferior group:

There is the phrase "A-bomb outcast community." This comes from the inferiority complex—physical, mental, social, economic—which *hibakusha* have, so that when people hear the word, they don't feel very good, but rather feel as though they are looked down upon. (Lifton, 1968, pp. 169–170)

Deep, long-lasting psychological scars resulted from the collapse of social order after the A-bomb explosions. These may in part have been due to the high value Japanese society places on social concern and sensitivity. But mostly they seem to have originated directly from the enormity of the catastrophe. Survivors have difficulty coping with the fact of their own survival. Similar feelings have been expressed by the survivors of the holocaust in the concentration camps of World War II. The literature about risk evaluation shows that the public has a greater fear of consequences that are catastrophic, unknown, not understood, and long term (Slovic, Fischoff, and Lichtenstein, 1979a and b). The effects of A-bombs have these characteristics: they certainly were catastrophic, the explosion came from an unknown source, the blast and radiation effects were mysterious, and the radiation sickness and cancers are long term. Reactions to nuclear bombs may well go far beyond fears of physical consequences.

Political Consequences of the A-bombs

One indication of the effectiveness of the A-bomb compared with conventional weapons might come from examining the results of using the two A-bombs in Japan. Why were they used and did they help to achieve the objectives? Did the bombs have an impact on the course of the war?

In the spring of 1945 the American military forces were approaching the Japanese home islands. The capture of intervening islands like Okinawa were expensive, as tens of thousands American and hundreds of thousands Japanese soldiers died. The strategic bombing campaign in the spring of 1945 was proving to be more successful in Japan than in Germany, for example, in affecting civilian morale, particularly when incendiary bombs created firestorms and large-scale conflagrations in Tokyo and other cities.

The American military plans included further bombings and naval blockades. Amphibious landings on the home islands were planned for the fall and winter of 1945. The Japanese in turn expected to meet these invasion forces on the beaches, hoping that the resulting bloody fighting would persuade the American toward a negotiated peace. Secretary of War Stimson reported that

> if we should be forced to carry this plan to its conclusion, the major fighting would not end until the latter part of 1946, at the earliest. I was informed that such operations might be expected to cost over a million casualties to American forces alone. (As quoted in Fogelman, 1964, p. 16)

The A-bombs were to persuade the Japanese toward unconditional surrender, thereby avoiding such bloody senseless combat.

Political circumstances increased the importance of early completion of the bomb. The Los Alamos laboratory was under pressure to get the first nuclear device tested in time for the Potsdam meeting between President Truman and Premier Stalin. The A-bomb might then give Truman an edge in the discussions. A final hope was that the A-bombs might help end the war in time to preempt the entry of the Soviet Union into the war with Japan.

It is difficult to judge whether the A-bomb gave Truman any advantage over Stalin when they met at the end of July 1945. When Truman mentioned to Stalin that the United States had a "powerful new weapon," Stalin only replied that he hoped it would be used to good purpose. Stalin probably knew about the existence of the A-bomb through espionage. While the A-bomb may have given Truman some self-confidence, it did not noticeably affect the Potsdam discussions or communiques.

The use of the A-bombs did, however, shorten the war. The two bombs of Fig. 2.11 were dropped. On August 6, 1945 the 5-ton "Little Boy" was exploded 1670 feet (510 m) above Hiroshima. Its small core of ^{235}U gave an explosion equivalent to 12,500 tons of TNT (12.5 kt). Three days later the "Fat Man" with a core of ^{239}Pu was exploded 1640 feet (500 m) above Nagasaki, with an explosive force equivalent to 22,000 tons of TNT (22 kt). President Truman stated on August 9, 1945 that the Hiroshima bomb had tactical objectives:

The world will note that the first atomic bomb was dropped on Hiroshima, a
military base. That was because we wished in the first instance to avoid, in so far
as possible, the killing of civilians. (As quoted in Fogelman, 1964, pp. 104–105)

And Secretary of War Stimson agreed that

Hiroshima was the headquarters of the Japanese Army defending Southern Japan
and was a major military storage and assembly point. (As quoted in Fogelman,
1964, p. 20)

But the official *Strategic Bombing Survey* reported after the war that

Hiroshima and Nagasaki were chosen as targets because of their concentration of
activities and population. (As quoted in Fogelman, 1964, p. 105)

Certainly the bombs successfully destroyed military-industrial targets.
They effectively killed and injured the civilian population as recorded
in Table 2.8, although they killed only about 1000 military personnel.
The bombs actually were even more effective than had been anticipated. The number of fatalities in Hiroshima had been predicted to be
20,000. However, the city's inhabitants did not go into bomb shelters
under the attack by only three bombers, and so the fatalities were many
times that number.

Whether the A-bombs had a major effect on the war is perhaps not
quite the right question, unless one adds: Compared with what?
Clearly the loss in population, housing, and war production had an
effect. Since the A-bombs were available, why should they not have
been used? The ultimate question, however, is whether the A-bomb is
a distinctively new weapon, with distinctively new effects. Was the
war shortened by the nuclear explosions more than would have been
the case if the same losses had been inflicted by means of incendiary
air raids leading to large conflagrations and firestorms.

Considerable evidence exists that the explosions at Hiroshima and
Nagasaki affected the decision-making process of the Japanese cabinet
and of the emperor. Toshikazu Kase, director of the Japanese Foreign
Office Information Bureau at that time, described that impact:

We were staggered. If a single bomb was equal in destructive power to the mass
raid of a fleet of two-thousand B-29s, with this lethal weapon the Allies could
exterminate all life in Japan in less than a week! . . . it also cannot be denied that
both the bombs and the Russians facilitated our surrender. Without them the
Army might still have tried to prolong resistance. (As quoted in Fogelman,
1964, p. 79)

The then Japanese Foreign Minister Shigenori Togo remembers that

> The Emperor . . . warned . . . we should not let slip the opportunity . . . to insure
> a prompt ending of hostilities. (As quoted in Fogelman, 1964, p. 75)

The nuclear weapons did hasten the end of the war. However, there is still no unanimity whether they shortened the war by only a few weeks, or by a much longer period of time. The Japanese experience leaves unanswered the question whether A-bombs are distinctively different weapons.

POSTWAR CONSEQUENCES OF THE A-BOMB

What effects did the A-bombs have on the postwar political arrangements? There had been considerable discussion whether the A-bombs should be used, and in what manner. The political initiator of the bomb project, President Roosevelt, died in April 1945 before a decision had been reached on those questions. Some of the scientists who had first proposed the A-bomb project were by then unsure whether the bomb should be used. They argued that the A-bomb had deep political implications for the postwar world and that restraint in its use might lead to a more propitious political climate for ultimately controlling the nuclear genie. The physicist James Franck said in his report of June 1945 that

> If the United States were to be the first to release this new means of indiscriminate
> destruction upon mankind, she would sacrifice public support throughout the
> world, precipitate the race for armaments, and prejudice the possibility of reaching
> an international agreement on the future control of such weapons. (Quoted in
> Smith, 1970, p. 45)

The immediate goals of ending the war and the rising distrust of the Russians led to an unrestricted bomb use. The bombs did not keep the Russians from entering the war on August 8, 1945 or from taking Manchuria from the Japanese. The use of the nuclear bombs did affect the relationship between the United States and the Soviet Union after World War II, culminating in mutual nuclear deterrence in the 1960s. This will be discussed in later chapters.

However, two additional important trends related to nuclear weaponry developed in the United States following World War II. First, the successful Manhattan project scientists began to play a role in political events aimed at control of nuclear energy and nuclear weapons. Second, the availability of nuclear weapons affected the power struggles between the various military branches. While the resulting public policies did not become firmly entrenched until the hydrogen bomb became a massive deterrent, internal antagonisms and competitions that had their origins in that time still help to fuel the arms race.

Scientists and Nuclear Politics

The A-bomb was a very prominent result of scientific involvement in World War II weapons developments. Scientists made many other contributions to the war effort; some would argue that the improvements in radar and the perfection of the proximity fuse were far more important to winning the war than was the development of the A-bomb. However, the atomic (nuclear) scientists had the high visibility at the end of the war, as they were called upon to explain the nuclear bomb to the general public.

The nuclear scientists felt they had a broad responsibility to exercise and, therefore, responded to the public's interest in nuclear matters. Scientists are used to open publication of all scientific information; they carried this view over to nuclear weaponry, believing strongly that citizens should be informed of the nuclear potential. Thus, scientists pushed through the publication of the Smyth report in 1945, which outlined the general features of the A-bomb and described the Manhattan project.

Scientists felt very badly about the secrecy aspects of their wartime work. They had not liked their experiences with the military compartmentalization (need-to-know) approach to knowledge. They, therefore, strongly supported civilian control of the development of nuclear power. In the fall of 1945, the War Department proposed the May-Johnson bill to establish an atomic energy commission. Under this bill that commission would have controlled all sources of nuclear energy and all activities related to research, production, and release of such energy. The commission would have included members of the Armed Forces and could have imposed secrecy on any research that was related to nuclear energy. The scientists formed a lobby against this bill, founding the Federation of Atomic Scientists for that purpose. Under their influence a civilian Atomic Energy Commission (AEC) was established through the McMahon bill signed by Truman finally on August 1, 1946. This bill put less emphasis on secrecy and strongly supported the concept of further basic research in the nuclear area.

Scientists became deeply involved in efforts to attain international control of nuclear energy. Even before the war had ended, some Manhattan project scientists concluded that only international control of atomic energy could prevent an ultimate arms race of nuclear weapons. In 1946 this viewpoint was incorporated into the Baruch plan for the control of nuclear weapons. The United States offered to give its nuclear secrets and nuclear weapons to an international control agency, if all other nations, including the Soviet Union, would agree not to develop their own nuclear weapons. This proposal failed because the Soviet Union insisted that the United States first give up its nuclear arsenal and was not willing to put its nuclear destiny into the hands of others.

In building the A-bomb, Oppenheimer claimed that "the physicists have known sin." Some physicists agreed with that claim and have tried to extirpate a feeling of guilt by developing peaceful uses of atomic energy. Many nuclear scientists switched into medicine, developing radioactive isotopes for diagnostic tracer work and for cancer therapy, and promoted the use of nuclear power reactors for the production of electricity.

Military Competition over Nuclear Power

The atomic bomb was built during World War II by the Army Corps of Engineers under General Leslie R. Groves. However, the McMahon bill in 1946 transferred all control over research, development, and production of nuclear weapons to the new civilian AEC. At that time, the roles to be played by nuclear weapons in the future of the military had not yet been determined. Each service had to define its own nuclear future and persuade the AEC and Congress to agree to it and provide it with the appropriate nuclear weapons. This led to interservice rivalry and competition that still continue.

Perhaps the most clear-cut nuclear role lay with the Air Force after World War II. It had used two A-bombs successfully and had developed the tactic of strategic bombing, which was well suited for powerful nuclear weapons. The Strategic Air Command (SAC) was established in 1946 to ensure adequate retaliation against the Soviet Union in case of an aggression. SAC was designed to carry out strategic (area) bombing of cities. This was the forerunner of the policies of massive retaliation and of deterrence. SAC's primary interest was therefore in the largest possible nuclear bombs; accuracy was secondary, as were tactical requirements for fighters and dive bombers. Another Air Force interest was the building of a nuclear-powered airplane.

Even though the Army had actually built the A-bomb, it did not get to keep it. After World War II, the Army was very much decreased in strength and was not equipped with nuclear tactical weapons, since there was not enough nuclear fissionable material to allow such a diversion from the strategic bombing role. The Army thus played only a very minor role in early nuclear controversies.

The Navy had finally become interested in nuclear power at the beginning of World War II. During the war it pursued diffusion isotopic separation processes for ^{235}U independently from the Army. But the award of the Manhattan project to its rival service branch kept it from developing this interest. After World War II the Navy did not pursue nuclear power strongly; it was more interested in retaining its aircraft carriers. A few individuals had an interest in nuclear propulsion for ships. However, not until the middle of the 1950s was Hyman Rickover able to convince the Navy that nuclear propulsion was ideal for submarines. The Navy became very interested in a large nuclear fleet only after the success of the nuclear submarine development program.

ARE NUCLEAR WEAPONS DIFFERENT?

Is the A-bomb a different weapon? In World War II it had no major impact on the military situation. The numbers of dead in Hiroshima or Nagasaki were no more than those killed by one incendiary raid in Tokyo, nor were they a major fraction of the tens of million dead for the whole of World War II.

Some think that nuclear weapons are not necessarily different, at least not unless a full-scale total war were to break out. The Nobel–prize winning physicist and operations-research pioneer Patrick M. S. Blackett made some of the strongest arguments in support of this view in his *Studies of War* of 1950. Fred C. Iklé in *The Social Impact of Bomb Destruction* (1958) shows that Hiroshima recovered as rapidly after World War II as various other cities subjected to large-scale destruction by conventional strategic bombing. Destroyed technical services were largely restored in Hiroshima within a few years. These authors, and others, argue that only through their enormous explosive power do nuclear bombs differ from other weapons.

In spite of such arguments, nuclear weapons do seem to have a qualitatively different character, precisely because of the quantitatively greater power. This greater power means that only a few delivery vehicles are required for total destruction of a city. One bomber destroyed Hiroshima, whereas 325 and 1200 were required to start firestorms in Tokyo and Dresden, respectively. This concentrated effect makes nuclear attacks seem more catastrophic and mysterious, potentially resulting in large psychological shocks for the survivors. This shock combines with little-understood and unpredictable physical after effects from radiation and fallout to make the aftermath of nuclear war seem potentially very different.

WAS THE DEPLOYMENT OF THE A-BOMB INEVITABLE?

It has been argued that both the scientific knowledge of the A-bomb and its technological availability were inevitable, although the time schedule for deployment was dictated by political events. Once available, the weapons were used and have been deployed in large numbers. High government officials debated this question prior to the first use of nuclear weapons in Japan. This debate involved responsible scientists and military and political leaders. In 1944 a scientists' review committee on the technical and political implications of the A-bomb, established at the University of Chicago under Franck, foresaw some of the political consequences of nuclear weapons. An Interim Committee was set up in May 1945 by President Truman to weigh the desirability of alternative ways of using the bomb. The final choice to use the A-bomb, and to use it as a strategic weapon, involved the considered judgment of a variety of people.

A lingering question remains whether that judgment was properly informed, whether true political control existed. The largest number of people who knew enough about the bomb to make a technically informed judgment were scientists. They were asked their opinion, but the methods of obtaining that opinion were poorly chosen, unevenly applied, and at times even censored. No consensus was ever reached among them whether or not to use the bomb as a strategic device. On the other hand, the military and political leadership that knew about the existence and potential of the A-bomb was very restricted and technically unsophisticated. Roosevelt, who initiated the project, died before the deployment decision was made, and Truman had never heard of the A-bomb before he became president in April 1945. There exists now the general feeling that once the A-bomb was available, its use, particularly under wartime circumstances, was inevitable.

The large-scale deployment of nuclear weapons after the war was a direct consequence of the wartime circumstances. The necessary secrecy meant that the potential political consequences could not be discussed until after August 6, 1945. By that time the cold war pattern of mistrust was already being established. The trust necessary to search for worldwide nuclear controls and disarmament did not exist.

References

Committee on the Biological Effects of Ionizing Radiations. *The Effects on Populations of Exposure to Low Level Ionizing Radiation (BEIR II)*. Washington, D.C : National Academy Press, 1980.

The Committee for the Compilation of Materials on Damage Caused by the Atomic

Bombs in Hiroshima and Nagasaki. *Hiroshima and Nagasaki: The Physical, Medical and Social Effects of the Atomic Bombings,* tran. by C. Ishikawa and D. L. Swain. New York: Basic Books, 1981.

Davis, N. P. *Lawrence and Oppenheimer.* New York: Simon & Schuster, 1968. A journalistic biography of two scientists deeply involved in the Manhattan project.

Fogelman, E. *Hiroshima: The Decision to Use the A-Bomb.* New York: Scribners, 1964. A reader.

Glasstone, S., and P. J. Dolan, eds. *The Effects of Nuclear Weapons,* 3rd ed. Washington, D.C.: Government Printing Office, 1977.

Hachiya, M. *Hiroshima Diary: The Journal of a Japanese Physician, August 6–September 30, 1945.* Chapel Hill: University of North Carolina Press, 1955.

Hershey, J. *Hiroshima.* New York: Alfred A. Knopf, 1946.

Hewlett, R. G., and O. E. Anderson. *A History of the U.S. Atomic Energy Commission: The New World, 1939–1946.* University Park: Pennsylvania State University Press, 1962. A detailed history of the Manhattan project.

Iklé, F. C. *The Social Impact of Bomb Destruction.* Norman: University of Oklahoma Press, 1958.

Irving, D. *The German Atomic Bomb.* New York: Simon & Schuster, 1968.

Lifton, R. J. *Death in Life: Survivors of Hiroshima.* New York: Random House, 1968. See also the review by J. Bronowski in *Scientific American,* Vol. 218, no. 6 (June 1968), pp. 131–135.

Peterson, J., and the *Ambio* editorial staff of the Royal Swedish Academy of Sciences. *Nuclear War: The Aftermath.* New York: Pergamon Press, 1983. A reprint of a special issue of *Ambio,* Vol. 11, nos. 2–3 (1982).

Slovic, P., B. Fischhoff, and S. Lichtenstein. "Rating the Risks." *Environment* Vol. 21, no. 3 (April 1979a), pp. 14–39; and "Weighing the Risks," *Environment,* Vol. 21, no. 4 (May 1979b), pp. 17–38.

Smith, A. K. *A Peril and a Hope: The Scientists' Movement in America: 1945–47.* Cambridge, Mass.: M.I.T. Press, 1970 (1965).

de Volpi, A. *Proliferation, Plutonium and Policy: Institutional and Technological Impediments to Nuclear Weapons Propagation.* New York: Pergamon Press, 1979.

CHAPTER
3

The Fusion Bomb

America can get what she wants if she insists on it. After all, we've got it, and they haven't and won't have it for a long time to come.

Bernard Baruch, speaking about
the A-bomb in December 1946

At the end of World War II, various knowledgeable people estimated how soon the Soviet Union would develop its own fission bomb. Some technical experts predicted that the first Soviet tests might come as soon as 1949. As time passed, however, that early date was forgotten and a more contemptuous view of Soviet technological capabilities pushed the estimates into the middle 1950s at the earliest. When the Soviets indeed exploded their first nuclear fission device in the fall of 1949, it came as a great shock to American policymakers and to the general public.

The technological surprise of *Joe I* was exacerbated by the military-political upheavals taking place at the same time. In 1948 Czechoslovakia had become a Soviet satellite state by revolution. In the same year Soviet troops blockaded Berlin, forcing the Western allies into a large-scale airlift of basic necessities. Furthermore, in early 1949 the People's Liberation Army of Mao Tse Tung captured all of mainland China and set up the Communistic People's Republic of China. These communistic political successes made the first "red" A-bomb seem doubly sinister, as the Western ability to respond to a Soviet conventional attack in Europe with unanswerable nuclear arms was thrown into doubt.

This political atmosphere prompted a reevaluation of a previously **58** proposed radical new nuclear weapon, the "Super" or fusion bomb.

This weapon is often called a thermonuclear device, since it uses very high temperatures to ignite nuclear reactions. The new Soviet challenge was in the nuclear area; hence, various nuclear responses were considered, such as increasing the number of deployed nuclear fission weapons and finding better ways of delivering them onto targets. Many policymakers saw the development of a thermonuclear fusion weapon as the militarily and politically most desirable way to meet the Soviet challenge.

The Super had first been proposed by Edward Teller in 1942. For various technological reasons, it had not been pursued intensively since then. The explosion of *Joe I* caused the political reasons for the Super to overcome not only these technological objections but also various moral and political considerations as raised by a scientific advisory committee chaired by Oppenheimer.

Under orders from President Harry S. Truman, the Atomic Energy Commission in 1950 instituted a crash program that led to the explosion of a first fusion device in 1952 and to the development of a usable H-bomb by 1956. The Soviet Union in the meantime developed an A-bomb augmented by fusion by 1953 and its own usable H-bomb by 1955. Ever since, both superpowers have relied on H-bombs as warheads for their strategic weapons.

The nature of fusion weapons will be described in this chapter. That description will include a discussion of the effects of global nuclear fallout. A review of the Soviet A-bomb program shows why *Joe I* came in 1949. The 1949 report of the scientists' General Advisory Committee to the AEC provides an outline of potential U.S. responses to *Joe I*, including the "technical" recommendation that the Super not be pursued as a crash program. That recommendation suggests that to some extent the development of the H-bomb might have been controlled. The Oppenheimer security clearance hearing of 1954 resulted from the impact of politics on the choice of this technology.

DESIGN OF A FUSION BOMB

Energy Conversion

Since 1934 it has been known that large amounts of energy can be released in the fusion of light elements. In 1937 Hans Bethe showed that fusion reactions release the energy in the sun that provides the sunlight. The strength with which nucleons are held together in a light nucleus increases with atomic mass. Thus, the nucleons in a helium (^{4}He) nucleus are more tightly bound together than are the nucleons in two deuterium (^{2}H) nuclei. Fusing two deuterium nuclei together therefore releases energy. The converse is true for heavy nuclei; the lighter fission product nuclei are more tightly bound together than are those of the heavier unfissioned parent uranium nucleus.

The hydrogen bomb releases energy by fusing together light nuclei such as deuterium and tritium. Five significant fusion reactions that can take place involve mixtures of deuterium (D = ^{2}H), tritium (T = ^{3}H), alpha particles (α = ^{4}He), ^{3}He, and neutrons (n):

$$^2\text{H} + {}^2\text{H} \rightarrow {}^3\text{H} + {}^1\text{H} + 4 \text{ MeV}$$
$$\rightarrow {}^3\text{He} + {}^1n + 4 \text{ MeV}$$
$$\rightarrow {}^4\text{He} + 23 \text{ MeV}$$
$$^3\text{H} + {}^2\text{H} \rightarrow {}^4\text{He} + {}^1n + 17.6 \text{ MeV}$$
$$^3\text{H} + {}^3\text{H} \rightarrow {}^4\text{He} + 2{}^1n + 11.4 \text{ MeV}$$

A helium nucleus (i.e., an alpha particle) is a particularly stable configuration of nucleons and hence is formed in many of these reactions. The indicated energy is released in the form of gamma rays and x rays, and as kinetic energy of the product nuclei.

The primary reaction that fuels the H-bomb is the deuterium-plus-tritium reaction (the D+T reaction). While it releases only one-eleventh the energy of a fission reaction, the mass of the reactants is much smaller, involving 5 nucleons as compared with 239 nucleons in fission. Hence the fraction of the reacting mass that is converted into energy is much larger for fusion than for fission; it is 3.5 million electron volts (MeV) per fusing nucleon compared with 0.84 MeV per fissioning nucleon, or to 10 eV per 227 nucleons in the explosion of TNT. Per unit mass, fusion is 40 million times more efficient than is an explosion of TNT. The energy released in the D+D reaction is 23 MeV, which is larger than the 17.6 MeV released in the D+T reaction. However, the less efficient D+T reaction is preferred because it is much easier to ignite. The 3.5 MeV per fusing nucleon in the D+T reaction corresponds to a 0.38% fractional mass loss, since the mass of a nucleon is equivalent to 938 MeV.

The fusion energy of 1 kg of ^{2}H is enough to lift 600 battleships (at 50,000 metric tonnes each) 1 km into the air, or to operate a 1000-megawatt (Mw) electric (3000 thermal megawatt) power station for 1.3 days, or to convert 500,000 tonnes of water into steam.

Ignition of the Fusion Reaction

The fusion reaction poses a problem not present for fission: How are the reactants to be brought together? In fission, the bombarding neutron has no difficulty penetrating the nucleus; it is electrically neutral and is not repelled by the nuclear protons. In fusion both reactants are electrically charged. Hence, when the two positively charged nuclei approach each other closely, a very large electrostatic repulsion forces them apart.

To bring these nuclei together, energy is added by heating them. As the temperature rises above a few thousand degrees Centigrade (°C), the orbital electrons separate from the nuclei, and a plasma is formed. The positively charged nuclei then repel each other, and large amounts of energy must be added to bring them still closer together. Temperatures of hundreds of millions of degrees Kelvin (K) must be achieved to cause the fusion reaction to take place at a reasonable speed. The required reaction rate depends on the density of the fusing material. For the D + T fusion reaction in the center of an H-bomb, a temperature of 2000 million K leads to a reaction time of about 0.000001 seconds (10^{-6} sec = 1 microsecond = 1 μsec) when the gas density is about 30 gm/cm^3. Other fusion reactions generally require a longer reaction time or a higher reaction temperature.

Once the electrostatic repulsion has been overcome, the nuclear forces lead to a large attraction between the nucleons. That results in a fusion of the reactants. As the fusion takes place, a large amount of energy is released. In some of the reactions (e.g., in the fusion of D + T) a neutron may be released. Most of the released energy is distributed as kinetic energy among the final products.

The problem of initiating a fusion reaction is to produce a temperature and pressure high enough to bring the fusing nuclei close together for a sufficient length of time. This is the nuclear equivalent of bringing any chemical fuel to its kindling point.

Source of Fusion Fuel

The most convenient fusion reaction is the combination of D and T into helium, as this reaction takes place at the lowest temperature. Deuterium is a readily available material; 0.015% of all naturally occurring hydrogen is ^2H; that is, there is one D atom for every 7000 ^1H atoms. Heavy hydrogen can fairly readily be separated from normal hydrogen through thermal diffusion or through the dissociation of water by electric currents during electrolysis. Heavy water (D_2O) presently costs about $250 per kilogram.

Tritium is radioactive, with a relatively short half-life of about 12.3 years; it does not occur in nature except in insignificant trace amounts produced by cosmic-ray bombardment. If T is to be used directly as the fuel for a hydrogen bomb, it must be artificially manufactured. Tritium can be produced by neutron bombardment of ^{6}Li:

$$^6_3\text{Li} + {}^1_0n \rightarrow {}^4_2\text{He} + {}^3_1\text{H} + 4.8 \text{ MeV}$$

Indeed, tritium is generally made by bombarding ^{6}Li in a nuclear reactor. ^{6}Li is a stable isotope, making up 7.4% of all naturally occurring lithium. Tritium can therefore be made from ^{6}Li, but only at some expense, and by using some neutrons produced, for example, in a nuclear reactor.

The Design of a Fusion Explosive

From the foregoing discussion, it is clear that a fusion reaction will take place only at a temperature of many millions of degrees Centigrade in a densely packed mixture of either liquid or solid deuterium and tritium. Such a high temperature cannot be achieved inside physical ovens since solid materials melt at a few thousand degrees Centigrade. In the H-bomb such very high temperatures are provided by a fission bomb that acts as a trigger for the fusion process.

In the H-bomb a fission bomb is placed near the material to be fused. This fission trigger is set off by implosion. The fission chain reaction provides the energy to heat some of the fusion reactants to the required temperature, while at the same time compressing them to enhance the fusion reaction rate. Thereafter, the energy from the fusion reactions can sustain further fusions, until the fusible material is all used up or the reactants have been blown apart so far that no further fusions can occur. There are several important design considerations involved in the H-bomb design of Fig. 3.1.

When the Super was first conceived, it was planned to incorporate D and T directly into the bomb and fuse them. Deuterium and tritium are gases at room temperature. In gases the atoms are too far apart for a fusion reaction to be sustained. To fuse D and T directly requires some appropriate liquid or solid compound of hydrogen in which the hydrogen can be replaced by D and T. This compound, however, should not absorb neutrons itself, nor should it absorb too much of the released fusion energy. This design criterion presents a problem. No liquid or solid chemical compound of hydrogen exists that has enough density for the fuel to sustain a fusion reaction. Another option is to cool the D and T down to $-250°$C below freezing, at which temperature both of these gases liquify. This cooling requires a superrefrigerator. A nuclear device including such a superrefrigerator would never be small enough to be delivered by aircraft, although it might be delivered by a ship. Tritium incorporated into such a fusion bomb would have to be produced in a nuclear reactor. That production would

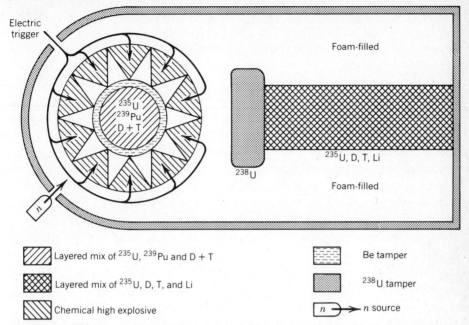

Electric trigger

Foam-filled

235U
239Pu
D + T

238U

235U, D, T, Li

Foam-filled

n

Layered mix of 235U, 239Pu and D + T

Be tamper

Layered mix of 235U, D, T, and Li

238U tamper

Chemical high explosive

n → *n* source

Figure 3.1 Design schematic of a hydrogen bomb fusing deuterium and tritium. At one end of the device is an implosion fission bomb with a core made up of an ingenious sequence of ^{239}Pu, ^{235}U, beryllium, natural uranium, D and T fusion boosters, and high explosives. Once the chemical implosion has taken place, the fission chain reaction is triggered by a burst of neutrons from a high-voltage generator. X rays from the fission reaction are focused by styrofoam onto the fusion component at the other end of the device. The pressure wave from the styrofoam compresses and heats the fusion cylinder, which includes some further fissionable material. Neutrons from the initial fission reaction produce tritium from the ^{6}Li to fuel the fusion reaction. High-energy neutrons resulting from the fusion reaction then further fission the uranium tamper that makes up the cylindrical enclosure of the H-bomb. (After Morland, 1981.)

consume many neutrons: within a nuclear weapons program, the neutron production of tritium becomes a competitor for the production of ^{239}Pu by the neutron bombardment of ^{238}U.

These two problems with D + T fusion devices were solved when an H-bomb was designed to be made out of lithium deuteride, ^{6}Li^{2}H. LiH is a solid material that does not have to be frozen. The neutrons from the fission trigger in the H-bomb produce the tritium within the bomb itself during the explosion. Both the fission explosion and the subsequent fusion reactions produce neutrons; these neutrons can be used to convert further ^{6}Li nuclei into additional tritium. This all occurs at the same time that the fission trigger provides the requisite high temperatures and pressures.

The fission bomb trigger has a tendency to blow apart the fusion material LiD. The fusion reaction must, therefore, proceed rapidly enough to be completed before this explosive effect can act, before explosive disassembly can take place. For this reason the D + T fusion reaction is preferred over the D + D reaction—it proceeds much more rapidly.

In the H-bomb design of Fig. 3.1, a block of uranium briefly shields the fusible mass from the fission bomb's shock wave. During that moment, the x rays that are emitted by the fission explosion provide compressional energy and high temperatures to the $^6Li^2H$ (LiD) by means of a styrofoam plasma, and they do so rapidly enough to complete the fusion reaction before the blast wave tears it apart. The physical arrangements involve layers of LiD, beryllium, fissile material, high-energy explosives, and so on; they are very complicated, as is the timing sequence. Fusion bombs are very complex and sophisticated in design, and the progress of their explosive processes is very difficult to calculate.

The explosive power obtainable from a fusion bomb is in theory unlimited. LiD can be made in large pieces, since there is no such thing as a critical mass for fusion; and this mass can be fused faster than it blows apart from the energy released in it. In addition, at relatively little expense, these fusion bombs can be made even more effective for strategic purposes. One can wrap some natural uranium around the fusion bomb. When this uranium is struck by the high-energy neutrons released by the fusion reactions, it too can fission. This increases the energy produced, enhances the blast, and makes the bomb "dirty" by producing large quantities of fission products. Each D + T fusion reaction produces one high-energy neutron. Table 2.1 shows that the high-energy neutrons released in the fusion processes are well able to fission natural uranium, even though not well enough to sustain a chain reaction by themselves. For every 5 kg of D + T that are fused, it is therefore possible to fission at least 238 kg of ^{238}U atoms (actually more, since the fission of ^{238}U produces some further neutrons). This added explosive fission energy is inexpensive, since natural uranium is relatively cheap (about $20,000 per tonne). A tonne of natural uranium may add as much as 20 Mt of explosive yield. The uranium jacket serves the additional function of a tamper, as it reflects some neutrons back into the fissioning and fusing masses.

The hydrogen bomb as such is relatively "clean." That is, fusion produces no fission products, only some tritium. The unavoidable major radioactivity comes from the fission trigger, which does produce such isotopes as ^{131}I and ^{90}Sr. The trigger can be made quite small. However, an almost pure H-bomb (one with a small fission trigger) is relatively inefficient as a weapon. Most of the energy released in the D + T fusion process will go into kinetic energy of the emitted neutrons and alpha particles. Of the 17.6 MeV of energy released in a D+T reaction, 3.5 MeV will be carried away by the alpha particle and 14.1 MeV by the neutron. Because of their short range, the alpha particles will give their energy to the fireball and add to the explosive yield. The high-energy neutrons travel a long distance in air ($d_{1/2}$ = 133 m), and most of them will, therefore, not add much of their kinetic energy to the fireball. Rather, they will heat up the air surrounding the fireball. That energy release in front of the shock wave will not enhance the blast from the explosion. Enhanced radiation weapons (neutron bombs) are of such a two-stage (fission-fusion) design. A uranium layer around the fusion bomb will increase the blast effects as it captures the kinetic energy from these high-energy neutrons and adds it to the fireball. For strategic effectiveness, H-bombs are fission-fusion-fission (F-F-F) devices, the combination that maximizes the explosive yield. The resulting large quantity of radioactive fission products additionally may make fallout areas dangerous for inhabitants.

THE EFFECTS OF FUSION BOMBS

Fusion bombs have all the major blast and radiation effects discussed in Chapter 2. Tables 2.4 and 2.5 show the various damage radii for this weapon. These radii are essentially extrapolations from the smaller fission bombs.

Consider the explosion of a 1-Mt bomb: (1) The crater radius for an explosion on the ground is about 183 m. (2) Third-degree burns range as far as 11 km. (3) The blast overpressure of 5 psi that was found to be indirectly lethal in Hiroshima and Nagasaki by collapsing buildings extends to about 5 km. (4) The lethal distance for prompt radiation is "only" 2.4 km, because over long distances absorption by air reduces the radiation intensity greatly (see also Chapter 12). Burn and blast effects overshadow radiation effects for very large nuclear bombs as shown in Fig. 2.19.

The "new" threat of a large hydrogen bomb compared with fission explosives is the potential effect of the large-scale fallout from the uranium fission jacket of the fission-fusion-fission combination. Fusion bombs up to 20 Mt have been tested by the United States, and the Soviet Union has exploded a fusion device with a yield of 58 Mt, although neither of those weapons is believed to be in the arsenal at present. The area badly contaminated by radioactive fallout increases more rapidly with yield than do other effects. The large fission-fusion-fission H-bombs continue this trend. The fissioning of the casing by the energetic fusion neutrons produces copious quantities of fission products. For a 1-Mt hydrogen bomb exploded at low altitudes so that its fireball touches the ground, Table 2.4 shows that the local area that could potentially receive 500 rem of fallout radiation could be very large at nearly 2000 km^2, which corresponds to the area of a circle with a radius of about 50 km. The much larger explosive yield of the fusion bombs ensures that the much larger quantity of fallout will also be deposited over much larger areas as the mushroom from the fireball penetrates higher up into the stratosphere.

Large H-bombs can produce global fallout. A large nuclear explosion produces a longer-lived fireball and a mushroom cloud that rises to higher altitudes. Consider the time evolution of a 1-Mt H-bomb exploded in the middle latitudes of the northern hemisphere. One minute after the explosion, the fireball has cooled off to the point that it barely glows, leaving behind the mushroom cloud made up of bomb fragments, water vapor, nitrogen oxides, and radioactive fission products (see Fig. 3.2). At that time the center of this cooled fireball will be at an altitude of 9 km and will be rising at 370 km/hr. After 2½ min the radioactive cloud will be at an altitude of about 16 km and its rise will have slowed to 225 km/hr. Ultimately the top of the mushroom cloud

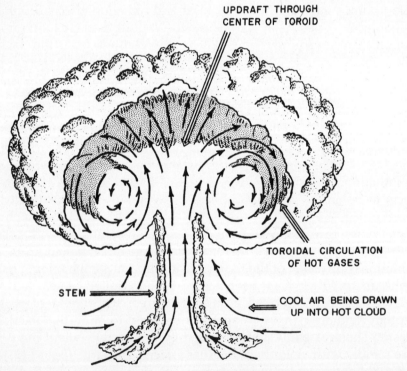

Figure 3.2 The mushroom cloud from a 1-Mt nuclear explosion 1 min after the explosion. (Glasstone and Dolan, 1977, Figure 2.07a, p. 29.)

from a 1-Mt explosion reaches a maximum altitude of about 20 km in the middle latitudes. Thus, for explosions greater than 1 Mt, most of the fission products are deposited in the stratosphere where they undergo worldwide circulation (Fig. 3.3). For explosions much less than 100 kt, no fission products will reach the stratosphere. Near the equator the mushroom will reach higher; near the poles it will not reach as high.

The uranium jacket of the fission-fusion-fission bomb introduces that major new strategic effect of extremely-large-scale fallout and its global effects. As in a fission bomb, radioactive isotopes such as ^{131}I, ^{90}Sr, and ^{137}Cs are produced as fission products; ^{14}C is generated through neutron capture by nitrogen in the air; and some ^{239}Pu is scattered from the Pu-bomb trigger and produced by neutron capture in the uranium jacket. Tritium is left over from incomplete fusion reactions. Some of the dirt in a ground-level explosion may be made radioactive by absorbing neutrons, but this effect is small compared with the direct radiation from bomb products. Once in the stratosphere, after some time this radioactivity drops back to earth, posing a long-time potential radiation threat to the survivors of direct blast effects. The H-bomb differs from an A-bomb both in the quantity of the fallout and in its distribution.

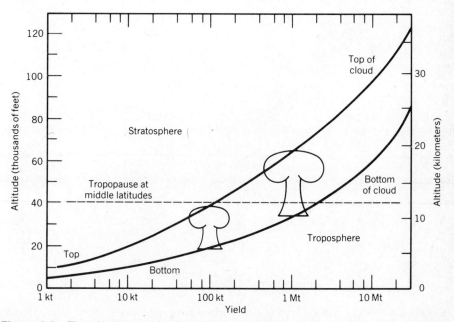

Figure 3.3 The altitudes reached by the top and bottom of the mushroom from surface or low-altitude nuclear explosions that have taken place in northern middle latitudes. (After Glasstone and Dolon, 1977, Figure 9.96, p. 431.)

Distribution of Fallout

Part of the fallout occurs rather promptly in the vicinity of the blast. Radioactivity that does not reach the stratosphere will drift a few hours or days (see Figs. 3.4 and 3.6) with the wind, coming down as fallout naturally or with rain, up to a few hundred miles away. The effects of this prompt fallout will be essentially on the near and not-so-near surroundings, extending the strategic effects of the bomb on the target area.

Table 2.4 gives a summary of the size of the area that might be made dangerously radioactive by such fallout. The details of the actual fallout pattern depend on wind direction and speed, and on the terrain; therefore, this table is only a very rough approximation to the real world. A 1-Mt bomb may contaminate with an integrated radiation exposure of 500 rem an area of about 2000 km^2, say, 17 km at its widest and 145 km at its longest. Figure 3.4 shows a calculated fallout pattern for a 1-Mt attack on the city of Detroit.

The primary initial harm from this prompt fallout will be caused by

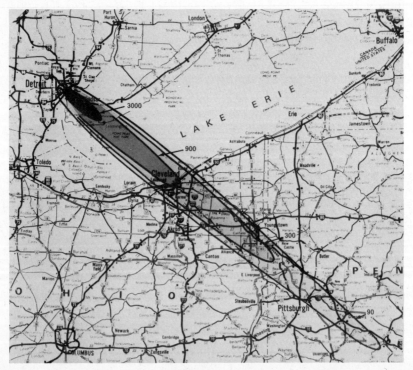

Figure 3.4 Fallout pattern from a 1-Mt surface burst on Detroit, Michigan. A 15-mph (24 km/hr) uniform northwest wind is assumed. The contours are for 7-day accumulated doses, without shielding, of 3000, 900, 300, and 90 rem. (Office of Technology Assessment, 1979, p. 25).

short-lived isotopes such as ^{131}I, with its 8-day half-life. ^{90}Sr and ^{137}Cs with their long half-lives of about 30 years will present longer-term contamination threats to the local fallout area. The longer-lived isotopes also present the global threats discussed in Chapter 4. For very large H-bombs the mushroom will penetrate into the troposphere and even the stratosphere; from there it will spread over the globe. The tropospheric fallout will be trapped there for a month, while the stratospheric fallout will reach the earth after a delay of a year or more. These delay times are long enough for ^{131}I and other shorter-lived isotopes to die out, so that only the long-lived isotopes will have a major global effect.

Effects of Fallout

$^3_1H.$ The amount of tritium released in a nuclear explosion depends on the bomb configuration, and on the efficiency of the fusion reaction. Once tritium reaches the ground, it will become intermingled with all normal hydrogen (^{1}H) in water and will quickly become diluted. Because of its chemical identity with normal hydrogen, there are no significant biological concentration processes. Hence, in spite of its 12.3-year half-life, tritium fallout is relatively harmless.

$^{14}_6C.$ Each megaton of explosive yield will produce about 3.4 kg of ^{14}C. Cosmic-ray bombardment of the atmosphere maintains a constant global supply of about 70 tonnes of ^{14}C, with 66 tonnes in the ocean, 3 tonnes in plants and animals, and 1 tonne in the air. Any ^{14}C fallout will initially be added to the part stored in the atmosphere and then, over a period of about 8 years, will mix into the ocean waters. Since the circulation and concentration paths of carbon are not well known, estimates of the long-term danger from ^{14}C range from essentially zero to being equal to those from ^{90}Sr.

$^{90}_{38}Sr.$ ^{90}Sr is very long-lived with a half-life of 28 years. Each megaton of nuclear explosives produces about 0.4 kg of ^{90}Sr. The more usual way of expressing radioactivity is in terms of curies (Ci) or millicuries (1 Ci = 1000 mCi). A curie is an amount of a radioactive isotope in which $3.7 \cdot 10^{10}$ disintegrations take place each second. One millicurie of ^{137}Cs, for example, gives a radiation dose of 0.33 rem/hr at a distance of 1 m. That 0.4 kg of ^{90}Sr, if evenly spread over a fallout area of 2000 km^2, would give a concentration of 0.02 mCi per m^2. In comparison, the allowed body burden of ^{90}Sr for workers is 0.02 mCi.

The biggest problem created by fallout of ^{90}Sr is probably due to its chemical resemblance to calcium. Like calcium it concentrates in milk; once ingested, it accumulates in growing bones. It emits 550-keV electrons when decaying; these electrons have a short range of about 2 mm in body tissue. Hence that decay energy is all deposited within the bones where the ^{90}Sr is accumulated. This radiation is particularly harmful to the marrow inside the bones that is constantly producing blood cells. ^{90}Sr is harmful for a long time; once inside the body, it stays there on average for 16 years, as shown in Table 3.1. While the presently allowed body burden of ^{90}Sr is 0.02 mCi, the bone burden is only 0.002 mCi.

$^{131}_{53}I.$ ^{131}I has a half-life of 8.1 days, so it presents no long-term fallout danger. But it concentrates biologically in milk products, and it collects in the thyroid gland of humans. Within 24 hr a normal thyroid gland will absorb one-third of all ingested iodine. Because of this rapid concentration effect, iodine presents a special danger in the vicinity of the bomb explosion where the prompt fallout occurs.

$^{137}_{55}Cs.$ ^{137}Cs with its radioactive half-life of 30 years also presents a long-term danger. Somewhat more ^{137}Cs is produced in fission processes than ^{90}Sr, about 0.75 kg for each megaton of nuclear explosive yield. Cesium is not particularly concentrated in biological processes, nor does it stay in the body as long once it has been ingested (see Table 3.1). Thus, it does not present as large a biological threat as ^{90}Sr. Its permissible body burden is 0.03 mCi for an adult. If the 0.75 kg of ^{137}Cs fallout from a 1-Mt H-bomb were spread evenly over 2000 km^2, a gamma-ray dose of about 0.06 mrem/hr will be received by anyone standing on the ground in the open. If this fallout is not cleaned up, over a half-life of that isotope this would come to a total dose of 15 rem.

$^{239}_{92}Pu.$ The amount of ^{239}Pu in nuclear fallout will depend on the bomb design. If the fission trigger of an H-bomb is made of ^{239}Pu, some of the plutonium may be scattered by the bomb explosion if the core is inefficiently fissioned. Some ^{239}Pu will be produced in the ^{238}U jacket of the bomb. The amount of the resulting fallout of ^{239}Pu will depend on the design of the bomb. Assume that 1 kg of ^{239}Pu is left over in the fallout after a 1-Mt explosion. If that ^{239}Pu is spread evenly over 2000

Table 3.1 Comparison of radioactive decay half-lives with the biological half-lives for various long-lived products of nuclear bombs.
The biological half-life indicates the time that a specific atom of that element on average remains in the body after being incorporated, before it is replaced by some other atom and leaves the body. The body burden is that allowed for workers. Based on Report No. 2 of the International Commission on Radiation Protection.

Isotope	Radioactive Decay $T_{1/2}$	Biological $T_{1/2}$	Allowed Body Burden
^{90}Sr	28 years	36 years	0.02 mCi
^{137}Cs	30 years	70 days	0.03 mCi
^{14}C	5,600 years	10 days	0.4 mCi
^{239}Pu	24,400 years	180 years	0.0004 mCi
^{235}U	$0.7 \cdot 10^9$ years	100 days	0.0004 mCi

km², it would be 0.04 μCi/m² ($4\cdot10^{-8}$ Ci/m²). The presently permitted whole body burden for workers is 0.4 μCi, but only 0.04 μCi for the bones. Table 3.1 shows that ^{239}Pu stays in the human body once it has been incorporated into it.

The global distribution of fallout will be considered in Chapter 4 as part of the consequences of full-scale nuclear wars. The focus here in Chapter 3 is on the effects of individual H-bombs.

An additional effect of nuclear weapons is the electromagnetic pulse (EMP) generated by the movement of electric charges from the explosion in the earth's atmosphere. This phenomenon does not affect people directly and is most related to the ability to control military activities during a nuclear war. Hence the EMP will be discussed in Chapter 12.

HISTORY OF THE H-BOMB

The development of the H-bomb led to the deployment of enough nuclear weapons to threaten destruction of all civilization. Controlling the H-bomb might have helped to keep the overkill factor low—although it would not have made nuclear war acceptable. Therefore, the history of the H-bomb will be considered in some detail. The history of the H-bomb has additional significance because it includes an early debate about tactical versus strategic nuclear war.

At the end of World War II, the United States had a nuclear monopoly. During the postwar period of 1949, the United States relied on its A-bombs to offset the large numerical military superiority of the Soviet land forces (Herken, 1980). There is now some debate whether the United States really had enough nuclear weapons before 1949 to carry out a nuclear war successfully; but certainly, after 1947, fission weapons were improved and mass produced. When the Soviet Union produced its first A-bomb in 1949, the shock to American political leaders was great and triggered a crash program aimed at a fusion bomb, against the advice of some technical advisors.

The Soviet A-bomb

The history of the Soviet A-bomb project suggests that attempts to control nuclear weapons would have been in vain, that further A-bomb and H-bomb development and deployment was most likely inevitable. At the beginning of World War II, several countries were actively engaged in nuclear research including the United States, Great Britain, France, Germany, Japan, and the Soviet Union. Each of these nations recognized the implications of fission. Once World War II started,

France could no longer pursue its well-advanced fission chain reaction research since it was defeated by Germany; not until 1960 did France explode its first nuclear device. Great Britain made considerable progress on the theory of an A-bomb early in World War II, inspiring the United States to pursue that project with vigor. Later Great Britain let the American industrial capacity produce the wartime weapon. After World War II, the United States reneged on agreements to share nuclear knowledge, so Great Britain had to start over and, hence, took until 1952 to develop its first nuclear device. Germany had a nuclear reactor research program during World War II but did not get far with it; since the end of the war, it has for political reasons declined to develop nuclear weapons. Japan invested some small effort in a nuclear weapons program during World War II; since then, it too has not developed nuclear weapons for political reasons.

The Soviet Union actively worked toward an A-bomb during and immediately after World War II. From 1941 to 1943, all nuclear research stopped in the Soviet Union due to the German invasion. Once the Soviets began their nuclear weapons program in 1943 in earnest under the physicist I. V. Kurchatov, it was clearly not aimed at winning the war but rather at establishing postwar power. It seems probable that the Soviets knew about the American Manhattan project during World War II, but

> there is no evidence that the Soviet espionage network was concerned with securing information on nuclear development. . . . In all probability, the collected information was not put to its best use until four or five years later. (Kramish, 1959, p. 53)

The first Soviet nuclear reactor went critical in August 1947; it was probably a prototype for ^{239}U production. In the same year, an effort was initiated to produce enriched ^{235}U by gaseous diffusion. On August 29, 1949 the first Soviet nuclear device was exploded, followed by the second in October 1951 and the third in August 1953. At that time the Soviet program thus was indeed about five years behind that of the Americans, but it seems to have experienced no undue technical difficulties.

The American Response
When the Soviet explosion was announced by President Truman a month later in 1949, most government officials and the public were greatly surprised, having perceived the Soviet Union as a technologically backward nation. This surprise led to the demand to develop

something to replace the now-broken U.S. nuclear monopoly. One proposal was to develop the Super.

The Super was a hydrogen bomb design put forward by Edward Teller during World War II. This design had been rejected repeatedly by the scientists on the General Advisory Committee (GAC) to the Atomic Energy Commission (AEC), because its fuel of deuterium and tritium would be hard to produce and would require liquification. The chance of the Super working had been estimated as 50%; if workable, it did not appear to be a usable weapon. The AEC instead had worked to use the fusion process in $^6Li^2D$ and $^6Li^3T$ to boost the power of fission bombs.

The Soviet bomb explosion triggered a reconsideration by the GAC (chaired by Oppenheimer) about whether a crash program to build the Super should be started. The GAC report of October 30, 1949, recommended that more tactical atomic weapons be made available, that the fusion booster program be pushed, and that on technical, military, political, and ethical grounds the Super bomb should not be produced. The ethical considerations included the suggestion that an agreement might be worked out with the Soviet Union not to develop this particular new weapon. The feeling was that very large fission bombs (up to the ½ Mt of the *King* shot of November 16, 1952) would be sufficient to counteract a Soviet H-bomb if the Soviet Union should go ahead to build one first. But under pressure from some scientists, including Teller and Lawrence, from two out of five of the AEC commissioners, and from various government officials, and acting on his own belief, President Truman announced on January 3, 1950 that a crash program for building the Super was being started. The general public was not involved in the policy debate; even after Truman had made his decision, there was great pressure on the participants in the debate not to talk about it in public. For example, there was a ruling by the AEC that its consultants should speak out not even on the unclassified details of the H-bomb—on the grounds that their association with the program might give hints to the Russians about the American plans.

The H-bomb

On May 8, 1951 the *George* nuclear test took place at the Eniwetok atoll in the Pacific Ocean. In this test a small fusion explosion was ignited by a large fission explosion. On May 24, 1951, the *Item* explosion tested the booster principle for a real nuclear device—proving that the yield of a fission bomb could be significantly augmented by a fusion reaction. These were not true fusion devices.

However, earlier in 1951 Stan Ulam and Edward Teller had an

ingenious idea, one that is still classified, although Howard Moreland (Moreland, 1979a, 1979b, 1981) claims to reveal the secret. A clever arrangement of the physical configuration of the fissile and fusible components of the H-bomb made it possible to produce fusion energy that greatly exceeded the released fission energy. It is such a neat idea that Oppenheimer changed his mind about the H-bomb:

> The program we had in 1949 was a tortured thing that you could well argue did not make a great deal of technical sense. It was therefore possible to argue also that you did not want it even if you could have it. The program in 1951 was technically so sweet that you could not argue about that. The issues become purely the military, the political and the humane problem[s] of what you were going to do about it once you had it. (*Bull. Atom. Sci.,* Vol. 14, no. 3 (March 1958), p. 66.)

This design allowed the use of LiD as fuel, made it possible to surround the fusion reaction by a fissioning ^{238}U tamper, and reduced the size of the bomb to the point where it could be carried in bombers and later in missiles.

On November 1, 1952 the *Mike* explosion, with a yield of 10.4 Mt, tested the Ulam-Teller idea for the first time, although it employed a configuration using refrigerated hydrogen. The explosion dug a hole almost a kilometer in radius into the test atoll, completely vaporizing one of the islands in the process, as shown in Fig. 3.5. Table 2.4 would predict for a 10-Mt bomb a crater radius of 364 m. The hole for *Mike* was larger than that because coral is very soft and is hence easier to crater than is typical soil.

On March 1, 1954 the 15-Mt *Bravo* shot tested a LiD prototype for a

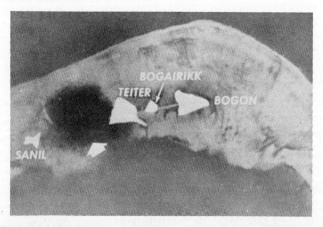

Figure 3.5 The 10-Mt *Mike* fusion explosion of 1952 replaced the island of Elugelab in the Pacific Eniwetok chain with a crater more than 1½ km in diameter (the distance between the epicenter and Bogon was 3 km). (Photo courtesy U.S. Department of Energy; see Hewlett and Duncan, 1969, opposite p. 595.)

useful bomb design, although no usable H-bomb was available to U.S. forces until 1956. This explosion is of additional interest because it first pointed out the very great dangers of radioactive fallout. It was boosted to an unpredicted magnitude by the ^{238}U tamper surrounding the fusion device. The wind direction changed during the test so that the fallout came down in an unexpected direction. Figure 3.6 shows the fallout pattern from that explosion and displays the radiation exposure due to the fallout. The explosion blew a lot of coral debris into the air. When that heavy dust settled three or more hours later, it carried with it the radioactive fission products.

Some islanders on Rongelap worked outside in this fallout for up to 48 hr before being evacuated. They received exposures up to 175 rem. A Japanese tuna trawler, the *Lucky Dragon #5*, was fishing 90 mi north of Rongelap. This vessel also was coated with fallout. When the *Lucky Dragon* returned to Japan two weeks later, most of the crew was suffering from radiation sickness. Because they did not clean off the fallout, ingested some of it, and were exposed to its radiations for two weeks, the 23 crew members had each received a radiation dose of about 200 rem. The victims suffered nausea the night of the explosion, then swelling and reddening of the face, neck, and hands, and complete loss of hair; within three months 17 cases of jaundice were reported. Seven months after the explosion one crew member died from a liver disorder brought on perhaps by a blood transfusion that replaced blood damaged by the radiation. Figure 3.6 shows that the area in which the fallout delivered a lethal dose of 500 rem within 48 hr is about 300 km by 60 km at its maximum, for a total area of about 15,000 km^2. Table 2.3 predicts a lethal fallout area for 15 Mt of about 30,000 km^2 (20,000 mi^2). Considering that the fallout radiation dose displayed

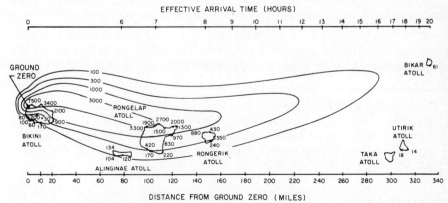

Figure 3.6 The fallout pattern from the 1954 Bravo test of a 15-Mt fission-fusion-fission bomb. The radiation exposure is that received outdoors during the first 48 hr after the explosion. (Glasstone and Dolan, 1977, Figure 9.105, p. 437.)

is for only the first two days, the observed fallout area is reasonably consistent with the predicted area.

This test demonstrated the biological danger of nonfatal fallout. Panic spread through Japan following the *Bravo* shot when it was found that a sizable fraction of the fish caught by Japanese fishermen at that time was radioactive. Plankton had concentrated some of the radioactive fission products from the seawater into their body tissue, so that they were thousands of times more radioactive than the water surrounding them. This indicates that ecological food chains can concentrate certain radioactive isotopes to a considerable extent.

The Soviet Union developed a fusion bomb quickly. It exploded its first device involving fusion on August 12, 1953. Herbert York, the director of the Livermore nuclear laboratory at that time, believes it was a fusion-augmented fission bomb of a few hundred kilotons of yield (see York, 1975). On November 23, 1955 the Soviet Union carried out its second fusion test. That device was apparently a true fusion bomb with a yield of a few megatons and was dropped from an airplane.

Was the H-bomb Inevitable?

The decision to develop the H-bomb was made only after extensive debate; the development was not as uncontrolled as that of the A-bomb. A recommendation against it had been made before it was built, it was not technologically obvious, and it took a special political event to trigger a developmental crash program. The ultimate decision to develop the H-bomb involved tactical versus strategic arguments, the McCarthy era, and the Oppenheimer security clearance hearings of 1954. It mixed political and technological considerations.

The controversy over the 1949 report of the GAC, recommending against a crash program development of the super, had an aftermath in 1953 and 1954. In the atmosphere of the anticommunist crusade that had been going on since 1949, Senator Joseph McCarthy asked why the American H-bomb had been so long in being developed:

> If there were no Communists in our government, why did we delay for eighteen months . . . our research on the hydrogen bomb . . . our nation may well die because of that eighteen-months deliberate delay. And I ask you, who caused it? Was it loyal Americans or was it traitors in our government? (Quoted in Shepley and Blair, 1954, p. 218)

In this atmosphere of a witch hunt for communists, Oppenheimer was accused of being a security risk. His security clearance was withdrawn in December 1953. This meant that he could see no more top-secret documents and was thereby rendered unable to act as scientific advisor on military matters. The hearings on these charges were held for three weeks starting in April 1954. They were not a trial in the ordinary sense; the final decision was only that it was not consistent with the security interests of the United States to reinstate Oppenheimer's security clearance. Twenty-three charges of the accusation dealt with Oppenheimer's association with communists and communistic sympathizers, mainly prior to his work at Los Alamos. The twenty-fourth charge and the testimony at the hearings show that the debate was as much over strategic versus tactical weapons as over espionage and that Oppenheimer stood accused in part because he was associated with tactical nuclear strategies. The H-bomb was seen by Oppenheimer's opponents as a symbol of strategic weaponry—even though many A-bombs were very large and usable only for strategic bombardments of civilian targets.

Strategic versus Tactical Nuclear War

The twenty-fourth accusation against Oppenheimer complained about his opposition in 1949 to the hydrogen bomb:

in the autumn of 1949, and subsequently you strongly opposed the development of the hydrogen bomb (1) on moral grounds, (2) by claiming it was not feasible, (3) by claiming that there was insufficient facilities and scientific personnel to carry on that development and (4) that it was not politically desirable. . . . you were instrumental in persuading other outstanding scientists not to work on the hydrogen-bomb project, and that the opposition to the hydrogen bomb, of which you are the most experienced, most powerful, and most effective member, has definitely slowed down its development. (Quoted in Stern, 1969, pp. 234–235)

By 1954 the H-bomb development program was far advanced. Why was Oppenheimer attacked at such a late date?

The attack appears to have been in part on Oppenheimer as a symbol of tactical nuclear warfare. Oppenheimer had since World War II been a very influential advisor on military matters; he consistently had recommended more tactical nuclear weapons. That advice attacked the orthodoxy of the Air Force, which believed that only strategic bombing would work. Oppenheimer's opinion was that

we must surely be prepared, both in planning and in the development of weapons, and insofar as possible in our "forces in being," for more than one kind of conflict. That is, we must be prepared to meet the enemy in certain crucial, strategic [read "tactical"] areas in which conflict is likely, and to defeat him in those areas. (Quoted in Wilson, 1970, p. 68)

This attitude in favor of tactical nuclear warfare showed up in the 1949 GAC report recommending against a Super crash program.

In Part I, the committee recommended

> an intensification of efforts to make atomic weapons available for tactical purposes, and to give attention to the problem of integration of bomb and carrier design in this field. (Quoted in York, 1975, p. 152)

One argument against building the Super had been that it would have reduced the number of "small" fission bombs that could have been made available.

The Air Force however was committed to the concept of strategic bombing.

> The USSR in the airman's view is . . . not really vulnerable to attack by sea. Furthermore, it has a tremendous store of manpower. . . . So my feeling is that it is relatively invulnerable to land attack. . . . Russia is . . . vulnerable only to attack by air power. (As quoted in Wilson, 1970, p. 72)

For this air attack, bombs with the very largest possible yields seemed desirable. The Super promised a very large yield.

Thus, the Strategic Air Command disagreed strongly with Oppenheimer. It seemed to officials of the Air Force that Oppenheimer opposed them at every point, favoring the other services. The SAC commander, General Roscoe Wilson, expressed this feeling when he complained that

> Dr. Oppenheimer also opposed the nuclear powered aircraft . . . but at the same time he felt less strongly opposed to the nuclear powered ships. The Air Force feeling was that at least the same energy should be devoted to both projects. (as Quoted in Wilson, 1970, p. 78)

The chief scientist of the Air Force, David T. Griggs, associated Oppenheimer with what he felt to be undue optimism in 1952 that an early warning system against bombers might work—an optimism he feared might lead to large expenditures at the expense of SAC. Oppenheimer's opposition to the H-bomb seemed one more objection to SAC's primary interest in the largest possible nuclear bomb for area strategic bombing.

It is not surprising that this attack on Oppenheimer flared up early in Eisenhower's presidency. During Truman's years as president, strategic bombing concepts were tempered by the demands for tactical capabilities, both nuclear and conventional, as expressed for example in the Korean conflict. President Eisenhower's reliance on massive retaliation made untenable Oppenheimer's advisory position favoring tactical nuclear weapons.

Was the H-bomb Inevitable?

It has often been suggested that new military technologies take on a life of their own once they have become feasible. The fusion bomb technology was adopted. Attempts to control the technological development failed. Does this case prove a general argument that attempts to control technologically new weapons are bound to fail?

The General Advisory Committee to the AEC in 1949 recommended an effort to halt the development of hydrogen bombs:

> We all hope that by one means or another, the development of these weapons can be avoided. . . . The majority feel that it should be an unqualified commitment [by the United States not to develop the weapon]. Others feel that it should be made conditional on the response of the Soviet government to a proposal to renounce such development. (Quoted in York, 1975, pp. 155–156)

Members of the committee in several statements clearly expressed the quantitative increase in danger to mankind represented by the H-bomb. It should not be produced:

> Its use would involve a decision to slaughter a vast number of civilians. . . . If super bombs will work at all, there is no inherent limit in the destructive power that may be attained by them. Therefore, a super bomb might become a weapon of genocide. . . . Mankind would be far better off not to have a demonstration of the feasibility of such a weapon until the present climate of world opinion changes. . . . In determining not to proceed to develop the super bomb, we see a unique opportunity of providing by example some limitations on the totality of war. (Quoted in York, 1975, pp. 156–157)

Might the delay of the American Super have persuaded the Soviet Union to stop or delay its development of an H-bomb? That question has no verifiable answer. If the Soviet H-bomb development had not stopped, would the security of the United States have become endangered? York has speculated about what might have been the possible consequences of a delay in the development of the American Super (York, 1975). In York's "most probable" alternative world, both the United States and the Soviet Union would have delayed their fusion bomb development. If both H-bomb programs had been delayed by agreement, it would proabably not have delayed the H-bomb forever. But it might have brought the decision on the H-bomb development into the era of President Eisenhower and Premier Krushchev. These leaders might have been more interested in arms limitation discussions on the development of the H-bomb. The ultimate nondevelopment of the H-bomb is unlikely, but perhaps some agreements might have limited the number deployed.

In York's "worst possible" case the Soviet Union would not have slowed down its H-bomb program and would have tested its first true fusion bomb in 1955. Would the United States have been in real danger in this case? Probably not. The concepts of the U.S. fusion bomb most likely would have been developed and improved even without a full-scale test, particularly since the 1951 fusion booster test would presumably have taken place. With the rapid development of computer technology in the early 1950s, a short delay in the H-bomb program most probably would have been made up by the much more improved simulation capabilities, leading to more rapid progress once development of the H-bomb was resumed. The U.S. fusion program might have caught up to build its first fusion device perhaps by 1955 or 1956.

York argues that the GAC was most likely right in 1949 when it suggested that a delay in the fusion program would be not very costly and might be very desirable for arms control. But York's argument can be turned around; the likelihood of such an arms control agreement on the H-bomb was very low. The fact that a delay in the Super crash program would probably have had little effect on the ultimate development of fusion devices suggests that technical developments made the H-bomb increasingly easier to design and, hence, increasingly more likely. Probably the H-bomb was indeed "technically so sweet" that it could not be resisted for long: probably the climate in the 1950s was not right for an agreement on H-bomb deployment. Existence of the mutual assured destruction provided by large stockpiles of A-bombs and H-bombs may have been necessary to provide the impetus for strategic arms limitations.

References

Golovin, I. N. *I. V. Khurchatov: A Socialist-Realist Biography of the Nuclear Scientist,* trans. by W. H. Dougherty from the Russian. Bloomington, Ind.: Selbstverlag Press, 1969.

Herken, G. *The Winning Weapon: The Atomic Bomb in the Cold War, 1945–1950.* New York: Alfred A. Knopf, 1980.

Hewlett, R. G., and F. Duncan. *Atomic Shield, 1947/1952: A History of the United States Atomic Energy Commission,* Vol. II. University Park: Pennsylvania State University Press, 1969.

Kramish, A. *Atomic Energy in the Soviet Union.* Stanford, Calif.: Stanford University Press, 1959.

Morland, H. "The H-bomb Secret." *Progressive,* Vol. 43, no. 11 (November 1979a), pp. 14–25; "Errata." *Progressive,* Vol. 43, no. 12 (December 1979b), p. 36; and *The Secret That Exploded.* New York: Random House, 1981.

Office of Technology Assessment. *The Effects of Nuclear War.* Washington, D.C.: Government Printing Office, 1979.

Shepley, J. R., and C. Blair, Jr. *The Hydrogen Bomb: The Men, the Menace, the Mechanism.* New York: David McKay, 1954.

Stern, P. M. *The Oppenheimer Case: Security on Trial.* New York: Harper & Row, 1969.

York, H. F. *The Advisors: Oppenheimer, Teller and the Superbomb.* San Francisco: W. H. Freeman: 1975.

Wilson, T. H., Jr., *The Great Weapons Heresy.* Boston: Houghton Mifflin, 1970.

CHAPTER
4

Massive Retaliation

We witness today, in the power of nuclear weapons, a new and deadly dimension to the ancient horror of war. Humanity has now achieved, for the first time in its history, the power to end its history.

President Dwight D. Eisenhower, 1956

The survivors would envy the dead.

Premier Nikita S. Khrushchev, 1962

The Oppenheimer case is an example of the struggle among U.S. policymakers after World War II over the proper military role of nuclear weapons. No clearly defined nuclear strategy existed until President Eisenhower formulated the concept of massive nuclear retaliation. When the assured destruction became mutual, this concept made deterrence possible through a balance of terror. Massive retaliation exploited the ease with which very large H-bombs could be built.

POSTWAR MILITARY NUCLEAR POLICY

At the end of World War II, the United States shifted its emphasis from a large Army and Navy to strategic bombing, including the use of the A-bomb. The Soviet Union was thought to have overwhelming superiority in military personnel. The American public was not prepared to pay for a very large military establishment. Consequently the nuclear monopoly of the U.S. Air Force was perceived as a necessary counterbalance to this conventional superiority. The public debate of this policy was limited, but in 1949 strategic bombing was accepted as the dominant U.S. military policy.

82   The U.S. Air Force believed Douhet's theory of air power. The results of strategic area bombing in World War II led it to believe that massive air bombardment would win any future war. The Air Force accepted the enemy's civilian population as a proper target of nuclear weapons. In 1949 too few nuclear weapons were available to attack a large number of separate military targets, and high-altitude bombing was too inaccurate to allow the attack of small tactical military targets. The Air Force, therefore, emphasized the role of the Strategic Air Command (SAC).

The Navy was not enthusiastic about the major role to be played by SAC. It was afraid that funds for aircraft carrier forces might be cut to pay for strategic bombers. It felt that the next war was likely to be a long one, so that long-term protection of sea lanes was important. The Navy argued on military, political, and ethical grounds that Soviet cities were improper targets for aerial bombardment. Neither did the Army appreciate SAC; it wanted an increased capability to fight tactical wars, possibly involving the use of small nuclear weapons.

These anti-SAC arguments were overridden in 1949 when it was decided to deploy the B-36 intercontinental bomber, develop inflight refueling, and launch the H-bomb crash program. Funding for the Army and Navy was kept relatively low; strategic rather than tactical objectives would be the primary targets in a major war.

The Doctrine of Massive Retaliation

The Korean conflict showed that nuclear weapons could not offer the United States national security against all kinds of military attacks. President Truman's response to this insecurity was to bolster expensive conventional military capabilities.

In 1953 Dwight D. Eisenhower became president, having promised during the campaign to balance the budget and remove the United States from Korea. His secretary of State, John Foster Dulles, viewed communism as a worldwide threat that needed to be contained by military means. The problem was to confront this threat yet at the same time limit defense spending. As Dulles put it, "We want for ourselves and others a maximum deterrent at bearable costs." This requirement produced the doctrine of massive retaliation. The United States would not develop a expensive conventional military capability to defeat the Russians in a tactical war. Instead, the policy of massive retaliation specified that any conventional attack on the United States or its allies would be answered by large nuclear blows at a time and place of America's choosing.

The objective of threatening massive retaliation was to deter the Soviet Union from any kind of military attack. How strong would a nuclear retaliatory threat have to be to act as an effective deterrent?

Alain C. Enthoven and K. Wayne Smith analyzed this question in their book *How Much Is Enough* (1971). They saw two parts to this question. What damage would a nation, such as the Soviet Union, find unacceptable, no matter how worthy a military or political objective was involved? And how many nuclear weapons, of what kind, are required to achieve a destruction in excess of this unacceptable amount?

In practice, this analytical process is complicated and uncertain. In the real world, the available destructive capability tends to affect the perception of what destruction is necessary, and the cost-benefit judgments of the enemy's leadership depend on circumstances and can only be guessed. Such judgments will be discussed in Chapter 8. The tendency in the past has been to reverse the program just outlined and ask first how much destruction can be achieved by how many nuclear weapons. The damage to two different types of strategic targets enter into such a calculation: What are the effects on civilian populations and on civilian industry?

Retaliatory Targeting

When the distributions of population and industry in the Soviet Union and in the United States are analyzed, it becomes evident that a considerable fraction of each is located in the major cities. Beyond these large cities, the remaining population and industry are widely dispersed. Table 4.1 shows that for the Soviet Union the 30 largest cities contain more than 25% of all the urban population and that another 25% of the urbanites are distributed over the next largest 100 cities. Even bigger concentrations hold for the industrial capacity, with the 10 largest cities containing 25% of all industry.

Given such concentrations, how much population and industrial capacity can a massive-retaliation nuclear attack destroy? A rough

Table 4.1 The cumulative distribution of Soviet population and industrial capacities as of 1970.
Based on Kemp, 1974, p. 5.

Number of Cities	Population (thousands)	% of Total Population	% of Urban Population	% of Industrial Capacity
10	21,317	8.8%	15.7%	25%
30	37,136	15.4	27.3	25 < % < 40[a]
50	46,004	19.1	33.8	40
100	59,828	24.8	44.0	50
200	74,532	30.9	54.8	62
300	82,997	34.4	61.0	62 < % < 72[a]

[a]The precise percentages are not known.

order-of-magnitude estimate can be made by developing some target-ing scenarios in which nuclear warheads are distributed to maximize some destructive measure (e.g., the civilian population killed or the industrial installation destroyed); estimating the area destroyed by a single warhead; multiplying the area destroyed by each warhead by the density of the target parameter in that area; and summing these individual destructions for all the warheads in the attack.

Civilian Casualties

Table 4.2 shows the result of a targeting exercise in which a Soviet military planner might have been asked to target 50 1-Mt warheads against U.S. population centers to maximize civilian fatalities. From Tables 2.4 and 2.5 it was argued that the area of lethality for popula-

Table 4.2 Results of an imaginary targeting exercise in which a Russian military planner has been asked to target 50 1-Mt H-bombs onto U.S. metropolitan areas with the objective of maximizing civilian casualties.[a]

The population data are taken from *U.S. Bureau of the Census Statistical Abstracts of the United States: 1982–83* (103 ed.), Washington, D.C.: Government Printing Office, 1982, pp. 22–24.

City	Population Density	Area	Bombs	Deaths
New York	26,000/mi^2	300 mi^2	10	7.8 M
San Francisco	15,700/mi^2	45 mi^2	1	0.5 M
Philadelphia	15,100/mi^2	129 mi^2	4	1.8 M
Chicago	15,100/mi^2	222 mi^2	7	3.2 M
Boston	14,000/mi^2	46 mi^2	1	0.4 M
Washington	12,300/mi^2	61 mi^2	2	0.7 M
First 25 1-Mt bombs			25	14.4 M
Newark	16,300/mi^2	24 mi^2	1	0.4 M
Baltimore	11,600/mi^2	78 mi^2	2	0.7 M
Detroit	11,000/mi^2	138 mi^2	4	1.3 M
St. Louis	10,200/mi^2	61 mi^2	2	0.6 M
Cleveland	9,900/mi^2	76 mi^2	2	0.6 M
Pittsburgh	9,400/mi^2	55 mi^2	2	0.5 M
Milwaukee	7,600/mi^2	95 mi^2	3	0.7 M
San Francisco	15,700/mi^2	(15 mi^2)	1	0.2 M
Minneapolis	7,900/mi^2	55 mi^2	2	0.4 M
Long Beach	7,400/mi^2	49 mi^2	1	0.2 M
Seattle	6,400/mi^2	84 mi^2	2	0.4 M
Los Angeles	6,100/mi^2	464 mi^2	3	0.5 M
Second 25 1-Mt bombs			25	6.6 M
Total of 50 1-Mt bombs			50	21.0 M

[a]M1 = 1 millions.

tions is about 75 km² (30 mi²), with the survivors inside that area balanced by the fatalities outside that area. In such an exercise, the major U.S. cities would be targeted in order of decreasing population densities. This particular attack is calculated to produce fatalities of 14 million for the first 25 Mt and 7 million for the second 25 Mt. In the real world, no Soviet planner (or American planner) would be likely to get such an assignment; industrial and military targets are sure to be at least as high on any target list.

Nonetheless, this order-of-magnitude calculation makes several points. If unevacuated cities are attacked, relative small numbers of nuclear weapons can cause large numbers of fatalities. There is a saturation effect, as increasing numbers of attacking warheads have decreasing effects at the margin; doubling the number of attacking warheads does not double the fatalities. Finally, careful targeting could presumably lead to even more effective destruction, since the populations within these cities are not evenly distributed but, rather, are clustered so that fewer bombs might achieve almost the same effects.

There exist many more sophisticated estimates of the effects of massive retaliation attacks. In such targeting exercises it is not the megatonnage (the yield Y) but the area destroyed that is important. Thus, generally, the calculations are done in terms of equivalent megatons (EMT). Table 2.5 shows that the radius of destruction by blast of nuclear weapons increases with $Y^{1/3}$. Hence the area of destruction of warheads increases with $Y^{2/3}$. Thus a 1-Mt warhead destroys 100 times the area that a 1-kt warhead does, even though its yield is 1000 times as large ($1000^{2/3} = 100$). Figure 4.1 shows the equivalent megatonnage for warheads of various yields. For example, it shows that the destructive effect of a 100-kt warhead is 0.22 EMT ($0.1^{2/3} = 0.22$); that is, it destroys one-fifth as big an area as does a 1-Mt warhead, even though its yield is one-tenth as large. In terms of the area destroyed per kt of yield, the smaller warhead is more than twice as effective.

All calculations of fatalities and industrial capacity destroyed under a nuclear attack for either the United States or the Soviet Union show results similar to those in Table 4.2. They show an initial rapid rise of damage with increasing levels of attack and then exhibit the saturation effects at high attack levels. The curve usually cited in discussions of how much is enough is in Kemp (1974, p.39). According to that figure, 50 Mt of nuclear explosives would cause about 25 million Soviet fatalities. This number is comparable to the 21 million fatalities in Table 4.2. The actual casualties could be much larger.

Figure 4.2 shows the percentage of the total populations (urban and rural) living cumulatively on increasing land areas in the Soviet Union

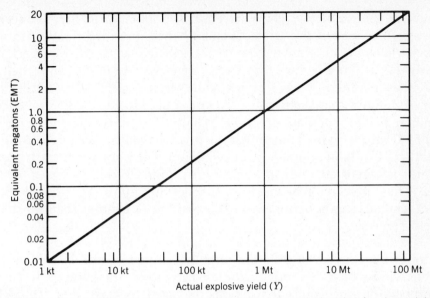

Figure 4.1 The equivalent megatonnage (EMT) of nuclear warheads of various yields Y. This is a plot of the equation EMT $= Y^{2/3}$, where both the EMT and the yield are given in megatons. The EMT is proportional to the area of destruction of the warhead when used on "soft" targets such as cities.

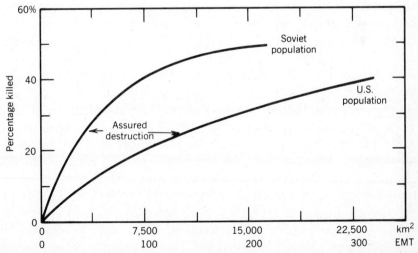

Figure 4.2 The Soviet and U.S. populations as a function of cumulative land area. (After Arms Control and Disarmament Agency, 1978, p. 3; also p. 311 of Katz, 1982.) If one assumes the destructive area of a 1-EMT warhead to be 75 km² (30 mi², see Table 2.3), then one can determine the explosive yield required to achieve that destruction. The total U.S. strategic arsenal contains more than 4000 EMT. The total Soviet and U.S. populations in 1980 were about 255 and 220 million, respectively.

and the United States. The Soviet urban population is more concentrated than that in the United States, hence one might expect more Soviet fatalities for a small strategic attack such as the 50-Mt attack of Table 4.2. If one assumes that 1 EMT destroys 75 km² (30 mi²), then a properly planned 50-EMT attack could destroy 3750 km² (1500 mi²); Fig. 4.2 shows that destroying 3750 km² could kill about 28% of the 255 million Soviet population, or 71 million. The curve suggests for a 50-EMT attack on the United States a possible fatality rate of about 12% for the 220 million population, or 26 million. The number for the United States is consistent with the order-of-magnitude calculation of Table 4.2. Thus, it seems reasonable to suspect that maximum possible Soviet fatalities might be more like those of Fig. 4.2 rather than those of Kemp (1974).

The disagreement between Fig. 4.2 and Kemp (1974) indicates uncertainties introduced by different targeting scenarios and by the precision with which the population distributions are known. If large numbers of small nuclear weapons are used to make up a strategic attack, they can be more selectively targeted on smaller population centers and can be more effective. The U.S. submarine-launched missiles form such a force of smaller nuclear warheads.

Many more sophisticated targeting scenarios have been evaluated, often in connection with the question of how many casualties a limited nuclear attack on military installations might produce. The estimated consequences depend very much on whether civilian or military installations are targeted, on the level of protection for the population through civil defense measures, and on the resulting fallout distributions. Some scenarios resembling massive retaliation will be described here. Chapter 12 will review the effects on civilians of attacks on military targets.

During a hearing before Congress in 1959, a Soviet nuclear attack on 71 population and industrial centers with 284 EMT (71 8-Mt warheads) plus 869 Mt on 111 Air Force installations, 21 AEC installations, and 21 other military installations was estimated to kill 28% of the U.S. population (Katz, 1982). This is low compared with Fig. 4.2.

The 1979 report on *The Effects of Nuclear War* by the Office of Technology Assessment (see Chapter 3) discussed the effects of a very large nuclear exchange involving thousands of warheads targeted on both urban-industrial and military targets. If all weapons are exploded at ground level, and if no civil defense measures exist, 155 million to 165 million Americans and 64 million to 100 million Soviet citizens might be killed. If air bursts predominate, and if enough warning exists to seek shelter, American fatalities might be reduced to 76 to 85 million.

With evacuation of the cities, American fatalities might range from 20 million to 55 million and Soviet fatalities from 23 million to 34 million.

Arthur Katz (1982) reviewed the expected effects of a very large nuclear attack on American cities and industries. He considered an attack with 500 1-Mt warheads on 71 U.S. standard metropolitan statistical areas, plus up to 300 100-kt warheads on industrial targets in 34 manufacturing sectors. This attack was estimated to have the potential to cause 50–60 million fatalities plus 20–30 million moderate to severe injuries. Figure 4.2 predicts Soviet civilian fatalities for this attack in excess of 50%, or more than 125 million, if the attack were only on strategic targets. The attack scenario described by Katz resulted in fewer fatalities than might be expected because its main goal was industrial and economic damage, with civilian casualties being a secondary goal.

In general, one may say that the vulnerabilities of Soviet and American civilians to strategic city attacks are roughly comparable, unless civil defense makes a major difference. For attacks that kill fewer than 50% of the population, the Soviet population is at least as vulnerable as that of the United States; the Soviet urban population is more densely packed in fewer large cities, and the United States has more suburbs. At the high end of the fatality ranges, for very large attacks, the United States may be more vulnerable, as a larger percentage of its population is urban; fewer Americans are engaged in agriculture.

The fatality rates just described represent prompt fatalities within 30 days after a nuclear attack. They do not take into account fatalities due to longer-term radiation sickness, lack of medical care, food and housing problems, and psychological effects. These effects will be discussed shortly in this chapter.

Industrial Damage

It is more difficult to estimate the industrial capacity that can be destroyed by a nuclear attack. A simple estimate may be made by assuming that industrial capacity is roughly proportional to the urban population living in cities with populations above 50,000. This assumption is reasonably consistent with the last two columns of Table 4.1. The fraction of the Soviet population that is urban is about 49% as defined by the U.S. Arms Control and Disarmament Agency (ACDA) (1978). Kemp (1974) calculates that 100 Mt can kill as much as 40% of the Soviet population or 80% of the urban population. Thus one would estimate that 100 Mt might destroy up to 80% of Soviet industry. Figure 4.3 suggests that 60% might actually be destroyed by 100 Mt.

Kemp estimates that 100 Mt of nuclear explosions might destroy 60%

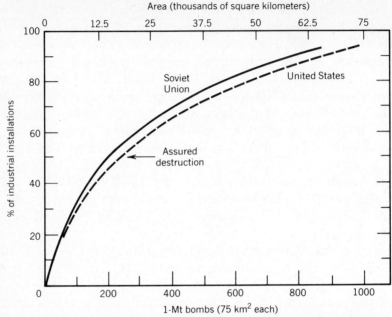

Figure 4.3 The cumulative land areas covered by U.S. and USSR industries. (After Katz, 1982, Figure 10.3, p. 313.) The EMT required to destroy that industry is calculated assuming that one 1-Mt warhead destroys industry over a 75-km² (30 mi²) area.

of Soviet industry, whereas the scenario of Katz shows enormous industrial damage for that 500⁺-Mt attack on American industry, namely, 60–65% of the total U.S. industry. It reduces eight key industries to less than 3% of their prewar level, namely, petroleum refining, iron and steel works, nonferrous metals smelting and refining, engines and turbines, electrical distribution products, drugs, office machines, and mechanical measuring devices.

Figure 4.3 demonstrates the comparative industrial vulnerabilities of the United States and the Soviet Union. This plot was derived by the U.S. Arms Control and Disarmament Agency (1978) by asking how many circles with a radius of 1.65 mi (an area of 9.34 mi² or 24 km²) would be required to cover the industries. Not only are Soviet and American vulnerabilities basically the same, but both industrial bases cover a relatively small area. About 70% of each industrial base covers less than 15,000 mi² (38,000 km²). If one assumes a vulnerability for industry of 5 psi, then 300 EMT are sufficient to destroy 50% of the industry of either country and 500 EMT would destroy 75%. These are somewhat lower estimates of vulnerability than Kemp's. Kemp's data are for destruction of "manufacturing value added," the additional value imparted to raw materials as they go through industrial processes in these plants. Figure 4.3 suggests that the least value-additive industries are also the least vulnerable, perhaps because they are more widely scattered.

More detailed attack scenarios have been explored. They generally not only confirm the foregoing destructive capabilities but further emphasize the extreme vulnerability of a complex industrial system due to weak points created by certain industries. The OTA study (see Chapter 3) points out that a 10-EMT attack could destroy 73% of the Soviet oil refining capacity and 16% of the national storage capacity. A Soviet attack with 80 EMT on U.S. oil refineries could destroy 64% of the national refining capacity. Similar vulnerabilities exist for aluminum and steel mills, as shown in Fig. 4.4.

In general Soviet and U.S. industry appear to be roughly comparable in their vulnerability. The Soviet Union is larger, but its industrial system is highly centralized, which keeps its industry very clustered in large complexes for economics of scale.

GLOBAL CONSEQUENCES OF NUCLEAR WAR

So far no questions have been asked about what would face the survivors if a nuclear attack were to take place on a national or global scale. Yet lack of medical facilities, economic ruin, and social chaos might conceivably make the survivors envy the dead, as civilization might

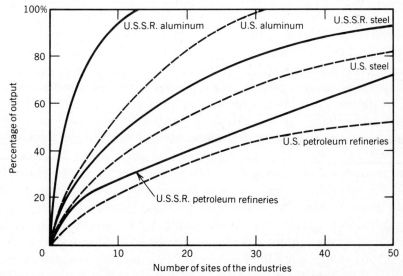

Figure 4.4 The vulnerability of oil refineries, steel mills, and aluminum mills to nuclear attack is very high because of their concentration in a very few locations. (After Lewis, 1979, p. 46.)

collapse. Might there also be global effects, of fallout or on the weather, that might wipe out humankind? Is it possible that the end might come with a whimper, as might everyone die of fallout as in Neville Shute's *On the Beach?* Might humankind die out as some atmospheric consequences spread throughout the world, as worries Jonathan Schell in *The Fate of the Earth?* Or might populations not directly exposed to nuclear attacks feel no major effects?

Survivors of Nuclear War

It is impossible to imagine all the consequences of a full-scale nuclear war. The journal *Ambio* of the Royal Swedish Academy of Sciences outlined a scenario for such a war (see Chapter 2). Its staff assumed that 14,747 warheads of 5742-Mt total yield would be used. These were assumed to be targeted on cities of 100,000 population or more in the major industrialized countries, on cities of 500,000 population or more in other nations in the northern hemisphere, on industry, and on military installations. In this strategic scenario, out of an urban population of nearly 1.3 billion in the northern hemisphere, 750 million would be killed outright and 340 million would be seriously injured, and of the 200 million initially uninjured urban survivors, many would ultimately die from latent radiation effects and infectious diseases such as cholera, tuberculosis, and dysentery.

To illustrate these postwar effects, consider some medical aspects of treating survivors with burns in the United States. In Hiroshima and Nagasaki, 65% of all survivors had burn injuries. In the *Ambio* reference scenario, 340 million out of 1300 million people, or 26% of the population, are seriously injured. For the United States this would be 35 million. If 65% of these had burn injuries, there would be 23 million Americans with burn injuries after a full-scale nuclear war, presumably many with extensive second- and third-degree burns requiring significant treatment. The United States has approximately 1000 to 2000 so-called "burn beds" in specialized institutions. Treatment of a severe burn now lasts as long as 100 days. Even if these burn centers and their staffs survived the nuclear war, and even if the economy and medical supplies would allow it, only a minute fraction of burn victims could be treated properly. Hospitals and physicians might unfortunately be more likely to be destroyed, injured, or killed than the general population because they are concentrated in the cities. The Federal Emergency Management Agency estimated in 1980 that in the United States, the preattack medical resources of 1.5 million hospital beds and 395,000 active physicians would be reduced, respectively, to 460,000 and 79,000 after a full-scale nuclear war.

Burns are only one of many probable medical problems. It has been estimated (Chivian et al., 1982, p. 231) that deaths from communicable diseases among the survivors of a full-scale nuclear war might approach 20–25%. The medical problems will be aggravated by the many other difficulties likely to face the survivors as the economy would be destroyed and crops ruined. One possible consequence of a full-scale nuclear war might well be a collapse of the present civilization, with all its technical, economic, political, and moral interconnections.

The Physical Effects of Full-Scale Nuclear War

So far the physical effects of individual H-bombs have been considered, together with the national and global consequences to society of a full-scale nuclear war. Are there any physical consequences of global nuclear war that might be serious enough to threaten not only the collapse of civilization, but the extinction of mankind? Possible global effects of nuclear wars have been discussed in several reports; in particular in those by the National Academy of Sciences (NAS) in 1975, the Royal Swedish Academy of Sciences in 1983, and Turco et al. and Ehrlich et al. in 1983. The NAS study presented a relatively optimistic technical view, the Swedish study raised concern about possible unexpected additional climatic consequences, and the Turco and Ehrlich studies represent a very pessimistic analysis of these additional climatic effects.

The NAS study considered the long-term world-wide effects of a large-scale nuclear war on environmental and ecological processes. The report did not consider what would happen in the directly involved nations, it did not ask what would happen to human society. The report seemed to support the conclusion that "the biosphere and the species, Homo Sapiens [will] survive," as the then President of the NAS, Philip Handler, put it in a cover letter when transmitting the report.

The NAS analysed the consequences of a large-scale nuclear war in which 10,000 Mt of nuclear bombs are exploded in the northern hemisphere. This would be the equivalent of 2½ tons of TNT per person on the earth. In World War II it was found that on the average 1 to 3 tons of high explosive bombs were required to kill one inhabitant of a city. In Great Britain 60,000 tons of bombs killed 40,000 people; in Germany ½ million fatalities were caused by nearly 1½ million tons of explosives; in Japan a similar number of fatalities were caused by a few hundred thousand tons of bombs. As the Swedish study showed, these 10,000 Mt are sufficient to wipe out most of the urban population in the major nations of the world.

But direct blast and radiation effects cannot wipe out the part of the world population that is widely scattered over rural areas. What might happen to those persons not directly exposed to bombs? The report considered the effects of 10,000 Mt, which equals the strategic mega-tonnage presently deployed (see Table 8.3) but is only about 20% of the present estimated nuclear arsenals (deployed plus stored) of the super-powers. An actual full-scale nuclear war, if continued for some time, might thus have considerably larger effects than those estimated by the NAS report. The report summary says that:

> There would be three primary global effects. An exchange of 10^4 Mt TNT equiva-lent yield in the northern hemisphere would produce an average cumulative fallout of ^{90}Sr of about 1 Ci/km^2 in the middle latitudes of the northern hemisphere. The corresponding latitudes of the southern hemisphere would receive about one third that amount. "Hot spots" of up to 30 times this magnitude could occur. Dust and NO [nitrous oxide] injection into the stratosphere could lead to significant climatological effects. Present understanding of climatological phenomena is insuf-ficient to predict these effects. They would probably lie within normal global climatic variability, but the possibility of climatic changes of a more dramatic nature cannot be ruled out. Preliminary results of a simplified model indicate that a 30–70 percent reduction in the ozone column in the northern hemisphere and 20–40 percent reductions in the southern hemisphere, with a recovery time of two to four years, are possible. (NAS, 1975, p. 7)

In contrast, Turco et al. (1983, p. 1283) conclude that

> For many simulated exchanges of several thousand megatons, in which dust and smoke are generated and encircle the earth within 1 to 2 weeks, average light levels can be reduced to a few percent of ambient and land temperatures can reach -15 to $-25°$C. The yield threshold for major optical and climatic consequences may be very low; only about 100 megatons detonated over major urban centers can create . . . subfreezing land temperatures for months.

The global fallout and ultraviolet radiation effects reported here are based on the NAS study. The description here of possible global effects due to soot and fine dust will be based on Turco et al. (1983), who coin the term "nuclear winter" to characterize the resulting climatic consequences.

Effects of Fallout

Following the 10,000-Mt war, there might be approximately 0.2 nanocuries ($0.2 \cdot 10^{-9}$ Ci) of ^{90}Sr per liter (per quart) in the milk of cows not directly exposed to local fallout, plus 3 nCi of ^{137}Ci. The body accumulation in a typical adult might be 50 nCi and 600 nCi of ^{90}Sr and ^{137}Cs, respectively 3 years after the war (Peterson et al., 1983, p. 127). These isotopes then leave the body with physiological half-lives of about 36 years and 70 days, respectively. Based on such numbers, the

NAS report estimated that the fallout will lead globally, in areas not directly exposed to local fallout, to a long-term total exposure to the average person of perhaps 8 rem in the northern hemisphere if the effects of ^{14}C are included, perhaps one-third as much in the southern hemisphere. The effects of the very toxic, but very diluted, ^{239}Pu in the fallout cannot be readily estimated. Altogether 2–20 million total additional global cancer deaths might occur, compared with an annual cancer fatality rate of about 5 million. This number is based on an estimate of 200 to 2000 cancer deaths per megaton yield of nuclear explosives burst in the air (OTA, 1979, p. 113). Overall, the global fallout effects do not appear to threaten the extinction of *homo sapiens* as a species, as has been hypothesized by Neville Shute, and feared by Jonathan Schell.

Changes in Ultraviolet Radiation

The 10^4 Mt of nuclear explosives predicated in the NAS study would produce 5 to 50 times more nitrous oxide than is presently contained in the atmosphere. The NAS study assumed the use of 1-Mt, 3-Mt and 5-Mt nuclear bombs. These would inject the NO into the stratosphere, where it would destroy ozone by catalytic reactions of the type

$$NO + O_3 \rightarrow NO_2 + O_2$$
$$O_3 + light \rightarrow O_2 + O$$
$$\underline{O + NO_2 \rightarrow NO + O_2}$$
$$Net: \quad 2O_3 \rightarrow 3O_2$$

Such an attack with 10^4 Mt of nuclear weapons might significantly deplete the ozone column. Combined with the 10^7 to 10^8 tons of dust that the NAS thought likely to be injected into the atmosphere by the explosions, this might reduce global average temperatures by a few tenths of a degree Centigrade, with the upper limit on the uncertainty being perhaps 1°C. Since 1°C of cooling is thought to threaten commercial wheat growing in Canada, such temperature changes might have a significant effect on food supplies and food distribution patterns.

The depletion of the ozone layer in the stratosphere greatly increases ultraviolet (UV) radiation at the earth's surface as shown in column 3 of Table 4.3. UV-B is the portion of the sun's ultraviolet radiation that penetrates the earth's atmosphere. The increased UV-B radiation would cause increased sunburn (second-degree burns), harm some aquatic species, and damage crops.

The NAS study reports that various species might be affected by an increased exposure to ultraviolet radiation. The extent of its effect depends on the sensitivity of the species to light. Some species may

Table 4.3   Erythema time in the tropics.
A minimal erythemal dose (MED) leads to a reddening of the skin. At about 15 MED blistering and other more serious effects develop. (After National Academy of Sciences, 1975, p. 177.)

% Decrease of Ozone	Yield (10^3 Mt)	Hemisphere (and limit)	Relative UV-B Factor	Minimal Erythema (minutes)	15 MED (minutes)
0%	0	No war	1	12	180
10%			1.6	7.5	113
20%	10	South (minimum)	2.2	5.4	81
30%	10	North (minimum)	3.3	3.6	54
40%	10	South (minimum)	4.9	2.4	36
50%			7.1[a]	1.7[a]	25[a]
60%			10.1	1.2	18
70%	10	North (maximum)	16.0	0.75	11
80%	15	North (maximum)	23[b]	0.52[b]	7.8[b]
90%	20	North (maximum)	34[b]	0.35[b]	5.3[b]

[a] These numbers are changed from the values given in the original tables; interpolations indicate that the original values are in error.
[b] Extrapolation beyond 70% ozone depletion.

now be at their upper level of tolerance; for such species a large increase in UV-B might be fatal.

> Many aquatic species appear to have relatively little reserve tolerance to existing solar UV-B—even a relatively small increase in UV-B exposure could be lethal. (NAS, 1975, p. 13)

Consider the median projected ozone depletion of 50% for three years after a 10^4-Mt attack, corresponding to a sixfold increase in ultra-violet radiation. Light-skinned human beings in the tropics might then get a blistering sunburn from a 30-min exposure to the sun. Unless protected from direct sunlight, no one could venture outside into the sun for a useful working period.

The NAS estimate is that such a 50% depletion of the ozone layer would lead to a 10% increase in skin cancers for the next 40 years. This 10% increase in skin cancers might lead to a worldwide annual skin cancer rate of about 2 million, with 20,000 fatalities a year, since 1% of all skin cancers are very malignant carcinomas.

Some plants might be affected by the increased ultraviolet radiation. Some legumes might be destroyed:

> [in] a tenfold increase in UV-B . . . peas and onions would be scalded and possibly killed. (NAS, 1975, p. 10)

This study by the National Academy of Sciences suggested that the major physical effect on the global survivors of a full-scale nuclear war might be the increased UV radiation due to ozone depletion. That effect would have a mean lifetime of 3–4 years. For that length of time, survivors might have to be careful about going out into the bright sunlight. Some animals and crops might have to be protected from sunburn.

The uncertainties in the predicted ozone depletion are very large. The threat to the ozone layer has in fact been recognized only within the last decade, so that the models on which the predictions are made are somewhat unreliable. In addition, the many possible scenarios of a full-scale nuclear war add great uncertainties. The protective ozone layer is located in the stratosphere. Thus ozone depletion occurs when the nuclear explosions inject the resulting NO high up into the stratosphere. Figure 3.3 shows that for explosions much smaller than 1 Mt the NO will penetrate mostly into the troposphere, which contains little ozone to be depleted. In fact, some people believe that NO in the troposphere might generate additional ozone (Peterson et al., 1983, p. 74–93).

Nuclear Winter
The increases in the UV radiation intensity may be significant over three to four years after a nuclear war. Turco et al. (1983) suggest that in the short term even more drastic effects will be due to climatic effects induced by fine dust and soot generated during the explosions and afterward in fires, and injected into the troposphere and stratosphere.

The consequences predicted by Turco, et al. are much worse than those predicted by the NAS, primarily because of two phenomena. First, Turco et al. argue that the dust raised by ground-level nuclear explosions contains smaller particles than previously assumed. That causes the dust to stay in the air longer and hence have larger effects. Second, Turco et al. argue that the burning of cities and forests induced by nuclear explosions will inject large amounts of very fine soot into the troposphere and stratosphere, to stay for an extended period. The effect of this longer-lived small-particle debris at altitudes up to 19 km is to shield the earth's surface from the sun's radiation. The earth's surface consequently will be much colder than normal, while the stratosphere will be much warmer.

The prediction of the global surface cooling effects depends on three separate estimates: the amount and kind of material injected into the air and its distribution in altitude, the effects of this material on the sun's radiation and the resulting thermal effects, and the global distribution of the material and the impact of the thermal effects on the climate. These estimates depend not only on the war scenario stipulated, for example on the areas assumed to be burnt and the amounts and kinds of dust and soot produced and where they are deposited in the atmosphere, but also on the models used in calculating the thermal and climatic effects and their global distributions.

Using a one-dimensional model for the vertical thermal effects, and assuming even distributions for the dust and soot, Turco et al. calculated the thermal effects shown in Fig. 4.5. This figure shows the effects of wars ranging from a full-scale 5,000-Mt nuclear war, to a 100-Mt attack aimed at inner cities. In all of these scenarios large temperature decreases are predicted to take place, particularly for the two cases involving fires in cities.

These calculations of Turco et al. (1983) must be seen as very preliminary in nature; they are currently undergoing extensive peer review. The assumptions concerning the burning of cities must be more comprehensively compared to the past experiences with firestorms and the climatic models must be made global in nature rather than restricting them to one dimension. For example, the spill-over of these effects to the southern hemisphere has not been calculated. An optimist can find many places in the calculations where pessimistic assumptions seem to have been made; a pessimist can find equally many places in the calculations where optimistic assumptions seem to have been made.

The most dramatic conclusion of Turco, et al. (1983) is that a small

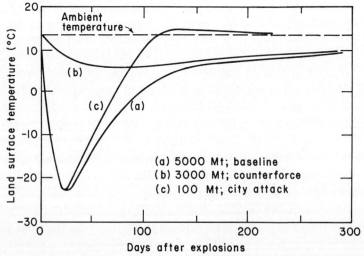

Figure 4.5 Hemispherically-averaged land surface temperature after various nuclear exchanges. (After Turco et al., 1983, Figure 1, p. 1286.)

100-Mt city-directed attack can have an enormous effect on the temperature at the land surface. This conclusion rests on the assumption that the centers of cities have much inflammable material in them which will burn and produce great amounts of soot. Even for attacks involving thousands of megatons of nuclear explosions, this soot from the burning city centers is responsible for the major fraction of the thermal effects. Hence the details of the potential burning of inner cities is crucial for the calculated conclusions.

It seems clear that the effects predicted by these preliminary calculations are so large that not only must they be checked exhaustively, but if they are even fractionally correct then the survivors of a nuclear war face a very complicated and undesirable climatic environment. Ehrlich et al. (1983) describe some of the biological consequences of such a nuclear winter. They are obviously potentially catastrophic for all biological systems dependent on regular supplies of light for sustaining photosynthetic processes.

One can conclude with certainty from such studies about the global effects of a full-scale nuclear war that physical phenomena such as ozone depletion and temperature reductions will take place. The magnitude of the consequences from these physical effects so far can be estimated only very crudely. It may well be that *homo sapiens* as a species would survive, particularly in the southern hemisphere, where the effects of fallout and ultraviolet radiation are reduced by factors of three or more, and where the climatic effects would be reduced and delayed. The existing calculations about nuclear explosions suffice to point out that the possible consequences of the climatic effects may be very large, and that the future following a nuclear war is very unpredictable.

HOW MUCH IS ENOUGH?

Having discussed the effects of nuclear war, one can go back to ask how much nuclear retaliation is enough. What levels of massive nuclear retaliation might be necessary to discourage attacks? Simple calculations may not only underestimate the fatalities but also ignore the problems faced by the survivors of a full-scale nuclear attack. The capability for massive retaliation (and what later will be called assured destruction) is that nuclear capacity that discourages the enemy from pursuing some undesirable action. In the 1950s the action to be deterred by the United States was a Soviet conventional attack anywhere in the American sphere of interest. Since the 1960s the action to be discouraged has been primarily a Soviet nuclear attack directly on the United States. How large must this nuclear retaliatory capacity be to deter these actions?

The level of this required capacity will of course depend on the goals of the Soviet Union. A cost–benefit calculation may persuade the Soviet Union that some large potential gains in a war may make a small nuclear retaliation by the United States acceptable. A wide range of retaliatory levels have been thought to be unacceptably massive. McGeorge Bundy in 1969 argued that

> Think-tank analysts can set levels of "acceptable" damage well up in the tens of millions of lives. . . . In the real world of real political thinkers—whether here or in the Soviet Union—a decision that would bring even one hydrogen bomb on one city of one's own country would be recognized in advance as a catastrophic blunder: ten bombs on ten cities would be a disaster beyond history: and a hundred bombs on a hundred cities are unthinkable. (*Foreign Affairs*, Vol. 48, no. 1 (October 1969), p. 10.)

The medium-sized nuclear power Great Britain has accepted as an adequate nuclear deterrent one nuclear submarine on patrol at all times, armed with 16 Polaris missiles, each carrying three 170-kt nuclear warheads. U.S. governments have in the past spelled out their thoughts on this minimum massive retaliatory capability. Former Secretary of Defense Robert McNamara in 1968 defined an assured destruction capability as follows:

> In the case of the Soviet Union, I would judge that a capability on our part to destroy, say, one-fifth to one-fourth of her population and one-half of her industrial capacity would serve as an effective deterrent. Such a level of destruction would certainly represent intolerable punishment to any twentieth-century industrial nation. (McNamara, 1968, p. 76)

If that judgment is correct, a retaliatory force able to deliver 200 EMT would seem to be minimally sufficient for meeting industrial retaliatory requirements, and 50 Mt would seem to satisfy the population requirement.

What are the origins and justifications for those three very different perceptions of what constitutes unacceptable destruction? Bundy's comment is true in a world where decision makers are both rational and humane. It has often been pointed out that the Soviet Union lost 20 million citizens in World War II and that a Soviet premier, Joseph Stalin, was willing to send that many Soviet citizens to their death in political purges. Hence, might not another such sacrifice be acceptable to the Soviet leadership if the cause warranted it? The Soviet Union of course did not start World War II, so this is not quite a correct analogy.

Presumably even Hitler would not have started World War II if he had been able to foresee its consequences. Nonetheless, one must ask whether the leaders of a nuclear power might not sometime be so far from humanity that they would judge the destruction of 1, 10, or even 100 cities an acceptable damage to risk in exchange for some overwhelming global political goal, yet shy away from risking the destruction of a thousand cities.

How did Great Britain determine that having four nuclear missile submarines, with one on patrol at all times, was a sufficient deterrent? It was all that the British could, or wanted to, afford. Because of the saturation effect, doubling the force would not have doubled the deterrence value. On the other hand, a smaller force would have meant that at some times no submarine would be on patrol; there would then be periods with no deterrent.

Finally, how did the U.S. government, how did McNamara, settle on the highest deterrent force limits? Enthoven and Smith (1971, p. 207) make the following guess:

> The level of destruction required—20 to 25 percent of the Soviet population and 50 percent of Soviet industry, commonly called our "assured-destruction" capability—was based on a judgment reached by the Secretary of Defense and accepted by the President, by the Congress, and apparently by the general public as well. That judgment was influenced by the fact of strongly diminishing marginal returns.

Figures 4.2 and 4.3 have shown that a nuclear attack beyond 400 Mt would produce little additional damage, as the curves for fatalities and for damage to industrial production have leveled off at that point. It would in fact take a considerable investment in strategic nuclear weaponry to push the damage levels significantly beyond the levels set by McNamara. It appears the feasible damage was accepted as the desired damage (Enthoven and Smith, 1971, p. 208):

> Thus the main reason for stopping at 1000 Minuteman missiles, 41 Polaris submarines, and some 500 strategic bombers, is that having more would not be worth the extra additional cost. . . . The answer to the question of how many strategic offensive forces are enough rests heavily on such flat-of-the-curve reasoning.

An alternative explanation for these numbers is offered in Chapter 6. But it is true that a technological society often decides that if the desirable course of action is unknown, then it will pursue the feasible course.

FLEXIBLE RESPONSE

This policy of massive retaliation was adopted by the Eisenhower administration under the guidance of Secretary Dulles. But it soon became clear that such massive retaliation could under some circumstances be too harsh (or rash?) a reaction against more limited aggressions. The Soviet crushing of the Hungarian revolution in 1956, for example, did not seem to warrant total nuclear war. To respond to such localized challenges, a system of mutual defense pacts was established and strengthened, like NATO (the North Atlantic Treaty Organization), CENTO (the Central Treaty Organization), and the Baghdad Pact. To make up for the small numbers of personnel involved in these military organizations, these forces were equipped with tactical nuclear weapons. By 1953 the United States had a stockpile of about 10,000 nuclear warheads, of which perhaps 7000 were located in Europe for tactical purposes.

A desire for flexible response had always existed, even immediately after the development of the H-bomb. But the economic pressures of balancing the U.S. budget forced a reliance on large strategic nuclear weapons, an emphasis that persisted through the 1960s well into the 1970s. The major changes since Eisenhower's presidency have been vast improvements in nuclear delivery systems and the establishment of a mutual balance of terror.

References

Arms Control and Disarmament Agency. *An Analysis of Civil Defense in Nuclear War.* Washington, D.C.: ACDA, December 1978.

Bottome, E. M. *The Balance of Terror: A Guide to the Arms Race.* Boston: Beacon Press, 1971. A good review of the development of the strategy of massive retaliation.

Chivian, E., S. Chivian, R. J. Lifton, and J. E. Mack, eds. *Last Aid: the Medical Consequences of Nuclear War.* San Francisco: W. H. Freeman, 1982.

Enthoven, A. C., and K. W. Smith. *How Much Is Enough? Shaping the Defense Program, 1961–1969.* New York: Harper & Row, 1971.

Ehrlich, P., et al., "Long Term Biological Consequences of Nuclear War." *Science,* Vol. 222 (1983), pp. 1293–1300.

Freedman, Laurence. *The Evolution of Nuclear Strategy.* New York: St. Martin's Press, 1981.

Katz, A. H. *Life After Nuclear War: The Economic and Social Impact of Nuclear Attacks on the United States.* Cambridge, Mass.: Ballinger, 1982.

Kemp, G. *Nuclear Forces for Medium Powers. Part I: Targets and Weapons Systems,* Adelphi Paper #106. London: International Institute for Strategic Studies, 1974.

Lewis, K. N. "The Prompt and Delayed Effects of Nuclear War." *Scientific American,* Vol. 241, no. 1 (July 1979), pp. 35–47.

McNamara, R. S. *The Essence of Security.* New York: Harper & Row, 1968.

National Academy of Sciences, Committee to Study the Long-Term Worldwide

Effects of Multiple Nuclear-Weapons Detonations. *Long-Term Worldwide Effects of Multiple Nuclear-Weapons Detonations.* Washington, D.C.: NAS, 1975.

Office of Technology Assessment. *Effects of Nuclear War.* Washington, D.C.: Government Printing Office, 1979.

Peterson, J., and the *Ambio* editorial staff of the Royal Swedish Academy of Sciences. *Nuclear War: The Aftermath.* New York: Pergamon Press, 1983.

Turco, R. P., O. B. Toon, T. P. Ackerman, J. B. Pollack, and Carl Sagan, "Nuclear Winter: Global Consequences of Multiple Nuclear Explosions." *Science,* Vol. 222 (1983), pp. 1283–1292.

THE NUCLEAR BALANCE

Nuclear weapons make it feasible for the United States and the Soviet Union to destroy each other. Delivery systems such as long-range bombers, intercontinental ballistic missiles, and missile-launching nuclear submarines have turned this feasibility into a destructive capability. A balance of terror now exists between the two superpowers through the ability to retaliate massively to any nuclear attack; mutual assured destruction (MAD) is an unavoidable fact of life. The concept of deterrence raises this balance to the level of doctrine; the assured second-strike retaliatory capabilities on both sides mean that nuclear war is controlled by a mutual overkill capability. The doctrine of deterrence using the existence of MAD has worked for almost two decades; can it continue to do so in the future?

This part of the text will consider the various delivery systems of strategic nuclear warheads, focusing on the strategic Triad of intercontinental bombers, intercontinental ballistic missiles (ICBMs), and nuclear missile submarines. Each part of the Triad has a history, a present balance, and a future potential. The main concern now is with the quality of each of these weapons systems; they can be improved much further, with no obvious limits to some of the technologies. Bombers will gain not so much in payload or speed but, rather, in survivability, penetrability, and accuracy. The future improvements in ICBMs will most likely be in acccuracy and possibly in mobility for survival. For the nuclear missile

105

submarines, while the range of the missiles is still being extended, the primary emphasis will be on navigational and missile guidance accuracy, and on quietness for survival.

After the technology of the Triad has been described, the strategic nuclear balance will be discussed. Several alternative ways of evaluating that balance will be developed. Differentiating between quantity and quality of weapons systems may force a major reassessment of the goals of deterrence; some improved weapons systems may increase the military stability in times of crisis more than other systems and might, therefore, be judged more desirable.

CHAPTER
5

Strategic Bombers

Let's just say the Air Force knew there was going to be a new manned bomber. They analyzed the need for it afterwards.

A high Pentagon official, 1976

As compared with missiles of any type the bomber is characteristically "slow to take offense" . . . [and] is also recallable.

F. P. Hoeber, *Slow to Take Offense*, 1980, p. 27

The fission bombs dropped on Hiroshima and Nagasaki in 1945 were delivered by B-29 bombers. With a range of 3000 km (2000 mi), the B-29 was designated the delivery vehicle for nuclear weapons as they became available after World War II. This B-29 strategic bomber force grew into the Strategic Air Command, with its B-36, B-47, and B-52 bombers that could threaten massive destruction of the Soviet homeland. The long-range bomber force has been one leg of the strategic Triad of delivery systems ever since. Some think it is now perhaps less important than the other two legs of the Triad, since the intercontinental ballistic missiles and the nuclear missile submarines seem both more reliable and better able to penetrate enemy defenses. Nonetheless, considerable effort is still being invested to keep bombers a viable strategic option.

BOMBER TECHNOLOGY

As do all aircraft, strategic bombers fly because the air flow past their wings creates lift. Aircraft design considerations balance lift and weight with desired rise times, and thrust and aerodynamic drag with desired acceleration. Since bombers are a component of the strategic **107**

Triad, additional design considerations include survival under fire from defenses and an ability to deliver the payload accurately on target. For bomber forces, the major question is whether they are obsolete for strategic nuclear retaliation. To answer that question, one must consider not only how bombers work but also what factors determine their obsolescence, and how much they might improve in the future.

Judgments about the future obsolescence of bombers may be based on the past rate of improvements. The development of the bomber force has been more evolutionary than revolutionary. The usefulness of bombers has been extended, not by exciting new discoveries but, rather, by gradual improvements in aerodynamic design, engine efficiencies, stronger, lighter, and more heatresistant materials for plane bodies and engines, electronic advancements in navigation and electronic countermeasures, and the replacement of free-fall bombs by missiles.

Aerodynamics

The technological capabilities of bombers are measured in part by such aerodynamic parameters as range, speed, payload, altitude of flight, and rapidity of takeoff. The value of the bomber force as one leg of the strategic Triad involves other technical parameters, including the ability to penetrate the enemy's air space and overcome his air defenses and the accuracy of delivery of the warheads. These factors depend largely on electronics.

The way in which these parameters enter into an analysis of the bomber force will be described later in the discussion of the deployment decision for the U.S. B-1 bomber. Here only a sketch of important aerodynamic characteristics will be presented to help understand how bombers came to be important and what is possible for them in the future. Various aerodynamic parameters are interrelated (Anderson, 1978).

Maximum Range

To achieve maximum range, an aircraft should be flown with as little fuel consumption as possible. For a jet engine, the power required to maintain a given speed decreases for higher altitudes, where the lower density of air offers less resistance to the passage of the aircraft. Thus, for best fuel consumption, a jet aircraft should fly at the highest possible altitude, close to the point where the lift no longer can support the aircraft. That best flight altitude is called the service ceiling, defined as the altitude where just enough lift remains that the plane could still rise at 100 feet per minute while retaining just enough control to avoid a stall. The B-52 most efficiently cruises as close to its service ceiling of

55,000 feet (16.8 km) as its payload allows. However, this technically ideal altitude is not necessarily the best for military strategy. When penetrating Soviet air defense, the B-52 would be flying at only 500 feet (150 m) above the ground, where it is hard to detect by radar but its fuel consumption is poor.

The ranges of bombers have improved as engines have become more efficient. This efficiency has come largely through the development of engines that operate at higher temperatures (Fig. 5.1). At higher operating temperatures, engines can convert a larger fraction of the fuel energy into thrust. Higher operating temperatures have become possible because of the development of ceramic materials and alloys capable of withstanding them (see Fig. 5.2).

Aircraft Weight and Speed

The fuel consumption of an aircraft increases almost directly with the weight of the aircraft. Modern alloying and ceramic techniques have allowed the increasing use of aluminum and titanium alloys and ceramic materials that have the same strength as stainless steels yet are much lighter. These alloys and ceramics also can better stand the high temperatures generated in aircraft surfaces as they are heated by air friction at high speeds.

Power requirements rise sharply with the speed at which the aircraft flies. The B-52 cruises at high altitudes at 77% the speed of sound in air, at Mach 0.77. Its fuel consumption at its maximum speed of Mach 0.9

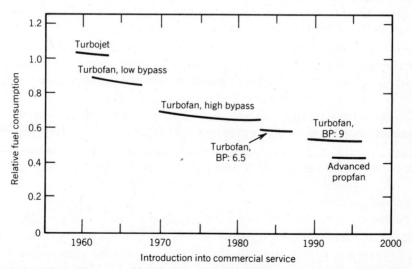

Figure 5.1 The efficiency of jet aircraft engines has been improving steadily in recent decades as the ratio of thrust of fuel consumption has been increased. (After Grey and Hamlan, 1981, p. 135.)

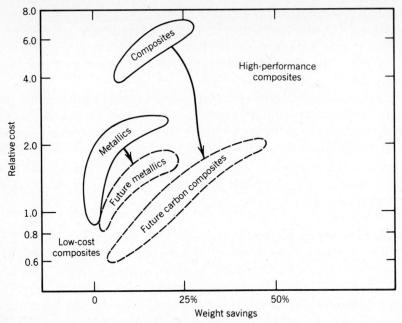

Figure 5.2 Cost and structural weight of metallics and composite ceramic materials used in aircraft. Weight savings up to 40% may be possible in future aircraft. (After Feuchtwanger and Mason, 1979, Figure 5, p. 111.)

is too large to be borne for any length of time. The power required also rises at very low speeds, for example, at takeoff or on landing.

Both fuel-consumption problems can be ameliorated by modifying an aircraft's aerodynamic configuration. Aerodynamic studies have helped to develop aircraft shapes with reduced air resistance. At high speeds, increased fuel consumption is caused largely by the drag resistance of the wings. At low speeds, upward thrust is needed to provide the lift that the wings no longer provide. Some contemporary aircraft, such as the FB-111, the Backfire, and the B-1 bombers, have variable geometry wings to adapt the aircraft shape to the particular operating speed. At low speeds, the wings are spread to provide maximum lift; at high speeds, they are swept back to minimize air resistance. This variable geometry technology also requires improved materials.

Payload
The range of an aircraft is greatly affected by its payload. The ferry range of an aircraft is the distance it can fly with no payload and with all unnecessary gear removed. How much a payload may modify the range of an aircraft is illustrated by L. Martin (1973) for the F-4D Phantom fighter bomber. If the payload is reduced to about one-third of the maximum from 6000 kg to 2000 kg, the mission radius can be

doubled from 155 km to 290 km. Even more effective is the replacement of payload by additional fuel. The weight of the 1340 gallons (gal) of kerosene fuel in three external tanks at 3 kg/gal is 4000 kg. Replacing 4000 kg of bombs by fuel extends the combat radius from 145 km to 700 km. Similar relationships hold for all aircraft.

Figure 5.3 shows the evolution of payload and range for a series of U.S. and USSR tactical aircraft. Over time the product of range times payload has improved constantly. Unfortunately, the price of the aircraft has increased as well, partially because fewer units are purchased, but mainly because of the higher costs of the better technologies.

Supersonic Speed

Ultimately the most important measure of the usefulness of the bomber is its survivability, its ability to reach the target despite defenses. For this purpose, a high-low-high flight profile may be employed. In this flight pattern, the bomber flies toward the boundary of hostile areas at high altitudes where the fuel consumption is the least. When approaching the target and likely to come under attack, it flies close to the ground to avoid being seen by ground-based radar. After bombing the target, the bomber may climb again to high altitudes for good fuel economy.

Supersonic speed (speeds greater than the speed of sound) can help

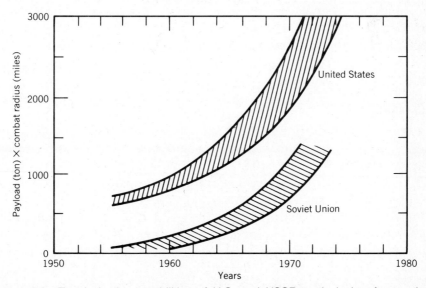

Figure 5.3 Trends in the capabilities of U.S. and USSR tactical aircraft over time, expressed in terms of the product of the range times the payload. (After Deitchman, 1979, Figure 3.2, p. 53.)

at various stages of this flight, as it not only can reduce the time of vulnerability, but can also make interception more difficult for defensive fighters. But supersonic flight consumes fuel rapidly, reducing the range enormously. Supersonic flight raises further problems at low altitudes, as ground turbulences badly buffet the aircraft. Ground-hugging flight using automatic radar altimeter guidance becomes very difficult as the reaction-time requirements become more stringent. Fuel consumption becomes enormous because of the tremendous air drag. Hence, low-altitude speeds can never be more than barely supersonic; it is uncertain how much that feature adds to the plane's survivability compared with the cost that it adds.

Bombing Accuracy

The accuracy of strategic bombers is potentially quite good. Deitchman (1979, p. 37) cites a best figure of 30 meters for tactical bombing, at least during exercises. On the other hand, A. Cockburn (1982, p. 148) claims that in all-weather attacks during the Vietnam war the F-111 bomber could "deposit half of its bombs no closer than three-quarters of a mile from the intended target." Obviously the bombing altitude, evasive maneuvers, and other circumstances may affect this accuracy. The highest accuracies can be achieved only by highly accurate navigation together with good bombing techniques.

The navigation of a bomber uses combinations of inertial guidance systems (see Chapter 6), observations of the ground below, and acquiring guidance signals from navigational systems, such as those provided by satellites. The new NAVSTAR satellite guidance system (see Chapter 6), for example, promises a three-dimensional location accuracy of 20 m or better anywhere on earth by comparing signals from 3 of the 18 planned satellites.

Electronics

The most rapidly improving technologies over the last decades have been electronic functions based on solid-state components, particularly computers but also radar. The growth in computer capabilities will be described in Chapter 13, and some aspects of radar will be discussed in Chapter 10.

Improvements in electronics over the last decades have increased the vulnerability of bombers during flight. Fighter aircraft can be guided toward interception by ground-based radar or by airborne warning and control aircraft (AWACS) flying above the battlefield. The interceptors can use on-board radar electronics to guide them to the interception and can use electronically guided missiles to shoot down the bombers. Alternatively, bombers can be attacked by surface-to-air missiles (SAMs). These missiles generally combine some guidance from the ground during the initial phases of the flight with built-in terminal guidance in the last phases of the interception.

As an illustration of missile functions, Fig. 5.4 shows the high-altitude intercept mode of the Soviet SAM-6. Two radars track the target and the missile in order to guide the missile toward the target. At the end of the flight, the missile uses a built-in infrared heat detector to guide itself into the jet exhaust. A variety of countermeasures have been developed against missiles such as the SAM-6, including steep dives and other evasive maneuvers, chaff, electronic countermeasures (ECM), and heat-flare decoys.

A developmental competition continues between builders of strategic bombers and defenders of air spaces. Past evidence indicates some potential successes for missiles such as the SAM; however, their success rate cannot begin to approach 100%.

Bombing tactics have adapted to the threats presented by surface-to-air missiles. The B-52 is to fly at altitudes on the order of 150 m during its penetration of Soviet air defenses, so that only radar from above can see and track it. The B-52s bristle with electronic countermeasure devices; one crew member out of six does nothing but operate ECM devices to detect all attempts to locate the bombers and foil these attempts and to deflect attacking interceptor fighters or missiles.

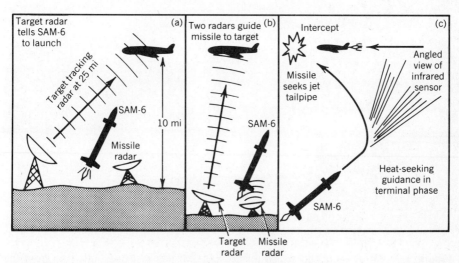

Figure 5.4 Interception modes of the Soviet SAM-6 surface-to-air missile: (a) radar detection, (b) radar guidance of the SAM toward the target aircraft, and (c) heat-seeking guidance for the final interception. (After one of the figures in The Insight Team, 1974.)

SRAM and Cruise Missiles

The ultimate way of overcoming enemy air defenses against strategic bombers is to use a stand-off (launch and leave) mode. The U.S. bomber forces are replacing free-fall gravity bombs by short-range attack missiles (SRAM). B-52Gs are being modified to each carry as many as 20 single-stage solid-fuel SRAMs (Model AGM-69A). These have a length of 4.25 m and a diameter of 0.45 m, and can be launched as much as 150 km away from the target. After being launched, they fly at supersonic speeds in excess of Mach 3 toward the target under the guidance of an on-board inertial guidance system. They deliver a 200-kt warhead on the target. The bomber firing the SRAM has to penetrate only to within 150 km of a heavily defended target.

Survivability can be extended even further by the use of long-range air-launched cruise missiles (ALCM). Cruise missiles are air-breathing unmanned aircraft. They are propelled by lightweight jet engines over ranges up to 2400 km. They can cruise at altitudes as low as 50 m. Guidance is in part by an on-board inertial guidance system and in part is based on optical or radar information gathered during the flight. The accuracy of cruise missiles may be better than 60 m over a 2400-km range. Cruise missiles can be launched from the torpedo tubes of any submarine (SLCM), from the ground (GLCM), or by bombers as shown in Fig. 5.5. They can carry either nuclear or conventional warheads.

Cruise missiles are not new. The German V-1 of World War II led to

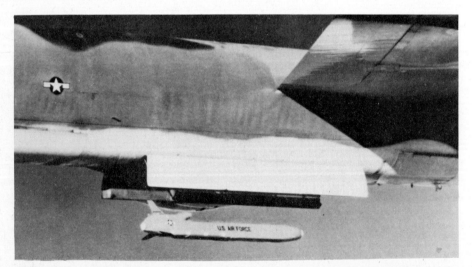

Figure 5.5 An air-launched cruise missile (ALCM) has just been released from the bomb bay of a B-52 bomber. The airscoop for the turbofan engine has popped up, the engine has ignited, the back wings are extended, and the vertical fin is unfolding. The larger forward wings are yet to be deployed. (Photo courtesy U.S. Air Force.)

U.S. designs such as the Houndog and the Navaho, while the Soviet Union has developed several ship-launched cruise missiles with ranges up to 720 km to be guided toward targets such as aircraft carriers by spotter aircraft. The recent improvements in U.S. cruise missiles are primarily in range, low-altitude flight, and accuracy.

The increased range has come through improved small-engine technology. The present U.S. cruise missile engine derives from a research program of the 1960s that aimed to develop a small backpack engine to carry soldiers for short distances above the Vietnamese jungles. New lightweight, yet strong, ceramic materials helped to make these engines possible. Such high-temperature engines produce long-distance flights.

Figure 5.6 illustrates the cruise missile's ability to fly at a very low altitude. It constantly emits pulsed radar signals. These are reflected off the ground; the time between the emission of a radar pulse and its return to the missile tells the altitude of the missile. An on-board computer translates this height information into control signals for the missile's engine and wing flaps. In this way the missile slips under the coverage of ground-based radar.

A most significant breakthrough for the cruise missile has been the terrain-contour matching (TERCOM) guidance system. The vehicle flies part of the time controlled by inertial guidance systems; but at various points along its flight path, it reorients itself with respect to the ground. It takes a picture of the terrain beneath it using a radar altimeter. The on-board computer compares this actual ground reading with an altitude map stored in the computer memory. From the comparison, the cruise missile computer evaluates how far the missile is off its course and instructs the missile-steering mechanism to make the appropriate flight corrections. The cruise missile may take several such map readings as it approaches the target where it homes in on a spot predesignated on a final terminal map. Alternatively, an optical reading of the terrain could be taken with a charge-coupled device

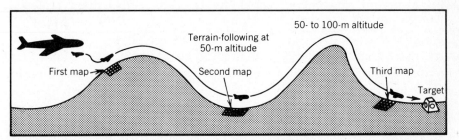

Figure 5.6 The terrain-contour matching system (TERCOM) of cruise missiles compares on-board numerical maps with altimeter readings taken by the missile's radar system. The altitude information also allows the missile to fly close to the ground.

array and compared with pre-prepared photographs in the computer memory; but that technique might be too dependent on the time of day and on the seasons.

The TERCOM system promises an accuracy limited only by the ability of the on-board computer to process the altitude data. Accuracies of 10 m are mentioned in the literature (Pfaltzgraff and Davis, 1977, p. 12; Lee, 1981, p. 165). Such map reading systems do work. Thousands of ALCMs are being built for B-52s and for the B-1 bomber (see Table 5.1).

THE BOMBER ARMS RACE

Why is the bomber force of the Strategic Air Command still so important in spite of some skeptics' doubts about bomber survivability?

The Bomber Gap

The strategy of massive retaliation demanded an absolute superiority in strategic nuclear weapons and their delivery systems. Until 1955 the United States ensured its strategic superiority by maintaining a monopoly on long-range bombers to attack Soviet cities. This monopoly was seen as vitally important, as illustrated by one of the early weapons myths, the supposed "bomber gap" of 1955 (Bottome, 1971).

After the first Soviet H-bomb explosion in 1953, some concern arose that the nuclear strategic balance might no longer strongly favor the United States. Soviet bravado turned these concerns into fears of a U.S. inferiority. In July 1955, the Soviets demonstrated their first intercontinental bomber, the Bison (the Myasishchev Mya-4). One squadron of 10 Bisons was flown past the reviewing stand six times, giving the impression that 60 of these planes existed. From this deception the United States concluded that 600 of these planes could be built quickly. This apparent new Soviet capability triggered the United States to produce rapidly about 1500 medium-range B-47 and 500 long-range B-52 bombers. However, the Soviet Union never possessed at any one time more than 300 bombers that could reach the United States. The bomber gap ultimately was 5-to-1 in favor of the United States rather than 2-to-1 against it.

This seeming challenge of U.S. superiority is typical of one component fueling the U.S.-Soviet arms race. Sometimes it has worked in the opposite direction, for example, when the Soviets built an air defense system against the never-deployed U.S. B-70 bomber. Often such challenges have led to spirals in the arms race (see Chapter 13). In the case of the bomber gap, it not only led to a very great expansion of the SAC bomber force and to the permanence of bombers as a part of the Triad, but it also made it easier to accept subsequently a missile gap as reality, leading to a missile arms race.

The B-70 and the Nuclear Airplane

The B-52 is still the mainstay of SAC. Over the last 20 years it has been constantly upgraded in performance and electronic capabilities. However, new versions of a manned bomber have frequently been proposed, for example, the B-70 bomber in the late 1950s before ICBMs became operational. It was to fly at Mach 3 (i.e., at three times the speed of sound), cruise for very long distances at an altitude of 100,000 feet (30 km), and carry a very large bomb load. The role seen for this plane was largely fulfilled in a much superior style by the ICBMs that were developed even as the B-70 program progressed. Yet great pressure developed to build 250 of these manned bombers. This program could be permanently restricted to prototype work only after President Kennedy and Secretary of Defense McNamara had been in office for some time.

A second major bomber development effort in the 1950s and 1960s was the ANP (the aircraft nuclear propulsion) program to produce a nuclear-powered airplane. In the ANP program, a nuclear reactor could be used to produce very hot air that then would be exhausted out of a nozzle to propel the airplane. With such a nuclear engine an aircraft would have a virtually unlimited range. From 1946 onward, the ANP was pursued with enthusiasm and money. The problems to be solved included materials difficulties, weight of shielding, and radiation leakage. Some of these problems, such as the shielding of the crew, were ultimately insoluble in any reasonable way. Yet repeatedly the project was passed from feasibility studies to development status. Thus,

> In July of 1952 the AEC and the Defense Department announced plans for a flight test of a nuclear-propulsion system . . . the directors bullheadedly insisted on flying something anyway, even if [it] was little more than a passenger in a conventionally powered aircraft. (York, 1970, p. 64)

Whenever attempts were made to cancel this project, protests arose. As shown on page 78, the conflict haunted Oppenheimer at his security clearance hearings in 1954 because he was not enthusiastic about this concept. In 1958 it was claimed that the Soviet Union had actually built a nuclear airplane. The semiauthoritative *Aviation Week* editorialized on December 1, 1958

On page 28 of this issue we are publishing the first account of a Soviet nuclear powered bomber prototype along with engineering sketches in as much detail as available data permits. . . . once again the Soviets have beaten us needlessly to a significant technical punch. (As quoted in York, 1970, p. 71)

The desire to develop such a plane was so great that the promoters translated Soviet theoretical speculations on nuclear airplanes into the actual existence of such a craft. Such self-driving enthusiasms are encountered frequently in arms race issues.

THE STRATEGIC BOMBER BALANCE

The Bombers

Three bomber types presently carry the primary intercontinental strategic bombing responsibility: the B-52, the Tu-95, and the Mya-4. Two newer medium-range supersonic bombers carry such a responsibility in Europe: the FB-111 and the Tu-26 Backfire bomber. The follow-on B-1 bomber for the United States will be discussed later in this chapter, together with a brief mention of the U.S. Stealth bomber.

The B-52

The mainstays of the U.S. strategic bomber force are the many variants of the B-52 (see Fig. 5.7) together with the KC-135 tankers that refuel them in flight. The first prototype model of the B-52 flew in April 1952. Through 1962, 744 production models were delivered to the U.S. Air Force; the most recent G and H models date from 1959 to 1962. All models have been enormously upgraded in capability since then, both mechanically and electronically. The range of an aircraft refers to the maximum distance it can fly with a given payload. Its operating or combat radius is then between one-third and one-half the range, depending on the fuel consumption during the attack on the target. The range of these eight-engined bombers is as much as 16,000 km when flying at high altitudes at Mach 0.77, although they have a maximum high-altitude speed of Mach 0.9 and a penetration speed at low altitudes of Mach 0.54. Their service ceiling is 17 km. These planes have a maximum payload of 32 tonnes. In the past these planes carried as many as four 10-Mt H-bombs, together with several air-to-surface missiles with megaton-yield warheads. Presently, 173 B-52Gs are being modified to carry 12 short-range attack missiles (SRAM) externally on pylons under the wings and are later in the 1980s to have their bomb bays converted to carry 8 more SRAM. They will then be able to carry up to 20 SRAMs, each armed with a warhead of 200-kt yield. A typical

Figure 5.7 A B-52 bomber of the U.S. Air Force Strategic Air Command during aerial refueling. It can carry 6 SRAM under each wing and will be modified to carry 8 more internally in the bomb bay. Some will carry 12 cruise missiles. (Photo courtesy U.S. Air Force.)

load for a converted B-52H bomber now might be 4 of these 200-kt SRAM plus 4 1-Mt free-fall gravity bombs. Sixty-four B-52Gs are being modified to carry up to 20 air-launched cruise missiles (ALCM). Present upgrading includes such features as quick-start capabilities for engines, the capability to fly at 150 m above the ground, and extensive electronic countermeasures for the penetration of Soviet air defenses. The B-52G and H models are projected to be structurally sound into the 1990s. The fleet of 646 KC-135 tankers gives these bombers not only a longer range but also allows long loitering times near the Soviet border in times of crisis.

Tu-95 Bear
The mainstay of the Soviet intercontinental strategic bomber force has been the Tupelov Tu-95 (or Tu-20) Bear bomber (Fig. 5.8). This turboprop aircraft first flew in 1952, with the final deliveries made in about 1962. Various reconnaissance, radar surveillance, and naval aviation models of the Bear have been built in addition to the strategic bomber version. Its range is 12,550 km when carrying a payload of 11.5 tonnes. Its maximum bomb load is 18 tonnes; typically, it carries perhaps three gravity bombs in the megaton range or a Kangaroo

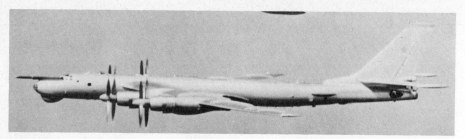

Figure 5.8 A Soviet Tu-95 Bear strategic bomber. (Photo courtesy U.S. Air Force.)

turbojet missile with a nuclear warhead of 800 kt. At 12,500-m altitude its maximum speed is Mach 0.78 (930 km/hr). The Bear's range is indeed intercontinental, although there are not a significant number of tankers to extend its range or flight time.

Mya-4 Bison

The Soviet Union strategic bomber forces include a few Myasishchev Mya-4 Bison bombers. This four-engined turbojet first flew publicly in 1954. Its maximum level speed at an altitude of 11 km is Mach 0.87 (1040 km/hr). Its service ceiling is 13.7 km. At 830 km/sec at high altitude its range with a 4.5-tonne bomb load is 11,250 km. It typically carries two bombs in the megaton range.

FB-111A

The FB-111A is a swing-wing medium-range bomber. It first flew in 1964 and final deliveries were made in 1968. Its range is 4700 km, and it can carry a maximum payload of 19 tonnes, including up to six SRAMs, although it is more likely to be carrying only two SRAMs. It is supersonic, with a maximum speed of Mach 2.5; that speed does reduce its range enormously, as does any supersonic flight at low altitudes. This bomber is of interest for its sweep-back design, for its ability to fly close to the ground through electronic ground-clearance controls, and for its supersonic speed. It is also interesting from a policy perspective; it represents a clear-cut failure by a secretary of defense to impose order on military procurement procedures. It was originally intended to be a multipurpose plane to serve all the military services, to be launched equally from air bases and aircraft carriers, and to serve equally as a fighter and bomber. Interservice squabbles over its design, payload, speed, and so on made it ultimately unacceptable for most of these roles.

Because of its relatively short range, the FB-111A is not considered to be an intercontinental bomber and is not counted under the SALT agreements. Some are stationed in Great Britain, from where they can reach targets as far away as 2350 km on a round-trip mission or farther with refueling. Although their main mission is probably tactical support for NATO operations in Europe, they could be used to some extent in strategic attacks on parts of the Soviet Union.

Tu-26 Backfire

Since 1976 the Soviet Union has been deploying increasing numbers of Tupelov Tu-26 (or Tu-22M) Backfire bombers (Fig. 5.9). This plane is comparable to the FB-111A, featuring wings whose geometry is partially variable. It has an estimated maximum speed of up to Mach 2.5 at high altitudes and Mach 0.9 at low altitudes, with an estimated range of 8000 km. It can carry a payload of up to 9 tonnes, which could be made up of a Kitchen liquid-propelled short-range rocket with a 350-kt warhead semisubmerged in its fuselage. The performance parameters of the Tu-26 are uncertain. One can find estimates of its range as low as 5700 km, perhaps derived from heavily loaded prototype flights; others have been as high as 10,500 km, which is perhaps the ferry range for an unloaded version; yet others claim the combat radius at high altitude to be 5440 km, which would correspond to a range of 11,000 to 16,000 km. The published speed estimates range from Mach 2 to Mach 2.5. Uncertainties about this plane's capabilities, about the planned production numbers, and about its intended use

Figure 5.9 The Soviet Backfire bomber with variable geometry wings. Is it only a medium-range aircraft, or can it be used as an intercontinental weapon? (Photo courtesy U.S. Navy.)

in China or in Europe have injected this bomber into the strategic arms negotiations.

The United States claims that the Backfire has the potential to be an intercontinental bomber. The Soviet Union claims that it is only intermediate in range and is intended for use against other enemies, such as the People's Republic of China. The USSR, therefore, argues that it should not be counted in any SALT agreement, unless the FB-111A and other nuclear-capable fighter-bombers are counted as well.

Figure 5.10 shows the portions of the United States reachable by Soviet bombers on round trips if launched from the northernmost parts of the Soviet Union. A refueled Backfire (or Bison) would have a range roughly equivalent to that of an unrefueled Bear; the Soviet Union never has had a significant refueling capability. Unless strategic air bases in the Arctic are used or one-way missions are flown, U. S. targets are not reachable by the Backfire. However, there remains a lingering doubt whether any agreement on strategic arms ought to

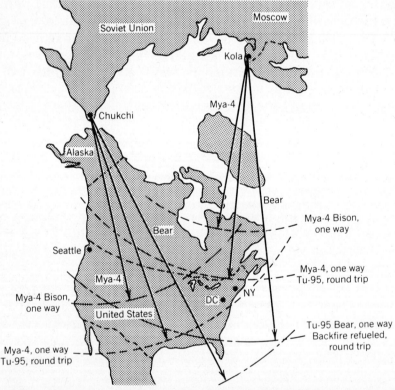

Figure 5.10 Areas of the United States reachable by Soviet bombers on round trips if launched from the northernmost parts of the Soviet Union. A refueled Bison or Backfire would have a range roughly equivalent to that of an unrefueled Bear. (After English and Bolef, 1973, p. 14.)

consider this bomber. The distinction between tactical and strategic nuclear weapons systems can easily become blurred.

The Bomber Balance

Table 5.1 shows the present situation in strategic bombers. The bomber balance favors the United States in the number of bombers and in bombing load as well as in quality parameters such as range, speed, and electronic capabilities; however, only the Soviets have a significant air defense system against bombers. The Bear is not even a jet bomber; it has turboprop engines. The imbalance in the bomber forces could be a significant contributor to strategic warfare if payload were to be important, since bombers can carry enormous payloads.

The bomb tonnage that could be delivered by bombers has always been very unequal between the United States and the USSR. Table 5.1 shows that for the United States, the total of the maximum bomb loads for the 272 B-52 and 56 FB-111A bombers is 9613 tonnes. For the USSR, about 43 Mya-4 and 100 Tu-95 bombers can carry a total bomb load up to 2187 tonnes. Excluding the medium-range FB-111A, the U.S. bomb load could be up to 8549 tonnes, or including the Backfire bomber, the USSR bomb load could be up to 3867 tonnes. The bombers actually use much reduced payloads to extend their range and to carry electronic gear to help in penetrating enemy air space.

The bomber situation might be summarized by pointing out that the American dominance is not surprising. The Soviet military leadership believes that bombers are not a viable strategic force.

Long-range bombers . . . whose flight is practically impossible to conceal . . . have become especially vulnerable. In covering great distances at relatively low flight speeds, long-range bombers will often be forced to be in the air defense zone for extended periods of time. . . . Consequently, the missions of destruction of targets deep in the enemy's territory will be executed more reliably by the Strategic Rocket Troops. True, "air-to-ground" missiles . . . have been developed. . . . But even in this case the strategic bomber aircraft cannot regain its lost importance. (Air Marshall V. D. Sokolovsky, as quoted in Quanbeck and Wood, 1976, p. 9)

Effectiveness of Strategic Bomber Forces

The balance of the nuclear bomber force in terms of numbers is only the beginning of any analysis. One really wants to know how reliable the strategic bomber force is as a deterrent against a nuclear attack. The answer to that question comes in three steps: (1) Within the warning time of a surprise first strike, how many bombers might survive to fly toward the Soviet Union in retaliation? (2) What fraction of these retaliating bombers might penetrate Soviet air defenses to reach the targets?

Table 5.1 The long-range and medium-range strategic bombing forces of the Soviet Union and the United States. Unless otherwise indicated, numbers are derived from the International Institute for Strategic Studies (1983).

Bombers	Range	Top Speed	Payload: Max; Typical	Number	Megatons Per Bomber	Megatons Total	EMTs[a] Per Bomber	EMTs[a] Total
United States								
B-52-D/F	9,900 km	0.95 Mach[b]	27 tonnes; 4 × 1 Mt[d] + 2 SRAM × 200 kt[e]	31	4.4 Mt	136 Mt	4.7 EMT	146 EMT
B-52-G	12,000 km	0.95 Mach[b]	32 tonnes; 4 × 1 Mt[d] + 4 SRAM × 200 kt[e]	135	4.8 Mt	648 Mt	5.4 EMT	729 EMT
B-52-G	12,000 km	0.95 Mach[b]	32 tonnes; 4 × 1 Mt[d] + 4 SRAM × 200 kt[e] + 12 cruise × 300 kt[f,g]	16[d]	7.2 Mt	115 Mt	10.7 EMT	172 EMT
B-52-H	16,000 km	0.95 Mach[b]	32 tonnes; 4 × 1 Mt[d] + 4 SRAM × 0.2 Mt[e]	90	4.8 Mt	432 Mt	5.4 EMT	483 EMT
B-52 models	Inactive storage			(187)				
FB-111A	4,700 km	2.5 Mach[h]	19 tonnes; 2 SRAM × 200 kt	(56)	0.4 Mt	(24 Mt)	0.7 EMT	(42 EMT)
KC-135 tanker		0.95 Mach		(646)				
B-1	9,800 km	1.6 Mach		(R&D)				
U.S. Total				272[i]		1331 Mt[j]		1530 EMT[i]
Soviet Union								
Tu-95 Bear[j]	12,800 km	0.78 Mach	18 tonnes;[k] 3 × 1 Mt[d,e,l]	100	3 Mt	300 Mt	3 EMT	300 EMT
Mya-4 Bison	11,200 km	0.87 Mach[m]	9 tonnes;[k] 2 × 1 Mt[d]	43	2 Mt	86 Mt	2 EMT	86 EMT

Tu-26 Backfire	8,000 km	2.5 Mach[h,n]	8 tonnes[k]	(210)		
Mya-4 Tanker				(35)		
Tu-19 Tanker				(10)		
USSR Total				143	386 Mt[i]	386 EMT[i]
United Kingdom Vulcan B2	6,400 km	1.6 Mach	9.5 tonnes	(48)[o]		
U.K. Total				0[i]	0 Mt	0 EMT

[a] EMT (megaton equivalent) is equal to $Y^{2/3}$, with Y in megatons. For the 0.2-Mt SRAM, the EMT = 0.342 Mt; for the 0.3-Mt cruise missile, the EMT = 0.448 Mt.

[b] At high altitude. The penetration speed at low altitude is Mach 0.66 (660 km/hr).[c]

[c] See Taylor (1982).

[d] See Stockholm International Peace Research Institute (1983). In general the data and numbers in this reference are similar to those in International Institute for Strategic Studies (1983).

[e] See Cordesman (1982, Table 5, p. 41). This table is slightly more detailed in listing the separate models; the totals are close to those in International Institute for Strategic Studies (1983).

[f] Starting in 1982, 173 B-52Gs are being modified to carry 20 SRAM, 6 on each wing, plus 8 inside the bomb bay; later in the 1980s this will be done to other B-52s.[c]

[g] The Stockholm International Peace Research Institute (1982) lists the yield of the cruise missile warhead as 200 kt.

[h] At high altitudes.[c]

[i] Counting only truly intercontinental bombers (i.e., not counting the F-111, the Vulcan B2, the Tu-95, Mya-4, the Tu-16 Badger, the Tu-26 Backfire, or the Su-24 Fencer).

[j] A turboprop aircraft; all others are jets.

[k] Taylor (1982) lists the speeds of the Tu-26 and the Su-24, respectively, as Mach 2 and as Mach 2 or more. It lists the payloads of the Tu-95, Mya-4, Tu-16, Tu-26, and Su-24, respectively, as 11.7 tonnes, 4.5 tonnes, 10.8 tonnes, and 1.8 tonnes. These payloads are probably the typical operational payloads listed, while the payloads given in the International Institute for Strategic Studies report (1983) may be the maximum payloads leading to a reduced range.

[l] A few carry the Kangeroo cruise missile.[c]

[m] At an altitude of 11 km.[c]

[n] At high altitudes. At low altitudes the maximum speed is Mach 0.9.[c]

[o] These were being phased out prior to the Falkland Island war.

(3) How many bombs of what yield could be delivered with what accuracy by these surviving bombers?

Bomber Prelaunch Survivability

Consider a scenario in which the Soviet Union launches a preemptive nuclear first strike, including a counterforce attack on the strategic bomber deterrent forces. Once the attacking missiles are detected, those bombers that are on ground alert will take off. The survivability of these bombers will depend on the time between missile detection and the nuclear explosions and on the rapidity with which the bombers can take off. It will of course also depend on the dispersion of these bombers and on the ability of the Soviet Union to target enough missiles on all possible bomber fields.

It is generally assumed that submarine-launched ballistic missiles (SLBMs) would be used to attack bomber fields. With their relatively long flight times, intercontinental ballistic missiles (ICBMs) would provide too much warning time. The time of flight of an SLBM launched just offshore toward air bases in the interior of the U.S. might range from 15 min for minimum energy standard trajectories to 7 min if the missile is launched into a depressed, nearly orbital, trajectory (see Chapter 6). The missile attack might be detected and messages passed on to the air bases. In day-to-day normal alert, the bomber crews might take 2 to 4 min to scramble into their planes. An additional minute might be required to start up the engines and taxi to the runway. Thereafter, the aircraft survival would depend on its blast resistance and on its acceleration during takeoff—that is, on how far it would be away from its base by the time the nuclear explosion takes place.

Figure 5.11 shows estimates of such survival rates made by Quanbeck and Wood (1976). They assumed the B-52 and B-1 bombers to have blast resistances of, respectively, 1 psi and 3 psi and slow and high (rocket-assisted) accelerations. They further assumed an attack of 300 1-Mt warheads (with 75% reliability) onto 75 dispersal fields in the U.S. interior. The figure suggests that for day-to-day alert most of the bombers will survive as long as the Soviet Union launches its SLBM on minimum energy trajectories, as long as their times of flight are on the order of 15 min. If the missiles, however, were to be on a depressed trajectory, very few bombers not on crisis alert would survive a surprise attack. Thus, if the Soviet Union were to test SLBM in the depressed trajectory mode, and if thereafter Soviet missile submarines were to maneuver close to the U.S. shores, then the bomber deterrent could become threatened at takeoff. The analysis by Quanbeck and

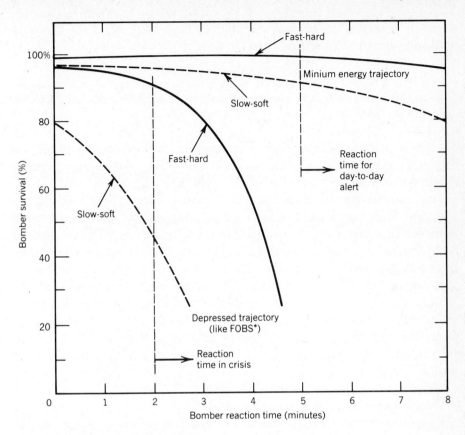

*Fractionally orbiting bombarding systems

Figure 5.11 Survival probabilities for slow and soft B-52 and fast and hard B-1 bombers dispersed on 75 bases and attacked by 300 1-Mt warheads launched from submarines. (After Quanbeck and Wood, 1976, p. 52.)

Wood suggests that at the present as many as 90% of the B-52 bombers might successfully take off under a Soviet first-strike attack.

Penetration of Soviet Air Defenses

The Soviet Union has an extensive antibomber defense system while the United States has none. It has about 2600 interceptor aircraft and 12,000 surface-to-air (SAM) launchers plus 4000 radar units. The SAM defense consists primarily of the SAM-2 units. The SAM-6 missiles that were so successful against Israeli planes early in the 1973 war are not presently used for strategic defense.

Any retaliatory U.S. strategic bomber attack would be carried out at low altitudes. Detecting such an attack and guiding interceptors and SAMs to an interception would be greatly helped by a radar system with an effective lookdown capability. Thus, Secretary of Defense Schlesinger in 1975 testified that

> without a "lookdown, shootdown" capability, the Soviet air defense interceptor aircraft are not likely to offer a serious obstacle to our bomber forces. (As quoted in Stockholm International Peace Research Institute, 1982, p. 65)

The Soviet Union is now trying to develop such lookdown capability through radar-carrying planes of the AWACS type. These must become effective for the USSR to have a truly useful air defense system.

The experiences that have been obtained with SAMs in North Vietnam and the Middle East support the feeling that as of now, bombers can penetrate Soviet air defenses. In North Vietnam against SAM-2 missiles over Hanoi, B-52 bombers experienced a 3% loss rate. In the 1973 Middle East conflict the SAM-6 missiles caused an overall loss rate of 1 to 1½% per mission. One estimate attributed to the U.S. Air Force placed the likely success rate of a strategic bombing attack on the USSR at 85%. The radar units and the SAM sites could be attacked by ICBMs or SLBMs to clear a path for incoming bombers. One reason put forward for maintaining a Triad deterrent is that it allows such mutual support.

Effectiveness of the Bomber Deterrent

Present American improvements in bomber alert capabilities and in bomber performance through low-level flight and electronic counter-measures (ECM) promise a high survival rate for the strategic bomber deterrent as long as it is not attacked by depressed trajectory SLBMs. Whether this force is sufficient for deterrence will be analyzed later in more detail. Chapter 4 indicated that 50 to 200 EMT are sufficient for massive retaliation. Consider an alert force of 200 B-52 bombers, with launch losses of 10% and further penetration losses of 15%. Then 150 (75%) of these bombers will arrive on target. These bombers could deliver about 800 EMT on their targets, according to Table 5.1.

MODERN STRATEGIC BOMBER ISSUES

The health of the strategic bomber force is an active issue in the nuclear arms race. In recent years, four particular weapons systems have been very much in the public spotlight. The range of the Soviet Backfire bomber has already been discussed. The most intense debate has been about deploying the B-1 bomber; side issues have been the develop-ment of a Stealth bomber and the American airborne warning and control system (AWACS). Each of these issues emphasizes different aspects not only of the strategic bomber debate but of the whole arms race as well.

The B-1 Bomber Debate

Most of the present U.S. bomber deterrent is quite old, dating from 1962 and earlier. The next generation of manned bombers has been planned ever since. The first proposals were for the B-70, with its high-altitude missions. The shooting down of the U-2 high-altitude reconnaissance plane in 1960 indicated that such a plane was vulnerable to attack by surface-to-air SAM missiles. Hence, gradually the plans changed to development of low-flying bombers, finally leading in 1970 to the B-1 bomber design. That plane was ready for deployment by 1977. The resulting deployment debate not only indicates the progress made in bomber technology but also explores alternatives to a straight-forward bomber force.

The B-1 Bomber Design

The B-1 bomber is a four-engine jet with variable-geometry wings (see Fig. 5.12). The B-1B design now proposed for deployment is a variant on the initial B-1 model. The B-1B is to fly supersonically at speeds of Mach 1.25 when at high altitude. It can also fly subsonically at Mach 0.9 as low as 60 m above the ground. In contrast, the B-52 cannot fly supersonically, and its combat altitude is above 150 m. Without refueling, the range of the B-1B may be as much as 12,000 km, perhaps 9800 km with a typical bomb load. The B-1B differs from the earlier B-1 version in being harder to detect and by incorporating even more advanced electronics (e.g., radar systems from the F-16 fighter aircraft). Its computer system alone weighs 2.4 tonnes; when jamming enemy signals, its ECM system consumes 120 kW of electrical power. By incorporating stealth technology (see p. 132), it is hoped that the B-1B may reflect 1% as much radar as does a B-52. This low reflectivity, combined with the very-low-altitude flight, will make the B-1B much

Figure 5.12   A B-1 bomber. (Photo courtesy U.S. Air Force.)

harder to detect by radar, helping it to avoid attacks by SAMs and interceptor aircraft.

The B-1 Debate

The debate over the deployment of the B-1 bomber has been going on since 1976. It has not focused on whether the bomber deterrent is necessary and desirable; rather, it has analyzed the various alternative ways of upgrading that force. Four major alternative options have been explored. (1) One could continue to improve the B-52s, modifying their engines and electronics. (2) The B-1 bomber could be deployed. (3) The stand-off capability of the B-52s could be improved by building more and better SRAMs and cruise missiles. (4) Some new bomber could be developed, based for example, on the Boeing 747 civilian airliner, a plane that would be relatively slow and vulnerable and would simply be a platform from which to launch long-ranged attack missiles. President Carter's decision was to pursue the third option—to add cruise missiles to B-52s. President Reagan's decision has been to deploy a new version of the B-1 bomber in addition to deploying the cruise missile while continuing to develop stealth technology for a new bomber.

The B-1 bomber project has been challenged on the basis of its cost. As is usual in new weapons programs, the estimated cost per B-1 aircraft has gone up from $9.9 million each in 1970, through $30 million each in 1973, to $87 million each in 1976, to about $200 million each in 1983. Research and development costs have been considerable, typically $400 million per year since 1973. Alternative programs also would be expensive; Table 5.2 shows the relative costs of various alternative options. Only the disbanding of the bomber deterrent altogether would lead to zero cost—and even in that case additional costs would probably arise from the strengthening of the submarine or the missile

Table 5.2 Estimated 10-year costs of the five bomber force options together with annual operating costs, expressed in billions of 1976 dollars.
After A. H. Quanbeck and A. L. Wood, 1976, p. 90.

Force	Number and Type of Aircraft	Ten-Year Costs (billion $)		
		Investment	Operations	Total
1	255 B-52s	$34.2	$35.4	$69.6
2	200 B-1s	$37.2	$34.2	$71.3
3	80 ALCM carriers	$27.3	$27.8	$55.1
4	100 fast-hard ALCM carriers	$29.0	$30.6	$59.6
5	120 high-acceleration ALCM carriers	$29.7	$31.0	$60.7

deterrent. A complete economic, military, and political analysis of all the various alternative options would be very desirable.

Such an analysis was done by Quanbeck and Wood (1976). This analysis is a reasonable review of the bomber deterrent, illustrating how to compare different weapons systems and how many assumptions must be made to allow a quantitative analysis. This analysis is complex: it considered five different options for improving the bomber force and four different levels of defenses by the Soviet Union against that force.

Five force options were considered: (1) Force 1 consists of 255 modified B-52s and an equal number of improved tankers. Included in the modifications would be new engines, rocket-assisted takeoff, new supercritical wings, improved guidance, low-level ride control, and a capacity of up to 24 SRAM stand-off missiles. (2) Force 2 consists of 200 B-1s, plus new tankers. (3) Force 3 uses a wide-bodied transport for air-launched cruise missiles (ALCM) plus new tankers. (4) Force 4 requires a new hard-fast–takeoff carrier, like the B-1, but without supersonic capability, to carry ALCM. (5) Force 5 is like Force 3, but would have rocket-assisted takeoff. The Soviet threats considered are (1) Level 1 includes 300 depressed trajectory SLBMs attacking bomber bases plus an estimated 400 interceptions of bombers by fighters plus the launching of 400 SAM missiles. (2) Level 2 is the same as level 1, except that the missiles are now minimum energy trajectory SLBMs, which take longer to reach bomber bases. (3) Level 3 has only the slow missiles and the fighter interceptions. (4) Level 4 offers no threat at all. The estimated costs of each of these five options, spread over 10 years, are shown in Table 5.2.

The success rate of these options is shown in Table 5.3. A distinction must be made between day-to-day alert and the strategic alert that goes into operation when major tensions arise between the United States and the Soviet Union. For strategic alert the time to takeoff is reduced by 3 to 4 min, and some fraction of the bomber force is constantly airborne. Tables 5.2 and 5.3 make two major points. The stand-off options are somewhat cheaper than are the options involving either the B-52 or the B-1 bombers; the deep-penetration capabilities of bombers are expensive. In all cases excepting one, a minimum of about 400 SRAMs or ALCMs will reach the target. Each SRAM and ALCM has, respectively, an explosive yield of about 200 kt or 300 kt, which is equivalent to a yield of 0.34 EMT or 0.45 EMT each or 135 EMT to 180 EMT total. This meets the definition of minimum population deterrent and comes close to the minimum industry deterrent described in Chapter 4. The only option in which insufficient bombers survive is the stand-off option involving ALCM on a slow and vulnerable wide-

Table 5.3 The estimated performance of the five bomber force options for various air defenses by the Soviet Union.
After Quanbeck and Wood, 1976, pp. 89–90.

Force	Number and Type of Aircraft	Prelaunch Survivability for Threat 1	Attack missile Delivered on Target for Various Threat Levels			
			1	2	3[a]	4[a]
With strategic warning						
1	255 improved B-52s	74%	1371	2010	2020	3960
2	200 B-1s	87%	1220	1500	1500	3110
3	80 ALCM carriers	100%[b]	1270[b]	1700[c]	2150[c]	2590[c]
4	100 fast-hard ALCM carriers	87%	1190	1500	1990	2270
5	120 high-acceleration ALCM carriers	74%	1220	1900	2380	2720
Day-to-day alert						
1	255 improved B-52s	22%	408	1180	1180	2800
2	200 B-1s	31%	434	850	850	2200
3	80 ALCM carriers	—[c]	—[c]	450	1270	1830
4	100 fast-hard ALCM carriers	31%	424	1020	1530	1600
5	120 high-acceleration ALCM carriers	22%	363	1020	1530	1920

[a] Adjusted to maximize the number of attack missiles delivered.
[b] For the airborne alert forces only.
[c] Negligible.

bodied carrier of the Boeing 747 type when attacked by SLBM missiles launched in a depressed trajectory.

The option chosen by President Carter, to improve the stand-off capabilities by deploying cruise missiles, is consistent with this analysis. The option chosen by President Reagan, namely, deploying B-1s and upgrading B-52s with ALCMs, tries to combine several of the survival features at some increased costs. The present bomber force appears to be a sufficient deterrent by itself for the foreseeable future. If the Soviet defensive (or SLBM offensive) capabilities develop further, the cheapest reaction would seem to be some specially designed delivery mode of ALCM.

Stealth Technology

Strategic bombers are potentially vulnerable to interception both by interceptor aircraft and by SAMs. For successful interception, the bombers must be detected as early as possible. This detection is usually done by radar systems. Once detected, interceptor aircraft and SAMs must be guided toward them. Guidance too is usually done by radar.

The final attack on the bomber is most likely carried out by missiles with on-board terminal guidance, such as from infrared heat-seeking systems.

It is possible to reduce the vulnerability of bombers if their visibility in all parts of the electromagnetic spectrum is decreased. The new stealth technology does that with a series of small improvements, which together may produce near invisibility.

Metals reflect microwaves most intensely at sharp edges. Radar microwave reflections can be reduced by rounding edges as much as possible or hiding sharp edges from direct line of sight to any radar detector.

Radar signals are well reflected by metallic surfaces. Replacing metals with nonmetallics, such as plastics or graphites, can reduce reflections greatly. As plastics and ceramics have become stronger and better able to resist the heat created by air flow past the aircraft exterior, it has become increasingly possible to replace or coat metal with such radar absorbing materials.

Very hot engines and exhausts emit much infrared radiation that infrared terminal guidance systems can detect. Baffles can be used to reduce the visible temperature of engine exhausts, and engines can be repositioned on aircraft so that they are harder to see.

When invisibility fails, electronic countermeasures can be used to make an aircraft "invisible" to attackers by radar jamming, by creating false and confusing return radar signals, or by other electronic counter-measures.

Stealth technology is very promising. The original B-1 bomber was said to have a radar signature one-third as large as that of the B-52; the newly proposed B-1B version is hoped to have a reflection a hundredth as much. This translates into a reduction by a factor of 10 in the range at which radar could detect the B-1B. Even if the aircraft is detected, a reduced radar or heat signature can help in confusing the defender; decoys or flares to simulate the aircraft's signature can then be a hundredth as large and still be successful.

AWACS

In the past the United States has mainly concentrated on a bomber deterrent, whereas the Soviet Union has focused on an air defense system against those bombers. The North American Air Defense Command (NORAD) has been neglected in past years, consisting now of less than 100 interceptor aircraft, few of them of recent vintage. SAM interceptors are almost nonexistent. A significant radar detection capability exists, but much of it is directed toward giving early warning of missile attacks. However, the perceived threat of the Backfire bomber has encouraged the United States to reconsider its air defenses. More recently, there has been a concern that by 1986 the USSR may have a new intercontinental bomber, the Blackjack, with a possible speed of Mach 2.3 and a range of 13,400 km. (Department of Defense, 1983).

An air defense proposal has suggested improvements in NORAD by adding an expanded airborne warning and control system (AWACS) together with upgraded F-14 and F-15 interceptor aircraft and a new SAM-D missile. This AWACS system would include 42 modified Boeing 707 jet liners to fly at 10 km and scan the air space both upward and down toward the ground to detect enemy aircraft and to direct intercepting fighters and SAMs. The low-altitude flight capability of the Backfire is of concern; only radar from above (lookdown radar) will be able to monitor such planes satisfactorily. AWACS would be supplemented by a long-range radar system, the over-the-horizon backscatter (OTH-B) system, which reflects radar signals off the upper atmosphere.

The 200 proposed F-14s or F-15s would be equipped with long-range Phoenix air-to-air missiles. Because of limited fuel capacity, these aircraft either would be on the ground until warning—in which case they would be vulnerable to a preemptive Soviet missile first strike —or else a tanker fleet would have to be built to refuel them in the air to allow for a longer time aloft. Finally, a SAM-D defensive system would be deployed, with four 160-km range missiles to be carried on a single launching trailer, accompanied by a phased array radar (see Chapter 10).

Total capital costs of this system, including research and development, have been estimated to be at least $10 billion. The need for such a system depends, of course, on the level of the Soviet bomber threat. However, it would also depend on the perception whether defense against a retaliatory second-strike bomber force is a part of a deterrence posture (see Chapter 8).

DISCUSSION

Is a bomber deterrent needed; are expensive new bombers and defensive systems necessary? It appears that at the present the U.S. bomber force by itself is sufficient for deterrence; only a coordinated Soviet SLBM system based on developing a depressed missile trajectory for the SLBM can threaten this deterrent. That system has not so far been developed by the Soviet Union. The bomber force does offer the attraction of being recallable after launch. The fact that bombers take much longer to reach their targets make them a true deterrent system. In that sense the bomber deterrent might be considered to be only a backup system, unless it were particularly inexpensive, which it is not.

If the bomber force is presently adequate, why then the expensive new systems? This chapter's introductory quotation from the Pentagon official is a cynical answer, implying that replacement of the B-52 by the B-1 is a matter of bureaucratic self-interest. However, if the demand is for certainty in matters of national security, if the preservation of the nuclear strategic Triad is a national policy for insurance purposes, then anticipated possible threats to the bomber force must be met. If there is indeed a need for new bombers, it arises in part because of better electronic capabilities, as described in Chapter 13. Both the defensive radar systems of the Soviet Union and the electronic ECM and bomber and missile guidance systems of the United States to overcome them can be greatly improved. Theories of the technological imperative (see Chapter 13) suggest that since the electronics can be improved, they likely will be improved; as long as national security demands the highest degree of certainty, an upgraded bomber deterrent will come. The various options ultimately chosen can be expected to be those that exploit to the utmost new electronic capabilities, rather than those that are most cost effective.

References

Anderson, J. D., Jr., *Introduction to Flight*. New York: McGraw-Hill, 1978.

Bottome, E. M., *The Balance of Terror: A Guide to the Arms Race*. Boston: Beacon Press, 1971.

Cockburn, A. *The Threat: Inside the Soviet Military Machine*. New York: Random House, 1982.

Cordesman, H., "M-X and the Balance of Power: Reassessing America's Strength." *Armed Forces Journal International*, Vol. 120, no. 4 (December 1982), pp. 21–51.

Deitchman, S. J., *New Technology and Military Power*. Boulder, Colo.: Westview Press, 1979.

Department of Defense, *Soviet Military Power*, 2nd ed. Washington, D.C.: Government Printing Office, 1983.

English, R. D., and D. I. Bolef, "Defense Against Bomber Attack." *Scientific American*, Vol. 229, no. 2 (August 1973), pp. 11–19.

Feuchtwanger, E. J., and R. A. Mason, *Air Power in the Next Generation*. London: Macmillan, 1979.

Grey, L., and L. A. Hamlan, eds. *International Aerospace Review*. New York: American Institute Aeronautics and Astronautics, 1981.

Hoeber, F. P., *Slow to Take Offense: Bombers, Cruise Missiles, and Prudent Deterrence*, 2nd ed. Washington, D.C.: Center for Strategic and International Studies, Georgetown University, 1980.

The Insight Team of the *London Sunday Times*. *The Yom Kippur War*. Garden City, N.Y.: Doubleday, 1974.

International Institute for Strategic Studies. *The Military Balance: 1983–1984*. London: IISS, 1983.

Lee, R. G., *Introduction to Battlefield Weapons Systems and Technology.* New York: Brassey's, 1981.

Martin, L., *Arms and Strategy.* New York: David McKay, 1973.

Pfaltzgraff, R. L., and T. K. Davis, *Cruise Missile: Bargaining Chip or Defense Bargain.* Cambridge, Mass.: Institute for Foreign Policy Analysis, 1977.

Quanbeck, A. H., and A. L. Wood, *Modernizing the Strategic Bomber Force: Why and How.* Washington, D.C.: The Brookings Institution, 1976.

Stockholm International Peace Research Institute. *World Armaments and Disarmament: SIPRI Yearbook 1982.* Cambridge, Mass.: Oelgeschlager, Gunn & Hain, 1982.

J. W. R. Taylor, ed. *Jane's All the World's Aircraft: 1982–83.* London: Jane's, 1982.

York, H.F., *Race to Oblivion: A Participant's View of the Arms Race.* New York: Simon & Schuster, 1970. See particularly Chapters 3 and 4, "The Bomber Bonanza" and "The Elusive Nuclear Airplane," pp. 49–59 and 60–74.

CHAPTER
6

Intercontinental Ballistic Missiles

So, there is a consensus that a world of absolute ICBM accuracy looms, and that the gradual march of technology is leading us to it.

Deborah Shapley, science writer, 1978

The second leg of the strategic Triad consists of intercontinental ballistic missiles (ICBMs). The history and development of military ICBMs is intertwined with the civilian desire to explore space, and it mixes technical feasibility and political will. The theory of rocket motion has been well understood ever since Isaac Newton published his three laws of motion at the end of the seventeenth century. Practicable rockets have to propel a significant payload over a useful range with enough accuracy at an acceptable price. The German V-2 rocket of World War II inspired some to dream that ICBMs might someday become feasible, and by 1954 rocket technology had progressed far enough.

The initial deployment decisions concerning ICBMs were made mostly on political grounds. For example, a perceived missile gap in 1960 led to a U.S. crash program that soon produced an overwhelming missile superiority compared with that of the Soviets. In the late 1960s and early 1970s, the Soviet Union caught up with, and surpassed, the United States in quantities of ICBMs.

Since the early 1970s, the numerical ICBM race has halted; it has been replaced by a quality race. Multiple warheads have been developed, and missile accuracy has increased tremendously. The present concern about ICBMs is no longer whether they would work if launched but whether they would survive a surprise attack by the **137** enemy. Concerns about quality are at the heart of most contemporary ICBM issues.

TECHNOLOGY OF ICBMs

ICBM Trajectories

The scientific understanding of rocket acceleration and of ballistic flight was completed with the publication of Isaac Newton's *Principia* in 1687. Newton's three laws describe the motion of masses in response to applied forces. Rockets experience several forces. Forward propulsion is caused by the high-temperature gases ejected backward out of the exhaust nozzle (see Fig. 6.1). The forward acceleration a is equal to the accelerating force F_a divided by the rocket mass m. This accelerating force F_a of the rocket is equal to the rate dm/dt at which masses of gas are ejected out of the rocket nozzle times the velocity v_e at which the ejected gases travel. The acceleration is thus described by the equation

$$\text{Force} = \text{mass of rocket} \cdot \text{rocket acceleration}$$
$$= \text{speed of exhaust gas} \cdot \text{gas ejection rate} \qquad (6.1)$$
$$= F_a = ma = mv_e \cdot \frac{dm}{dt}$$

This acceleration force not only provides an increasing rocket velocity, but it also helps the rocket to overcome the force of gravity and the drag of the atmosphere. Gravitational forces act on the rocket throughout the flight. In contrast, the atmospheric drag acts only in the initial launch phase and during the final reentry process. Figure 6.2 shows a typical flight plan of a long-range ballistic missile. The launch phase takes several minutes during which time the various stages of the rocket sequentially ignite, burn all their fuel, and separate from the remainder of the rocket. After launch, the warheads and the "bus" that carries them float under the influence of gravity in an elliptic trajectory with the center of the earth at one of the foci, a trajectory called ballistic because the only force acting on the rocket is that of gravity. Finally, during reentry through the atmosphere, the payload is protected against burnup from friction with the air and may be guided toward the target by control flaps or by shifting weights inside the reentry vehicle (RV).

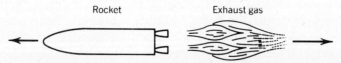

Rocket   Exhaust gas

Figure 6.1   A rocket is propelled by exhaust gases ejected through the exhaust nozzle.

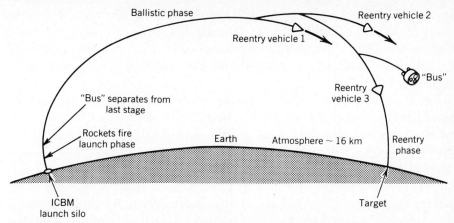

Figure 6.2 The three phases of the flight of an intercontinental ballistic missile.

In considering the range of a ballistic missile, as a first approximation the launch and reentry phases can be ignored (i.e., one can act as if the ballistic rocket instantaneously reaches the final ballistic velocity v_b and as though it flies at all times in a vacuum). The range of a rocket depends very strongly on its ballistic, or terminal, velocity.

Figure 6.3 shows this relationship for various ballistic velocities of a rocket fired at 45° with respect to the earth's surface. It shows, for example, that an increase of 33% in the ballistic velocity from 5.5 km/sec to 7.4 km/sec increases the range of the missile by 108% from 3450 km to 7180 km. For a velocity of 8 km/sec, the missile can go into orbit at an altitude of 160 km just above the atmosphere, circling the earth in 1

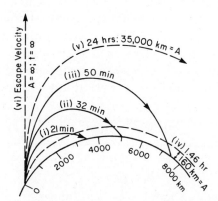

Figure 6.3 Trajectories of ICBMs launched at 45° to the horizontal, with instantaneous velocities of (i) 5.5 km/sec, (ii) 6.4 km/sec, (iii) 7.4 km.sec, (iv) 8 km/sec, (v) 10.7 km/sec, and (vi) 11.2 km/sec. Case (iv) involves enough ballistic speed to put the missile into orbit just above the earth's surface; case (v) can put the rocket into a geosynchronous orbit 38,000 km above the earth's surface; in case (vi) the rocket will leave the earth altogether. The flight times are indicated for (i), (ii), and (iii); for (iv), (v), and (vi), the times required to complete one orbit are shown.

hr and 28 min. A velocity of 10.7 km/sec can put the missile into an orbit 35,000 km (22,000 mi) above the earth's surface, circling the earth once every 24 hr. For velocities in excess of 11.2 km/sec, the rocket will escape from the earth's gravitational field altogether and will never return to it.

For a given ballistic velocity, the range also depends on the angle the final ballistic velocity makes with the horizon. Figure 6.4 shows some of the ranges achievable with a ballistic velocity of 7.4 km/sec. For launch angles of 6° and 51° the rocket travels 7360 km in 17.5 and 49 min, respectively. For a launching angle of 19.3°, the rocket lands 11,300 km away from the launch point after a flight of 35 min. This latter range is the longest that can be achieved for that ballistic velocity, and hence it is called the maximum range. This flight path is called the minimum energy trajectory, as it demands less fuel to reach 11,300 km than any other trajectory. If the earth were flat, the maximum range would be achieved for a launch angle of 45°.

ICBM Velocities

The V-2 rockets of World War II achieved a terminal ballistic velocity of 1.6 km/sec. Modern ICBMs have velocities at the end of the propulsion phase in excess of 7 km/sec. For historical reasons the velocities and ranges of missiles and even strategic bombers are often given in terms of nautical miles (nm). The nautical mile is defined as 1 min of the earth's circumference at the equator, and hence 1.0 nm = 1.15 mi = 1.85 km. This ballistic velocity of 7.3 km/sec is equal to 4 nm/sec. Missiles with ballistic velocities in excess of 8 km/sec will go into orbit; above 11.2 km/sec, they will leave the earth altogether, as shown in Fig. 6.4. Thus there is an upper limit to the rapidity with which ballistic missiles can reach targets on the earth's surface.

This ballistic or terminal velocity is a product of the acceleration due to the rocket exhaust times the period for which the rocket firing

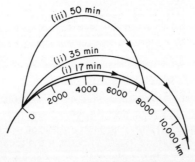

Figure 6.4 Trajectories for a ballistic velocity of 7.4 km/sec, with launch angles of (i) 6°, (ii) 19.3°, and (iii) 51°.

provides this acceleration. This acceleration is on the order of one to two times that due to gravity. Equation 6.1 shows that the acceleration is large when the gas exhaust velocity v_e is large. Large accelerations are produced by high-energy fuels that provide high-temperature exhaust gases in which the individual molecules move at high speeds, by a large rate of mass exhaust dm/dt, and by the smallest possible rocket mass m. Large amounts of rocket fuel can produce long acceleration times, but they increase the mass of the rocket.

The energy content of liquid rocket fuel has not increased greatly over the years. Generally, liquid-fueled rockets operate by mixing two liquids within the engine itself during the firing process. Oxidizers such as liquified oxygen or liquid nitrogen pentoxide combine with a hydrogen-based fuel such as aerozine 50 to give high exhaust velocities. Rocket development work has aimed to produce storable liquid fuels or solid fuels with equivalent energy content or to build larger rockets. High-energy liquid fuels give exhaust velocities of 3.6 km/sec (12,000 feet/sec). Liquid fuels have problems of expense, degradation during storage, toxicity, corrosiveness, and instability. Unless the liquid fuel is stored in the rocket itself, the time between the decision to launch and the actual launch could be many hours. The expense is large if fuels such as hydrogen or oxygen are used that must be liquified by refrigeration. Liquid fuels require that the rocket be strong enough to contain the lateral forces of the liquids in the two separate fuel tanks inside the rocket itself. Refrigerated fuels will become gaseous if warmed and present a potential explosion hazard. Storable liquid fuels are very toxic and chemically unstable and, hence, must be handled with great care. Storable liquids do degrade in time and must regularly be chemically treated.

In contrast, solid fuels are cheaper and do not present storage or toxicity problems. However, their energy content is generally not as high as that of liquid fuels; their exhaust velocities have been less than 2.7 km/sec. Firing solid-fuel rockets presents some difficulty because the magnitude of their thrust cannot be varied as it can be with liquid fuels where liquid flow rates can be accurately adjusted. Solid-fuel rockets have difficulties in controlling the termination moment, restarting the engines, and coordinating the firing of multiple rockets. Solid-fuel rockets tend to have more difficulties with vibrations. Finally, to achieve the even firing of a solid-fuel rocket, it is desirable to manufacture and transport the complete rocket fuel loading in one piece; this presents difficulty for large rockets.

The rate of fuel burning has increased over the years both for liquid- and solid-fuel rockets. Not only have the exhaust nozzles become larger: for liquid-fueled rockets the fuel handling inside the rocket has much improved, and for solid-fueled rockets large amounts of fuel can now be burned simultaneously. For example, the thrust of solid fuel rockets grew from 100 pounds (lb) in 1951 for the Falcon air-to-air missile to 40,000 lb for an early version of the Minuteman missile in 1959, to 200,000 lb for the Minuteman II in 1964. The length of time of fuel burns similarly improved as it was learned how to lengthen the chunk of solid fuel within the rockets and to shape the burning surface inside that chunk. The mass of the rocket required to contain a given amount of fuel too has been decreased; rocket walls have been made thinner and lighter by the use of modern alloys. However, the decrease in the mass of rockets has come primarily through the use of multiple-stage rockets. For a single-stage rocket, the thrust has to accelerate a large mass of empty fuel casing to the final ballistic velocity. In contrast, a multistage rocket ejects the empty fuel tanks as each smaller stage is fired (Fig. 6.5). The first stage reaches only a relatively low velocity, but the ballistic velocity v_b of the final stage will be large. For example, a rocket like the Minuteman III might give a 1½-tonne payload a ballistic velocity of 4 km/sec if constructed of a single stage or 7.5 km/sec if made up of three stages.

The final ballistic velocity v_b of a rocket approximately equals the velocity of the exhaust gases times the logarithm $\ln(m_0/m_b)$ of the ratio of the initial takeoff mass m_0 of the rocket to the final ballistic payload mass m_b.

$$v_b = v_e \cdot \ln \frac{m_0}{m_b} \tag{6.2}$$

In turn the range of the rocket depends on the ballistic velocity. Thus the range of a given rocket can be increased by using a more powerful

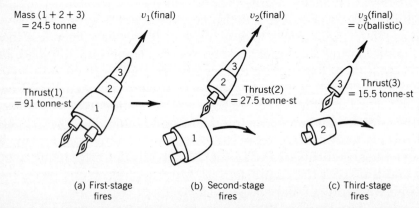

Mass $(1 + 2 + 3)$ = 24.5 tonne v_1(final) v_2(final) v_3(final) = v(ballistic)

Thrust(1) = 91 tonne-st   Thrust(2) = 27.5 tonne-st   Thrust(3) = 15.5 tonne-st

(a) First-stage fires   (b) Second-stage fires   (c) Third-stage fires

Figure 6.5 Multiple-stage rockets release fuel casings once they are ejected. The masses and thrusts shown here are for the Minuteman III missile. (Data from Pretty, 1982.)

rocket fuel with a higher exhaust velocity v_e or by making the payload smaller (higher m_0/m_b ratio); there is in fact no uniquely determined range for a given missile.

Liquid-fueled rocket engines generally have larger thrusts than do solid-fueled engines, and they can have larger payloads. This advantage can be exploited by having larger warheads or by utilizing fewer rocket stages. Table 6.2, which appears shortly, shows that solid-fueled ICBMs usually have three stages, liquid-fueled missiles only two stages.

ICBM Accuracy

The V-2 rocket of World War II was a very inaccurate weapon. Over the short range of 320 km, only 33% of all V-2s fell within 5 km of their targets. The accuracy of modern ICBMs has been achieved by combining inertial guidance mechanisms with on-board computers. Completely self-contained gyroscopes and accelerometers measure the rocket's motion during the propulsion phase, requiring no information from outside sources. The computers translate the inertial information into thrust-direction and thrust-termination instructions that allow the rocket to follow the preplanned flight trajectory.

Inertial Guidance

Inertial guidance systems are typically made up of a combination of three gyroscopes plus three accelerometers, as shown in Fig. 6.6. Spinning at very high speeds, these gyroscopes resist any changes in the directions of their axes and, therefore, define constant reference orientations in space, for example, one pointed at the North star. Changes in the rocket's orientation are detected by a computer as it compares the gyroscopically defined reference directions with the direction of the rocket's axis.

The velocity and position of the rocket in space are monitored by three accelerometers mounted on this stable inertial platform. The three accelerometers constantly measure the acceleration of the rocket in three independent dimensions (e.g., up-down, north-south, and east-west). Since speeds can only be measured by constant reference to some outside points, the computer must use the measured accelerations to calculate the instantaneous velocities in three dimensions. The computer then averages the velocities over the flight time to calculate the actual rocket position in space. The calculated velocities and positions are compared by the computer with those required to achieve the desired trajectory. The computer can correct deviations from the preprogrammed rocket orientations by inserting deflecting vanes into the rocket exhaust, rotating the rocket nozzle, or activating small

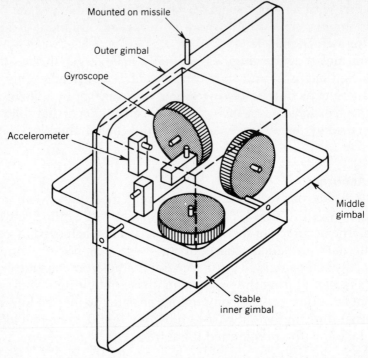

Figure 6.6 The arrangement of gyroscopes and accelerometers in an inertial guidance system.

supplementary guidance-control rockets. When the desired terminal velocity and direction are finally attained, the computer shuts off the engines.

Missile Accuracy

The accuracy of a missile is ordinarily expressed in terms of a circular error probability (CEP). The distance by which a warhead may miss its target in the direction of its flight is known as the range miss; the miss perpendicular to the line of flight is called the track miss. Figure 6.7 shows how these two misses combine to a CEP, where the CEP is equal to three-fifths of the vector sum of the range and track misses; that is,

$$CEP = 0.6 \text{ (average track miss + average range miss)} \quad (6.3)$$

This definition of the CEP means that one-half of all warheads with such an accuracy will impact near the target in an area equal to that of a circle with radius CEP and one-half will fall outside that area.

Various factors can contribute to the range and track misses. Table 6.1 shows estimates of possible contributions to the CEP for typical present land-based and sea-based U.S. missiles. Initial condition errors

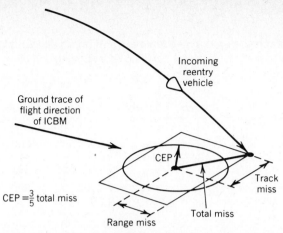

Figure 6.7 The accuracy CEP of an ICBM warhead is determined by a vector combination of the track miss and the range miss. The particular missile shown was one of the 50% that would fall outside the area defined by the CEP.

Table 6.1   Estimates of sources of inaccuracies in the targeting of nuclear warheads of a hypothetical contemporary inertially guided intercontinental ballistic missile. The total circular error probability is equal to three-fifths of the sum of the average range miss plus the average track miss.
These numbers come from Bunn and Tsipis (1983), except for the initial condition parameters for SLBMs, which are derived by scaling the values given in Tsipis (1975) for 1975 missiles to current missiles. See also Feld et al. (1971).

Source of Errors	Land-Based Missiles		SLBM Missiles	
	Range Miss	**Track Miss**	**Range Miss**	**Track Miss**
Knowledge of initial conditions				
Initial position and				
targeting	20 m	20 m	200 m	20 m
Velocity	0 m	0 m	400 m	60 m
Vertical alignment	60 m	6 m	200 m	50 m
Azimuth alignment	0 m	77 m	10 m	400 m
Inertial sensing				
Accelerometer problems				
(e.g., bias, calibration,				
misalignment,				
vibrations)	60 m	70 m	60 m	70 m
Gyroscope problems				
(e.g., initial and				
acceleration induced				
drift, vibrations)	85 m	30 m	85 m	30 m
Thrust termination	40 m	0 m	40 m	0 m
Gravitational anomalies	50 m	15 m	50 m	15 m
Guidance computation	15 m	5 m	15 m	5 m
Reentry buffeting and				
fuzing	100 m	60 m	100 m	60 m
Total range or track error	170 m	105 m	515 m	420 m
CEP = 0.6 · total error		165		560

Table 6.2 ICBM missiles presently deployed and under development.
All data are derived from the International Institute for Strategic Studies, 1983, unless otherwise indicated.

Missile	Fuel	Stages	Launch	Range	Accuracy	Payload
United States						
Titan II	Liquid	2	Hot	15,000 km	1300 m	3.8 tonnes
Minuteman II	Solid	3	Hot	11,300 km	370 m	0.7 tonnes
Minuteman III	Solid	3	Hot	13,000 km	280 m	1.1 tonnes
Minuteman IIIA	Solid	3	Hot	13,000 km	220 m	1.1 tonnes
MX	Solid	3[c]	Cold	11,000 km[d]	80 m	3.6 tonnes
Soviet Union						
SS-11 (MOD 1)	Liquid	2	Hot	10,500 km	1400 m	0.9 tonnes
(MOD 3)	Liquid	2	Hot	8,800 km	1100 m	1.2 tonnes
SS-13	Solid	3	Hot	10,000 km	2000 m	0.5 tonnes
SS-17 (MOD 1)	Liquid	2	Cold	10,000 km	450 m	2.7 tonnes
(MOD 2)	Liquid	2	Cold	11,000 km	450 m	1.6 tonnes
SS-18 (MOD 1)	Liquid	2	Cold	12,000 km[f]	450 m	7.5 tonnes
(MOD 2)	Liquid	2	Cold	11,000 km[g]	450 m	7.6 tonnes
(MOD 3)	Liquid	2	Cold	10,500 km	350 m	7.2 tonnes
(MOD 4)	Liquid	2	Cold	9,000 km	300 m	7.6 tonnes
(MOD 5)	Liquid	2	Cold	(9,000 km)	(250 m)	(7.0 tonnes)
SS-19 (MOD 1)	Liquid	2	Hot	11,000 km	500 m	3.6 tonnes
(MOD 2)	Liquid	2	Hot	10,000 km	300 m	3.3 tonnes
(MOD 3)	Liquid	2	Hot	(10,000 km)	300 m	3.6 tonnes

[a] Equivalent megatonnage (EMT) is equal $Y^{2/3}$, with the yield Y in megatons.
[b] Often cited as 0.2 Mt (e.g., by Pretty, 1982).
[c] The postboost bus has a rocket fueled by storable liquid propellant.
[d] See Office of Technology Assessment (1981).
[e] See Chapter 5, Cordesman (1982), p. 41. This reference gives subtotals for the various modifications and assumes that 52 more SS-11s have been replaced by SS-19s.
[f] Pretty (1982) says 10,500 km.
[g] Pretty (1982) says 9,250 km.
[h] Out of service.

come from insufficient knowledge of the launch and target locations and of the velocity of the launching platform if it is a submarine, for example. Inertial sensing errors are introduced by miscalibrations, biases, and drifts in the gyroscopes and accelerometers. Errors in thrust termination come from imprecision in shutting off the engines, a particular problem for solid-fuel engines. Gravitational anomalies introduce errors due to uncertain knowledge of mass concentrations on earth, such as mountains and ocean valleys, that lead to local changes in gravitational forces (i.e., errors that might come when

Warheads	No. in 1982	No. of Warheads	Mt TOTAL	EMT/RV[a]	Total EMT
1 @ 9 Mt	45	45	405 Mt	4.33 EMT	195 EMT
1 @ 1½ Mt	450	450	675 Mt	1.31 EMT	590 EMT
3 MIRV @ 0.170 Mt[b]	250	750	127 Mt	0.31 EMT	230 EMT
3 MIRV @ 0.335 Mt	300	900	302 Mt	0.48 EMT	434 EMT
10 MIRV @ 0.335 Mt	(R&D)	0	0 Mt	0.48 EMT	0 EMT
U.S. total	1045	2147	1509 Mt		1449 EMT
1 @ 1 Mt	518(−)[e]	518(−)	518 Mt	1.00 EMT	518 EMT
3 MRV @ 0.1–0.3 Mt	Some	Some	(0 Mt)	0.34 EMT	(0 EMT)
1 @ 0.75 Mt	60	60	45 Mt	0.83 EMT	50 EMT
4 MIRV @ 0.75 Mt	120[e]	480	360 Mt	0.83 EMT	396 EMT
1 @ 6 Mt	32[e]	32	192 Mt	3.30 EMT	106 EMT
1 @ 20 Mt	58(−)[e]	58(−)	1160 Mt	7.37 EMT	427 EMT
8 MIRV @ 0.9 Mt	175[e]	1400	1260 Mt	0.93 EMT	1305 EMT
1 @ 20 Mt	Some[e]	Some	(0 Mt)	7.37 EMT	(0 EMT)
10 MIRV @ 0.5 Mt	75[e]	750	375 Mt	0.63 EMT	472 EMT
(10 MIRV @ 0.75 Mt)	(R&D)	0	0 Mt	0.83 EMT	0 EMT
6 MIRV @ 0.55 Mt[f]	0[h]	0	0 Mt	0.67 EMT	0 EMT
1 @ 5 Mt	60[e]	60	300 Mt	2.92 EMT	175 EMT
6 MIRV @ 0.55 Mt	300[e]	1800	990 Mt	0.67 EMT	1208 EMT
USSR total	1398	5158	5200 Mt		4657 EMT

sending missiles over an untested polar route). Reentry errors come from the buffeting by the atmosphere of the warheads during the reentry phase of its flight, from uneven ablation (wear) of the reentry vehicles, or from fuzing problems.

The accuracies in Table 6.1 impose very high demands on the inertial guidance components. A speck of dust (less than 10^{-10} kg) on one of the accelerometers may cause a track miss of 70 m and a range miss of 200 m. An imbalance of $5 \cdot 10^{-10}$ m in the center of a 1-kg gyroscope can produce a track miss of 50 m and a range miss of 100 m. If the rocket thrust is terminated one-thousandth of a second too late, the target may be missed by 600 m. The various accelerations must be measured to an accuracy of one part per million over a magnitude range in excess of a million.

Tables 6.2 and 7.2 list the best present accuracies for actually deployed missiles as 220 m and 450 m for land- and sea-based missiles, respectively. This is an improvement by a factor of more than 1000 since World War II. Figure 6.8 shows the improvements in missile accuracy of U.S. and Soviet ICBMs since 1960. Missile accuracies have been doubling approximately every 7 years, with the Soviet accuracies lagging those of the United States by about 7 years. Improvements in accuracy have come through technological improvements in the inertial sensing techniques coupled with better computer controls on the rocket engine firings from better knowledge of gravitational anomalies and through improved reentry vehicle technologics. The proposed improved accuracy of the MX missile involves for example a greatly improved inertial guidance system.

In the future, major improvements may come from guidance after the propulsion phase as the payload and warheads become maneuverable during the ballistic and reentry phases. External information will be fed into the missile from satellite navigation systems (such as NAVSTAR), from star sightings (for the Trident II), or from radar mapping of the target as described in Chapter 5 and in Chapter 12 for the Pershing-II missile. Accuracies of tens of meters seem feasible for such systems. Figure 6.8 does not provide a definitive prediction of future missile accuracies. But these potential guidance technologies suggest that accuracies may well continue to improve rapidly. The past guidance improvements in the missile accuracy by both the United States and the USSR suggest that, while there is not likely to be a sudden breakthrough by either side in the future, the significant gap

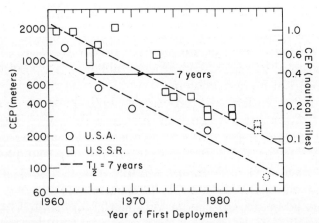

Figure 6.8 The accuracy of U.S. and USSR missiles as a function of the date of first deployment (from Table 6.2 and International Institute for Strategic Studies, 1982). The straight lines representing a 7-year doubling time in the missile accuracy are rough fits to the data.

will continue into the future (see, e.g., Amann, Cooper, and Davies, 1977; Amann and Cooper, 1982).

ICBM Payloads: MIRV

The payloads of ICBMs can be very large or quite small. The Soviet SS-18 missile has a 7.6-tonne payload; the single-warhead modification has an explosive yield of 20 Mt. In contrast, the Minuteman-III missile has a payload of 1.1 tonnes, containing three warheads each with an explosive yield of 170 kt or 335 kt. The mass of the payload, and hence the possible explosive yield of the warheads, is significant. For many targets, the number of separate warheads that are contained in the payload of any one missile is even more important.

Separate warheads are delivered by separate reentry vehicles (RVs). Systems with more than one warhead are labeled by the acronyms MRV, MIRV, and MARV, referring to "multiple reentry vehicles," "multiple independently targetable reentry vehicles," and "maneuverable reentry vehicles" (some write it MaRV). The MRV systems were first developed to penetrate antiballistic missile (ABM) defenses, to flood them with too many targets to be intercepted (see Chapter 10, and York's (1970) Chapters 5, 6 and 7). The MIRV system extended the MRV concept by giving a single missile the ability to strike several independent targets several hundred kilometers apart. Through their greatly increased accuracy, MIRVs have at the same time acquired an improved capability to attack hardened military installations. (See Chapter 12 for a discussion of the war fighting capabilities of MIRV, Chapter 8 for the destabilization it induces, and Chapter 13 for the role played by the technological imperative in this case.)

In the multiple reentry vehicle system, shortly after the propulsion phase the reentry vehicles separate from each other and pursue independent ballistic and reentry paths. They stay close together and strike in a cluster around the target. The accuracy of MRV systems is usually low, and they are designed to destroy a broad area comparable in size to the separation between the impact points of the separate RVs.

ICBMs carrying MIRV warheads can successfully attack separate targets. The final stage of the MIRVed ICBM is a "bus" carrying the warheads. Figure 6.9 shows the MIRV system in an MX missile nose cone. After the propulsion phase, during the ballistic phase, this bus varies its angle of orientation and sequentially lobs unpropelled warheads at different targets, as shown in Fig. 6.2. Inaccuracies introduced by the MIRVing separation technique can be overcome by increasing the accuracy of the maneuvers carried out by the postboost bus.

MARV technologies add maneuverability to each separate reentry

Figure 6.9 A mockup of the MIRV payload for the MX missile. (Photo courtesy of the AVCO Corporation.)

vehicle. As discussed in Chapter 5 for the cruise missile, that maneuverability can exploit targeting information received by the reentry vehicle during its ballistic flight, and even during reentry. The intermediate-range Pershing-II missile discussed in Chapter 12 has a single MARV reentry vehicle with radar terminal guidance. Initially, the MARV technology was sought to overcome ABM defenses. Now this maneuverability opens the way to very high accuracy.

THE ICBM ARMS RACE

Prior to World War II, rocketry had been the field of amateurs including the Russian Konstantin E. Tsiolkovskii, the American Robert H. Goddard, and the German Hermann Oberth. In the 1930s the military establishments of these countries began to support some of these efforts. As a result of this support, various Soviet artillery and anti-aircraft rockets were extensively used during World War II, while in Germany about 3700 V-2s were launched toward Great Britain under the direction of Wernher von Braun and Walter Dornberger.

At the end of World War II, the U.S. ICBM program began with a collection of V-2 rockets accompanied by von Braun and many others of the German engineers who had developed that weapon. Yet the first satellite, the Soviet *Sputnik,* was not launched into orbit until 1957, and the first Soviet intercontinental rocket reached the deployment stage only in 1958. Why were long-range rockets not developed earlier?

At the end of World War II little interest could be raised for a weapon that could deliver a 1-tonne warhead over a few hundred km with an inaccuracy exceeding several miles. The B-29 strategic bombing techniques were highly developed, and nuclear weapons weighed several tonnes and thus were too heavy to be delivered by such missiles. Technologists were skeptical about ICBMs. Consequently, much research effort went instead into the development of air-breathing ramjet missiles. Rocket research focused on short-range, solid-fuel rockets. Satellites might be launched with long-range rockets. But for what purpose? A satellite could not function well as a bomb-launching platforms; satellite photoreconnaissance did not appear very interesting at a time when offensive doctrines predominated. The ICBM engines in the end were a spinoff from the effort to develop booster rockets for intercontinental cruise missiles such as the Navaho.

Finally in 1954 President Eisenhower gave top priority to developing an ICBM. At that point it appeared that the requirement of an intercontinental range could be met, and the feasible accuracy and warhead size seemed adequate. The improved accuracy came from the new high-precision inertial guidance first installed in 1953 in the Redstone rocket. The use of transistors, discovered in 1949, made on-board computers feasible. Small but powerful nuclear warheads followed the development in 1952 of the H-bomb and its subsequent miniaturization.

The development of ICBMs was also fostered by a rocket competition with the Soviet Union. In 1955 the United States promised to launch an earth satellite as part of the 1957 scientific International Geophysical Year. But the USSR was the first to launch an artificial earth satellite, *Sputnik 1,* on October 4, 1957. This was taken by many as symbolizing superior Soviet rocket capabilities. Once the feasibility and desirability of military rockets seemed established, fierce competitions developed between the various branches of the Armed Services. Both the Army and the Air Force developed intermediate-range, liquid-fuel rockets, the Jupiter and the Thor (see Armacourt, 1969). The Thor/Atlas/Titan sequence of the Air Force ultimately produced the Titan-II intercontinental missile first tested in 1962. Fifty-two remaining U.S. Titan-II missiles are now being gradually decommissioned.

The development of the solid-fuel Minuteman ICBM required more radical improvements in technology. Solid fuel had been worked on since World War II. The difficulty lay in making a single unit of solid fuel large enough for an intercontinental rocket. By 1955 that problem was solved in the United States, solid-fuel rockets large enough to transport nuclear weapons were developed by 1957. The competition induced by the launch of *Sputnik* accelerated this program to a commitment to deploy the Minuteman missile before it was even flight tested. In contrast, the Soviet Union was not as able to miniaturize its warheads; hence, it required more powerful rockets and committed itself to liquid fuels. This difference in ICBM fueling has persisted to this day; the USSR still has no satisfactory solid-fuel ICBMs.

The U.S. decision to deploy large numbers of ICBMs was made in the atmosphere of the purported missile gap (Bottome, 1971). From 1957 to 1959 the suspicion grew that the Soviet Union was far ahead of the United States in ICBM production; late in 1959 it was predicted that by 1961–1962, the USSR would have between 1000 and 1500 ICBMs whereas the United States would have only 130. The United States, therefore, committed itself to build 1000 Minuteman missiles, although by 1962 the Soviet in fact produced fewer than 100 ICBMs. Why build exactly 1000 missiles? Herbert F. York argues that this was the minimum number of missiles that President Kennedy could offer the military hawks:

> Secretary (of Defense) Gates . . . had set in motion programs for manufacturing and reworking a force somewhat less than 1000. The Air Force . . . was urging figures more like 2000 to 3000, and [the] commander of SAC talked of 10,000. McNamara . . . set . . . it to 1000. (York, 1970, p. 15)

The single warhead on the Minuteman-II missile was designed to have a yield of 1 Mt because

> It is true that the damage radius of a one-megaton bomb is more or less compatible with the (5 mile) accuracy prescribed for the missile. However, the accuracy goal itself was arbitrary. . . . So, why 1.0 megaton? The answer is because and only because one million is a particularly round number in our culture. We picked a

one-megaton yield . . . for the same reason that everyone speaks of rich men as being millionaires and never as being ten-millionaires or one-hundred-thousand-aires. It really was that mystical. (York, 1970, p. 89)

THE ICBM BALANCE

In comparing the strategic ICBM arsenals of the United States and the USSR, one must take into account more than just numbers of missiles and their ranges. One needs to consider such factors as throw weight, number of warheads, explosive yield of warheads, accuracy, survivability, and even readiness and reliability. Some of these factors are easily determined; the number of missile silos can easily be counted. Other factors, such as accuracy and reliability, clearly are much harder to determine and are even statistically uncertain. The two super-power ICBM arsenals of Table 6.2 can be analyzed with such questions in mind.

The ICBMs

U.S. ICBMs

The Titan II is the last liquid-fueled ICBM still deployed by the United States, although in limited and decreasing numbers. It is very large; its two stages have a length of 32 m and a mass of 150 tonnes. Its liquid fuel gives the first stage a thrust of 200 tonnes. It can deliver a single 9-Mt warhead over a 15,000-km range. Its liquid fuel is stored in the rocket, allowing the Titan II a short reaction time to a launch order. But the aerozine fuel is very toxic and potentially explosive, as demonstrated by the two recent explosions of Titan IIs.

Between 1965 and 1970, the United States deployed 450 Minuteman-II missiles. The Minuteman is a three-stage all-solid-fuel rocket (Fig. 6.9). The first stage is made by Thiokol and provides a thrust of 90 tonnes; the second is by Aerojet with a thrust of 27 tonnes; and the third is by Hercules with a thrust of 16 tonnes. Its length of 18 m and diameter of 1.8 m contain a launch mass of 37 tonnes. The Minuteman-II Mark-1 warhead contains a 1½-Mt warhead plus some anti-ABM penetration aids. The reentry vehicle has a range in excess of 11,300 km. The missile rocket ignites inside the silo in a so-called "hot launch."

After 1970, the United States replaced its older Minuteman-I missiles by 550 Minuteman-III missiles. Of these, 250 are still deployed. The major difference between models II and III lies in the warhead. The Minuteman-III carries a postboost MIRV bus with three Mk-12 warheads. These three warheads are independently targetable with an explosive yield of 170 kt each (many reports say 200 kt). The reentry vehicles can reach targets more than 13,000 km away with an accuracy of 280 m.

Since 1978 the warheads in 300 Minuteman III have been upgraded. Each of these improved Minuteman ICBMs now carries three MIRV Mk-12A warheads of 335-kt yield. The accuracy has been improved by 20%. Otherwise, the Minuteman III(A) is the same in physical dimensions and range.

These Minuteman missiles are buried in silos (see Fig. 6.10) grouped together in missile farms in Missouri, Montana, North and South Dakota, and Wyoming. Within the farms, the silos are separated from each other by at least 9 km and are at least 5.5 km from any control center. Within each control center two officers control the missile launch; both must take independent active action to launch a missile. The various control centers have some overlap in launch control functions. The targeting of the Minuteman-III missiles can be reprogrammed in less than 36 min.

For many years the United States has had a new ICBM under devel-

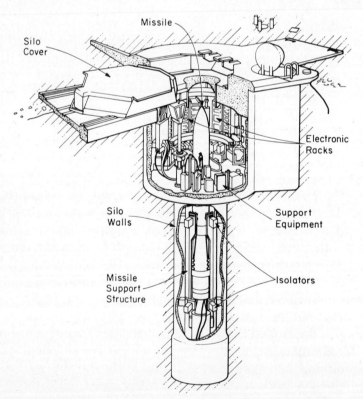

Figure 6.10 Cross-sectional sketch of a Minuteman missile silo. The silo cover is more than 1 m thick. (Photo courtesy Boeing Corporation.)

opment, the so-called "MX" (missile experimental, see Fig. 6.9). This solid-fuel missile is designed to be the largest "light" missile possible under the SALT II agreements, with a length of 22 m, a diameter of 2.3 m, and a weight of 78 tonnes. In addition to the usual three solid-fuel stages, it will have a liquid-fueled fourth stage. It will be cold launched (i.e., it will be ejected from its silo before the engines ignite). It will incorporate the newest warhead technology, including a 10-MIRV payload, with a yield of 335 kt per warhead, and it will have a greatly improved accuracy—100 m (0.05 nm) is the figure usually mentioned. The justification for the MX in the past has been its mobility for survival under attack. But the large numbers of reentry vehicles with big yield and superb accuracy make this missile very suitable for attacking hardened military targets, such as missile silos.

Soviet ICBMs

The Soviet SS-11 Sego of Fig. 6.11 is an older liquid-fueled two-stage rocket. It is nominally a "light" ICBM. It has been deployed since 1966, mostly in a single warhead version. The accuracy of that 1-Mt warhead is only 1400 m. It is hot launched. There are still about 500 SS-11s in service. Other SS-11s have since 1975 been gradually replaced by SS-17 and SS-19 missiles. These carry, respectively, four and six MIRV warheads of ½- to ¾-Mt yield with much higher accuracy. The SS-17 has been converted to the cold-launch technique in which the missile is ejected from the silo by cold gases before the rocket engines are ignited.

The SS-18 missile is defined in the SALT-II agreement as a "heavy" missile. This large two-stage liquid-fueled rocket has a length of 35 m and a diameter of 3 m. Its storable liquid fueling allows it to deliver a 20-Mt warhead over a distance of more than 12,000 km. It went into service in 1974, replacing the older SS-9. This missile is cold-launched; that is, it can fit more tightly into the silo. Therefore, it can be 10%

Figure 6.11 The Soviet SS-11 liquid-fuel intercontinental ballistic missile. (Photo courtesy U.S. Department of Defense.)

larger in each dimension than the older SS-9 it replaced. The majority of SS-18s carry eight MIRV warheads, each with a yield of about 1 Mt. These large missiles have caused great concern to U.S. planners because their very large warheads threaten the silos of the U.S. Minuteman missiles.

The Soviet Union has not deployed significant numbers of solid-fueled ICBMs. The SS-13 was first deployed in 1968, but no more than 60 are in service. Under the terms of the SALT II agreement, its follow-up, the 1975 model SS-16, has not been deployed. The SS-16 has been described by a Pentagon expert who followed its development closely "a dog of a missile—it was just no good, and it wasn't getting much better" (Talbott, 1979, p. 134). Two of its stages make up the SS-20 intermediate-range ballistic missile (see Chapter 12). A new Soviet solid-fuel ICBM, known as the Plesetsk-5, is under development.

The ICBM Balance

Table 6.2 summarizes the ICBM balance between the United States and the Soviet Union. No French, British, or Chinese missiles are listed, as there are presently none with intercontinental range, although the Chinese are trying to develop one. An analysis of the ICBM balance must take into account more than just the numerical balance in numbers of missiles, warheads, and yield; it must also consider accuracy, survivability, reliability, and retargeting capability. Each of these parameters will be discussed briefly, keeping in mind the distinction between the use of the ICBM forces as a deterrent (as strategic counter-value weapons) and in a warfighting capacity (as tactical counterforce weapons).

ICBM Quantities

The number of ICBMs favors the Soviet Union. The USSR is mostly landlocked and has a large land mass. Therefore, it has focused its strategic efforts on its ICBMs rather than on submarine-launched missiles. The imbalance is large for the number of ICBMs and very large for the explosive yield. This latter is a direct consequence of the much larger payload carried by the Soviet liquid-fueled rockets. Accuracy of the U.S. missiles are presently superior, as indicated in Table 6.2 and in Fig. 6.8. Soviet accuracy has been improving as the inaccurate SS-9s and SS-11s have been replaced by the SS-17, SS-18, and SS-19 and as the last is being upgraded further. In turn, the Minuteman III(A) has increased U.S. accuracies as well, and the MX missile is planned to be superaccurate. The accuracies cited in Table 6.2 are uncertain, particularly those of Soviet missiles. The accuracy of the SS-18, Mod 4, for example, had earlier been thought to be considerably better than 300 m.

On the basis of past overestimates of accuracy and of the internal consistency of Fig. 6.8, one should be suspicious of any announced abrupt breakthroughs and skeptical of any figures that are very inconsistent with extrapolations from past performance data.

ICBM Qualities

The ICBMs of the United States are qualitatively superior to those of the Soviet Union in several respects. Some U.S. technologies, such as computers and machine tools, are much ahead of those of the Soviet Union (see Amann et al., 1977; Amann and Cooper, 1982; and Chapter 13). This superior technology is reflected in better guidance capabilities. Better guidance translates into the greater U.S. missile accuracy shown in Fig. 6.8. It also improves flexibility, as in the retargeting capabilities of American Minuteman-III missiles. The reliability of the electronic guidance of U.S. ICBMs is thought to be better as well, producing greater overall reliability.

Except for the Titan II, all American missiles use solid fuel. Although this has cost in payload, it gives benefits of stability and reliability. Solid-fuel missiles are less vulnerable to enemy attack; they are not as fragile as liquid-fuel missiles, and their smaller size makes it easier to build silos with high levels of blast resistance. Soviet missile silos built before 1969 to 1970 are thought to have a protective capability of about 300 psi, those built since then about 1000 to 2000 psi. Some of the new SS-18 silos have been said by some to be resistant to overpressures up to 3000 psi (even 5000 psi has been mentioned); but the general consensus uses 2000 psi as a "canonical" hardness for Soviet missiles. U.S. missile silos have protection up to 300 psi for the Titan II missiles; the Minuteman silos are thought to be protected to 2000 psi.

Table 6.2 thus says that the Soviet ICBM force is considerably superior in the most quantitative aspects such as the number of missiles and their throw weight. The U.S. missiles are superior in qualities, with Soviet missiles so far still trying to catch up in such parameters as accuracy. In the context of mutual assured destruction through nuclear retaliation, neither of those imbalances are very important, so long as enough ICBMs of adequate accuracy and reliability survive a surprise attack to deliver an unacceptable second strike. If the retaliatory requirement is between 50 and 200 EMT, as argued in Chapter 4, both ICBM forces are more than adequate for this task (see Chapter 8 for further discussions of this point). The quantitative and qualitative parameters do matter in the context of a limited nuclear war in which attempts are made to destroy military targets by precision ICBM attacks; then the relationship of Table 6.2 to specific scenarios must be analyzed in detail, as in Chapter 12.

CONTEMPORARY ICBM ISSUES

Nuclear arms technology is advancing very rapidly. In spite of this progress, certain issues are recurrent. For ICBMs the recurring issues are related to the stability of the strategic balance; that is, the concerns are about missile survivability, surprise attacks, and verification.

MX and Future Survivability of ICBMs

The present ICBMs are located in fixed silos. Their locations are, therefore, well known through satellite reconnaissance to both the United States and the Soviet Union. A significant fraction of these silos are likely to survive most nuclear attacks. However, at some level of accuracy, even the most hardened silos would become vulnerable. Figure 6.12 shows the accuracies required to destroy missile silos hardened to resist overpressures of 2000 psi (130 atmospheres). Various weapon developments threaten to raise this vulnerability to a high level. However, one must remember that this vulnerability concerns only one leg of the Triad, and it would require great coordination in timing and high reliability of the attacking missiles.

Soviet Heavy Missiles

The Soviet Union under the SALT II agreement is allowed to deploy 308 "heavy" missiles while the United States cannot deploy any other

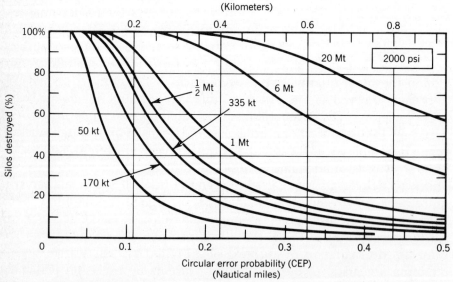

Figure 6.12 Probabilities of destroying ICBM silos hardened to 2000 psi by attacking missiles of different yields and accuracies. (Based on Tsipis, 1975.)

than the Titan II. A heavy missile is defined as any that is heavier than the SS-19 in either launch weight or throw weight. The SS-18 is that heavy missile. It has good accuracy (see Table 6.2 and Fig. 6.8) and carries up to 10 MIRV warheads each with a yield up to 1 Mt. The fear is that in the 1980s the SS-18 might be able to destroy as many as 90% of the U.S. ICBMs if its accuracy were to be sufficiently improved and if its reliability were high enough. Chapter 8 presents calculations that under pessimistic assumptions a large danger to ICBM silos now exists. But even if the vulnerability of ICBM silos does not now exist, it surely could do so in the future. The SS-19 missiles add to this fear, as they have supposedly exhibited further improved accuracies in some tests.

MARV

The United States, in turn, has improved the Minuteman-III(A) missile with the Mk-12A warhead and the NS-20 guidance system; these have not only increased yield but have also improved accuracy. In the longer term, the United States is deploying a system of navigational satellites, called NAVSTAR. By measuring the frequency shift and the time delay of the radio signal from these satellites, the position of a receiver can be determined to better than 20 m. Receivers for NAVSTAR signals might someday be installed in ICBM warheads. Newer maneuverable warheads could use guidance signals from such systems for more precise flight corrections after ejection by the postboost bus of the ICBM. MARVs (maneuverable reentry vehicles), when combined with such location information, could increase the accuracy of U.S. warheads tremendously. Accuracies of tens of meters would seem feasible. Alternatively, great accuracies may become available in the future through terrain-reading systems, as described in Chapter 5, or by using stars as directional guides. The accuracies of U.S. missiles could grow so much that they would threaten enemy silos just as much as the Soviet heavy missiles (see Chapter 8).

Mobile Missiles and Verification

One way to solve the problem of ICBM survivability is to make them mobile so that they cannot be targeted with sufficient precision. A mobile missile, however, is also easier to hide and hence harder to verify under any arms limitation agreements. Under the SALT II treaty, the USSR has agreed not to deploy its mobile SS-16 solid-fuel rocket. But the United States feels strongly enough about its ICBM vulnerability to desire a mobile missile, even if it is not quite verifiable within the letter of the law of SALT agreements.

The MX Missile in the Mobile Mode

For the United States the issue of mobile missiles has most recently been aired in the debate about the MX missile deployment; the United States had been actively planning the deployment of its new MX missile in a mobile mode. The original justification for the development of the MX had been its decreased vulnerability due to its mobility. The MX was to be located not in silos but, rather, was to be hidden. Early ideas were to move 200 mobile MX missile launchers inside covered trenches. On command, the missile would be raised through the trench cover into launch position. The hope had been that if the trench were long enough, with the missile located anywhere along its length, a large number of attacking missiles would be required to destroy all the trench to be certain that the missile inside the trench is destroyed. The trench idea was ultimately rejected beccause of its expense, the impossibility of verifying the number of missiles hidden inside a trench, and the danger of blast waves focusing inside and along the trench.

The next plans for MX deployment were for a multiple aiming point system (MAPS) or multiple protective shelters (MPS). In this scheme, 200 MX missiles would be shuffled among 4600 empty concrete launching sites (as shown in Fig. 6.13). A closed transporter would move the missiles around in a random manner, so that even with 100% reliability

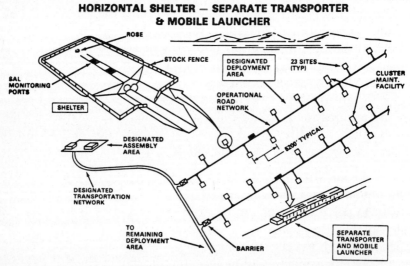

Figure 6.13 Horizontal shelter–separate transporters and mobile launchers. In the MPS system, transporters were to shuffle 200 MX missiles among 4600 launching sites. Together with the MX missiles inside the protective container, each transporter would have weighed 720 tonnes. (Photo from *Department of Defense Annual Report, Fiscal Year 1982*, p. 110.)

and accuracy, the Soviet Union would have to target at least 4600 warheads to be sure of destroying these 200 MX missiles. For verification purposes, the lids on the launching points would be raised periodically so that the reconnaissance satellites of the Soviet Union could verify that indeed only 200 missiles were located in these launching sites.

Both the trench and the MPS basing modes posed the problem of any mobile missile system: Can the number of mobile missiles be verified by national technical means (i.e., by reconnaissance satellites)? If the USSR were to build a similar system, would the United States accept it as verifiable? The MX mobile basing modes were projected to be very expensive; a preliminary estimate for the costs of MPS, for example, was more than $30 billion. The system would take up very large land areas to keep the various launching points safely separated; perhaps as much as 50,000 mi^2 (125,000 km^2) might be involved. Large amounts of concrete would have to be poured, perhaps equal in area to one-third of the whole U.S. interstate highway system. The combination of expense and potential environmental damage made the MPS basing mode politically unacceptable.

Another proposal for the MX basing was to build densely packed fields of MX missiles. The MX silos would be placed in fields of three north-south rows with sufficient spacing between the silos so that each attacking warhead could destroy no more than two silos. The dust raised by one attacking warhead would produce a cloud through which subsequent warheads could not pass for some time (an effect called fratricide). Thus destruction of one silo would thus protect its siblings. Carefully timed MX missiles could be launched through that dust cloud some of the time, because a just-launched ICBM passing through that cloud could have such a low velocity that it would not be disturbed as much by the dust particles as would the high-speed reentry vehicles of the attacking missiles. This dense-pack idea too met with little enthusiasm; it was perceived as increasing the risks to MX missiles because of their proximity to each other and as offering uncertain protection by a phenomenon that is relatively unknown, little understood, and untested.

Alternative basing modes for the MX will continue to be explored, including underground tunneling systems, ballistic missile defenses (see Chapter 10), placing the MX on aircraft or submarines, or building smaller and hence more easily transportable new missiles, such as the Midgetman missile, instead of the large MX. None of these alternatives is particularly appealing, and all are likely to be expensive. The long-term vulnerability problem for land-based missiles may be insoluble at an acceptable price.

SS-20

The Soviet Union has an intermediate-range mobile missile, the SS-20, made up of the upper two stages of the SS-16 solid-fuel ICBM. Concern has been expressed in U.S. circles that this mobile missile represents a verification problem. The fear is that a large number of such missiles might be built, that a number of third stages for the SS-16 might be clandestinely produced, and that in a surprise move the two could be combined so that suddenly a number of SS-16 ICBMs would be available. The SS-16 has been judged to be a poor missile so far; it has been tested only a few times, mostly unsuccessfully. It has been given up by the Soviets under the (unratified) SALT II treaty; hence, this may not be a major problem at the moment. However, it does symbolize the recurring problem of the verification of mobile missiles.

Surprise

The military of both superpowers have frequently proposed locating nuclear weapons in space (or even on the moon). This has so far been rejected as a poor idea, and a treaty has been signed forbidding such placements (see Chapter 16). Satellites, unless in synchronous orbit 35,000 km above the earth, will come in range of their targets only infrequently, as their orbits are constantly moving with respect to the earth. Hence the time from receipt of a firing order to an actual launch and attack from a satellite could be long. A derivative of this orbital technique is the so-called "FOBS method" (Fig. 6.14). In this fractionally orbiting bombarding system, an ICBM places its payload into a low orbit 160 km above the earth. Near the target a retrofire rocket would slow the payload, causing it to reenter toward the target. Such a system reaches the target in a relatively short time, and its lower trajectory gives a short warning time, just like the depressed trajectories discussed in Chapter 5. Hence, FOBS could be a system that allows surprise attacks. The Soviet Union tested its SS-9 missile in this mode,

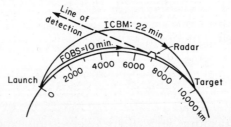

Figure 6.14 In the fractionally orbiting bombardment system (FOBS), the missile would arrive at the target more rapidly than via the minimum energy ballistic trajectory. This would give less warning time to the attacked nation.

but it has not pursued this method with more modern ICBMs. The United States has not specifically developed such a system, and SALT II forbids testing of FOBS. However, for both nations, their space program clearly contains the relevant technology.

DISCUSSION

The ICBM component of the strategic Triad for a long time has been considered most important. Missiles could carry much larger payloads than can the SLBM submarines, they could be launched from the homeland, and they were much less likely than bombers to be intercepted before reaching the target.

Increasing accuracies of missiles can threaten this force. The United States led the way in using the less vulnerable SLBMs to make up for this potential deficit in the ICBMs. Hence, for the United States the ICBM force does not have the singular importance that it has for the USSR. The United States has a somewhat smaller number of missiles, and these do not carry the large fraction of the total payload (throw weight) that the Soviet ICBM force carries. The United States has aimed for very high reliability through solid fuel, for very high accuracy, and for high penetration ability of ABM defenses through multiple MIRV warheads. Soviet missiles are achieving similar qualities only now— although most still use liquid fuel and the accuracy appears to be continuing to lag.

Two dangers are arising in connection with the ICBM force. These dangers come from the decreasing survivability of ICBMs created by very accurate MIRV warheads. The response of deploying more survivable mobile missiles creates the danger that missile numbers may no longer be verifiable by satellite observations, thereby endangering arms control agreements. Only by halting the progression of improving missile qualities and limiting the number of MIRV warheads can the ICBM force remain viable in the long run.

References

Amann, R., and J. Cooper, eds. *Industrial Innovation in the Soviet Union*. New Haven, Conn.: Yale University Press, 1982.

J. Cooper, and R. W. Davies, eds. *The Technological Level of Soviet Industry*. New Haven, Conn.: Yale University Press, 1977.

Armacourt, M. Y., *The Politics of Weapons Innovation: The Thor-Jupiter Controversy*. New York: Columbia University Press, 1969.

Bottome, E. M., *The Missile Gap: A Study of the Formulation of Military and Political Policy*. Rutherford, N.J.: Fairleigh Dickinson University Press, 1971.

Bunn, M., and K. Tsipis. *Ballistic Missile Guidance and Technical Uncertainties of Counter*

Silo Attacks, M.I.T. Report #9. Cambridge, Mass.: Program in Science and Technology for International Physics, M.I.T., 1983; and "The Uncertainties of a Preemptive Nuclear Attack." Scientific American, Vol. 249, no. 5 (November 1983), pp. 38–47.

Feld, B. T., T. Greenwood, G. W. Rathjens, and S. Weinberg, eds. *Impact of New Technologies on the Arms Race*, Cambridge, Mass.: M.I.T. Press, 1971. Has an excellent article by D. G. Hoag on "Ballistic Missile Guidance," pp. 19–106.

Ordway, F. I., III, J. P. Gardner, M. R. Sharpe, Jr., and R. C. Wakeford. *Applied Astronautics: An Introduction to Space Flight*. Englewood Cliffs, N.J.: Prentice-Hall, 1963. Some technical details.

Office of Technology Assessment. *MX Missile Basing*. Washington, D.C.: Government Printing Office, 1981.

Pretty, R. T., *Jane's Weapons Systems: 1982–83*. London: Jane's 1982.

Talbott, S., *Endgame: The Inside Story of SALT II*. New York: Harper & Row, 1979.

Tsipis, K., "The Accuracy of Strategic Missiles." *Scientific American*, Vol. 233, no. 1 (July 1975), pp. 14–23.

York, H. F., *Race to Oblivion: A Participant's View of the Arms Race* (New York: Simon & Schuster, 1970). See particularly Chapters 5, 6 and 7, "Rockets and Missiles," "Sputnik," and "Missile-Gap Mania," pp. 75–105, 106–124, and 125–146.

CHAPTER
7

Nuclear Missile Submarines

In the future, given enough time and warheads, it may be possible to conduct nuclear barrage attacks against SSBN [nuclear missile sub] bases and suspected SSBN patrol areas. Nonetheless, both sides still have reason to be confident that major elements of their sea-based nuclear strike force would survive these initial exchanges because of the continuing difficulty of detecting and localizing at sea submarines that are not obliged to give away their general location.

Paul H. Nitze, SALT negotiator, *Securing the Seas*, 1979.

The third leg of the nuclear strategic Triad consists of submarine-launched ballistic missiles (SLBMs). They are considered to be essentially invulnerable to a surprise attack. Since the first deployment of U.S. Polaris submarines in 1963, the nuclear-powered SLBM submarines have become faster, larger, quieter, and more accurate in navigation. At the same time the missiles they carry have become larger and more accurate and have incorporated multiple independently targetable reentry vehicles (MIRVs).

The SLBM component of the Triad is considered by most to be by itself quite adequate as a strategic retaliatory force. The 34 current U.S. SLBM submarines carry 568 missiles with 5152 separate warheads; once the planned nine additional Trident submarines are built, 760 missiles will carry 6688 warheads. This force appears invulnerable far into the future as antisubmarine warfare (ASW) technology has not been able to catch up with SLBM-submarine technology. This force continues to be upgraded; the United States is building the Trident submarine and its associated missiles, and the Soviet Union is building the Delta submarines with MIRVed long-range missiles. All these new missiles have increased accuracy.

HISTORY OF THE SLBM FORCE

The sea-based nuclear deterrent is based on two separate technological developments. Nuclear reactor power plants allowed submarines to become true submersibles; missiles of appropriate range and accuracy had to be mated to the nuclear submarines (see Hewlett and Duncan, 1974).

Nuclear Propulsion for Submarines

The use of nuclear power to propel submarines under water is an obvious idea. It was first proposed by Ross Gunn, a nuclear physicist at the U.S. Naval Research Laboratory early in 1939, soon after fission was discovered. After World War II ended, the Navy was able to pursue the idea, but by then aircraft carriers had so proven their worth that this new concept found little enthusiasm in the naval leadership. The very junior Captain Hyman Rickover was selected in 1946 to cooperate with the Atomic Energy Commission (AEC) and persuade it to develop a reactor for a submarine. By a combination of mastery of nuclear technology, energy, frankness, abrasiveness, and administrative ability, Rickover was unexpectedly successful. He played off the AEC against the Navy, he instilled a drive for perfection in his staff and industrial concerns, and he led the project by total personal commitment.

In 1949 the Navy was convinced by Rickover; nuclear reactor development was placed at the top of the AEC's military list of priorities. Water-cooled and sodium-cooled reactors were developed in parallel with submarines to carry them. On January 17, 1955 the first nuclear submarine *Nautilus* sailed for the first time on power provided by a pressurized-water nuclear reactor. The sodium-cooled reactor of the *Seawolf* never was equally satisfactory and was phased out. The $90 million *Nautilus* covered 60,000 miles (100,000 km) in two years while averaging up to 22 miles per hour (35 km/hr) under water for some long trips. Once the *Nautilus* demonstrated its speed and underwater endurance, the submarine forces accepted a nuclear future. For the first time submarines were truly submersible; they could stay under water, fully mobile, as long as the crew could stand it.

Until his recent retirement in 1982, Admiral Rickover continued to influence the application of nuclear power in the Navy. He pushed for bigger nuclear reactors, and for large Trident submarines to carry them. He promoted the use of nuclear reactors in various naval vessels, particularly in aircraft carriers. This has placed him on the side of those naval officers who want a Navy made up of fewer but larger ships. Interestingly, in his last testimony to Congress, he expressed some doubt about the value of the SLBM forces.

Submarine-Launched Ballistic Missiles

Launching long-range strategic missiles from submarines had been seriously considered even before World War II. During that war the Germans separately developed and improved both rockets and submarines. Combining these two technologies was an appealing idea; but World War II did not allow much progress on this combination.

In 1955 a combination of events triggered the fleet ballistic missile (FBM) program. The Soviet Union exploded its first useful hydrogen bomb; the large explosive yield of that weapon threatened the survivability of the bomber air bases and of above-ground launch sites for rockets. This made submarines more attractive, since they could hide and survive a nuclear attack beneath the ocean surface. Subsequently, the Soviet Union came to be perceived as having a lead in space technology; crash programs to develop missiles became the accepted way to overcome this lead. The *Nautilus* dramatically demonstrated the capabilities of nuclear submarines, so that the submarine missile program was perceived as a way in which the Navy could compete on equal terms with the other services for strategic weapons funds.

Many problems had to be overcome by the SLBM program. Solid-fuel rockets were desirable for SLBMs, but they had not been developed; the SLBMs were difficult to incorporate into the hull of a submarine; and guidance for missiles launched from mobile platforms had to be developed. In an effort to balance the budget, President Eisenhower was opposed to large new expenditures; the Army and Air Force opposed such large new naval projects; and within the Navy, conflicts raged between the submarine advocates and those committed to aircraft carriers.

In 1955 President Eisenhower accepted a large SLBM program. Admiral Raborn was selected as its manager; in a warlike atmosphere, he got the job done very rapidly. The solid-fueled 1500-mile (2400 km) Polaris missile was ready by 1959 and the first SLBM sub *George Washington* launched it underwater in 1960.

Why was the Polaris program so successful? Technologically, this development was even more technically obvious and ripe than was the nuclear submarine when Rickover first began pushing it. The leadership by Raborn was managerial and organizational rather than technological:

the FBM program managers were political entrepreneurs as well as technological innovators and military strategists. . . . FBM introduced PERT [Program Evaluation and Review Technique], CPM [Critical Path Method], . . . stressed decentralization, and fostered fierce competition, total dedication and religious fervor. (Sapolski, 1972, pp. 225 and 227)

Many improvements have been made in the SLBM system since the deployment of the original Polaris. The Poseidon program provided longer-ranged and MIRVed missiles; the Trident program has developed much larger submarines with SLBMs of truly intercontinental ranges and will provide the Trident-II missile with stellar navigation leading to very high accuracy. However, these programs are only refinements and improvements on the original Polaris concept; they have not provided or required equivalent breakthroughs in either technology or management.

SLBM TECHNOLOGY

Submarine-launched ballistic missiles are part of a system that includes the submarines and their nuclear propulsion system, the missiles, and the command and control of the whole SLBM fleet. A Poseidon submarine is quite large: it displaces about 7500 tonnes of water when submerged, is 130 m long with a diameter of 10 m, and its crew has up to 147 members. Inside that volume it houses the nuclear reactor and its associated propulsion system, tubes to hold and launch the SLBM, the control center, crew space, and auxiliary armaments such as SUBROC torpedos (submarine-launched rockets that carry a nuclear depth charge).

Nuclear Submarines

The heart of the nuclear submarine is its nuclear reactor. The first nuclear reactors were build during World War II to produce ^{239}Pu for nuclear weapons. After the end of the war, thought was given to utilizing the heat produced in such reactors to produce electric power and in propulsion systems. The basic operation of a nuclear reactor will be described in Chapter 14. The heat generated in the fission processes is extracted from the core of the nuclear reactor to produce power.

As shown in Fig. 7.1, the radioactive primary water that has been circulated through the reactor core gives its heat in a heat exchanger to a secondary water circuit in which it generates steam. The nonradioactive steam passes over turbine blades, turning them, and is then condensed back to water to reduce the back pressure. The turbine wheels turn the propellers through reduction gears. The steam also drives a second turbogenerator to generate electricity for ship operations. Backup systems of electric batteries and diesel engines can provide power for a short time in case the reactor must be turned off.

The core of the nuclear reactor in U.S. nuclear submarines contains uranium enriched to 90% in fissile ^{235}U. These reactors are designed to

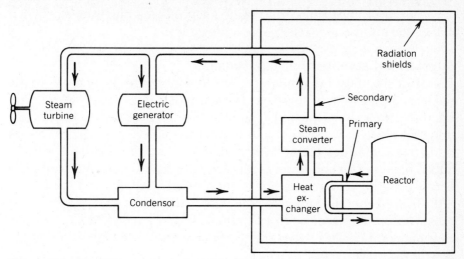

Figure 7.1 The drive system of nuclear-powered submarines. The turbogenerator produces electricity for shipboard electrical systems; the steam turbine is coupled to the propeller drive shaft.

operate for very long times without being refueled. The Poseidon nuclear submarines can go 600,000 kilometers (400,000 miles) on one reactor core over a period of 9 years; Trident submarines are intended to be refueled once every 10 years. These long operating times can be achieved because of the very high level of enrichment of the uranium core; a large fraction of the ^{235}U can be fissioned without destroying the reactor's ability to become critical.

A typical nuclear submarine has a power rating at the propeller shaft of about 15,000 horsepower (hp). At that power rating the submarine may go somewhat in excess of 50 km/hr (30 mph) underwater. This power corresponds to 11 megawatts (MW). Assuming that this mechanical energy is produced with an efficiency of about 30%, the thermal energy released within the nuclear reactor must be about 37 thermal MW. The actual core could contain as little as 35 kg of uranium; this mass occupies a volume represented by a cube on the order of 12 cm on a side.

Except that they have a nuclear reactor as propulsion unit, nuclear submarines operate similarly to conventionally powered submarines. They submerge by filling auxiliary tanks with water until the weight of the water they displace just equals their own weight; they surface by expelling water from these auxiliary tanks. Diving depth is limited by the strength of the hull. They maneuver underwater by rudders and winglike planes. They use electricity to separate CO_2 into carbon and oxygen for the crew to breathe. The underwater speed is generally higher than that possible on the ocean surface. But in either case high speed is rarely used in combat since it produces much noise, which makes the submarine susceptible to detection.

Submarine-Launched Ballistic Missiles

The most significant distinction of SLBM submarines is their cargo, the nuclear-tipped ballistic missiles. These missiles impose special requirements on the submarine hull design and on the precision of the navigation and place particular value on undetectability. The missiles carried by U.S. submarines are solid fueled, whereas those of the USSR are liquid fueled. The solid-fuel technology is greatly preferred for SLBM because of its instant readiness, nontoxicity, safety, and longevity. SLBMs are generally similar to the ICBMs described in Chapter 6. The major differences are the need to make SLBM smaller, the constantly changing launch site, and passage of the missiles through water on the way to the target.

Figure 7.2 shows the arrangement of the launching tubes on SLBM submarines in cross section. The missiles are launched from these tubes inside the hull while the submarine is submerged. The hatches shown in Fig. 7.3 are opened, and the missiles are ejected by gas pressure, at a rate of up to one missile launch per minute. The rocket engine ignites once the missile is above the ocean surface.

To be guided successfully to the target, the missile must know both the position and velocity of its launching submarine and its planned trajectory to the target. The launch site information is provided by the submarine. The submarine has an on-board ship's inertial navigation system (SINS) whose gyroscopes, accelerometers, and computers keep

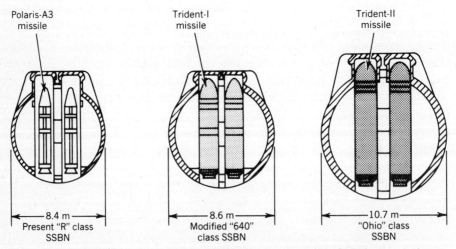

Figure 7.2 Installation of the Polaris, Trident-I, and Trident-II SLBMs into Lafayette class Poseidon, modified Poseidon, and Ohio class Trident submarines.

Figure 7.3 The U.S.S. *Sam Rayburn* Poseidon SLBM submarine at Newport News in 1964. The missile tube hatches are opened as they would be during an underwater missile launch. (Photo courtesy U.S. Navy.)

track of its movements. The data in the SINS are updated, perhaps once a day, by stellar observations and by listening to navigational signals from land-based transmitters and from satellites.

Figure 7.4 shows a navigational aid similar to the naval LORAN system. Known radio signals are emitted simultaneously by several sending stations. Measurement of the time differences between arrival of several signals allows the receiver to calculate its location. Such signals can also be sent by sets of earth satellites. The signals from these require, however, more complex analysis of the received information since the satellites are constantly moving. The ship location information is used to update the SLBM's planned trajectory. Once the missile has left the submarine, it uses its own built-in inertial guidance system to guide itself to the assigned target, taking into account such factors as the buffeting it receives in penetrating to the water's surface, the rocket firings, and so on. Table 6.1 has shown the relative contribution to the missile inaccuracies due to launch and flight uncertainties.

Improvements in the SLBM payload and range have come through larger missile size and better fuel. Figure 7.2 shows the relative sizes of various SLBMs, including the Polaris A-3 (first deployed in 1964 and now taken out of service), the Trident-I C-4 (first deployed in 1980), and the Trident-II D-5 (to be deployed at the end of the 1980s). The first

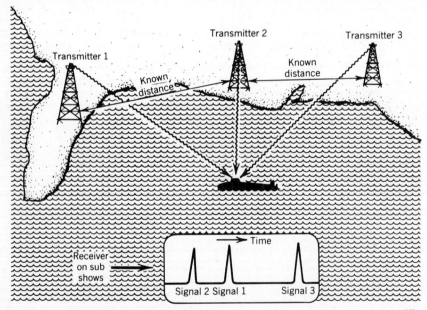

Figure 7.4 LORAN-type navigational aid. The time delays between receiving different signals allow determination of the receiver position.

two (as well as the Poseidon missile) all fit into the Poseidon submarines of the Lafayette class, while the Trident-II missile will fit only into the Trident submarines. The ranges of SLBM have improved greatly from the 2750 km of the Polaris A-1 and A-2 to the 7400 km of the Trident I. Increasingly larger payloads have permitted the warheads to go from a single 800-kt warhead on the Polaris A-1 through three MRV 200-kt warheads on the A-3 Polaris, ten MIRV 50-kt warheads on the C-3 Poseidon, to eight MIRV 100-kt warheads on the C-4 Trident I. The future D-5 Trident II is to have a range of 11,000 km and will carry 14 MARV warheads, each with a yield of 150 kt; improvements in the reentry vehicles and the guidance systems have allowed great improvements in missile accuracies over those longer ranges.

THE SLBM BALANCE

The SLBM-submarine balance between the United States and the Soviet Union is difficult to evaluate without reference to specific objectives. In the unlikely event of a prolonged conventional war between the two superpowers, nuclear submarines might have to play defensive and offensive roles in support of surface ships. The SLBMs could be useful in a limited tactical nuclear war if they were very accurate. But given the SLBMs' present inaccuracies, their strategic retaliatory capability is most relevant in the nuclear context. In that role, the equivalent megatonnage, survivability, and communication capabilities are most important. The major types of submarines and missiles relevant to the balance of retaliatory forces are listed in Tables 7.1 and 7.2.

The SLBM Submarines

U.S. Nuclear Submarines

Polaris. The first U.S. submarines were generically known as Polaris submarines. They were somewhat smaller than the later Poseidon submarines, displacing approximately 6090 to 7200 tonnes, with lengths of 116 to 125 m, and a crew of 140. Their nuclear reactor could drive them at speeds in excess of 35 km/hr on the surface or 55 km/hr underwater. The Polaris submarines had 16 missile tubes holding A-3 Polaris missiles, which were the third improved version of the original Polaris missile. This solid-fuel missile had a length of 9.5 m, which allowed it to fit also into the later Poseidon submarines. But the tubes of the Polaris submarines could not hold the Poseidon missile. Since the Polaris missile with only three MRV warheads is considerably inferior to the Poseidon missile, the Polaris submarines have been decommissioned.

Table 7.1   Listing of the submarine deterrent[a].

All numbers are from Cordesman (1982), as those are somewhat more detailed than are those of the International Institute for Strategic Studies (1983), but basically the two sets of numbers are in agreement.

Submarines	Function	No. of Missiles	No. of Subs
United States			
Polaris	SLBM nuclear subs	16 Polaris A-3	Decom. 1982
Poseidon	SLBM nuclear subs	16 Poseidon C-3	19
Poseidon	SLBM nuclear subs	16 Trident I C-4	12
Trident	SLBM nuclear subs	24 Trident I C-4	3
SSN-688	New nuclear attack subs	Harpoon and SUBROC	(18)[a]
Other nuclear subs	Other nuclear attack subs	SUBROC	(67)[a]
		U.S. total	34
Soviet Union			
Golf	SLBM diesel sub	6 SS-N-8	(1)[b]
Hotel II	SLBM nuclear subs	3 SS-N-5	(6)[b]
Hotel III	SLBM nuclear sub	6 SS-N-8	(1)[b]
Yankee I	SLBM nuclear subs	16 SS-N-6	25
Yankee II	SLBM nuclear sub	12 SS-N-17	1
Delta I	SLBM nuclear subs	12 SS-N-8	18
Delta II	SLBM nuclear subs	16 SS-N-8	4
Delta III	SLBM nuclear subs	16 SS-N-18	13
Typhoon	SLBM nuclear sub	20 SS-NX-20	1[c]
Other nuclear subs	Nuclear cruise missile subs	24 SS-N-19, etc.	(49)[a]
Other nuclear subs	Nuclear attack subs	SS-N-15/16, etc.	(56)[a]
		USSR total	62[a]
United Kingdom			
Resolution	SLBM nuclear sub	16 Polaris A-3	4
Other nuclear subs	Nuclear attack subs		(11)[a]
		U.K. total	4
France			
Redoutable	SLBM nuclear subs	16 MSBS M-20	5
Rubis	Nuclear attack sub		(1)[d]
		French total	5

[a]See the International Institute for Strategic Studies (1983).

[b]Missiles but not submarines are counted in SALT II.

[c]The Stockholm International Peace Research Institute (1982) thinks that this submarine will become operational in the mid-1980s.

[d] Henri le Masson, *Les Sous-Marins Français* (Paris: Editions de la Cite-Brest-Paris, 1980).

Poseidon. After 1963 the Poseidon class of SLBM submarines was built. Some label all the pre-Trident submarines as Polaris boats and make the distinction by class; all Lafayette class boats can carry the Poseidon missiles. The Poseidon submarine is about 270 tonnes heavier and 5 m longer than the Polaris submarines and has a slightly larger crew complement of 140 to 168 sailors. It is more sophisticated in its propulsion and electronic features. And it can accommodate 16 of the 1 m longer C-3 Poseidon missiles. The 4600-km range of the Poseidon missile is the same as that of the Polaris A-3 missile. The C-3 weighs 30 tonnes and can deliver 10 to 14 independently targetable MIRV warheads with a thermonuclear yield of 50 kt each. A new warhead with double the explosive yield per pound has been developed. The warhead accuracy is about 450 m. Twelve Poseidon submarines have been converted to carry the longer-ranged Trident-I missile. The Poseidon's four torpedo tubes can launch the SUBROC missile to deliver depth charges.

Trident. In the 1980s the United States is deploying the Trident system. The Trident submarine is much larger than its predecessors, with a displacement of 17,000 tonnes and a length of 170 m (Fig. 7.5). The crew consists of about 150 sailors, but it has 24 tubes that will accommodate not only the new Trident-I (C-4) missile but also the proposed Trident-II (D-5) missile. The Trident submarine is faster, quieter, more reliable, and more roomy than its predecessors. And it is more expensive; the cost per Trident submarine is on the order of $2 billion.

Figure 7.5 The first Trident submarine *Ohio* (SSBN-726). (Photo courtesy U.S. Navy.)

Table 7.2 Listing of nuclear-tipped SLBMs carried on submarines. The payload is given in metric tonnes. All numbers, unless otherwise indicated, are derived from the International Institute for Strategic Studies (1983).

Missiles	1st Deployed	Max. Range	Payload	RV/SLBM	CEP	Number of Reentry Vehicles		Y Total	EMT Total[a]
						1978	1983		
United States									
Polaris (A-3)	1964	4600 km	?	3 MRV @ 200 kt[b]	900 m	480	0	0 Mt	0 EMT
Poseidon (C-3)	1971	4600 km	1.5 t	10 MIRV @ 50 kt	450 m	4960	3040	152 Mt	413 EMT
Trident (C-4)	1980	7400 km	1.3 t	8 MIRV @ 100 kt	450 m	0	2112	211 Mt	455 EMT
Trident (D-5)	(1985)	11,000 km	?	14 MARV @ 150 kt[c]	?	0	0	0 Mt	0 EMT
	U.S. total		799 t			5440	5152	363 Mt	868 EMT
Soviet Union									
SS-N-5	1964	1400 km	?	1 @ 1 Mt	2800 m	54	18	18 Mt	18 EMT
SS-N-6[d]	1968	3000 km	0.7 t	1 @ 1 Mt	900 m	528	400	400 Mt	400 EMT
SS-N-8[d]	1972	7800 km[e]	0.7 t	1 @ 1 Mt	900–1300 m[f]	370	292	292 Mt	292 EMT
SS-NX-17	1977	3900 km	1.1 t	1 @ 1 Mt	1500 m	16	12	12 Mt	12 EMT
SS-N-18[d]	1978	8300 km	2.3 t	7 MIRV @ 0.2 Mt	600 m	0	1456	291 Mt	498 EMT
SS-NX-20	(1985)[g]	8300 km	?	(12 MIRV, dev.)	?	0	(240)[f]	0 Mt	0 EMT
	USSR total		994 t			968	2178	1013 Mt	1220 EMT
Great Britain									
Polaris (A-3)	1967	4600 km	?	3 MRV @ 170 kt	900 m	192	192	33 Mt	60 EMT
Chevaline	(1983)[b]	N.A.	N.A.	3 MRV[b]	?	0	0	0 Mt	0 EMT
	U.K. total		?			192	192	33 Mt	60 EMT

	Year		Range	Warheads		Number		Mt	EMT
France									
MSBS M-2	1974	?	1900 km	1 @ 0.5 Mt	?	8	0	0 Mt	0 EMT
MSBS M-20	1977	?	3000 km	1 @ 1 Mt	?	48	80	80 Mt	80 EMT
M-4	(1985)	?	4000 km	MRV	?	0	0	0 Mt	0 EMT
French total					?	56	80	80 Mt	80 EMT

N.A. – Not applicable.

[a]The EMTs of the Polaris, Poseidon, and Trident I are, respectively 0.31 Mt, 0.136 Mt, and 0.215 Mt.

[b]See Pretty (1982).

[c]See the Stockholm International Peace Research Institute (1982).

[d]These missiles are liquid fueled, although the International Institute for Strategic Studies (1983) lists the SS-N-18 as containing solid fuel.

[e]Mod 2 is listed by Pretty (1982) as having a range of 9100 km with a payload of 3.6 tonnes and a single 800-kt warhead; that payload seems much too large to be reasonable.

[f]Pretty (1982) reports a claim that the accuracy of this missile might be 400 m due to combining stellar with inertial guidance.

[g]The Stockholm International Peace Research Institute (1982) considers this an experimental model, not becoming operational until 1985; others, such as Department of Defense (1983), claim first deployment in 1983.

The Trident is initially carrying the Trident-I (C-4) missile. With a length of 10.4 m and a weight of 29.5 tonnes, this solid-fuel rocket is similar in size to the Poseidon missile. The Trident-I missile has a range of 7400 km; it carries at least 8 MIRV warheads, each with a 100-kt yield and an accuracy of about 450 m.

Near the end of the 1980s the United States will deploy the Trident-II missile. That solid-fuel missile will have a greatly extended range of 11,000 km. Its 10 or more reentry vehicles may be independently maneuverable (MARV) after being released by the last missile stage. The MARV capability may be combined with stellar guidance to give the Trident II a much improved accuracy—CEPs comparable to that of the Minuteman III(A) have been mentioned.

SSN-688-Class Attack Submarine. The SLBM nuclear submarine deterrent cannot be completely separated from the remaining naval configuration. Not only must it compete in funding with the aircraft carrier force, but it may have to combine its operations with other nuclear submarine forces, particularly with those forces designed to defend American naval fleets. Symbolic of these competitors is the SSN-688 Los Angeles class of nuclear attack submarines. This submarine is quiet and fast and carries very sensitive sound detection (sonar) gear. Its 6300-tonne weight, 110-m length, and 127-sailor crew compare with those of the Poseidon SLBM submarine. It carries the SUBROC missile system with a range of 56 km. It has been estimated that a 10-kt nuclear underwater blast at a depth of 150 meters can destroy a submarine at a distance of 1.9 km (Stockholm International Peace Research Institute, 1970, p. 117). If the SUBROC were to carry a 1-Mt warhead, its kill radius might be 9 km. This is consistent with the 5- to 8-km radius often cited but is smaller than the 16-km damage radius cited by Trident critics (Moore, 1982, p. 244).

Soviet Nuclear Submarines

Yankee. The Soviet Union has a large number of missile-carrying submarines, both with diesel and nuclear propulsion. Some, such as the Golf and Hotel models, offer no significant strategic threat because the range of their missiles is 1200 km or less or because they must surface to fire them. The Yankee class missile submarine was the first significant Soviet SLBM submarine to be deployed (after 1968). It is very similar to the U.S. Polaris class with a displacement of 7500 tonnes, a length of 130 m, and a submerged speed of about 40 km/hr produced by 24,000-shaft horsepower. It has 16 launching tubes for the SS-N-6 missile as well as 8 torpedo tubes.

The SS-N-6 is a 12.8-m liquid-fuel rocket existing in three different modifications. The Modification 1 has a limited range of 2400 km and carries one warhead; the Modification 2 has a longer range of perhaps 3000 km with a single warhead; the Modification 3 has a range of perhaps 3000 km carrying two MRV reentry vehicles. The single warhead is estimated to have a yield on the order of 1 Mt. The accuracy of the SS-N-6 is estimated at best to equal that of the Polaris A-3 missile at 900 m.

Delta. Since 1972 the Soviet Union has been deploying improved SLBM submarines of the Delta class. The Delta I displaces about 7600 tonnes with a length of 130 m. Its submerged speed is 45 km/hr. This first model has 12 missile launchers for the SS-N-8 missile, as well as 8 torpedo tubes. The Delta-II and Delta-III submarines, first deployed in 1976, are much larger, displacing about 14,500 tonnes (Fig. 7.6). This additional size accommodates a total of 16 launching tubes for SS-N-8 missiles.

The SS-N-8 missile is a liquid-fuel missile about 14.6 m long. Its range is on the order of 7800 km with a single warhead of perhaps a 1-Mt yield. A modification of this missile has been tested with three MIRV warheads. Some have claimed that improved missile propulsion and a stellar inertial guidance system could produce a very high accuracy for the missile of 400 m, but Table 7.2 represents the consensus that this is not presently the case.

Since 1978 the SS-N-18 SLBM is being deployed. Although the International Institute for Strategic Studies of London (1983) lists it as using solid fuel, it is liquid fueled, as indicated by other sources such as *Jane's* (Pretty, 1982). It can carry as many as 7 MIRV warheads with 200-kt yield and has an accuracy as low as 600 m. A new solid-fuel missile,

Figure 7.6 The Delta III class Soviet nuclear SLBM submarine. (Photo courtesy U.S. Navy.)

the SS-NX-20, is under development; it may carry up to 12 MIRV warheads.

Typhoon. An even larger SLBM submarine called Typhoon is under development. This 23,000-tonne ship is to carry 20 of the SS-NX-20 missiles.

Victor Class Submarine. The Soviet Union has not invested as much effort in its patrol and fleet submarines as in the SLBM fleet. Consequently, most of its non-SLBM submarines are not nuclear powered and tend to be relatively obsolete. The best of the attack submarines built in any numbers is the Victor class, first deployed in 1967. It displaces 3800 tonnes and is 87 m long. Its nuclear reactor gives it a submerged speed of 56 km/hr. It has only torpedoes as armament. Because it has the traditional upper-deck casing with free-flood holes, it is noisy underwater and hence sonically easy to detect. A small number of new Alpha attack submarines are being built; these are supposedly faster and can dive deeper because of a titanium-containing pressure hull, and their operating noise level is supposedly comparable to that of the U.S. Thresher class of the early 1960s.

The SLBM-Submarine Balance

An assessment of the balance of SLBM submarine forces between the United States and the Soviet Union must include more than just the numerical balances in submarines, missiles, warheads, yield, accuracy, and missile range. It must also take into account the relative effectiveness of the forces in terms of survivability, fraction of time on patrol, and quality of crews. These parameters shall be briefly discussed, keeping in mind the present primary objective of the SLBM-submarine force to act as a strategic retaliatory force.

Table 7.1 lists the present nuclear submarine balance. The Soviet Union has presently 62 SLBM submarines, compared with the 34 of the United States. The United States is building more Trident submarines to replace the Polaris models just decommissioned, and the number for the United States will go back up to 42 by the end of the 1980s. The relative explosive yield deliverable by the two forces favors the USSR at 1013 Mt versus 363 Mt for the United States, although in terms of megatonnage equivalents the ratio is closer to 1 at 1220 EMT to 868 EMT. The number of deliverable SLBM nuclear warheads on SLBMs favors the United States at 5152 to 2178; more United States SLBMs carry MIRV warheads.

The range of the SLBM missiles in the past favored the United States. The Soviet SS-N-4 and SS-N-5 missiles are so short ranged that they are not even counted as SLBMs in the SALT II agreements, and the SS-N-6 is comparable in range to the early Polaris A-1 missiles. However, the SS-N-8 and SS-N-18 have ranges that are in excess of that for the Polaris A-3 and Poseidon C-3 missiles and are comparable to that of the Trident-I missile. It is actually difficult to compare these ranges, since the range of a missile depends on the payload. For one configuration of the new Trident-I missile, a 10% increase in range could be achieved at the expense of a 30% decrease in payload. The Poseidon missile supposedly could be redesigned to go 6400 km if it were to carry only a single warhead. Stated ranges are meaningful only if the payload for the particular configuration is also known. The proposed Trident-II missile is planned to have a range considerably in excess of the SS-N-8.

The accuracy of the missile warheads generally favors the American SLBM forces. To achieve high accuracy for SLBMs, the location of the submarine must be accurately known at all times. This location information requires frequent updating; whenever the submarine surfaces—or trails an antenna near the ocean surface—it can get an accurate fix from signals emitted by land, air, or ocean-based transmitters, or even from navigational satellites. The NAVSTAR system of 18 satellites, once completed, will allow positions to be fixed anywhere on earth with an accuracy of perhaps 20 m. Once the submarine resubmerges, it keeps track of its position with an inertial system in which a computer translates various measured accelerations into position information. This information is used to revise constantly targeting instructions for the missiles. Once the missile is launched, it corrects its flight for tilts in the submarine during launch and for buffeting by the water through which it has passed.

Table 7.2 shows that the accuracy of U.S. missiles is superior to that of Soviet missiles. This is consistent with the relative accuracies of ICBMs shown in Fig. 6.8. These accuracies can be expected to improve in the future through in-flight measurements of star positions or satellite triangulations. The maneuverable MARV warheads can then adjust their flight paths in accord with these measurements. As argued in Chapter 6 for ICBMs, one might expect Soviet SLBMs to duplicate U.S. accuracies typically seven years later.

Strategic Balance

The quantitative parameters in the missile balance are most relevant insofar as they allow a lesser or better fulfillment of the SLBMs retaliatory mission. In that sense the most important parameter is the assured area of destruction in retaliation to an enemy first strike. High survivability is as important as the EMT yield that is carried by the submarines, but the missile accuracy needs only be moderate. One might, however, also evaluate the SLBM potential for a successful first strike or for nuclear war fighting. Then the number of accurate warheads would be important, as would be control capabilities.

Assured Destruction. According to Chapter 4, the defined requirements for destruction might be satisfied if the SLBM force surviving an enemy's first strike can deliver a 50- to 200-EMT retaliatory second strike. That is equivalent to 6–25% of the present U.S. SLBM force or the payload of two to eight SLBM submarines.

Time on Station. The Soviet Navy has a major geographical disadvantage; it is largely landlocked. Soviet submarines must travel considerable distances before they are reasonably safe from antisubmarine warfare (ASW) detection on their patrol station in the open ocean. In contrast, U.S. submarine bases on the American east and west coasts adjoin the open ocean. The Soviet Union lacks forward naval bases in which it can service nuclear submarines, whereas the U.S. SLBM force has stations in Spain, Scotland, and Guam. Thus Soviet SLBM submarines must return more frequently to their home bases and take a longer time doing so.

In reliability and repair frequency the U.S. submarine force is considerably better; quality control and maintenance tend to be neglected in the Soviet Union where the industrial system pays more attention to fufilling production quotas than to repairs. Even crew conditions enter into the calculation as the U.S. concern with crew comfort and its two-crew system for each submarine increases effectiveness and greatly reduces the turnaround time between missions. The United States has usually more than 50% of its SLBM submarines on station compared with about 10%–15% for the Soviet Union; some of this difference relates to quality problems.

Patrol Area. Figure 7.7 shows the patrol area for USSR submarines from which their missiles can reach 300 km or more into the continental United States. The advantage of longer ranges for SLBMs is the much larger ocean area in which the submarines can hide. The Soviet submarines carrying the short-range Soviet SS-N-6 missile have to travel great distances to get close enough to the United States to reach even coastal targets; the extended range of the SS-N-8 and SS-N-18 missiles greatly enlarges the possible patrol areas.

Detectability. Soviet submarines face two handicaps in trying to escape detection by ASW forces. On the way to ocean patrol, the Soviet SLBM submarines must either pass between Greenland and the United Kingdom or through the Sea of Japan. During that passage, antisubmarine forces have a prolonged chance to detect and trail them. Such ASW detection and tracking risks are minimal for U.S. submarines.

Soviet submarines are also more exposed to detection by antisubmarine units. As noted, Soviet submarines are noisier than their Amer-

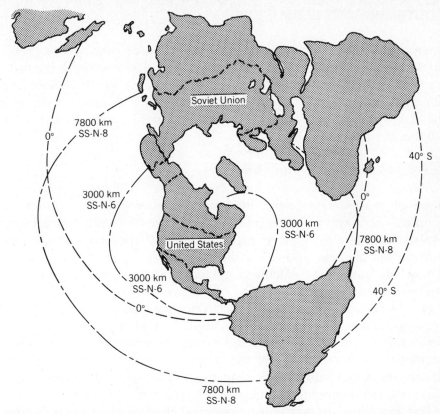

Figure 7.7   The operational areas from which Soviet submarines could strike 300 km into the continental United States. The 3000-km and 7800-km ranges correspond to those of the SS-N-6 (Yankee class) and the SS-N-8 or SS-N-18 (Delta class) SLBM.

ican counterparts. In general, the design and quality of Soviet submarines cannot ensure the sound and vibrational damping required to make a submarine truly quiet (Paine, 1980). Furthermore, the ASW efforts of the United States and its allies are much larger than are those of the Soviet Union. The Soviet Navy does not have the requisite access to the ocean and has concentrated more of its efforts on vessels to attack surface ships and on protecting its own SLBM forces. The relative quality of ASW forces is clearly in favor of the United States; the inequality is illustrated, for example, by the inability of Soviet aircraft carriers to launch long-range surveillance airplanes. U.S. submarines, therefore, should survive better than Soviet subs in case of attack. This does not mean Soviet submarines are now necessarily in danger. The inability of Scandinavian ASW forces to catch Soviet submarines in their fjords suggests that ASW may not be very good at present.

CONTEMPORARY SLBM ISSUES

Some SLBM issues resurface regularly in old or new guises. These might be classified into (1) the conflict of the SLBM force with the other legs of the Triad—and with other naval programs, (2) the question of whether improved SLBM systems are necessary or are just the next inevitable step in the technology, and (3) ensuring the survival of the submarine deterrent.

SLBMs versus the "Other" Navy

Generally, the SLBM forces have been funded separately from other naval programs. The desirability of such systems as the Trident has been decided largely on its own merit. However, some conflict with other naval systems is inevitable, not only because of economic competition but also because of conflicting requirements for support systems. This conflict is particularly evident with respect to large nuclear aircraft carriers.

As has the Trident submarine, each nuclear aircraft carrier costs billions of dollars. They demand an orientation of the rest of the Navy toward their support; large aircraft carriers require a fleet of vessels to protect them from attack by the enemy, including missile cruisers, destroyers, attack submarines, and support vessels, all preferably fast and nuclear powered to keep up with the carrier.

This emphasis on large nuclear aircraft carriers has a twofold effect on the SLBM program: it strips SLBM submarines of some potential protection from the enemy that would trail and attack them, and it instills in the nuclear navy a bias toward large vessels. This emphasis on large vessels has led to constantly larger and better nuclear submarines and constantly larger and better SLBMs. The public debate about the purposes and advantages of having a few large vessels rather than many smaller units has been so far inadequate.

Improved SLBM Submarines

The United States intends to replace at least the 10 Polaris submarines with Trident submarines during the 1980s. This new submarine has been justified on the grounds that the Polaris/Poseidon system is aging and that the Trident will be less vulnerable to antisubmarine warfare. The Tridents form a more survivable retaliatory force because they are technologically more sophisticated and because the missiles they will carry in the future have a longer range, allowing a wider and hence safer dispersal of the submarine. Is this Trident submarine system a needed follow-on to the Polaris system, or is it a naval example of the inevitable adoption of superior technologies?

The Polaris submarines were indeed aging; the last one was completed in 1963. All had been continually upgraded in performance since then. If the objective of the SLBM fleet is to provide platforms to launch retaliatory missiles in a second strike, it is not clear that the Polaris submarines were becoming obsolete. In a retaliatory sense, obsolescence would exist only if they were unreliable or became vulnerable to Soviet ASW in the foreseeable future. If the Polaris was becoming obsolete, one might then still ask whether it must be replaced. This replacement would seem necessary only if the remaining submarine force of 31 Poseidon submarines were inadequate. Finally, assuming that the Polaris subs must be replaced, must they be replaced by a system like the Trident? One could, for example, picture a larger fleet of smaller submarines, each carrying a few missiles, rather than a small fleet of very large Tridents carrying 24 missiles each. For invulnerability, a dispersed force of small and easier-to-hide submarines might seem desirable, although the economics might be against it.

It is argued that the Trident submarines are needed because they are less sensitive to ASW detection and, hence, less vulnerable. There is, however, no evidence that the Soviets have the air surveillance capability or the needed forward naval basing to detect and destroy any significant number of SLBMs. If a Polaris sub had been located, it could only have been destroyed by nuclear explosives delivered most reasonably by nuclear hunter-killer submarines. Soviet hunter submarines, however, lag in technology, as in the level of noise they make, so that U.S. subs can readily escape them if they are followed. In 1978 a U.S. Navy representative stated that the Soviets had never detected a single Polaris/Poseidon submarine in 1500 60-day patrols (Paine, 1980, p. 4).

The Trident submarine is technologically superior to both the Polaris and Poseidon subs. It is faster and mechanically quieter through better insulation and more precise designing and machining of reactor and drive components. Not only is its electronics newer, but there is much more room in the 17,000-tonne ship to install more of it. The Trident can more readily detect ASW efforts and therefore perhaps avoid detection.

The Trident-I missile is superior to the Poseidon missile. It carries warheads that have twice the explosive yield of those in the Poseidon C-3. The larger explosive yield makes the Trident I somewhat better for retaliation; the equivalent megatonnage per warhead goes up from 0.14 to 0.22 Mt. The increased range of the Trident I and of the future Trident-II missiles will give the submarines much greater ocean areas in which to hide from ASW. However, the Trident-I missile is being backfitted into Poseidon submarines; hence, only the Trident-II missiles require Trident submarines. If the SLBM submarines were in danger of detection by Soviet ASW forces, these improvements in technology might be very useful.

A major distinction of the Trident system is probably its potential for greatly improved missile accuracy with the Trident-II missile. With stellar or other navigation, this missile will have accuracies approaching those of land-based ICBMs. The increased accuracy is not necessary for strategic retaliation; it would be useful in tactical attacks on military targets.

The Trident deployment debate contained hints of a technological imperative: the decision for the Trident seems to have been made to a considerable extent on the grounds that old equipment must be replaced when much better technology becomes available and that large nuclear ships are better than small ones. Detailed analyses of various alternative options in terms of strategic versus tactical uses were not seriously debated in public. When debates took place, they had little effect on policy decisions. One gets the feeling that better submarines and missiles were feasible, and hence were developed, and are being deployed regardless of any analyses that might suggest militarily and politically preferable alternatives.

Antisubmarine Warfare

An ASW force can undertake either area or point naval defenses. A point defense protects some specific naval unit, such as an aircraft carrier or a freighter convoy. This ASW defense involves a task force, including carrier-based aircraft and helicopters, destroyers, and possibly hunter-killer submarines. The U.S. Navy is well prepared for this kind of ASW; since the United States is very reliant on sea-carried imports such as oil, it intends to be able to protect its sea lanes in any future conflict. One might question whether a major threat against the sea lanes is realistic and whether a limited oceanic war can be fought without escalating to a full-scale nuclear conflict.

> [The] submarines and ASW forces [of the Soviets] are primarily designed around such a nuclear confrontation. Their two prime ASW tasks are to provide a counter for the United States Polaris and Trident fleets, and to defend their own SLBM submarines against attack. They are allowing their large conventional submarine force to rust in obsolescence and do not seem to be enchanted by the numbers of submarines on their active rolls. They are building hunter-killer submarines to support Soviet surface units and missile-carrying submarines. The Soviet admirals do not seem to be concerned with blockade or the role of aggressor against merchant shipping. They see no clash of fleets in a total nuclear war context—only the exchange of thermonuclear warheads. (Moore, 1982, p. 97)

When asking whether the present ASW capabilities of the United States and the Soviet Union constitute a significant threat to SLBM submarines, area ASW is more relevant, that is, defenses in which large portions of the ocean are kept under surveillance and are patrolled to detect enemy submarines. Submarines are detected by sonar (sound navigation and ranging) techniques, either passively, by listening for noises they make, or actively, by reflecting sound signals off them. The detection may be carried out by long-range aircraft or helicopters, some survey ships, and hunter-killer submarines. Once detected, submarines may be tracked by continuous monitoring of the sonar signals. They may be destroyed by acoustic homing torpedoes carrying conventional explosives or by depth charges carrying nuclear warheads.

Detection

Passive Acoustic Detection. The most sensitive listening for submarines can be done by other submarines, as they are in the same medium, unaffected by surface wave noises. Clusters of hydrophones (underwater microphones) to detect very weak sonic noises can be carried by hunter-killer submarines; they achieve high sensitivity by adding the signals from the component detectors and can determine the position of the noise source by computer analysis of the signals. Passive detection works best if the hunting submarine is intrinsically very quiet and is moving very slowly to keep its own noise level to a minimum. Effective detection distances can range from less than 1 km to more than 100 km, depending on sea conditions and the noise level of the hunted and the hunter submarines.

Alternatively, an aircraft or a helicopter can drop a set of sonobuoys onto the ocean surface. Hydrophones are hung deep into the ocean from these buoys to pick up sonar noise (see Fig. 7.8). Amplified transmissions from the sonobuoys can be monitored. Arrays of hydrophones transmit signals that can be computer analyzed for more sensitivity and directionality. A sonobuoy weighs a few kilogram; an aircraft or helicopter can establish a large sonar-sensing array.

Active Acoustic Detection. Active sonar detection involves emitting an acoustic pulse and listening for echoes from submerged objects (see Fig. 7.8). The sound may be generated either by a vibrating mechanical transducer or by an underwater explosion. The latter is more likely to be used as the sound source for a large array of hydrophones.

Localization. A system of sonar detectors mounted on the ocean floor may be used to detect a submarine and determine its position within a very large area. The SOSUS network of hydrophones covers the U.S. continental shelf and is deployed around the Azores, Hawaii, and the northern coast of Japan, off the Aleutians, north of Norway, between Iceland and the United Kingdom, and elsewhere. The

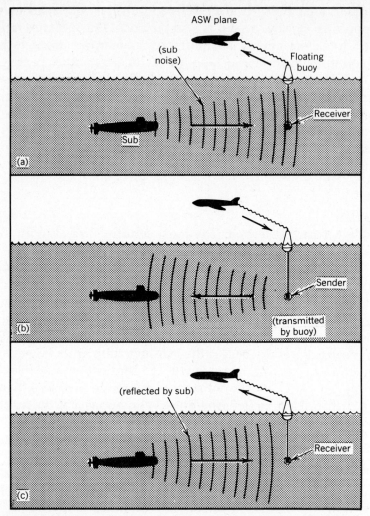

Figure 7.8 Passive and active acoustic detection. (a) In passive detection, one listens for noises emitted by a submarine. In this illustration the signals detected by a sonobuoy are relayed to an aircraft for processing to distinguish submarine noises from the acoustic background. In active detection (b), sound is generated, and (c) one listens for echoes as that sound pulse might be reflected from the hunted submarine.

CAESAR underwater surveillance system has many active and passive sonar detectors mounted on the sea floor. Its fixed active detectors use narrowly focused beams of sound of very low frequency (a few hundred cycles per second) and power levels of several megawatts. They consequently have detection ranges of hundreds of kilometers and can localize the sound source to within perhaps 50 km.

Once a submarine has been located within such an area, aerial surveys are used to pinpoint the submarine more accurately (see

Garwin 1972; Tsipis, 1974). A group of nine helicopters, dropping sonobuoys with a detection range of 3 km, may be able to determine in one hour the location of that submarine with an accuracy of 3 km. Finally, the submarine might be located even more precisely using a magnetic anomaly detector. This device can detect the presence of large submerged steel bodies at perhaps a distance of ½ km.

Tracking

The destruction of SLBM submarines makes the most sense in a first-strike scenario, where prompt nuclear retaliation needs to be reduced to a minimum. To make that scenario a success, all SLBM submarines that are on station would have to be tracked continuously so that they could all be destroyed simultaneously on command. Tracking requires not only detecting the submarines but also using active sonar to trail them with another submarine, some aircraft, or a surface vessel. The tracking vessel would have to stay continuously within a few hundred meters of the pursued submarine. Ideally, such tracking vessels should be small and simple, be specially designed for long-term operations, and be produced in large numbers. Such trailing fleets have not been built so far by either the United States or the Soviet Union.

Destruction

The U.S. Navy has two main torpedoes for destroying enemy submarines. The Mark 46 is an active acoustic homing torpedo. It is lightweight and can be carried by aircraft and helicopters as well as by ships and killer submarines. The Mark 48 is a longer-range torpedo with a larger warhead: it uses both active and passive hunting modes, and hunter-killer submarines can guide it after launch by means of control wires. Both torpedoes can carry nuclear warheads with lethal radii in excess of 1 km. Once an SLBM submarine is located within a few hundred meters, it can be destroyed.

It has been suggested that SLBM submarines could be prevented from reaching their patrol stations after leaving their home port by a mine barrier blocking some narrow passage through which they all might have to pass. However, such a barrier would be useful only in a protracted oceanic war.

The major issue in ASW in the near future is likely to be the extension of Project CAESAR, of the underwater sound surveillance system (SOSUS). The technology of sonar detectors combined with very advanced computer processing capabilities makes such a system technically appealing. The arrays of detectors allow computers to recognize and analyze the sonar signature of various ships, to untangle the noise of submarines from the noise of surface ship traffic. If such extended surveillance comes, its potential for destroying SLBM submarines would have to be analyzed thoroughly.

Sea-Launched Cruise Missiles

It has been proposed that long-range cruise missiles be developed for lauching from submarine torpedo tubes. These would be boosted above the surface of the ocean by small rockets until their air-breathing engines could be turned on. Then the missile would fly low above the ocean surface until it reached land, where it would use a TERCOM system (Fig. 5.6) to fly to a predesignated target with very high accuracy.

Such a system would combine the very high accuracy of the cruise missile with the very high survivability of the nuclear submarine. The maximum 2400-km range of the present generation of U.S. cruise missiles makes them relatively unsuitable for sea-launched strategic retaliatory missions; the launching submarine would have to hide close to shore to reach the enemy heartland. But the high accuracy makes them useful as tactical weapons for example in a European war.

Long-ranged, sea-launched cruise missiles would present a problem for arms limitations; since any submarine or surface ship could launch them from torpedo tubes or shipboard launchers, they would be difficult to count.

Submarine Communications

SLBM submarines must be in frequent communication with their home base (e.g., to know whether a nuclear attack has taken place). Present methods of communication by electromagnetic radiation require that the receiving antenna of the submarine be near the ocean surface; therefore, to receive messages submarines must come fairly close to the ocean surface. At that moment they are potentially vulnerable to detection and attack.

For many years it has been the hope of SLBM strategists to transmit messages by extremely-low-frequency (ELF) electromagnetic waves that can penetrate deeply below the ocean surface (see Fig. 7.9). This proposed transmission system was initially known as Project Sanguine. Because of feasibility questions and environmental opposition, this antenna was redesigned and renamed Project Seafarer. No site acceptable both to the Navy and to local inhabitants has so far been found for this revised project, and it is presently largely in abeyance. But because of the desirability of having more secure communications, such ELF antenna systems continue to be proposed.

Very-low-frequency (VLF) antennas communicating at around 15 kilohertz (kHz, 15,000 cycles per second) already exist. These antennas

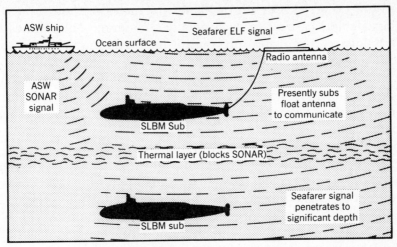

Figure 7.9 An extremely-low-frequency (ELF) communications system could help SLBM submarines such as the Trident hide at greater depths from ASW forces.

can radiate several megawatts of power with perhaps 30% efficiency. In contrast the ELF Seafarer system would radiate at around 60 hertz (Hz). This system would have two main attractions. First, it would inject the electromagnetic energy into the space between the earth's surface and the ionosphere, where it would propagate around the earth. Its intensity would only drop to one-half after traveling about 4500 km through the air. ELF waves could, therefore, constitute a good global communications system. Second, the system has a reasonable ability to penetrate water. Typically, the radiation intensity will decrease by a factor of 10 in 25 m, or by 10,000 in 100 m, of water. If enough power were emitted by the antenna, even a deeply submerged sub could receive some information.

The main problem with ELF systems is the very large size required for the antenna. The lower the frequency of ELF, the more effective it is in penetrating water. Antennas radiate most efficiently when their dimensions are comparable to the wavelength of the emitted waves. For a frequency of 60 Hz, the wavelength is 5000 km; thus an ELF antenna should be very large.

The Sanguine antenna was to be a crossing grid 240 km on a side, with 10,000 km of copper cable buried 6 feet underground. Because of its electrical properties, the most desirable ground was in Wisconsin. At one point the antenna was to take up 60,000 km², or 40% of that state's area.

Even at that size, some thought that the system was likely to be quite inefficient, radiating perhaps 1 watt (W) of ELF energy for a power input of 25 MW. The submarine 10,000 km away might then receive

10^{-15} W of power at a depth of 100 m. Estimates of the rate at which messages could be sent to such deeply submerged submarines have been as low as 5 min to more than 3 hr to communicate one bit of information (Klessig and Strife, 1980). Such a system would be best used to transmit simple go/no-go information for the release of nuclear missiles. Questions have been raised about enemy strikes at the antenna, danger from emitted electromagnetic radiation, and falling property values.

Political objections drove the Sanguine system from Wisconsin. The Navy then proposed to build a significantly smaller Seafarer system in Upper Michigan to cover only 10,000 km², requiring 100 times less power, but producing much weaker signals. Michigan too rejected the system. For the moment large-scale ELF communications with SLBM submarines is on the shelf. But if enough concern arises about the detectability of submarines near the ocean surface, this project might well be resurrected.

DISCUSSION

The present purpose of the SLBM submarines is to act as an invulnerable retaliatory force. However, an unspoken policy seems to be that the U.S. SLBM force ought to be at least as good as that of the Soviet Union. The number of SLBMs favors the Soviet Union by 930 to 568. The United States can presently deliver 5152 SLBM warheads, the USSR 2178. Because of this forward bases and crew rotations, the United States has a 4 to 1 advantage in time on station. Soviet submarines are more vulnerable to tracking because they must pass through unfriendly channels to reach the open ocean. In ability to strike targets deep in enemy targets, the USSR may have an advantage since its major cities are further inland. The accuracy of missiles is perhaps counterproductive to deterrence, but it may be useful in nuclear war fighting. The U.S. submarine missiles are more accurate, but the missiles on both sides are quite accurate enough for deterrence purposes as their CEP is smaller than the soft-target lethal radius of the nuclear warheads. The continuing improvements in SLBM accuracy might begin to threaten land-based missiles by the end of this decade.

The major concern for the SLBM force must be its vulnerability. Improvements in electronics and computer capabilities might someday (although not in the foreseeable future) give ASW forces the ability to detect, track, and destroy SLBM submarines. As long as the United States maintains the lead in electronics and computers (see Chapter

13), one might expect the Soviet Union to be more concerned about this problem than the United States. Actually, as long as some of the other retaliatory strategic forces would survive a surprise first strike, the SLBM submarine force does not have to be totally invulnerable. The debate about SLBM improvements then should come down to the levels of expenditures that can be justified to pay for absolute invulnerability. At the present, that question is not seriously asked. Instead, SLBMs as a retaliatory force often become involved in questions of conventional warfare to protect the sea lanes.

Reference

Cordesman, H. "M-X and the Balance of Power: Reassessing America's Strength." *Armed Forces Journal International*, Vol. 120, no. 4 (December 1982), pp. 21–51.

Department of Defense, *Soviet Millitary Power*, 2nd ed. Washington, D.C.: Government Printing Office, 1983.

Garwin, R. L. "Antisubmarine Warfare and National Security." *Scientific American*, Vol. 227, no. 1 (July 1972), pp. 14–25.

Hewlett, R. G., and F. Duncan. *Nuclear Navy: 1946–1962*. Chicago: University of Chicago Press, 1974. A detailed history of the U.S. nuclear submarine and the Polaris program.

International Institute for Strategic Studies. *The Military Balance: 1983–1984*. London, IISS, 1983.

Klessig, Lowell L., and Victor L. Strife. *The ELF Odyssey: National Security versus Environmental Protection*. Boulder, Colo.: Westview Press, 1980.

Moore, T., ed. *Jane's Fighting Ships: 1982–3*. London: Jane's, 1982.

Nitze, P. H., L. Sullivan, Jr., and the Atlantic Working Group on Securing the Seas. *Securing the Seas: The Soviet Naval Challenge and Western Alliance Options*. Boulder, Colo.: Westview Press, 1979.

Paine, C. "The Triad Game," *FAS Public Interest Report*, Vol. 33, no. 10 (December 1980), pp. 4–8.

Pretty, R. T. *Jane's Weapons Systems: 1982–83*. London: Jane's, 1982.

Sapolski, H. M. *The Polaris System Developments: Bureaucratic and Programmatic Success in Government*. Cambridge, Mass.: Harvard University Press, 1972. Examines why the Polaris program was so successful.

Stockholm International Peace Research Institute. *World Armaments and Disarmament: SIPRI Yearbook (1969–70)*. New York: Humanities Press, 1970.

———— . *World Armaments and Disarmament: SIPRI Yearbook 1982*. Cambridge, Mass.: Oelgeschlager, Gunn & Hain, 1982.

Tsipis, K. *Tactical and Strategic Antisubmarine Warfare*. Cambridge, Mass.: M.I.T. Press, 1974. See also K. Tsipis, A. H. Cahn, and B. T. Feld, eds., *The Future of the Sea-Based Deterrent*. Cambridge, Mass.: M.I.T. Press, 1973.

CHAPTER 8

Nuclear Deterrence and Stability

What in the name of God is strategic superiority? What is the significance of it politically, militarily, operationally at these levels of numbers? What do you do with it?

Henry Kissinger, Secretary of State, 1974

We have placed ourselves at a significant disadvantage voluntarily.

Henry Kissinger, former Secretary of State, 1980

When discussing the nuclear balance between the United States and the Soviet Union, the "doves" emphasize the mutual overkill in the strategic area, the "moderates" argue the existence of sufficiency and rough equivalency, and the "hawks" worry about the U.S. inferiority in some important nuclear areas. Are the two statements by Kissinger mutually inconsistent?

The issue has recently become more polarized: the "hawkish" position has become accepted by many Americans as truth, whereas at the same time referenda on a nuclear "freeze," based largely on the concept of overkill, have passed in about a dozen states. The SALT debates raised the specter of inferiority for the strategic nuclear arsenal. What is the nuclear balance between the United States and the Soviet Union?

DEFINITION OF A NUCLEAR BALANCE

Any analysis of the balance in nuclear strength between the United States and the Soviet Union first requires a definition of the objectives **194** to be achieved by the nuclear weapons. Chapter 4 shows that nuclear weapons have produced the capability for massive retaliation if the retaliatory forces survive an attack. Both the United States and the Soviet Union have built up a strategic nuclear inventory that is survivable enough to retaliate effectively following an attack by the opponent; a state of mutual assured destruction (MAD) now exists. Many people believe that the assured destruction is so large as to be unacceptable under any conceivable circumstances, that MAD therefore deters everyone from launching a surprise first-strike nuclear attack.

The policy of relying for peace on such a MAD nuclear balance is called deterrence. To deter an enemy, a country must have a second-strike capability; it must have so many nuclear arms that an attack by the opponent would let it retain sufficient retaliatory arms to inflict damage on the attacker that is so large as to be totally unacceptable. If this threatened country also shows a credible intent to retaliate under an attack, then the opponent would be deterred from such a first-strike attack. A country has a first-strike capability if it can destroy in an attack so much of the opponent's nuclear weaponry that the retaliatory strike would not inflict unacceptable damage on the attacker. When both sides in this balance have a second-strike capability (i.e., if neither has a first-strike capability), then both countries are deterred from attacking each other from fear that an attack would be suicidal. If this state of mutual deterrence existed, an attack could only be initiated by irrational leaders.

Nuclear weapons could, however, serve purposes other than acting as a deterrent through MAD. They could be used not only in the strategic countervalue mode against soft civilian targets, such as cities, but if accurate enough they could be used also in the tactical counterforce mode against harder military targets, such as missile silos. Paul H. Nitze, the current U.S. negotiator at the intermediate force reduction talks, has outlined five nuclear strategic concepts (1976, pp. 2–3), including four alternatives to the MAD deterrence policy:

1. *Minimum Deterrence.* This means a capacity to destroy a few key cities with little if any counterforce capacity to attack a hostile nation's military forces. The effect of this level of deterrence would be to provide limited deterrence of a full-scale attack on the U.S. population.

2. *Massive Urban/Industrial Retaliation.* As the name implies, this posture is designed to destroy many cities, many millions of people and much productive capacity, and to do so on an assured second-strike basis. This level of deterrence, sometimes called "Assured Destruction," would concede to the Soviet Union the potential for a military victory if deterrence failed, but (it would be anticipated) would make any such victory worthless in political terms.

3. *Flexible Response.* In this form of deterrence the United States would have the capability of reacting to a Soviet counterforce attack without going immediately to

a countercity attack. It would thus increase the credibility of deterrence. . . .

4. *Denial of a Nuclear War–Winning Capability to the Other Side.* This means a nuclear posture such that, even if the other side attacked first and sought to destroy one's own strategic striking power [read: "tactical" in the sense defined in this text], the result of such a counterforce exchange would be sufficiently even and inconclusive that the duel would be extremely unattractive to the other side. . . .

5. *A Nuclear War–Winning Capability.* This would be a position so superior that, whatever the initial forms of nuclear exchange, one's own surviving capacity would be enough to destroy the war-making ability of the other nation without comparable return damage.

Evidence exists that the Soviet Union at the very beginning of its nuclear development in the 1950s and early 1960s was interested mostly in minimum deterrence coupled with strategic defense of the homeland. Indeed, the inferiority of Soviet nuclear strategic forces at that time hardly allowed any other posture. In the late 1960s the USSR built its nuclear forces up to the massive-retaliation level. Now such weapons as the highly accurate MIRVed SS-18 and SS-19 may be providing the Soviets with, at least, a flexible response ability. For the United States, the massive-retaliation doctrine has become the doctrine of deterrence through MAD. A flexible response option has often been discussed and has been adopted at least nominally.

It is possible to analyze approximately how well the deterrence criteria are presently satisfied and how stable the balance may be in the future. However, the enormous nuclear arsenals and the constant technological improvements force analyses as well of alternate strategies, such as limited tactical nuclear wars, flexible response capabilities, and second-strike counterforce doctrines. Some aspects of weapons that make them useful for tactical nuclear war may also make them a threat to a successful and stable deterrence posture.

THE STRATEGIC BALANCE

The policy of deterrence relies primarily on the MAD capabilities provided by the intercontinental strategic weapons described in Chapters 5, 6, and 7. Which of the weapons' performance parameters help to maintain MAD? Which may be useful for counterforce actions? And which may be threatening to deterrence? Table 8.1 summarizes some aspects of these weapons. The parameters range from the quantitative numbers of missiles and their throw weight to the qualities of MIRVing, the missile accuracies, and the missile hardening.

Table 8.1   The strategic nuclear balance between the United States and the Soviet Union
The missile-silo blast resistances are particularly controversial. The 2000 psi listed is that generally used by experts in calculations. Older silos may be considerably less protected; the newer Soviet SS-17/18/19 silos may have higher levels of hardening. Data represent a summary of Tables 5.1, 6.2, 7.1 and 7.2

| Delivery Systems | Quantities | | Yield | | | Qualities | |
	Number of Launchers	Throw Weight max. tonnes	Y (Mt)	Y (EMT)	Number of Warheads	Accuracy (median)	Protection (median)
United States							
ICBM	1045	1091	1509	1449	2147	280 m	2000 psi
Submarines	568	799	363	868	5152	450 m	NA
Bombers	272	8549	1332	1530	2306	NA	NA
U.S. total	1885	10,439	3204	3847	9605	NA	NA
Soviet Union							
ICBM	1398	3724	5200	4657	5158	450 m	2000 psi
Submarines	930	994	1013	1220	2178	600 m	NA
Bombers	143	2187	386	386	386	NA	NA
USSR total	2471	6905	6599	6263	7722	NA	NA

NA – Not applicable.

The Soviet Union is significantly ahead in the quantitative parameter of actual throw weight in tonnes of their ICMBs. If bombers are counted to the maximum bomb loads they could carry, the numbers favor the United States somewhat; however, bombers do not carry such maximum bomb loads. The more significant parameter is the megatonnage of explosive yield that actually might be delivered. Overall, the USSR has an advantage in explosive yield, although it is less when expressed in terms of equivalent megatons (EMT) to account for the greater efficacy of smaller warheads (see Chapters 3 and 4). The major difference between the United States and the USSR lies in the fact that the United States has its largest yield carried by bombers, whereas the Soviet Union has its yield concentrated in the land-based missiles. The United States has the lead in parameters such as the number of warheads it can deliver and their accuracy.

A comparison of the numbers in Table 8.1 really is meaningful only in the context of some strategy. Table 8.2 translates these parameters into the more meaningful terms of destructive capability, vulnerability to attack, and ability to carry out counterforce strikes. These parameters will be discussed next.

Table 8.2 Details of the strategic balance between the United States and the USSR.
Damage area is calculated as 75 km² (30 mi²) per equivalent megaton (see Chapter 4). The hard-target kill parameter K is explained on page 202. A summary of Tables 5.1, 6.2, 7.1, 7.2 and 8.1

Missiles	No. of Warheads	Mt per Warhead	EMT per Warhead	Area Destroyed Each	Area Destroyed Total	Silo Protection	Vulnerability (K required) 90% Each	90% Total	97% Each	97% Total	Counterforce Capability (K available) Accuracy	Each	Total
United States													
Titan II	45 × 1	9.0 Mt	4.3 EMT	325 km²	14,600 km²	300 psi	30	1400	52	2,300	1300 m	9	400
Minuteman II	450 × 1	1.5 Mt	1.3 EMT	98 km²	43,900 km²	2000 psi	120	54,000	184	82,800	370 m	32	14,600
Minuteman III	250 × 3	0.17 Mt	0.31 EMT	23 km²	17,400 km²	2000 psi	120	30,000	184	46,000	280 m	7	5,400
Minuteman IIIA	300 × 3	0.335 Mt	0.48 EMT	35 km²	32,400 km²	2000 psi	120	36,000	184	55,200	220 m	33	29,700
Poseidon C-3	304 × 10	0.05 Mt	0.14 EMT	10 km²	31,900 km²	NA	NA	NA	NA	NA	450 m	2	6,700
Trident I	264 × 8	0.10 Mt	0.22 EMT	15 km²	34,800 km²	NA	NA	NA	NA	NA	450 m	4	8,400
Bombers													
Bombs	272 × 4	1.0 Mt	1.0 EMT	75 km²	81,600 km²	NA	NA	NA	NA	NA	NA	NA	NA
SRAM	1026	0.2 Mt	0.34 EMT	25 km²	26,200 km²	NA	NA	NA	NA	NA	NA	NA	NA
Cruise	192	0.3 Mt	0.45 EMT	35 km²	6,500 km²	NA	NA	NA	NA	NA	NA	NA	NA
U.S. total	9603	NA	NA	NA	289,300 km²	NA	NA	121,400	NA	186,300	NA	NA	65,200

Soviet Union

SS-11	518 × 1	1.0 Mt	1.0 EMT	75 km²	38,800 km²	300 psi	30	15,500	52	26,900	900 m	2	880
SS-13	60 × 1	0.75 Mt	0.83 EMT	63 km²	3,700 km²	300 psi	30	1,800	52	3,100	900 m	1	40
SS-17 (Mod 1)	120 × 4	0.75 Mt	0.83 EMT	63 km²	29,900 km²	2000 psi	120	14,400	184	22,100	450 m	14	6,480
SS-17 (Mod 2)	32 × 1	6 Mt	3.3 EMT	248 km²	7,900 km²	2000 psi	120	3,800	184	5,900	450 m	54	1,700
SS-18 (Mod 1)	58 × 1	20 Mt	7.4 EMT	553 km²	32,200 km²	2000 psi	120	7,000	184	10,700	450 m	121	7,700
SS-18 (Mod 2)	175 × 8	0.9 Mt	0.93 EMT	70 km²	97,200 km²	2000 psi	120	21,000	184	32,200	450 m	15	21,300
SS-18 (Mod 4)	75 × 10	0.5 Mt	0.62 EMT	48 km²	34,900 km²	2000 psi	120	9,000	184	13,800	300 m	23	17,400
SS-19 (Mod 2)	60 × 1	5.0 Mt	2.9 EMT	220 km²	13,000 km²	2000 psi	120	7,200	184	11,000	300 m	108	6,500
SS-19 (Mod 3)	300 × 6	0.55 Mt	0.67 EMT	50 km²	90,500 km²	2000 psi	120	36,000	184	55,200	300 m	25	44,500
SS-N-5	18 × 1	1 Mt	1 EMT	75 km²	1,300 km²	NA	NA	NA	NA	NA	2800 m	0	0
SS-N-6	400 × 1	1 Mt	1 EMT	75 km²	30,000 km²	NA	NA	NA	NA	NA	900 m	4	1,640
SS-N-8	292 × 1	1 Mt	1 EMT	75 km²	21,900 km²	NA	NA	NA	NA	NA	900 m	4	1,200
SS-N-17	12 × 1	1 Mt	1 EMT	75 km²	900 km²	NA	NA	NA	NA	NA	1500 m	2	20
SS-N-18	208 × 7	0.2 Mt	0.34 EMT	25 km²	37,100 km²	NA	NA	NA	NA	NA	600 m	9	13,400
Bombers bombs	386	1 Mt	1 EMT	75 km²	29,000 km²	NA	NA	NA	NA	NA	NA	NA	NA
USSR total	7722	NA	NA	NA	468,300 km²	NA	NA	115,700	NA	180,900	NA	NA	122,760

NA – Not applicable.

199

DETERRENCE

Many possible alternative strategies exist for the use of strategic nuclear forces. The most prominent among these is the policy of deterrence through mutual assured destruction by retaliatory second strikes after an attack. This policy not only requires sufficient forces but also that they be adequately survivable.

Destructiveness

The easiest damage to inflict in a MAD scenario is on the civilian population and on industry. It has been shown in Chapters 3 and 4 that civilians can be killed and industry destroyed by an overpressure of about 5 psi. According to Table 2.3, a 1-Mt H-bomb then has a radius of ground destruction of 5 km (3 mi, slightly less for an air burst). This corresponds to an area of about 75 km² (30 mi²) destroyed by a 1-Mt bomb and hence by each EMT of yield. Tables 8.2 and 8.3 show a translation of the EMT available into area destroyed for the various weapons systems.

The strategic weapons in the United States and the Soviet Union are comparable in destructiveness, although the larger number of U.S. warheads does not quite make up for the larger total yield of the Soviet

Table 8.3 The USSR/U.S. strategic balance expressed in terms of the area each can destroy, the counterforce available, and the counterforce each country would need for a 90% or 97% successful attack on the enemy's missile silos, if missile reliability were 100% and assuming only one RV is targeted on each silo. A summary of Tables 5.1, 6.2, 7.1, 7.2, 8.1 and 8.2

| | Area Destroyable | Silo Kill Factor K | | |
		Available	Required for 90%	Required for 97%
United States				
ICBMs	108,300 km²	50,100	121,400	186,300
Submarines	66,700 km²	15,100	NA	NA
Bombers	114,300 km²	NA	NA	NA
U.S. Total	289,300 km²	65,200	121,400	186,300
Soviet Union				
ICBMs	348,100 km²	106,500	115,700	180,900
Submarines	91,200 km²	16,260	NA	NA
Bombers	29,000 km²	NA	NA	NA
USSR Total	468,300 km²	122,760	115,700	180,900

NA – Not applicable.

missile payloads. The McNamara criteria for minimum unacceptable damage were found in Chapter 4 to be equivalent to a retaliatory force delivering 50–200 EMT. This corresponds to an area of destruction of 3750–15,000 km² (1500–6000 mi²). It is tempting to define an overkill factor as the number of times that McNamara's minimum MAD criteria are met. By such a definition these destructive capabilities represent an overkill capacity of 20 for the United States and 30 for the USSR. However, these criteria are only guesses as to what threatened damage would deter the Soviets. They certainly do not mean that every Soviet citizen could be killed 20 times over; some would probably survive any level of nuclear retaliation. Nor do these overkill factors ask what fraction of the available megatonnage would actually survive to reach the enemy in a retaliatory strike.

Counterforce Capability

The counterforce capability of a weapon system measures its ability to carry out tactical attacks on specific military objectives, particularly on the enemy's strategic forces. For some years now there has been concern that the increasing accuracy of missiles is threatening the survivability of the land-based Minuteman ICBM forces. Figure 8.1 shows the nature of a successful counterforce attacks by missiles.

The determining characteristics for the success or failure of a counterforce attack are the accuracy (CEP) and yield (Y) of the attacking missile and the hardness (H) of the attacked missile silo. It is possible to define a lethality parameter K that describes the counter-

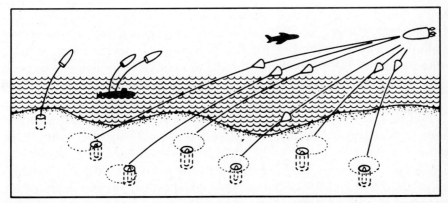

Figure 8.1 In an effective counterforce attack, accurate MIRV missile warheads would destroy most of the targeted missile silos. Yet the alert bomber force and the SLBM would survive to retaliate.

force capability of a missile reentry vehicle as (Tsipis, 1975 and 1983; Feld and Tsipis, 1979).

$$K = \frac{[Y \, (\text{Mt})]^{2/3}}{[\text{CEP} \, (\text{nm})]^2} = 3.4 \, \frac{[Y \, (\text{Mt})]^{2/3}}{[\text{CEP} \, (\text{km})]^2} \tag{8.1}$$

Here the yield Y is to be expressed in megatons (Mt) and the accuracy (CEP) in nautical miles or in kilometers. To improve the lethality of a reentry vehicle by a factor of four, either its accuracy must be improved by a factor of 2 (its CEP halved) or its yield must be increased by a factor of 8; this suggests that increases in warhead accuracy are far more effective in improving counterforce capabilities for hard targets than are equal increases in warhead yield. Tables 8.2 and 8.3 show the lethalities K of the U.S. and Soviet missiles individually and in total, derived from the yields and accuracies in Tables 5.1, 6.2, 7.1, and 7.2. At the moment, the Soviet Union is believed to have about twice the value of the K kill parameter as does the United States; the larger number of U.S. warheads combined with their greater accuracy does not make up for the larger yield of the Soviet warheads.

The question is how much the land-based ICBM silos are actually threatened by this counterforce capability. The blast resistance of various missile silos are controversial. Kosta Tsipis (1975) says that Titan-II and Minuteman-II silos are hardened to 300 psi, Minuteman III to 1000 psi; later (1979), Tsipis assumes 2000 psi for Minuteman III-silos and again (Feld and Tsipis, 1979) he reports that Soviet silos built before 1970 were hardened to 100 psi and to 300 psi thereafter. One finds claims in the literature that some contemporary Soviet missiles may be superhardened to resist overpressures in excess of 3000 psi. Apparently, silo hardnesses are not well known, at least not outside the intelligence community. Hence, most analysts presently simply use some "canonical" number for the hardness of missile silos on both sides; usually 2000 psi is the number chosen. That number will be used here, except that 300 psi will be used for the older Titan-II, SS-11, and SS-13 silos.

Figure 6.12 has shown silo kill probabilities for 2000-psi silos of various combinations of missile yield and accuracy. Figure 8.2 shows the same information in terms of the warhead lethality and missile-silo hardness. Tables 8.2 and 8.3 show the K values required to destroy more than 90% or 97% of the enemy silos in an attack with a single RV on each silo. If such attacks were totally successful, they would still leave 10% or 3% of the missiles, enough for a retaliatory strike destroying 10,000 km² or 3300 km² of Soviet territory, or 35,000 km² or 10,500 km² of U.S. territory. Such calculations assume perfect missile reliabil-

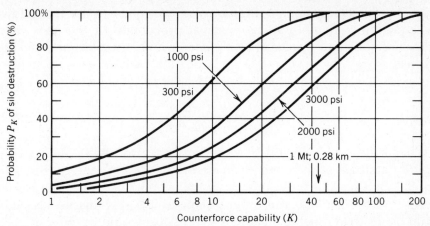

Figure 8.2 The probabilities P_K and P_s of destroying a missile silo or of its survival, respectively, when it is hardened to various levels of hardness and is attacked by warheads of various degrees of lethality K. $K = 44$ for a yield of 1-Mt and a CEP of 0.15 nm = 0.28 km.

ity, which is not the case; they ignore the fact that each RV can destroy only one silo (i.e., that a K greater than 100 for a warhead is partially wasted), and they overlook the possibility of targeting two RVs on a silo. They ought to take into account that the alert bomber forces and the SLBMs would also be available for a retaliatory second strike. The K calculations show that the counterforce capabilities are considerable, but do not now seem sufficient to destroy retaliatory strategic forces unless the accuracy of Soviet missiles were much larger than is usually reported.

In fact, neither side now has sufficient kill capability to threaten the other's silos enough to endanger its retaliatory capabilities. The actual strategies for an antisilo counterforce strike would likely have to be far more complex than the K parameter calculations suggest. They might include cross-targeting several warheads from different missiles on each silo. The general consensus says that it makes little sense to target more than two warheads on each silo because the explosion of one warhead will interfere with the subsequent warheads through the so-called "fratricide" effect.

We can estimate the survivability of the U.S. Minuteman missiles. Assume that each Minuteman is indeed attacked by two enemy warheads. Further assume that each silo is hardened to withstand an overpressure of 2000 psi, that the attacking Soviet warheads are from the MIRVed SS-18s and SS-19s with a yield $Y = 0.5$ Mt and an accuracy of CEP = 300 m (0.16 nm), and that these missiles have a reliability $R = 0.85$. The kill capability K for each warhead in this case is 25. To calculate the probability P_K of destroying any one Minuteman missile silo of hardness H (in psi) with two warheads, one can use the following equation, where P_s is the survival probability of the silo when attacked by a single warhead and where n is the number of attacking warheads

$$P_{nK} = 1 - [1 - R(1 - P_s)]^n \tag{8.2}$$

$$P_s = \exp \frac{K}{0.22 \cdot H^{2/3}} \tag{8.3}$$

When setting $K = 25$ and $H = 2000$ psi, the probability of surviving a hit by a single such reentry vehicle is $P_s = 0.5$, in agreement with Fig. 8.2. Setting $R = 0.85$ and $n = 2$, the overall kill probability would be $P_{2K} = 0.66$. The maximum percentage of 2000-psi missile silos that could be destroyed using such $K = 25$ missiles would be 66%.

The results of this calculation depend very critically on the values assumed for the accuracy of the attacking missiles. Table 8.4 shows the probability of destroying an ICBM silo with warheads of various sizes and accuracy. Increasing the accuracy of a ¾-Mt warhead from 460 m (0.25 nm) to 220 m (0.12 nm) increases its ability to destroy a missile silo in a double strike from 0.43 to 0.87. The reliability of the attacking missiles is also very important in this calculation; this parameter is not well known. Finally, these calculated silo vulnerabilities may not be very directly related to the results of a real attack. A real attack would involve a very complex targeting procedure to ensure simultaneous attacks on all missile silos. The targeting of several warheads on each silo would create major problems. The explosion of one warhead may interfere with the subsequent warheads through fratricide phenomena. The dust cloud, turbulence, nuclear radiation, and electromagnetic

Table 8.4 The calculated destructiveness of warheads on a silo hardened to 2000 psi, based on Equation 8.3.

Accuracy	Yield	K	Reliability	Probability P_K	
				One RV	Two RV
220 m (0.120 nm)	0.75 Mt	57.3	85%	69%	90%
220 m (0.120 nm)	0.75 Mt	57.3	70%	56%	81%
220 m (0.120 nm)	0.50 Mt	43.8	85%	61%	85%
220 m (0.120 nm)	0.50 Mt	43.8	70%	50%	75%
300 m (0.163 nm)	0.75 Mt	31.1	85%	50%	75%
300 m (0.163 nm)	0.75 Mt	31.1	70%	41%	65%
300 m (0.163 nm)	0.50 Mt	23.7	85%	42%	66%
300 m (0.163 nm)	0.50 Mt	23.7	70%	34%	57%
450 m (0.245 nm)	0.75 Mt	13.8	85%	28%	48%
450 m (0.245 nm)	0.75 Mt	13.8	70%	23%	40%
450 m (0.245 nm)	0.50 Mt	10.5	85%	22%	39%
450 m (0.245 nm)	0.50 Mt	10.5	70%	18%	33%

pulse from the first explosion may create enough disturbances to disable the subsequent warheads or at least reduce their accuracy. Most targeting strategies allocate two reentry vehicles from different ICBMs to each silo, with the first explosion to take place on the ground, followed promptly by a second explosion in the air above the silo; this would minimize fratricide interference, since the second warhead would not have to pass through the explosion effects of the first explosion. The timing requirements for such an attack are very rigorous.

Stability

From the foregoing discussion it is clear that MIRVed missiles with high accuracy can endanger at least the ICBM portion of the deterrent balance. Legault and Lindsey (1976) present a technique using deterrence diagrams to analyze the deterrence balance. This is a steady-state method that cannot describe the dynamics of an arms race; it begins to break down when the counterforce capabilities become too large; and it ignores invulnerable retaliatory forces beyond the ICBMs. Nonetheless, it clarifies the concept of stability in a nuclear balance.

Deterrence Diagrams

In deterrence diagrams, one plots the number of strategic missiles N_A deployed by the United States and the N_S deployed the the Soviet Union on a two-dimensional plane, as shown in Fig. 8.3(a). The minimum number of missiles required for deterrence is indicated by the numbers U_A and U_S. Different areas of this plot correspond to different kinds of deterrence and stability. The bottom left of the diagram shows the situation where neither side has enough missiles to inflict unacceptable damage, where no deterrence exists. In areas in the lower right and upper left of the diagram, only one side has enough warheads to survive an attack with an assured retaliatory second-strike force; these are areas of unilateral deterrence. In the upper right-hand area of the diagram, both sides have an assured second-strike force, and mutual deterrence exists; this is the regime of mutual assured destruction.

Such diagrams can be used to sketch the effects of various weapons options, such as MIRVing, ABM systems, and civil defense, on deterrence. Consider the effects of MIRV warheads with very high accuracy. If attacking missiles are used to attack missile silos, then a larger number of missiles may be needed for assured deterrence, to ensure that some will survive to retaliate. Label the kill probability of a single reentry vehicle P_K and the number of MIRV warheads on each missile n. Then, as the product nP_K increases, that is, as missiles become more threatening to missile silos, the area of mutual deterrence shrinks, as

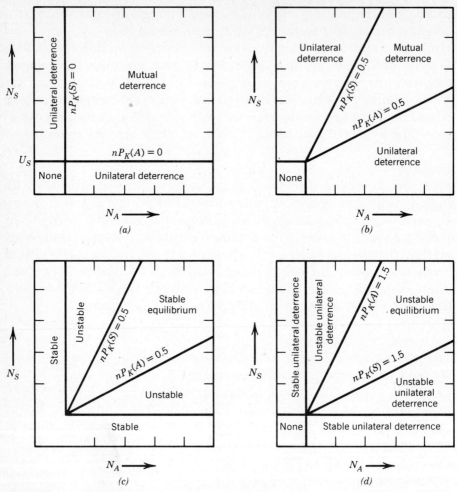

Figure 8.3 Deterrence diagrams. N_A and N_S are the number of missiles possessed by sides A and B, while U_A and U_S are the minimum deterrence requirements for sides A and B. Various kinds of deterrence and stabilities exist, depending on the balance between N_A and N_S. The parameter distinguishing these figures is the ability nP_K of a single ICBM to destroy a retaliatory second-strike missile in its silo. When a warhead is MIRVed with n warheads, each with a kill probability P_K, then nP_K may be larger than one, since that missile might destroy more than one silo. (After Legault and Lindsey, 1976.)

shown in Fig. 8.3(b). A point may be reached where the accuracy and number of reentry vehicles per ICBM become so large, as in Fig. 8.3(d), that an attack by either side can reduce the retaliatory second-strike capability of the opponent's missile forces below the minimum required for assured destruction. Then there is no area at all for mutual deterrence. Consider a case where both sides have 1000 superaccurate and totally reliable missiles with 10 warheads each. Either side could then kill all of the enemy's 1000 missiles with a surprise attack made up of 100 missiles with a total of 1000 warheads. After the surprise attack, the attacker could come out ahead with 900 missiles to none. And, of course, vice versa. In this case, whoever strikes first would win an overwhelming advantage in ICBMs. For mutual deterrence the number of warheads per missile, or their accuracy, should be small.

Stability

Deterrence diagrams can be used to discuss the stability or instability of various levels of the nuclear balance. There may be conditions under which it might be to the advantage of one side to attack the other if sufficiently provoked. These conditions represent instabilities in the nuclear balance.

Figure 8.3(c) shows a deterrence diagram for ICBM forces with a certain missile accuracy. For areas in which one side or the other has insufficient missiles to inflict unacceptable damage, there would be no inducement for either side to attack. The inferior side could not damage the opponent sufficiently to inflict unacceptable damage; the superior side would not be enticed into a surprise attack because it does not feel threatened. Such a balance exists between any nonnuclear nation and either of the superpowers; neither side has an incentive to launch a surprise attack. Another area of stability is the region of mutual deterrence. For that situation, no matter which nation strikes first, that nation would suffer unacceptable damage from the opponent's second strike.

Areas of unilateral deterrence, where the ICBM forces of both sides exceed the assured destruction threshold, are areas of instability. In those areas the superior country might be tempted during a tense situation to strike first and decrease the enemy forces below the level of assured destruction. In turn, the inferior country is aware of this possibility and might be tempted to carry out a surprise attack to avoid having its deterrent destroyed.

The previously described situation, where MIRVed missiles on both sides have such high accuracy that nP_K is greater than 1, is one of double or mutual instability. In that regime in Fig. 8.3(d), it might be to the advantage of either side to carry out a preemptive first strike, since whoever strikes first would reduce the retaliatory ability of the opponent's ICBMs below the threshold of unacceptable damage.

Antiballistic Missile Defenses

Such deterrence diagrams graphically illustrate the effects of antiballistic missiles systems, as shown in Fig. 8.4. If an ABM system is used to defend a city, some retaliatory second-strike missiles might not reach their targets. Hence, more missiles would have to survive a first strike

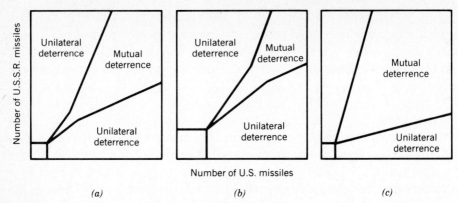

Figure 8.4 Different thresholds of minimal deterrence and zones for unilateral and mutual deterrence for (a) no ABM, (b) ABM defending cities, and (c) ABM defending ICBM silos. (After Legault and Lindsey, 1976.)

to maintain deterrence, to exhaust the ABM missile defenses. A city-oriented ABM system raises the threshold of minimally required missiles. This decreases the area of mutual deterrence as shown in Fig. 8.4(b). In contrast an ABM system that defends missile silos increases the area of mutual deterrence, as shown in Fig. 8.4(c), since missile site ABMs reduces the probability P_K that an attacking ICBM can destroy retaliatory silos.

The U.S.–USSR Balance

If one were to diagram the nuclear balance between the United States and the Soviet Union for ICBMs only, one would find that the area of mutual stable deterrence has been shrinking as MIRV accuracies have been increasing. For the ICBMs only, the present trend is toward double instability. At the moment an actual first-strike surprise attack would at best be able to target two RVs on each silo with perhaps 85% reliability. If an attack by the ICBMs listed in Table 8.2 on silos were carried out right now, and if it worked perfectly, then the Soviet Union could destroy perhaps 68% of all U.S. silos; the United States would only be able to target a maximum of 1076 silos with two ICBM warheads and, thus, could destroy only 45% of all Soviet silos.

Such deterrence diagrams, as is perhaps true for all calculations of the nuclear balance, are actually too rational to hold cleanly during crisis situations. Levels of acceptable damage are subjective and depend on circumstances; missile accuracies cannot be relied upon in a large-scale first strike and so on. Most important, an ICBM deterrence diagram would ignore the other strategic forces. For SLBMs mutual assured destruction now exists, since SLBM forces are presently invulnerable; hence, in a deterrence diagram that includes all nuclear forces, mutual stability would exist. If one part of the Triad is in the region of mutual stability because it is invulnerable, then the whole Triad of deterrents is stable.

In spite of their limitations, deterrence diagrams do indicate the effect on stability of various weapons developments. In particular, they make it clear that equality in weaponry does not necessarily guarantee peace; a state of mutual instability may increase the chances of war even if the armaments are equal.

COUNTERFORCE ATTACKS

For the time being mutual assured destruction seems to exist. Since MAD is a prerequisite for deterrence, one might expect then that both superpowers would accept the policy of deterrence. Yet both sides continue to discuss alternatives to deterrence, such as limited nuclear war and counterforce strikes. These strategies are feasible only if the damage from such wars is small enough to distinguish them from a full-scale nuclear war and if escalation to a full-scale nuclear war is not inevitable.

Soviet and U.S. Views of MAD

The Soviet Union accepts the fact that nuclear war would cause grievous damage to all participants. In 1979 Aleksandr Bovin, a political observer for *Izvestia*, stated that

> Can one consider a general nuclear-missile war as a normal, sensible means of pursuing some particular political aim? Obviously one cannot do this because the consequences of such a war would be a catastrophe for mankind, and in the current situation the one to risk making a first nuclear strike would inevitably be doomed to destruction by the forces available for a retaliatory strike. This is in fact what is called the balance of terror, and although this position is far from ideal . . . it does nonetheless exist. (As quoted in Leebaert, 1981, p. 96)

Many Soviet political leaders, including the late Soviet President Leonid Brezhnev have made almost identical arguments that any nuclear war would "spell annihilation for the aggressor himself." Based on extensive readings of Soviet literature, Leon Gouré concluded that

> There can be no doubt that Moscow is anxious to avoid nuclear war with the U.S. . . . Soviet spokesmen . . . consistently acknowledge the enormous damage that would result from such a war. . . . They contend that under current conditions its inception would be irrational in the extreme. (Gouré et al., 1974, pp. 8, 10)

Even when paying lip service to the politically grounded Clausewitzian thesis that war is a continuation of politics by forcible means, Soviet leaders and theoreticians agree that nuclear war is no longer an expedient usable instrument of policy. They do believe in deterrence on the nuclear level, and are always trying to enhance it. They view nuclear forces as a means to deter by threatening retaliatory punishment. Raymond L. Garthoff summarizes it as follows:

> both sides accept the basic premise that war is a matter of policy or political motivation; both sides also accept the fact that resort to nuclear war would not be expedient as a matter of policy. The underlying debate is whether war is recognized as so unpromising and dangerous that it can never occur. Such a question has profound implications for military requirements. Is a force dedicated to deterrence enough? And if war were to occur, is a war-waging capability needed to seek a pyrrhic "victory"? (Leebaert, 1981, p. 93)

The Soviet view of deterrence does go beyond reliance on the threat of a nuclear retaliatory second strike. The Soviets make military provisions for the failure of nuclear deterrence in order to increase the credibility of such deterrence. Gouré summarizes the Soviet view as saying that

> The better the Soviet armed forces are prepared to fight and win a nuclear war, the more effective they will also be as a deterrent to an attack on the Soviet Union; at the same time, the ability of Soviet forces to fight and win a nuclear war provides indispensable insurance against the failure of deterrence. Thus, Soviet statements tend on the one hand to laud the armed forces as effective guarantors of the security of the Soviet Union from nuclear attack, and on the other to warn persistently of the danger of nuclear war and of the necessity of being fully prepared to meet it. (Gouré et al., 1974, p. 8)

Garthoff agrees:

> Soviet military power, and the constant enhancement of its capability and readiness, is thus justified primarily for deterrence, as well as to wage a war if one should come despite Soviet efforts to prevent it. This view is consistently held by the Soviet military and political leaders. It is not accurate, as some Western commentators have done, to counterpose Soviet military interest in a "war-fighting" and hopefully "war-winning" posture to a "deterrent" one; the Soviets see the former capability as providing the most credible deterrent, as well as serving as a contingent resort in the event of war. (Leebaert, 1981, p. 95)

Within this framework of deterrence on multiple levels, the Soviet Union does not think in terms of an attack on purely civilian targets. Soviet plans include counterforce strikes, possibly preemptive first strikes against U.S. strategic and tactical military targets, once a war has become inevitable due to a U.S. threatened or actual attack. Such counterforce strikes would reduce the damage inflicted by the United States on the Soviet Union.

> Soviet comment consistently emphasizes the necessity of being able to face an enemy with an ability to "frustrate" or "disrupt" any attack, and makes clear that in Soviet thinking the only way in which this can be done is to have the capability to strike first, that is, a capability to launch a first counter-force nuclear strike which would seek not only to disarm an opponent but simultaneously to destroy his defense industry and major industrial complexes, as well as his administrative, military-political command and control, and vital communications and transportation centers. (Gouré et al., 1974, p. 5)

On the other hand, the Soviet Union does not think in terms of a limited nuclear war. It recognizes that nuclear escalation would be inevitable, that nuclear weapons will of course be a major component of any war between the nuclear powers.

> Soviet doctrine does not discuss the possibility of using nuclear weapons in a controlled, escalatory fashion or for war bargaining purposes (except possibly in terms of a residual nuclear force either withheld or newly produced in the course of the war), and Soviet spokesmen are scornful of such Western theories, which they claim are intended to allow the West and especially the U.S. the possibility of avoiding retribution and to establish rules which will facilitate the initiation of war. (Gouré et al., 1974, p. 17)

The position of the United States has been officially different, but tactically similar. The United States has accepted the existence and desirability of maintaining MAD and believes in the validity and usefulness of deterrence. U.S. policymakers accept that a full-scale nuclear war would lead to unacceptable damage for all participants. But U.S. political and military leaders have not accepted the notion that nuclear escalation is inevitable. The standard integrated operating plan (SIOP), the targeting plans for U.S. strategic Triad forces under President Carter's Presidential Directive #59 (PD-59), for example, includes flexibility for attacking tactical military or strategic civilian targets. Counterforce options to limit nuclear war are frequently discussed and proposed by U.S. secretaries of defense. Counterforce attacks are seen as a possibility. For example, tactical nuclear weapons are intended as the last line of defense for NATO in Europe—clearly an inevitable escalation to full-scale nuclear war would make such a policy as suicidal as a preemptive nuclear strike under the existence of assured retaliatory destruction.

The Counterforce Balance

The consequences of a limited counterforce strike will be examined in Chapters 9 and 12. But what is the balance of forces if the two superpowers were to engage in a flexible response type of war, if they were to exchange counterforce strikes aimed at each other's military targets? A scenario that has often been considered is that the Soviet Union carries out a limited nuclear attack on U.S. strategic arsenals. Then the United States might possibly be confronted with the choice of either retaliating by striking Soviet civilian targets for assured destruction— and be totally destroyed in return—or by striking back at Soviet military targets to minimize the consequences of a second Soviet large-scale strike.

For the second alternative scenario, some people have argued that the United States is now lagging so much behind the Soviet Union that it would be unacceptably inferior after such a first counterforce exchange. Paul H. Nitze (1976, p. 225) represents this viewpoint:

> It is a situation *after* attack, of course, that is most important. And here, since the targets remaining after the exchange would almost all be soft ones, missile accuracy and other refinements in the original postures no longer have the same significance. Surviving throw weight thus becomes an appropriate *total* measure of the residual capabilities on both sides.

The situation after a nuclear attack depends on the targeting strategies used by both sides. Sample calculations by the U.S. Department of Defense in 1980 of the nuclear balance left after a U.S.-USSR counterforce exchange are shown in Fig. 8.5. The calculations suggest that if no alert were called before the exchange the United States would have an advantage in warheads after such an exchange, whereas the USSR would have a megatonnage advantage. Conclusions about the balance after a counterforce exchange are uncertain. The targeting strategies are not predetermined, their success cannot be evaluated in advance, the problems of command and control may be very large. Even more uncertain is the reasonableness of such a counterforce strategy. It makes sense to plan for it only if escalation to a full-scale nuclear war were unlikely or if planning for it were to deter it from ever happening.

FUTURE CONCERNS

In thinking about the future of deterrence, stability, and the nuclear balance, a variety of questions present themselves. Some of these

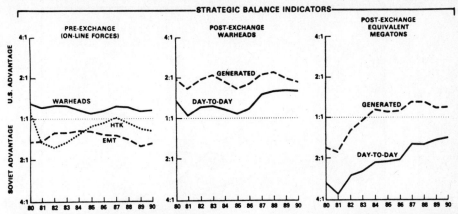

Figure 8.5 Strategic balance indicators. The nuclear balance left after a U.S.-USSR counterforce exchange as calculated by the DOD in 1979. The preexchange graph shows the ratio of strategic forces in terms of warheads, equivalent megatonnage (EMT), and hard target kill capability K (HTK). The scenario is that the Soviet Union attacks the U.S. strategic forces and that the United States in return then attacks Soviet strategic forces. The postexchange graphs show the ratio of warheads and EMT in case of counterforce exchanges with no prior warning (day-to-day alert) and with strategic warning (generated alert), for example, during an escalating war in Europe.

relate to the nuclear balance itself. But many also relate to the problem of stability.

Arms Technologies

What will be the future of the arms balance? The SALT agreements described in Chapter 16 aim to control the growth of strategic arms. Indeed, they have placed some quantitative limits on the numbers and sizes of the strategic arms of the United States and the USSR. But SALT has had only limited success in controlling qualitative improvements; consequently, the concern with the increasing ICBM vulnerability shown in Fig. 8.6 will continue to grow. There is considerable uncertainty in the exact levels of missile vulnerability, but most probably the vulnerability will continue to get worse. Whether the vulnerability of one leg of the Triad disturbs the existence of MAD is another question.

Nuclear Decision Making

In the nuclear arena the concern is not only about relative force strengths, but also about stability. Who will decide under what circumstances nuclear forces will be used?

In the United States the president makes that decision. While he is not on his own in the sense that Congress must approve any declaration of war, under the War-Powers Resolution of 1973 the president

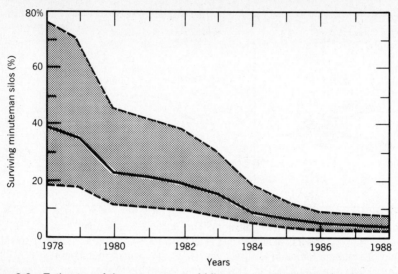

Figure 8.6 Estimates of the percentage of Minuteman missile silos surviving a Soviet surprise attack. The solid line represents best estimates from the DOD; the dashed lines represent the DOD 90% confidence levels. The uncertainties are caused by imprecise knowledge of Soviet missile accuracies, yields, and reliabilities. The calculations of page 208 estimate a survival rate of about 32% in 1983, in reasonable agreement with this figure. *(Department of Defense Annual Report, Fiscal Year 1980.)*

can engage in hostilities in an emergency for as long as 60 days without congressional approval. Since any escalation from a major conventional war to a nuclear war is likely to happen rapidly, the president can initiate a nuclear exchange without obtaining approval from anyone. He is in complete control of the nuclear forces.

One could imagine an alternative policy, a declaration that the United States will engage in "no first use of nuclear weapons," with the requirement that any escalation to first nuclear use would require congressional approval. Such a policy might enhance stability because it would remove one element of uncertainty that might lead to an escalation of a conventional war to a nuclear war. If a single individual could no longer trigger a nuclear war, then the value to the Soviet Union of a preemptive nuclear strike might be reduced. Such a renunciation of a first nuclear use would interfere with the NATO strategy of deterring a Soviet conventional attack in Europe with the threat of nuclear weapons. A renunciation of the first use of nuclear weapons would likely require that NATO strategy be changed, for example, by greatly expanding conventional armaments in Europe. This has so far been politically unacceptable.

Launch on Warning

Another issue that bears on nuclear stability is the sensitivity of the retaliatory trigger. Under what circumstances will one of the superpowers launch an unrecallable missile strike? When international tensions rise, U.S. nuclear forces are placed on alert; this increases the survivability of the bomber force. The ICBM forces also could be made more survivable if they were no longer in their silos when those are attacked. This could be done by adopting the policy of "launch on warning," the launching of ICBMs on the first indication that an attack is underway. ICBM launch procedures take less than a minute; the 30-min intercontinental flight time of attacking missiles provide sufficient time to empty the silos. Such a policy would make the ICBM deterrent invulnerable and thereby would strengthen MAD.

Such a "launch on warning" procedure, however, would be risky. In the past, flocks of birds have been interpreted as possible incoming Soviet missiles, and improper computer tapes have accidentally simulated a Soviet attack. Once an ICBM is launched, it cannot be recalled; an ICBM launch would be an instant, irreversible start of a nuclear war.

The U.S. policy has been to be able to wait out a Soviet attack until it is confirmed by actual strikes. Only then would a decision be made to retaliate by the launching of ICBMs. In this policy the retaliatory deterrent must be safe even against a surprise first attack. But with the increasing vulnerability of the ICBMs in their silos, this policy might well be reconsidered.

Multiple Actors

Nuclear proliferation destabilizes nuclear deterrence (see Chapter 14). The possibility of playing off other major powers such as China against the Soviet Union may help in some political situations. However, when these powers have nuclear weapons, the usage of MAD to achieve stability becomes more complicated and difficult. If a nuclear attack were to take place in a multinational MAD situation, one would first have to determine who is the attacker. One would have to decide the level of the retaliatory strike. The question arises whether one should involve the other nuclear powers, either by inviting them to also retaliate or by launching preemptive first strikes against them. Under such circumstances it is unclear what forces might be sufficient for a MAD strategy. As nuclear proliferation spreads, these questions are likely to become more and more difficult and critical.

CONCLUSIONS

The policy of deterrence through mutual assured destruction is not universally accepted. At present, it appears to operate insofar as both the United States and the Soviet Union agree the consequences of a full-scale nuclear war would be devastating. In the sense of MAD, there is nuclear balance between the two superpowers.

However, some on both sides think about nuclear superiority, at least for limited counterforce strikes. Some would argue that a counterforce capability and MAD may be mutually exclusive, that developing the missile accuracy required for counterforce strikes to some extent threatens the deterrent required for MAD. In the sense of MAD, nuclear superiority is destabilizing: some see the chances of a nuclear war increasing whenever the consequences of such a war are reduced by counterforce capabilities, city-defending ABMs, and civil defense measures.

References

Feld, B. T., and K. Tsipis. "Land-Based Intercontinental Ballistic Missiles." *Scientific American*, Vol. 241, no. 5 (November 1979), pp. 50–61.

Gouré, L., F. D. Kohler, and M. L. Harvey. *The Role of Nuclear Forces in Current Soviet Strategy*. Coral Gables, Fla.: Center for Advanced International Studies, University of Miami, 1974.

Leebaert, D., ed. *Soviet Military Thinking*. London: George Allen & Unwin, 1981.

Legault, A., and G. Lindsey. *The Dynamics of the Nuclear Balance*, rev. ed. Ithaca, N.Y.: Cornell University Press, 1976.

Nitze, P. H. "Assuring Strategic Stability in an Era of Detente." *Foreign Affairs*, Vol. 54, no. 2 (January 1976), pp. 207–232.

Tsipis, K. "Physics and Calculus of Countercity and Counterforce Nuclear Attacks." *Science*, Vol. 187 (1975), pp. 393–397.

———. "Minuteman Vulnerability." *Science*, Vol. 203 (1979), p. 510

———. "How to Calculate the Kill Probability of a Silo." In *Physics, Technology and the Nuclear Arms Race*, D. Hafemeister and D. Schroeer, eds. pp. 353–356. New York: American Institute of Physics Conference Proceedings #104, 1983.

PART
3

ALTERNATIVES TO NUCLEAR DETERRENCE

At present nuclear weapons are designed primarily to deter nuclear war by threatening mutual assured destruction (MAD). The existence of MAD, it is hoped, will ensure that no nation will use nuclear weapons because of the certain knowledge of their own destruction through retaliation. Unfortunately, MAD cannot promise a situation that will be stable in the long term.

One analogy to MAD has been the image of two scorpions in a glass jar, each afraid to strike the other because they are both sure to die after an attack by either "partner" in the jar. This image is hardly reassuring when one worries about the long-term survival of nuclear civilization. Another image is that of overkill: the presently stockpiled nuclear explosive yield is equivalent to 10 tons of TNT for every person on earth. Can such an unstable deterrence situation be kept under control to avoid the outbreak of nuclear war by accident or irrationality?

No matter how unappealing mutual assured destruction may be, it cannot be abolished unless an alternative is found for it. The next four chapters explore some possible alternatives to deterrence by the threat of MAD. Defenses against strategic nuclear weapons might be developed: (1) Civil defense would be a passive defensive system. (2) An antiballistic missile defense system would be an active defense, whether made up of interceptor missiles, lasers, or particle-beam weapons. (3) Chemical and biological warfare weapons have existed for many years without being used. One could imagine deterrence through CBW weapons. (4) Under the umbrella of nuclear deterrence, smaller-scale wars as in Vietnam are still being fought. How do such wars connect to the nuclear situation? Might MAD be avoided by strictly limiting the use of tactical nuclear weapons, to avoid escalation to the strategic level?

The technological feasibility of each alternative policy must be analyzed. Their economics ought to be more cost effective than MAD. One must consider for each alternative whether technological surprises are less likely, whether escalation can more readily be monitored, and whether the technologies can proliferate. Ultimately, any alternative to MAD must be able to provide more short- and long-term stability at a bearable price.

The costs to civilizaton of each policy alternative must be evaluated. Some of them, such as full-scale civil defense, might impose social costs through increased governmental controls as in building codes and evacuation rehearsals. Some alternatives might require an impossible future political rigidity if small wars of liberation are suppressed. New ethical components may enter into the analysis; some forms of biological warfare could produce genetic modifications possibly leading to changes in the human gene pool. Careful detailed analyses of all policy alternatives to MAD are necessary, comparing their probabilities and consequences with the likelihood and the local and global consequences of full-scale nuclear war.

CHAPTER
9

Civil Defense

Everybody's going to make it if there are enough shovels to go around. . . . Dig a hole, cover it with a couple of doors and then throw three feet of dirt on top. It's the dirt that does it.

Thomas K. Jones, Deputy Undersecretary of Defense, 1982

qualified Russian observers concede that Russian civil defense is a phony, a Potemkin village.

Admiral Noel Gayler (Ret.), 1982

Standard military wisdom says that defense is easier than offense. In conventional warfare, one often hears the estimate that a successful attacking force must be at least three times as strong as the defending force. If this is so, why should one not develop defenses against strategic nuclear forces? During World War II, defenses were sometimes quite successful against strategic bombing. At times the losses to Allied bomber forces were staggering; overwhelming air superiority was needed to overcome air defenses. The passive defenses of air-raid shelters kept civilian casualties in most bombing raids low enough to prevent strategic bombing from becoming an unqualified success. Similarly, the offensive Axis submarine forces were decimated by defensive antisubmarine forces once detection systems became sophisticated enough. These experiences raise the question whether one might not circumvent mutual assured destruction (MAD) by defending civilian populations. The introductory quotes represent opposite points of view of the efficiency of air defense.

Defenses against nuclear attacks can be developed. Both the United States and the Soviet Union have at various times promoted civil defense efforts. The Soviet Union has an extensive air defense (antibomber) system. Both sides work to improve antisubmarine warfare. And both sides have developed antiballistic missile (ABM) **219** systems, although they are limited by treaties in their deployment. Civil defense and the ABM are two specific defenses to bypass the MAD of deterrence. Civil defense is a passive defense of civilians. The ABM was originally conceived to actively defend cities. The status of these defenses will be considered here: Are they feasible? And are they desirable? This chapter will focus on passive civil defense.

Civil defense was actively promoted in the United States in the early 1960s. Thereafter, its importance in U.S. planning receded for over a decade. In 1976 civil defense against strategic nuclear attack was resurrected as a potential military policy. Thomas K. Jones, then an employee of the Boeing Aerospace Company and a former member of the U.S. SALT negotiating staff, testified before Congress that the Soviet Union was expanding its civil defense effort at a threatening rate (see e.g., Shapley, 1976). He reported that under some conceivable circumstances, that effort might allow the Soviet Union to reduce its casualties in an all-out nuclear war to 2% of its population and to recover in its industrial effort to the prewar level within two to four years. He argued that this damage level would be far below that required for MAD, as it would be less drastic than the damage the Soviet Union suffered during World War II. Such effective civil defense would upset deterrence. The Soviet Union might then be able to apply nuclear blackmail by threatening a nuclear first strike. To counteract this possibility, either some U.S. civil defense or increased offensive spending might be needed.

The projections made by Jones about the efficacy of civil defense are generally seen as being extremely optimistic. Nonetheless, many debates have been carried on about civil defense ever since. The civil defense effort of the Soviet Union is thought by some to be a major program. Civil defense could save some lives in a nuclear war; some argue that civil defense could make a significant difference to the outcome of a nuclear war. Hence it must be taken into account in strategic planning; perhaps civil defense ought to be either limited by treaty or else undertaken? This chapter will summarize the history of civil defense, analyze its feasibility, and discuss its desirability.

HISTORY OF NUCLEAR CIVIL DEFENSE

During World War II, two rather different perceptions of strategic bombing developed. The Soviet Union was attacked and experienced the benefits of civil defense. In contrast, the United States carried out extensive strategic bombing and experienced its benefits. The effects of these experiences have survived to today: the United States still places reliance on bombers as one leg of its strategic Triad, and the Soviet Union still is interested in civil defense.

The Soviet Union was the first to try to develop some antinuclear civil defense, since until the middle 1950s only the United States could deliver nuclear weapons onto Soviet cities. That defensive effort continued after Soviet long-range missiles became operational; the Soviet Union has continued to operate a civil defense program at a level of perhaps $1 billion per year. The USSR civil defense program appears to have been somewhat revitalized after 1972.

The American civil defense program reached its high point during the early 1960s when the Berlin and Cuba crises coupled with the perceived missile gap to promote a great defense effort. The desire was for a bomb shelter in every backyard; many public buildings were equipped as fallout shelters with food and medical supplies; some highways were designated as city evacuation arteries; and an emergency radio network was developed. As the U.S. missile force clearly became much larger than the Soviet ICBM arsenal, civil defense decreased in importance in the later 1960s. Since then the U.S. civil preparedness program has cost perhaps $300 million per year, compared with military budgets of a hundred billion dollars; about $100 million of this sum has been allocated specifically to military civil defense against nuclear attacks. The Reagan administration has shown some inclination to increase U.S. civil defense efforts. But on the whole the United States has done very little toward defense since it gave up its efforts to deploy an ABM system.

THE FEASIBILITY OF CIVIL DEFENSE

Civil defense is the protection of the nonmilitary aspects of a country from an attack, plus preparations for the nation's recovery after an attack. It can include the building of blast and fallout shelters, the stockpiling of critical supplies such as food and medicine, the dispersal and protection of industry, the education and training of the population toward the eventuality of a nuclear attack, and the dispersal of the urban population.

A civil defense effort intended to protect against a small nuclear attack by The People's Republic of China or the fallout from a counterforce strike might have a different configuration than one designed to protect against a full-scale nuclear war. The expected warning time of an impending attack would affect the nature of the civil defense effort. The ultimate objective of the civil defense would have to be considered in designing it: Is it to protect the war-making capability, to ensure the survival of civilization, or to prevent the occurrence of nuclear war?

Generally, civil defense is discussed as an alternative to deterrence by mutual assured destruction in the context of a U.S.-USSR full-scale nuclear confrontation. Such civil defense will be the focus of this chapter. It is argued by some that a small civil defense effort could make a significant difference under some specific nuclear war scenarios. Are some types of limited nuclear wars sufficiently more likely to warrant developing very specific protective measures?

A Soviet counterforce attack against U.S. missile silos would endanger civilians primarily through fallout effects. Then a civil defense program restricted to fallout shelters might be the most useful defensive measure. However, if such a counterforce attack is likely to aim also at militarily important industrial targets in major cities, then protection against blast effects could not be neglected. In the latter case, civil defense would have to be developed as though any future war would at best be a scaled-down version of a full-scale nuclear war. Then the number of lives saved by civil defense would be proportional to the number of people at risk in the attack, to the level of protection developed. Some experts, including Eugene P. Wigner (1969), Leon Gouré (1979), and Arthur A. Broyles (1976), not only feel that civil defense is worthwhile even at a low level but cite Soviet and some European civil defense programs as proof for their arguments.

To be a viable alternative to MAD, the technical objective of an American civil defense effort would have to be quite ambitious. Ideally, it should help both in a surprise attack and in an attack after days of rising confrontations. It should reduce the civilian casualties from the expected level for an all-out Soviet attack of 100 million to an "acceptable" level of a small percentage of the civilian population. Both the civilian economy and the military industries should survive at a level where no essential items are in unacceptably short supply. As far as possible, the existing way of life should survive basically intact. On a political level, such a civil defense effort should be cost effective as compared with alternative uses for the money. Finally, civil defense should not significantly increase the chances of a nuclear war—this may well be the most controversial point in any analysis. The following is a consideration of the effectiveness of various aspects of civil defense effort designed to meet these goals.

Blast Shelters

If a nuclear attack on industry or cities were to take place suddenly, with no prior increase in the level of alert, then an effective civil defense effort would require bomb shelters reachable by much of the urban population within a few minutes. The maximum warning time of a surprise attack might be 30 minutes for ICBMs coming over the North Pole. Only if bomb shelters are available near places of work and play and at home, and only if warnings could be communicated quickly, could civil defense work in the case of a surprise attack.

The persons to be protected by bomb shelters for a full-scale surprise attack would include the whole urban population, as many as 150 million persons each in the United States and the Soviet Union. These shelters would have to protect in the short term against blast, fires in the area, and prompt gamma radiation, and in the longer term against fallout.

Blast

How strong must shelters be to protect civilian populations against blast? Consider an attack on the United States limited to the minimal industrial retaliatory level of 200 EMT. Such an attack would cover 15,000 km^2 (6000 mi^2) with an overpressure of 5 psi. According to Figure 4.3, this would kill 30% of the U.S. population or about 50% of the Soviet population. What would be the effect if shelters with 100-psi resistance were available? Some 14% of that area, or 2100 km^2 (800 mi^2), would be covered with an overpressure of 100 psi. This would kill about 7% of the U.S. population or 20% of the USSR population. A program making 100-psi blast shelters available to all urban residents might save 50 million American or 75 million Soviet lives, reducing fatalities to 15 million or 50 million, respectively. Shelters protecting to less than 100 psi would be correspondingly less effective. Costs for such shelters were put at $300 and up per person in 1965. The lower figure was for expanding existing subway tunnels to hold one person per 1½ cubic meter (m^3) which is a floor space of 0.6 m · 0.9 m (2 feet · 3 feet) by 2.5 m (8 feet) high per person as shown in Fig. 9.1. This is to be compared with present construction costs for homes of at least $15 per 0.09 m^2 for an unfinished basement that offers relatively little shelter against blast effects. Assuming that the cost of true fallout shelters is $1000 per person ($500 plus inflation since 1965), the total cost of a full-scale blast shelter program would be $1000 · 150 million = $150 billion to reduce the number of blast victims to 15 million

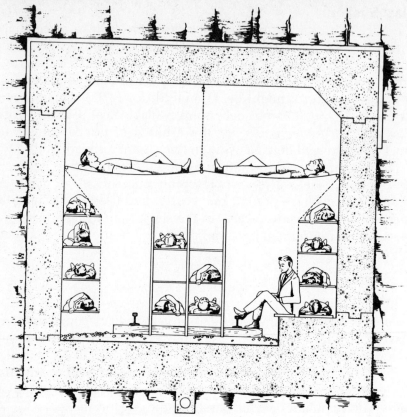

Figure 9.1 A subway tunnel equipped for emergency habitation. (Wigner, 1969, p. 215, photo used with permission.)

in a minimal Soviet attack. The Swiss are developing a full-scale shelter program with an annual per capita expenditure of $50 per year, or $1000 over 20 years.

How long would it take a population to reach these shelters?

> Assuming the warning was heard, understood, and believed, significant movement toward shelter would begin within approximately five minutes and would continue until all were under cover. The total movement time might be as long as an hour (high-rise building evacuation might require twenty to thirty minutes) in large and congested cities. (Wigner, 1969, p. 222)

The warning time of less than 30 min for a surprise attack seems hardly enough to allow the reaching of shelters, unless they are in very close proximity to everyone's workplace and home.

It has been generally accepted that the very large expenses of building bomb shelters occupiable for a long time, and the probable short available evacuation time, make a maximal civil defense impossible for the United States and the USSR. Hence, evacuation of the urban areas has more generally been the scenario under which protection is to be provided. The blast problems then are less severe. The Soviet civil defense program is based on a scenario in which rising tensions give a three-day warning period in which to evacuate the cities. The Soviets plan to build shelters out of timber and bound saplings (*fascines*) during this evacuation period. These shelters are primarily designed to protect against prompt radiation; their blast resistance may range between 7 and 28 psi. The construction of a shelter for 60 persons has been estimated to require 200 to 250 person-hours of work; if the proper material and organization is available, it could thus be built in one day by half the occupants.

Prompt Radiation

Thick layers of dirt make a good shield against the prompt high-energy gamma rays from a nuclear blast. A 0.3-m (1-foot) layer of earth would reduce the intensity of prompt gamma rays from a nuclear explosion by a factor of three, a thickness of 1½ m provides a protection factor of 300. According to Tables 2.4 and 2.5, for large hydrogen bombs, the prompt gamma radiation is not much of a threat compared with the danger of blast effects, since the intensity of the prompt radiation is greatly reduced by intervening air. Civil defense efforts that protect against the other bomb effects will most likely also provide sufficient protection against the prompt radiation.

Heat Radiation

Heat radiation is a danger even at very considerable distances from a nuclear explosion. Direct exposure leading to skin burns can be held to a minimum by taking prompt cover behind opaque objects. The secondary danger from fires started by the heat is harder to reduce. Shelters need to be thermally insulated against such fires, particularly if they are in densely populated areas where conflagrations may occur. A proper urban shelter might need both its own oxygen supply and cooling system.

Air normally contains 0.04% carbon dioxide. In a sealed bomb shelter with 1½ m^3 of space per person, the CO_2 level would reach 4% in about 2 hr and 11% in about 6 hr. Consider that 4% CO_2 leads to considerable discomfort such as labored breathing and possibly nausea, 11% can produce unconsciousness, and a few hours at 30% can result in death. CO_2 must be removed from the shelter or fresh air must be added.

If the occupants of the shelter each radiate 100 w of heat, then the temperature would rise to 33°C (92°F) and 76% relative humidity in 4 to 8 min. These are dangerous levels. Therefore, some cooling might be needed, for urban shelters as much as 100 w per person. The fires could last several days, so this sheltering would have to be fairly long term. Gas masks, portable oxygen supplies, and firefighter outfits would be desirable equipment for urban shelters if they are to be evacuated quickly.

Fallout

The most long-term protection problem for civil defense will be against fallout, which is likely to cover a large area, as was shown in Table 2.4. The minimal problem is illustrated by Fig. 9.2, which shows the fallout resulting from a limited Soviet nuclear attack (a counterforce strike) on U.S. missile silos. The fallout from a typical 1-Mt bomb, giving a total dose of 500 rem, may cover 2000 km^2 (800 mi^2). Figure 9.2 shows the fallout covering about 500 km^2 per warhead to a level leading to a dose of 1350 rem outside or 450 rem inside homes above ground. For a higher wind velocity in the upper atmosphere, this value could easily be 750 km^2. In this example, the fallout from the attack on the Whiteman missile base in Missouri could reach nearly to the coast, 1300 km away.

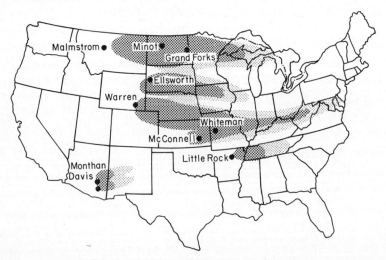

Figure 9.2 The fallout from a Soviet counterforce attack on all Titan-II and Minuteman ICBM bases, with two 1-Mt surface bursts per silo. The solid lines correspond to a 1350-rem outdoor exposure (or 450 rem indoors), and the dashed line indicates a 600-rem exposure outdoors. The attack is assumed to take place in winter, with typical west winds. (After Drell and Hippel, 1976.)

At the extreme, if the Soviet Union were to carry out a full-scale attack, optimally spacing its 8000-plus warheads and exploding them near the ground to produce maximum fallout, enough fallout could be produced to cover a total area of 500 km^2/warhead $\cdot$ 8000 warheads = 4 million km^2. The land area of the mainland United States is about 7.5 million km^2. Thus as much as 50% of the U.S. land area could be blanketed with enough fallout to give doses of 450 rem inside houses with a radiation protection factor of three. Basements that are fully underground provide a higher protection factor of 20 to 40, thus, within some of this area occupants of deep basements could survive. Obviously no attack of this kind is likely. But it illustrates how much fallout may be released—any attack would most likely include thousands of ground-level nuclear explosions aimed at missile silos and other hardened military targets. Hence large areas would have to be supplied with fallout shelters.

How long would people have to remain inside the shelter? Within 1 hr after a groundburst, about 60% of the fallout will be deposited locally. If 60% of the fission products from a 1-Mt H-bomb (50% fission, 50% fusion) were spread over 2000 km^2, the gamma-ray dose 1 hr, 10 hr, 100 hr, and 1000 hr after the explosion would be 2000 rem/hr, 125 rem/hr, 8 rem/hr, and 1 rem/hr 1 m above the ground. Figure 9.3 shows how the total dosage would be distributed over the time after the explosion. The first quarter of the total fallout dose occurs between the first and the fourth hour after the explosion, assuming that the 60% of the fallout does reach the ground 1 hr after the bomb explosion. The second quarter of the fallout dose is received between 4 hr and 17 hr after the explosion; and the third quarter of the fallout dose comes between 17 hr and 1 week (wk) after the explosion. The final quarter of the fallout dose stretches out beyond that 1-wk period.

This curve suggests that prolonging the stay in a fallout shelter beyond a week or so will not significantly reduce the total fallout dosage received unless it is extended to months. The remaining long-term fallout exposure must be reduced other than by sheltering; plans must be made for a later dispersal of the population or for decontamination.

Evacuation

To be the most useful, civil defense must include preattack evacuation of the cities; sufficient shelters are not likely ever to be available in urban areas. Both the U.S. and Soviet civil defense plans include the transport of populations out of urban areas.

A crude technical measure of evacuation capabilities might be the ability to move people. For the United States the capacity exists in automobiles; for the Soviet Union it is in buses and trains. The United

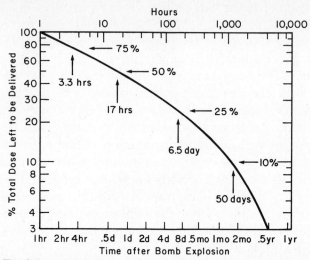

Figure 9.3 The fallout dosage left to be delivered after a nuclear bomb explosion as a function of the time after that explosion. The dose is expressed as a percentage of the total integrated fallout dose delivered beginning 1 hr after the blast. The total integrated fallout dose is equal to about 4.5 times the dose rate at 1 hr after the explosion. For example, if the rate at the 1-hr mark is 250 rem/hr, then the total integrated dose would be 1125 rem; anyone subjected fully to that fallout radiation would receive an exposure of 560 rem in the first 17 hr. (Based on Glasstone and Dolan, 1977, Figures 9.16a and 9.16b, pp. 392–393.)

States has 1 car for every 2 people. The bus system of the Soviet Union moves on the order of 50 million persons to and from work each day inside the cities. Intraurban trains and buses, however, move only about 1 million persons per day. There might be other means of emergency transportation, such as trucks and freight cars. The technical capacity for short-range evacuation may exist for both sides; longer-range interurban movement may be harder for the USSR.

The real question about evacuation is whether it can be organized under crisis circumstances. For this, one can look at rush-hour traffic in big cities. When the destinations and routes are known, very high densities of commuters can be handled over short distances in reasonable times. But destination plans must exist and must be made available to everyone in advance.

Industrial Protection
Civil defense should protect not only populations but also industry; otherwise, the postattack society may not be able to sustain the technological level of production needed to keep up a minimal civilization. If assured destruction is to be avoided, industrial protection must be enough to preserve better than 50% of all the major industries, and it must ensure that no critical industry suffers undue damage. Industry

can be protected in three ways. It can be dispersed in a long-term plan for plant construction; it can be hardened against the effects of nuclear weapons; or, in some cases, it can be temporarily dispersed and protected during crisis periods.

Long-term industrial dispersal has frequently been suggested in various countries; this seems desirable on other grounds as well, since concentrations of industry often present traffic, pollution, and energy-supply problems. But the economics of large-scale manufacture argue for industrial concentrations. Some geographic dispersal of industry is possible, particularly when new industries are establised to exploit new resources. But many industries have limits to how much large plants can be broken up or how far interlocking industries can be separated. The Soviet industrial relocation experience of World War II suggests that much could be done if it were deemed desirable.

Hardening of industry costs money. It may be possible to raise the blast resistance of some particularly vulnerable industries from a typical level of 3 psi toward 7 psi. The ideal protection would be placing industries in underground shelter. Sweden has done this with some of its industry. During World War II, some essential German plants were moved into mines, and 1.5 million m^2 of underground plants were constructed (a few times the size of the diffusion plant in Fig. 2.7). However, considering that not even U.S. nuclear power plants are underground—plants where an underground location would provide safety advantages even in peacetime—such large-scale relocations are not likely.

Postwar Resources

To sustain an industrial civilization, its economy must operate at some minimal level, its industry must produce necessities from mineral resources, and foodstuffs must be available. Because unpredictable shortages of various resources may occur, stockpiles ought to be preestablished. Obviously, shelters must have food, medical supplies, communications, and radiation detectors.

Longer-term shortages of vital agricultural and industrial resources must be anticipated. Items to be available include perhaps a year's supply of food for the whole population, particularly of grain. That would overcome the possible disruption of one planting season by fallout, fuel scarcities, or general disorder. Various raw materials would need to be stocked, including metals for industry and fuel for transportation and for those electric power plants that have not been destroyed. A detailed plan might be prepared in advance for postwar recovery and the needed stockpiles be accumulated in protected facilities.

THE SOVIET CIVIL DEFENSE EFFORT

Much of the recurrent U.S. interest in civil defense arises because the Soviet Union seems to be putting a considerable effort into it, an effort that is extensive compared with U.S. programs. Whether it comes close to meeting even the technical requirements for civil defense is a question.

In the late 1970s, the subject of Soviet civil defense once again became topical. Several new developments indicating increased Soviet interest in civil defense were reported (see, e.g., Shapley, 1976). A 0.7 million m^2 (½ mi · ½ mi) underground factory had been discovered "west of the Urals and east of Moscow," and new industrial plants were being established in dispersed locations away from urban centers. Population shelters were observed near apartment complexes in Moscow, Leningrad, and Kiev. About 40 underground grain silos were periodically being refilled. About 30,000 shelters were being built for military equipment, troops, and communications, including 75 shelters near Moscow and bunkers for the political leadership. The civil defense effort was being directed by an aggressive general, A. T. Altunin, who had a rank equal to the heads of the armed forces. It was argued that these items indicated a trend toward a comprehensive civil defense program.

Leon Gouré (1976) has for many years been keeping track of Russian literature about the Soviet civil defense effort. Based on his readings, he says that this effort has been growing since 1951, particularly since 1961, with another upsurge after 1972. The Soviets view civil defense as being critical for winning a nuclear war. The USSR now spends more than $1 billion per year on civil defense, a level it has been maintaining for two decades. Extensive evacuation plans exist that would remove nonessential personnel to distant rural locations while essential workers would commute back into the cities from 60 to 100 km away. In 1974 new blast shelter construction in cities was resumed after such construction had been judged too expensive in the late 1960s. Gouré (1976, p. 12) thinks that

> the cumulative construction of shelters . . . has resulted in a shelter capacity for a large fraction of the population. . . . The population is also being trained in the construction of hasty shelters, and according to Soviet plans, the entire population should be able to secure protection in either blast or fallout shelters within 72 hours of an announcement by the government that a "threatening situation" exists.

Extensive dispersal of industry is being practiced; it is claimed that since 1966, at least 60% of all new industrial plants are being located in small towns. There are "clear indications" of hardening of industrial plants. About a year's war reserve of grain is stored.

Do these reported efforts meet the technical requirements for civil defense just outlined? The present shelter program is not sufficient for protection against a war with only a 15-min warning without evacuation. If the 30,000 shelters indeed exist and can protect occupants against a major blast or fallout, they might help perhaps 200 people per shelter survive a nuclear attack. That would mean a maximum of 6 million people might be protected out of the 150 million urbanites vulnerable to attack. Subways might provide some additional shelters. Gouré estimates that the Moscow subway might protect as many as 1 million inhabitants against blast and fallout; this is 15% of the Moscow population. If the price for complete fallout shelters is indeed $1000 per person, the required $150 billion cost of a complete shelter program has not been available in the USSR in the past, with its total annual civil defense budget averaging about $4 per year per person over the past 20 years.

Consequently, the Soviet planners count on having several days' warning of an impending attack. During that time they propose to evacuate their nonworking urban population 150 km or more into the countryside. Essential workers are to be relocated perhaps 50 km from the cities. The interurban railway system, which normally moves 1 million people a day, supplemented by some of the intraurban buses, is to disperse 150 million people over distances of several hundred kilometers each and then commute a substantial work force of perhaps 30 million each day over 100 km back into the cities. Part of the plan is to have as many as 20% of the urban residents evacuate the cities on foot. Evacuation plans have been drawn up, but large-scale realistic evacuation practices have never taken place.

Education on civil defense does take place in the schools. Perhaps as much as 50 hr is devoted to this subject during the first grades. College students and industrial workers may get another 50 hr of civil defense training. The civil defense personnel who would supervise the evacuation and protection activities are supposed to undergo an additional 20-hr training course. The evacuees are to build their own fallout shelters in the countryside. Large-scale building exercises and realistic studies of the survivability of such shelters have not been carried out. In the frozen winter and the muddy spring, self-built shelters might be impossible to erect in some areas. The long-term danger of fallout would depend on the U.S. targeting plans.

Thomas K. Jones, now Deputy Undersecretary of Defense, has argued that Soviet industry can survive a full-scale nuclear war. In his view, adapted from that of Herman Kahn (1959), recovery basically depends on the number of workers available, so that if the population survives, industry can be rebuilt.

Figure 9.4 shows his projections for postwar recovery for various levels of population survival. For example, if most of the population survives and 50% of the industry is destroyed, then, he claims, within 2½ yr industrial production would be back to the prewar level. If all industry were destroyed and 50% of the work force (as well as 50% of the nonworking population) were killed, the curves of Fig. 9.4 suggest that within 15 yr the prewar GNP would be reached, doubling the prewar GNP per capita.

During World War II the Soviet Union lost or relocated 66% of the industrial production of the occupied territories making up 33% of the gross output of industry. Thus, perhaps 20% of Soviet industry was destroyed. Soviet casualties during the war were perhaps 20 million, or 10% of the population. Figure 9.4 would have predicted a 3-yr recovery period; in fact, the Soviet GNP reached prewar levels in 1951—6 yr after the end of the war. But it is hard to believe that after a nuclear attack, a prewar GNP could be reached in 5 to 7 yr if most of the Soviet population were to survive while most of its industry were destroyed.

Jones argued that much industrial equipment could be preserved if several days of advance warning are available. Many industrial machines can be surrounded by sandbags to achieve blast resistance up to 80 psi. Packing equipment in plastic foam could further increase

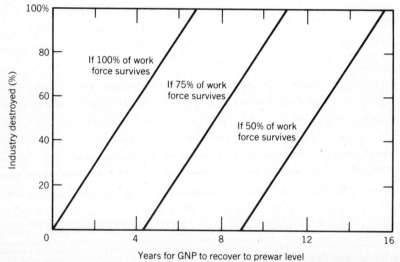

Figure 9.4 Estimates by T. K. Jones of postwar recovery periods of the Soviet Union's industry following a nuclear war in the 1985 time period. (Boeing Aerospace Co., "Industrial Survival and Recovery after Nuclear Attack," Report to the Joint Congressional Committee on Defense Production, November 17, 1976.)

that protection factor. He estimated that for an expenditure of $200–300 million, preparations could be made for protection to 40–80 psi, and for $2–3 billion, protection to 200–300 psi could be planned. The industry would have to be shut down to achieve that protection level, and in the long run it would have to be evacuated.

Could the Soviet civil defense effort produce survival of that nation as a social entity following a full-scale nuclear war? At present, the money invested in civil defense ($4/yr per capita) is perhaps 10 times that spent by the United States on antinuclear civil defense, is comparable to that spent by Sweden, and is one-twelfth that spent by Switzerland, which allocates $50/yr per capita. These sums are small compared with the $150 billion required for large-scale bomb shelters; similar large sums would be needed to harden or relocate existing industry. Evacuation would be cheaper, but it has not been practiced; the building of millions of expedient bomb shelters in a few days has not been attempted. Food and resource storage may or may not be sufficient; the Soviet Union now imports many millions of tons of wheat each year to make up for its own crop failures. The industrial recovery rates projected by Jones are thought by most experts to be very high.

THE DESIRABILITY OF CIVIL DEFENSE

If the USSR civil defense effort has not achieved a level affecting the existence of mutual assured destruction, the much smaller U.S. effort is unlikely to be more successful. Civil defense seemingly could be useful: evacuation and shelters would save some lives in case a nuclear war begins to break out; industrial hardening and resource storage could somewhat speed postwar industrial recovery. In a strictly technical sense, one would need to make a cost-benefit calculation to estimate whether civil defense expenditures would be worthwhile. However, an equally important question is whether civil defense is in fact desirable. The primary objective of the superpowers has so far been to rely on deterrence to avoid a nuclear war. Might the existence of civil defense become a self-fulfilling prophecy by increasing the probability of a nuclear war? Or might civil defense add credibility to the nuclear deterrent by giving some choices beyond mutual nuclear suicide? Within the deterrence framework, civil defense is harmful; Figure 8.4 argues that since civilian populations are hostages in mutual assured destruction, significant protection for them is destabilizing by threatening the existence of MAD, just as does a city-oriented ABM system.

To maintain MAD, any significant civil defense effort ought to be countered by an increase in the second-strike force. These forces might be used to destroy transportation lines, dispersed industries, and resource stockpiles. Some nuclear warheads might be redesigned to increase the fallout to overcome the expedient shelters. One must ask whether that increased second-strike expenditure by the "offense" would cost more or less than that spent on the civil defense effort. One might expect that additional warheads would be less expensive than civil defense; people, industry, and a technological society are relatively immobile and fragile.

Civil defense offers some attraction for the strategies of tactical nuclear wars, counterforce strikes, and flexible response. If the civilian population could be protected from nuclear attack, then the ability and willingness to fight lower-level nuclear wars might be more credible. The NATO strategy of using tactical nuclear weapons to halt a Soviet advance in Germany might seem more reasonable if Germany were to have an extensive civil defense effort. The country with the largest civil defense budget, Switzerland, relies on a purely defensive posture to discourage attacks, it has no nuclear weapons—or even a conventional offensive capability. Civil defense makes some sense for Switzerland. For the superpowers, it is not clear whether the increased capability to survive a limited tactical nuclear war via civil defense is worth the loss in stability. A true civil defense capability might encourage a preemptive first strike. If the defense plans require a 3-day evacuation, then this could exert pressure never to allow that much time to pass between the beginning of a crisis and the use of nuclear weapons.

The disturbing aspect of the Soviet civil defense effort is not so much its existence at the present level; it does not now assure sufficient protection to a significant fraction of the Soviet population. What is disturbing about the Soviet civil defense effort is its possible growth. Historically, the Soviet Union has always had some civil defense, dating back at least to World War II. In the last half of the 1960s, the Soviet Union seemingly accepted the existence of mutually assured destruction. The fear is that this acceptance of MAD might now be weakening. The evidence that Soviet civil defense is now significantly increasing is not overwhelming, although it has perhaps been too much ignored in intelligence circles. Very active, ambitious generals have been placed in charge of civil defense; this may be the source of the new impetus. But that explanation begs the question; the fact that such ambitious persons are placed in charge suggests that the Soviet government is interested in civil defense.

A second explanation is that with the cancellation of the ABM systems, institutional pressures forced the transfer of those funds into equivalent defensive activities (i.e., into the civil defense program). This explanation too raises the question of whether the Soviets' belief in any form of defense means that they no longer accept the existence of MAD. From the discussions in Chapter 8, it appears that the Soviet civil defense effort is part of its ambivalence in accepting the unacceptable destructiveness of nuclear war while at the same time wanting to come better out of one if it were forced on them.

The United States might respond to the Soviet civil defense program by building up its own effort. That might, however, produce a parallel expansion in the second-strike forces, with no net gain for greatly increased at great financial expenses. On the strategic level, civil defense is destabilizing. It is not now an alternative to MAD.

References

Broyles, A. A., E. P. Wigner, and S. D. Drell. "Civil Defense in Limited War—A Debate," *Physics Today*, Vol. 29, no. 4 (April 1976), pp. 44–57.

Drell, S. D., and F. von Hippel. "Limited Nuclear War." *Scientific American*, Vol. 235, no. 5 (November 1976), pp. 27–37.

Gouré, L. *War Survival in Soviet Strategy: USSR Civil Defense.* Coral Gables, Fla.: Center for Advanced International Studies, University of Miami, 1976. Professor Gouré has read vast numbers of Soviet sources that he interprets as demonstrating a strong and growing Soviet civil defense effort.

Kahn, H. *Thinking the Unthinkable.* Princeton, N.J.: Princeton University Press, 1959.

Shapley, D. "Soviet Civil Defense: Insiders Argue Whether Strategic Balance Is Shaken." *Science*, Vol. 194 (1976), pp. 1141–1145. The testimony of Thomas K. Jones before the Congressional Joint Committee on Defense Production on the new Soviet civil defense efforts, and the reactions from various sides to this testimony.

Wigner, E. P., ed. *Survival and the Bomb: Methods of Civil Defense.* Bloomington: Indiana University Press, 1969. This collection of essays summarizes some of the more pertinent aspects of civil defense.

CHAPTER
10

Ballistic Missile Defense

[We need] a comprehensive and intensive effort to define a long-term research and development program . . . on measures that are defensive . . . [to intercept and destroy Soviet missiles] before they reach our own soil or that of our allies.

President Ronald Reagan, 1983

it's really a declaration of a new arms race.

Jerome Wiesner, former presidential science advisor, 1983

it won't work.

Richard Garwin, science advisor, 1983

On August 6, 1969 Vice President Spiro Agnew cast a tie-breaking vote in the U.S. Senate in favor of deploying an antiballistic missile (ABM) system. It was a vote for an active nuclear defense against missiles. Since then, the 1972 SALT I agreement and an addendum to it have restricted the deployment of the ABM to one site of 100 launchers each for the United States and the USSR. It is important to understand the reasons the ABM became an issue in 1969, why the vote in the Senate came to be so close, how the ABM came to be included in the SALT I agreement, and in what way the debate about the ABM relates to the MIRVing of missiles. The ABM story includes questions of technical feasibility, nuclear tactics, and economics. It goes to the heart of nuclear defense policy; the SALT I agreement limiting the ABM seemed to recognize the futility and expense of a nuclear defense when the capability for mutual assured destruction (MAD) exists.

The ABM of 1969 was designed to shoot down incoming enemy missiles, whether launched from submarines or from enemy territory. **236** One could try to prevent the launch of attacking missiles by destroying enemy missile silos with a preemptive counterforce first strike and by tracking and destroying enemy SLBM submarines. But these would be provocative defenses; the 1969 ABM was intended to defend without provocation.

The goal of destroying missiles in flight is currently being revitalized under the label ballistic missile defense (BMD). New generations of interceptor missiles and guidance radars are being planned. However, thoughts about BMD now go far beyond interceptor missiles, to considerations of steel curtains, swarm jets, and pellet defenses and of particle-beam and laser defenses deployed both on the ground and in earth orbit. Some of these weapons may be consistent with a continuing mutual assured destruction (e.g., if they are to defend the silos of retaliatory missiles). Some of the newer systems are, however, being thought of as possible total defenses against any nuclear attacks. If missiles could be reliably intercepted shortly after launch, such defenses could, for the first time, offer a potential real defense against nuclear weapons, conceivably removing both the need for and the continuing existence of mutual assured destruction.

The 1969 U.S. ABM system and the debate about its deployment will be described in this chapter. The history of that system illustrates how technical developments may make new weapons systems possible. The deployment debate about the 1969 ABM system considered the technical details of the system, but it also involved some quantitative cost-benefit analyses. Proposed BMD applications of the new technologies of particle beams and laser weapons will be discussed. The new technologies at the moment have limited technical feasibility. But they can also be analyzed in terms of their impact on the overall strategic and tactical nuclear situation.

THE ABM

The ABM system developed in the 1960s, partially deployed in the early 1970s, and placed under SALT I limitations in 1972 will be discussed here. It is an important system to consider, because some of its technical problems would characterize any BMD efforts.

History of the Safeguard ABM System

The history of the 1960s' ABM illustrates how technologies are promoted. Its ancestors included the radar detection systems for detecting possible Soviet bomber attacks after World War II; its missiles were derived from the Polaris solid-fuel technology; and its nuclear warheads were modifications of those carried in ICBMs. Specific development of an ABM was an offshoot of surface-to-air missile (SAM) defenses. In 1956 all offensive surface-launched missiles were assigned to the Air Force together with all area defense SAMs. The Army was given the job of point defenses using SAMs; it turned that role into ABM systems.

Antiballistic missile systems must fulfill five functions: (1) The enemy warhead has to be detected; (2) the reentry vehicle carrying the warhead has to be distinguished from the missile debris and from penetration aids such as decoys and chaff; (3) the path of the warhead has to be predicted into the future; (4) the interceptor missile has to be guided to the attacking reentry vehicle; and (5) the incoming warhead has to be destroyed in a verifiable way by the explosion of a nuclear warhead. Based on its experience with the Nike-Ajax nuclear antibomber defenses, the Army developed such a system, calling it Nike-Zeus. By 1957, 10–15% of the Army budget went for missile air defense; General James Gavin, who was in charge of the missile R&D effort, assured Congress that a fully effective air defense was attainable. In 1959 and 1960 the Army asked for a commitment by the president for early deployment of the system, with the estimated total costs of $5–15 billion to be spread over nine years.

The technologically oriented advisors to President Kennedy's new Secretary of Defense Robert McNamara were not particularly impressed with the usefulness and technical adequacy of the Nike-Zeus. Hence, while this system was well funded in R&D, it was not brought toward deployment. By 1963 the improved Nike-X ABM system was developed. Its improved radar and second missile for a two-layer defense were perfected to such an extent that by 1965 some of the ABM's opponents agreed that this ABM system could do on a limited scale what it was designed to do. But by this time McNamara was interested only in an ABM that could be essentially perfect. Early in his tenure he had been interested in damage limitation for a potential nuclear war, including civil defense; by 1965 he was committed to deterrence by mutual assured destruction. As was argued in Chapter 8, an imperfect ABM would result in instability by encouraging a preemptive first strike during a tense situation; only a nearly-perfect full-scale ABM might lead to a new stability of total safety from nuclear attack. Consider an enemy ABM screen that could intercept 100 missiles with 90% reliability and a missile force of 1000 missiles that is so vulnerable that in a first strike by the enemy only 100 retaliatory missiles would survive. Then of these 100 retaliatory missiles only 10 would penetrate the ABM screen to retaliate against that first strike. But if a preemptive strike with 1000 missiles were launched, 910 missiles would penetrate the ABM screen. A preemptive first strike would become a more attractive option.

In the middle 1960s the international situation created pressure toward building an ABM system. In 1964 the Soviet Union began work on its Galosh ABM system around Moscow, and in 1965 a possible Chinese nuclear threat began to worry some analysts. Gradually McNamara lost political power as a result of opposing the full-scale bombing of North Vietnam. The ABM system continued to be improved. The deployment of a small ABM system thus became a political compromise that was not too expensive and partially satisfied everyone. In 1967 a commitment was made to deploy the Nike-X in the Sentinel system to guard U.S. cities primarily from a possible small-scale nuclear missile attack by the People's Republic of China. With the 1968 presidential election coming up, McNamara approved the deployment of what some called a "Republican-oriented" ABM.

The ABM System

The Missiles

The ABM system proposed in the late 1960s was a two-layer system, consisting of Sprint and Spartan missiles armed with nuclear warheads, a parameter acquisition radar (PAR), and a missile site radar (MSR) (Fig. 10.1). The Spartan missile was to be the first line of defense. It was to be launched when the PAR first detected the incoming enemy reentry vehicles (RVs) up to 4000 km (or 10 minutes) away. The Spartan was to be guided to the interception by the shorter-ranged but more accurate MSR. The three-stage, solid-fueled Spartan was to intercept the incoming RV above the atmosphere as far away as

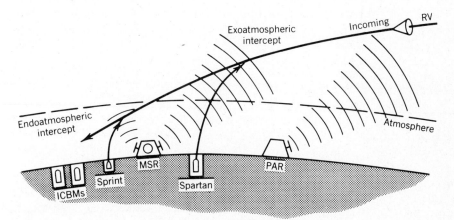

Figure 10.1 A two-layer ABM defense system like the 1969 Safeguard concept with long-range and short-range missiles and with long-range perimeter acquisition radar and short-range missile site radar.

600 km. Since blast would not be effective with no air to transmit a shock wave, x rays and neutrons from a megaton thermonuclear explosion would destroy the RV. Those incoming RVs that escaped the Spartan barrage would be attacked by the Sprint missile. This two-stage, solid-fueled rocket had tremendous acceleration so that it could be launched after the surviving RVs had entered the atmosphere and still reach and destroy them. Since the interception would be at low altitudes, the nuclear weapon would explode in the atmosphere; not only x rays and neutrons but also blast effects could be used to destroy the reentry vehicle.

The Radar

Both the PAR and MSR radars consisted of multiphase arrays. They would not scan the sky mechanically but, rather, would electronically analyze the time differences of the arrival of radar signals at the separate components of the multiphase array to determine the direction of their arrival. This electronic scanning allows hardening the radar to resist overpressures of 20 psi rather than 2 psi for mechanical models. The PAR (Fig. 10.2) faced toward Soviet launch points, the MSR had multiple sides to scan in all directions.

The PAR and MSR combined with farms of Spartan and Sprint missiles to form a single defense unit. The Nekoma site near Grand Forks, North Dakota, housed the only U.S. ABM system ever built. The PAR and MSR together with 30 Spartans and 70 Sprints cost $5.5

Figure 10.2 An early warning Pave Paws phased-array radar similar to the perimeter acquisition radar of the Safeguard ABM system. Next to it is its power plant. (Photo courtesy U.S. Air Force.)

billion to build. It became operational in 1975 and was decommissioned soon thereafter.

The ABM Kill Interactions

Of the three types of emission from a nuclear explosion, only blast and prompt radiation can be useful for ABM kills. For kills above the atmosphere, only the prompt radiation of both x rays and neutrons can be used, with no air to transmit a blast shock wave.

X rays. The Spartan missile was to intercept the incoming reentry vehicle above the atmosphere. The prompt radiations then would not be absorbed by any air molecules and could travel unimpeded to the RV. The x rays from the explosion of a Sprint at sea level are reduced in intensity by a factor of two for every 170 m of air they have to traverse; above the atmosphere there is no absorption of such x rays.

The x rays from a 1-Mt nuclear warhead exploded about 1 km from an enemy RV could heat a top layer of 1 cm of the missile to a temperature of about 5000°C. The resulting vaporization of the missile skin would send a shock wave through the missile that might disable the warhead, particularly by destroying or detaching the protective shielding of the RV.

Neutrons. A nuclear explosion releases neutrons with large kinetic energies. These neutrons can disable the warhead in a reentry vehicle by damaging some of the semiconductor devices in the computerized guidance system or by causing some fissions inside the fissile bomb core located inside the nuclear warhead to melt the fissile core out of shape so that it could no longer be made critical. This neutron interaction can be used at long range outside the atmosphere. Thus a 1-Mt Spartan warhead of a standard design (fission-fusion-fission) could release enough neutrons to damage some computer components at a distance of 1 km (Hafemeister, 1973). The effectiveness of such intercepts can be increased by redesigning the nuclear explosive to have enhanced neutron radiation. As discussed in Chapter 12, enhanced radiation weapons (ERW) or "neutron bombs" have been designed in which the number of neutrons produced per explosive yield is larger by a factor of six than for a normal nuclear explosive and where the neutrons have seven times larger kinetic energies and hence travel much farther before being captured.

Such ERW warheads were designed for both the Spartan and Sprint missiles. An 1-Mt ERW warhead in the Spartan might have a kill radius up to 6 km, and a 2-kt warhead in the Sprint might destroy an RV up to 1 km away. An advantage of such ERW explosives is that there would be much less radioactive fallout.

Blast. The warhead on the Sprint missile was to explode inside the atmosphere. It would produce a blast wave to shake the incoming RV apart; to damage the RV the shock wave would have to produce accelerations of the RV on the order of 100 times that of gravity or more. A lesser shock wave might deflect the RV enough to cause it to miss its target. If shock is to be the primary kill interaction, the warhead would be designed for maximum blast and might consist of a pure fission bomb.

Ways of Overcoming the ABM

An ABM system might be negated in a variety of ways. The reentry vehicle and warhead could be hardened against the various kill interactions. A stronger structure for the RV would reduce the effects of a blast shock wave. The effect of x rays could be overcome by adding an ablative surface layer that would not transmit the shock of vaporization to the rest of the RV. The effect of neutrons could be reduced by shielding, say, with paraffin that absorbs neutrons well (see Chapters 2 and 12). This strengthening or shielding would increase the mass of the RV, which would have to be counterbalanced by a reduced payload; either fewer or smaller warheads could be carried by the ICBM.

Payload could also be traded for missile survival by modifying the flight path of the ICBM. As discussed in Chapter 6, the most efficient missile trajectory is one that takes the ICBM to an altitude of about 1300 km. In that trajectory the ICBM can be seen by a direct-line radar system at a distance of about 4000 km, giving about 10 min warning time for the ABM system to work. The ICBM could, however, also be put into an earth orbit for a fraction of its trajectory (Fig. 6.14 shows the trajectory for such a fractionally orbiting bombarding system). The FOBS missile is launched into an orbit 150 km above the earth's surface, and then near the target it is deflected downward. This is not only the fastest possible trajectory, but it also gives the least warning to the ABM defense. For the Safeguard ABM system, the PAR radar would have seen those low-flying FOBS ICBMs only 1400 km away, equivalent to a 3-min missile flight time. If a missile could somehow be put into an even lower orbit, this warning time could be further reduced; but at lower altitudes the atmosphere would slow down ballistic missiles, causing them to crash short of the target.

Reducing the warning time for the defense costs the offense some payload. An FOBS mode reduces the payload of a missile between 25% and 50%. It requires guidance and maneuvering capability at the end of the flight to slow down the warhead and aim it toward the target. Such a technology resembles that of MARV warheads.

It is probably most desirable for the offense to destroy or confuse the defensive ABM radar rather than attack the ABM missiles. The radar is probably the weakest link in the ABM system, both physically and electronically. ABM missile silos could be hardened to resist overpressures of 2000 psi, but the exposed radar is vulnerable to as little as 30 psi. In the Safeguard system, one PAR and one MSR were assigned to each group of 100 ABM missiles; it would be tempting to blind these radars quickly. A 1-Mt nuclear explosion gives a 30-psi overpressure at 1.6 km; this accuracy is now easily available for ICBM and SLBM warheads.

Even if the ABM radar cannot be destroyed, it might be confused. Penetration aids could give the ABM system such a large number of objects to analyze and destroy that its capabilities become saturated. The attacker might launch so many ICBMs with multiple warheads that insufficient ABM missiles could be deployed to intercept them all. Multiple reentry vehicles (MRV) and multiple, independently targetable, reentry vehicles (MIRV) in fact were developed initially mainly to exhaust ABM missile defenses. If each ICBM launch vehicle were to carry as many as 10 separate nuclear warheads, at least 10 defensive ABM missiles would be required to provide a defense against a single ICBM.

The radar and missiles might be further exhausted by fake warheads; these decoys might include fragments of the booster rockets, metallized balloons, small pieces of metal, and metal-wire chaff. These decoys must be made to resemble the reentry vehicle: the booster may be broken into pieces of the proper size, the metallic balloons could be blown up into the proper conical shape, and the chaff would be made up of fine metal wires cut to a length equal to about half the wavelength of the defensive radar so that thousands of these wires could form a cloud to hide the real warhead.

Most of these decoys can be distinguished from the warheads if a terminal defense can be carried out inside the atmosphere. In the atmosphere light balloons and chaff would be slowed by air resistance, while the heavier warheads and booster fragments would continue on. The booster fragments would fly in uneven trajectories because of their very asymmetric shapes. A short-range Sprint defense could then detect and destroy the reentry vehicles as they continue on a true ballistic trajectory. An active shoot-look-shoot tactic could be used to separate the chaff from the real RV. A nuclear warhead could be exploded by the defense among the decoys and real RVs. The heavier and stronger RVs would survive this blast; the radar could pick these out and guide the ABM missiles to them. These tactics could to some extent be negated by using more solid decoys, but in general decoys to overcome an ABM system reduce the payload and present technical problems that raise the costs of ICBMs.

Finally, the ABM radar may be hampered by blocking radar signals. Some of the penetration aids may carry electronic devices emitting radio signals to jam the defensive radar. Nuclear explosions can be used to reflect and absorb radar signals in the upper atmosphere. As shown in Fig. 10.3, two blackout effects predominate. The fireball from the explosion is ionized. These ions deflect and absorb radar signals. At an altitude of 50 km, a 1-Mt explosion will produce a fireball 10 km in diameter. A radar signal passing through this fireball would be attenuated by a factor of 10 on each passage. At altitudes above 100 km, blackouts may be produced lasting tens of minutes over areas of thousands of square kilometers.

Electrons emitted by the fission products after the explosion can produce the so-called "beta blackout." These electrons from a high-altitude explosion can ionize air to within 60 km of the earth's surface. The fission products from 1 Mt of fission yield can produce beta blackout over a circular area about 400 km in diameter. These nuclear blackouts would be produced both by defensive nuclear explosions and by

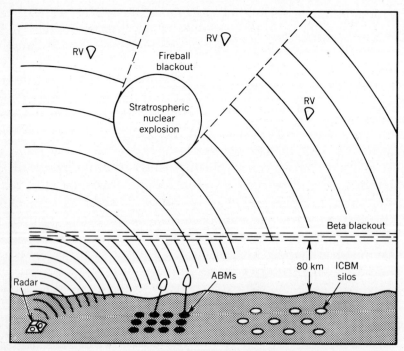

Figure 10.3 The fireball from a nuclear explosion, or the beta particles from the radio-active fission products, may ionize enough air to block radar transmissions.

explosions set off by the offense to interfere with the ABM radars. This blackout would not interfere with the radar signals for a terminal defense inside the atmosphere.

The electromagnetic pulse (EMP) from a high-altitude nuclear explosion, described in Chapter 12, can interfere with the electronic communications needed to operate ABM defense systems.

The Safeguard ABM Deployment

The history of the Safeguard ABM deployment decision is interesting because it tells a great deal about the making of weapons policy. The ABM has technological appeal that makes it attractive to research and develop. The deployment came when the ABM technology seemed riper—and when political circumstances made the ABM desirable. In the end ABM was controlled by the SALT I agreement in the interest of strategic stability and because the technology was not quite so attractive after all.

Secretary of Defense McNamara prevented the deployment of the ABM between 1961 and 1967. The ABM became very difficult to resist because it seemed to have become feasible. In 1964 one of the more prominent science advisors to the Department of Defense, Freeman Dyson who had originally opposed deployment of the ABM, said (*Bulletin of the Atomic Scientists*, Vol. 20, no. 6 [June 1964], p. 13),

> Problems that ten years ago seemed unapproachably difficult are now either solved or close to being solved. The builders of antimissile systems . . . can now justifiably claim to be able to provide a partial defense, a defense which would make some significant difference to the strategic balance.

A variety of technologies became available in 1964 and by 1967 seemed even better; missiles, warheads, and computers all by then had become much more advanced.

The Spartan and Sprint missiles of 1967 could be built using solid fuels derived from the Polaris and Minuteman programs. Only solid fuel could allow the quick reliable launch needed for an ABM system and the high acceleration for the smaller Sprint missile. In the 1960s, sophistication entered the nuclear weapons program. Enhanced-neutron and x-ray warheads could be developed for the Spartan and Sprint missiles to reduce the fission products that might contaminate the defended territory. The computer technology was very rapidly improving, as will be discussed in Chapter 13. Computer improvements were reflected in improved missile and radar accuracy, in much better radar discrimination ability, and in the greater blast resistance of the phase-array switched radars. Faster computers allow more frequent and more accurate signal analysis so that more targets can be tracked and discriminated simultaneously. The 1969 ABM debate showed that the technology of the arms race can become so interesting that it is hard to resist (see Chapter 13). Particularly the new computer capabilities may have made the development of better ABM technologies very difficult to resist.

The debate about the ABM deployment involved not only technological sweetness but also political and economic considerations (Garwin and Bethe, 1968; Brennan et al., 1968; Chayes and Wiesner, 1969; Yanarella, 1977). The ABM was ultimately not deployed on a large scale. This may be proof that technologies can sometimes be controlled if there is enough political will. Although Secretary of Defense McNamara did not want the ABM, and delayed it as much as possible, throughout the 1960s large political pressures worked toward deployment of the ABM. Deployment of the American ABM was presented as a response to various perceived weapons developments in the Soviet Union. The Soviets have long had extensive air defense systems against American bombers, which evolved into an ABM system. They constructed the Tallin air defense system to ward off the U.S. B-70 bomber that was never built. The United States in turn assumed that the Tallin system was a real ABM and pushed its own development of the MRV and MIRV technologies. When the Soviet Union deployed the Galosh ABM system around Moscow (with rotating antennas), the United States decided to incorporate the MIRV into its ICBMs and to deploy the more advanced electronically steered Nike-X ABM system. (Only now is the USSR finally deploying phase-array radars in its Moscow ABM system.)

The ABM system was possibly the first major U.S. weapons system whose fate was decided following an open public debate. In June 1968 the Senate voted $250 million toward the Sentinel system. This thin area defense required that the ABM missile farms be located near the cities they were to defend. When the Army began to purchase these city missile sites, popular protests arose, as the inhabitants of these cities thought the ABM installations made their cities more attractive targets.

After President Richard M. Nixon took office in 1969, he announced his Safeguard version of the Nike-X. Safeguard was primarily to be a protection of ICBM bases against an all-out Russian preemptive strike on U.S. missile silos. After considerable debate, the Senate approved in 1969, by a vote of 51 to 50, the deployment of Safeguard.

In the debate technical experts testified on both sides of the argument (Cahn, 1974). The argument hinged primarily on the question of whether the ABM might make a difference in the survivability of the American deterrent under the assumption of some very specific possible future Soviet missile developments. Some argued that this system could ultimately be expanded into a full-area defense saving millions of American lives in an all-out nuclear exchange. The debate considered the capabilities of the ABM system, the future Soviet threats, the economics of offense versus defense, the cost of saving American lives, and the destabilizing nature of ABM.

Much of the technical debate focused on the reliability of the ABM, particularly in a large attack with penetration aids. One major argument against the ABM was the narrowness of the range of assumptions under which the small-scale missile site ABM system could make a difference in the foreseeable future. The pro-ABM forces argued that in national security matters worst-case assumptions must be made, an approach that is illustrated by a report published in 1971 by the Operations Research Society (Caywood et al., 1971). This report judged that the opponents of ABM had not presented their arguments properly. Specifically, they felt that

> The proponents of the ABM should show that there exists a reasonable set of future circumstances for which the ABM is desirable. The opponents must show that for *all* reasonable sets of future conditions the ABM is undesirable. Desirability in both cases should be represented in terms of cost-effectiveness or cost benefits. The postulation of a particular set of future conditions for which the ABM is undesirable cannot show that the program should not be pursued. (Caywood et al., 1971, p. 1237)

The ABM economic agruments were couched in terms of dollars per American life that might possibly be saved. Both sides in the debate could use numbers to prove their point. The pro-ABM strategists could point out (see, e.g., Halstead, 1971, p. 250) that for a $20 billion heavy ABM defense U.S. fatalities in a Soviet first strike could be reduced by at least 20 million no matter how much effort the Soviet Union put into overcoming the ABM; surely 20 million Americans are worth $20 billion. Opponents of the ABM could point out that while such a defense system would cost at least $20 billion to build, a combination of penetration aids, MIRV, and mobile missiles could bring the U.S. fatalities back to essentially the pre-ABM level for a much lower offense expenditure of perhaps $5 billion. The projected costs for the Safeguard system were $25 million for each of 200 missiles; in contrast the Poseidon MIRV conversion ultimately cost only $½ million for each additional warhead—for $3.2 billion, 656 missiles received 9 additional warheads each.

McNamara had objected to the original city-guarding ABM system on the grounds that it would destabilize mutual assured destruction. An ABM would be likely to provoke new technical developments, such as MIRV, leading to a new spiral in the arms race. The pro-ABM analysts argued that a defense of the retaliatory deterrent force would increase stability. Figure 8.4 has illustrated these arguments. For a missile-site Safeguard ABM system, fewer retaliatory missiles are needed to have an assured second-strike destruction; however, for an area defense ABM, more retaliatory missiles would be needed to achieve assured destruction. The city-defending Sentinel ABM system would have been destabilizing.

The Salt I agreement of 1972 limited the deployment of ABM systems; thus the ABM continues to be an improving technology looking for a use. Some analysts claim that its development led to a new spiral in the arms race with MIRV. Others argue that the Soviets accepted the SALT I agreement because they were afraid of the U.S. ABM technology; they complain that the United States gave away a large technological advantage. Still other analysts say that the limited ABM deployment served a useful function as a bargaining chip in the SALT discussions and as such was worthwhile.

DIRECTED-ENERGY WEAPONS

The ABM may have been the first major weapon system that was controlled at birth. However, the promise of applying futuristic technologies to ABM systems continues to draw the attention of technologists and policymakers. Two interests predominate. Some would like to defend missile silos as the ICBMs are becoming more and more vulnerable to high-accuracy first strikes. Others dream of an antimissile defense so complete that it could remove the horror of MAD.

For many years both the United States and the Soviet Union have been working to develop ever more intense beams both of laser light and of particle beams. For the United States one of the motivations for such research has been an interest in using the very strongly focused energy of such beams to trigger the fusion of very small quantities of deuterium and tritium. This research has been in part in anticipation of a time when underground nuclear explosions might be banned by treaty. Then the controlled fusion explosions could be used to test in miniature the effects of H-bomb explosions on various electronic circuitry.

Since the late 1970s General George J. Keegan, Jr., former director of Air Force Intelligence, has tried to redirect that research effort toward directed-beam weapons; he claims the USSR is already developing such weapons. Now President Ronald Reagan, under the influence of Edward Teller and the High-Frontier group directed by retired Army

Lt. General Daniel O. Graham, former chief of the Defense Intelligence Agency, has expressed the dream that directed-energy weapons might someday be a complete defense against nuclear weapons. He has asked for a study in the style of the World War II Manhattan project to develop a research agenda leading to defense against attacking missiles, including the use of directed-energy beams.

The opportunities of directed-beam weaponry come from rapid developments in the energy intensity of lasers, from promised developments in particle beams, and from potential improvements in beam guidance techniques derived from great strides in computer capabilities. In reviewing the potential for the future of directed beam weapons, one must distinguish between ground- and space-based systems and between lasers, charged-particle beams, and neutral-particle beams. One must also consider the performance of complete weapons systems, including the detection of ICBMs during flight, the discrimination of ICBMs from decoys, the generation of the directed beam, the aiming of the beam and locking it onto the target, the propagation of the beam through air or space, the verification of damage to the missiles, and the engagement of as many as 1000 targets in a few minutes.

Particle Beams

The effects of radiation on living tissue were discussed in earlier chapters. Intense beams of very energetic charged or neutral particles could cause damage to solid materials as well, including melting holes in the metal skins of missiles or damaging the electronics of guidance mechanisms inside missiles. Accelerators have long been creating beams of high-energy particles; the new proposals want to develop accelerators suitable for applications to defenses against missiles. The use of high-energy particles in defensive systems is appealing because such particles travel close to the speed of light making a rapid defense imaginable. This section will describe two of the most conceivable particle-beam systems. Figures 10.4 and 10.5 sketch these two systems, one located on the ground and one in orbit around the earth.

Beam Propagation

Many different kinds of beams can be created in high-energy accelerators, consisting, for example, of positively- or negatively-charged hydrogen ions or of negatively-charged electrons. These charged particles, say, the H^- (or H^+), could be converted into neutral particles by sending them through a stripper, a foil in which an electron would be removed from (or added to) them.

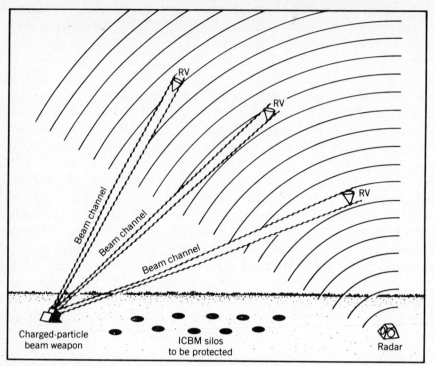

Figure 10.4 A particle-beam defense of missile silos against attacking reentry vehicles. The defense would have a range of about 1 km, and with several successive shots, it would bore channels in the air to hold the beam together.

Beams that would be suitable for missile defenses are limited. In outer space (exoatmospheric) only neutral beams would be usable, beams made up, for example, of neutral hydrogen atoms. A beam of charged particles would spread very quickly as the particles repel each other and as the earth's geomagnetic field would deflect it. Charged particles such as electrons would be used in the atmosphere (endo-atmospheric). As such a beam travels through the air, it creates the effect of an evacuated tube in which the air becomes so hot that its density decreases to less than one-tenth normal; around this tube a sheath of positive charges is formed, which keeps the negatively-charged electrons traveling tightly together.

A ground-based beam defense most likely would use a beam of electrons. It might consist of a 5000-ampere (A) beam of 500-million electron volt (MeV) electrons aiming toward a target 1 km or less away; this could be useful in protecting missile silos from ICBMs as in Fig. 10.4 or large ships from cruise missiles. The power of this beam might be equivalent for a moment to 2500 billion watts (gigawatts or GW), equivalent to 2500 large electricity-generating stations operating for a

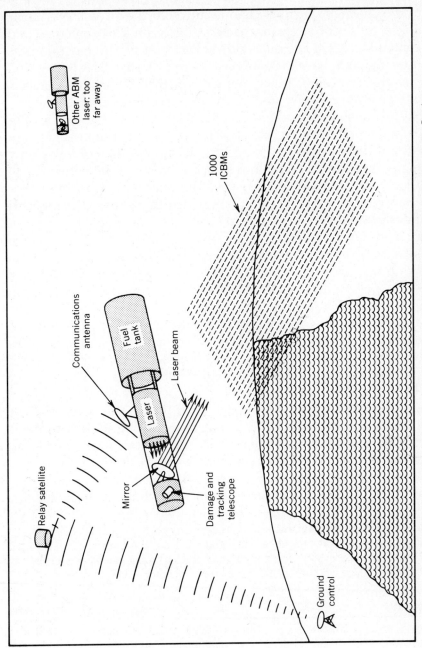

Figure 10.5 A laser beam defense of the whole United States that intercepts Soviet missiles during the boost phase before they fractionate into many MIRVs. Out of 50 laser stations in orbit at an altitude of 1000 km, only one would be in sight of each launch site at any time and, therefore, might have to destroy over 1000 missiles within 400 sec.

short time. It might burn its channel through the air with perhaps a few dozen pulses of electrons, each lasting a tenth of a microsecond, and containing a 250 kilojoules (kJ) in each pulse. The repetition rate of this beam might have to be on the order of 10,000 pulses per second, representing an average power demand of 2500 MW or the equivalent of 2½ large electric power stations operating continuously.

Table 10.1 shows the present best feasible values for various accelerator parameters. Current accelerators tend to be either high-energy and low-current units used in high-energy physics research or low-energy and high-current units used in research to generate miniature fusion explosions and weapons diagnostics. The required mix of high energies and high currents is presently provided by neither of these accelerator designs. It may be possible to build an accelerator of the required energy and beam intensity by scaling up some present systems. Present extrapolations suggest that such an accelerator might be on the order of 500 m in length and would have a weight of 250 tonnes or more. It is presently unresolved whether the requisite beam focusing and pulse repetition rate could be achieved.

A space-based particle accelerator would be used to intercept missiles above the atmosphere, most likely during the boost phase as close to launch as possible before the MIRV warheads could be separated from the bus carrying them. A system of 50 or more satellites would have to be placed in orbit about 1000 km above the earth's surface so that all ICBM silos would be in range at all times. The boost phase of ICBMs lasts about 8 min, with 2 min spent inside the atmosphere. Thus such a particle-beam station would have about 400 seconds (sec) to destroy up to 1000 ICBMs. A particle beam of 200-MeV neutral hydrogen atoms might require a current of 1 to 10 A and would have to fire several pulses per second during the whole of those 400 sec.

Table 10.1   Performance parameters of present-day particle-beam accelerators.
A satellite-based accelerator might have to produce a 1- to 10-A beam of 200-MeV neutral hydrogen ions several times a second, whereas a ground-based accelerator might have to produce a 5000-A beam of 500-MeV electrons 10,000 times a second. After Parmentola and Tsipis, 1979, p. 57.

Accelerator	E_{max} (MeV)	I_{max} (A)	Pulse Length	Pulse Rate
Stanford	20,000	0.00003	2500 nsec	360/sec
Saclay	600	0.0002	1000 nsec	1000/sec
MIT	400	0.0001	1500 nsec	1000/sec
Glasgow Univ.	130	0.0003	3500 nsec	240/sec
Sandia Labs	1.5	4,500,000	80 nsec	3/day
H. Diamond Lab	15	400,000	120 nsec	1/day
MIT	1.6	20,000	30 nsec	5/hr
Sandia Labs	0.35	30,000	30 nsec	100/sec

Table 10.1 shows that such combinations of energy, current, and pulse rate are not presently available in the existing accelerator styles. An accelerator capable of producing a 200-MeV, 10-A neutral hydrogen beam with a cross-section of several meters after traveling for 1000 km might conceivably be constructed over the next 10 years. Such a device might be about 20 m long and might damage a missile at 1000-km range with a continuous 10-sec burn, or it might damage the ICBM electronics with a burn of a tenth of a second.

Target Destruction

Once particle beams of the right characteristics are available, they must be focused and aimed at the target. It is thought that about 2000 joules (J) of energy would be required to burn a hole in 1 cm^3 of the walls of a missile. It is desirable to focus the beam as tightly as possible to make it at least as small as the size of the target missile. In creating the neutral hydrogen beam for exoatmospheric beams, stripping the electrons induces a spread in the beam that might be kept to 20 m at 1000 km, but only if geomagnetic shielding inside the accelerator could maintain the beam alignment to one part in a million. The charged beam would have to be magnetically aimed, after leaving the accelerator but before being neutralized; this operation too would have to be shielded from geomagnetic effects. The energy contained in some tens of tonnes of chemicals would be required to provide the beam energy for the destruction of a single missile.

Charged particle beams inside the earth's atmosphere would not have a great focusing problem if the target is to be intercepted less than a kilometer away and if a channel indeed can be bored through the atmosphere. Each destruction of a reentry vehicle might require a few dozen pulses of ½ million J of energy each; at 4 million J of energy per kilogram of high explosives, this would correspond to the burning of a few tens of kilograms of fuel material per attempt to destroy a missile.

Firing Procedure

The ground-based particle-beam defense would have to intercept enemy reentry vehicles during the last kilometer of their flight. At 10 km/sec, this corresponds to interception during the last tenths of a second before the reentry vehicle impacts. The particle-beam weapon would have to track the RV and fire at it in an atmosphere probably disturbed by previous nuclear explosions and beam weapon firings. All the problems described above for missile-based defensive systems hold here, that is, decoys, chaff, and radar interference from previous nuclear explosion, as in Fig. 10.3, can be used here to overcome the defense. There would not be as much need to ascertain destruction of any one incoming RV if the objective of the beam weapon defense were the preservation of only some of the retaliatory missiles for deterrence purposes. A partial defense is much easier than a complete and perfect defense.

The demands placed on a space-based defensive system would be more stringent. If cities are to be defended, not even a few reentry vehicles could be allowed to penetrate the total defense. Anyone of the 50 or more space stations would always have to be prepared within 400 sec to detect 1000 missiles, track all of them simultaneously using an optical telescope, fire sequentially with an accuracy of one part in 100,000 at least one shot at each one of the 1000 ICBMs, move onto the next one only after visible damage has been seen to have occurred on the first one, and continue the cycle until all 1000 ICBMs are destroyed. For countermeasures to overcome such interceptions the attacker could use penetration aids as well as some additional defenses, such as blowing some air into the stratosphere to defocus the beam.

Laser Beams

Lasers are devices that generate very intense, narrowly-focused beams of light. These beams travel at the speed of light (300,000 km/sec) much faster than the 7 km/sec of an ICBM; lasers offer the potential for very rapid interception of targets. The rapid advancement in laser technology over the past two decades has made it seem interesting to try to incorporate lasers into defensive systems. Much effort has gone into using lasers in conventional warfare where they mark targets for smart bombs that detect the reflected laser beam. The use of lasers in an antisatellite (ASAT) mode could, possibly, make technical sense, since satellites are very soft targets and therefore require relatively little energy deposition to be destroyed and since satellites follow a steady course in orbit, offering a long time period for interception.

The use of lasers for endoatmospheric defenses of ICBM silos would be hard to accomplish because of atmospheric problems. Any cloud cover or particulates in the air would negate a laser system. The light intensities required to disable a reentry vehicle might cause atmospheric effects through thermal blooming (hot air spreading the beam) or ionization of the air that would defocus the beam enough to stop its operation. The present review will deal only with the use of lasers to intercept on a massive scale ICBMs shortly after their launch (Fig. 10.5), with the goal of a city defense.

Lasers

Lasers of the types likely to be used in high-intensity operations may be of a design like that in Fig. 10.6. Two gases such as hydrogen and

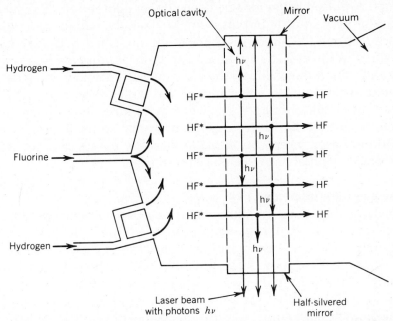

Figure 10.6 Chemical lasers for BMD might utilize the reaction of hydrogen with fluorine to produce many HF* molecules in an excited state. Lasing takes place when all these excited molecules give up their energy simultaneously. (After Tsipis, 1981, p. 52.)

fluorine are reacted together. The resultant hydrogen fluoride molecules are in an excited state HF* after the reaction. When these excited HF* molecules decay into the ground state, they emit a photon of a very specific energy. The photon from one decaying molecule may trigger the deexcitation of other molecules; in a group of excited HF* molecules, an exponentially growing avalanche of deexcitations is possible. The growing photon beam is reflected inside the laser cavity back and forth between a set of parallel mirrors (one of which is partially transmitting). This produces an intense beam of well-collimated light that comes out through the partially transmitting mirror. High-intensity laser beams could also be generated by cooling a very hot gas such as CO_2 to create many molecules in the highly excited states, or by using electron beams to populated excited states.

For all these lasers, the critical problems in beam production are the available light intensities, the wavelength of the light and diffraction broadening, whether the beam is continuous or pulsed, and most important, the efficiency of converting chemical energy into light. The wavelength of the laser light is important particularly with respect to transmission through the atmosphere, which is much better for visible and some infrared light; shorter-wavelength ultraviolet light is scattered greatly by haze, but it is easier to focus with smaller reflecting mirrors. A pulsed beam may be desirable for some applications where a series of very short light pulses might crack the surface of a missile. Melting the missile surface might be accomplished better by longer exposures to lower-intensity light. The laser light intensity obviously places a limit on the ability of the laser to cause damage at the desired targeting distance. The reflectance of the target and the efficiency of converting chemical energy into light determines how much fuel is needed to operate the laser. This might not be so much of a problem for ground-based lasers, but it matters greatly for space-based operations where the fuel has to be placed into orbit.

Damage Requirements

Consider the energy requirements for a laser system designed to intercept all Soviet ICBMs during that 400-sec part of the launch phase when they are above the atmosphere but have not yet fractionated into MIRVs. Some 50 or more stations would have to be placed into 1000-km earth orbit to have the Soviet Union launch sites under fire at all times. Each of the laser stations would have to be able to detect the missile launches and must track up to 1000 ICBMs at the same time— distinguishing them from chaff and decoys. The lasers would have to operate continuously or in a pulsed mode for at least 400 sec. A large mirror would have to aim the laser beam toward the 1000 targets one after the other under the control of an aiming optical telescope. After each shot, the damage to the target missile would have to be assessed to decide whether to go on to the next target and so on, until all targets are destroyed.

The focusing and energetic requirements of such a laser system are formidable. For highest efficiency, the beam should be focused to an area no larger than the target missile, and it needs to be aimed with a precision equal to the smallest dimension of the target (a 10-m missile at a range of 1000 km would require an aiming precision of one part in 100,000). Large reflecting mirrors would be required both to focus the beam narrowly and to avoid melting the mirror surface. The effectiveness of such exoatmospheric laser operations involves a series of energy conversions that must independently be as efficient as possible. The energy conversion inside the laser is likely to be less than 30%. The energy transfer out of the laser into a final beam again is not likely to reach an efficiency above 30%. The reflectivity of the guiding mirror must be nearly 100% to avoid damaging its surface. Energy from the beam must be absorbed by the target. If the target surface is shiny, as for an aluminum missile skin, more than 90% of the incident light might be reflected, although very rapid vaporization of the surface layer might create a plasma that could increase the energy absorption to as much as 30%.

The overall energy requirements start from the assumption that perhaps 400 J/cm² might be needed to melt through a 2-mm thick missile skin. A 100-MW CO_2 laser with a 4-m optically perfect mirror would need 1 sec to cause such damage at a range of 1000 km. The fuel consumption might then under ideal conditions be ½ tonne of fuel per missile destroyed. Thus each of the 50 or more laser satellite stations would require more than 500 tonnes of fuel just for the operation of the laser. The present U.S. space shuttles would need to make 1000 flights with a 25-tonne payload just to transport the fuel for a minimal global defense system. At the present cost of $2000 per kg, the cost would be $50 billion just to place the fuel into low earth orbit; taking it up to a 100-km orbit would be an additional expense.

Defenses against such a laser battle station are obvious. Any chaff or decoys during launch would cause discrimination problems for the station's tracking and discrimination system. The satellite station with its telescopes, lasers, and mirrors would be very vulnerable to an anti-satellite attack; its sensors and communications systems could be jammed or blinded, and its laser or mirror destroyed. The missiles, in turn, could be protected against laser attack by increasing their surface reflectivity with a mirrored surface, by coating them with some ablative material that would separate on heating, by flowing a continuous liquid layer over the surface of the missile to remove some of the heat, or by rotating the missile continuously to spread the incident heat over a larger surface area.

On balance, space-based lasers do not seem a near-term weapons system. A recent study by Tsipis (1981) concluded that "lasers have little or no chance of succeeding as cost-effective defensive weapons." In defending cities the problems of generating intense beams, providing the fuel for these beams, focusing the beams, aiming the beams, damaging the targets, and doing so for 1000 targets with near 100% reliability within 400 sec seem large indeed.

ACTIVE DEFENSES

If either particle beam or laser weapons were feasible for a working ABM system, one would have to consider the strategic and tactical consequences. In the sense of strategic stability, systems defending countervalue targets such as cities would be undesirable. On the other hand, systems defending missile silos might well appear stabilizing by preserving retaliatory capabilities.

Some dream of a perfect antimissile defense that might end mutual assured destruction as a way of coping with strategic nuclear weapons. However, there are a few problems with this dream. It seems unlikely that any defensive system could ever be so perfect as to reduce the consequences of a full-scale nuclear strike below the level of unacceptable damage. Only a few percent of a thousand ICBMs would have to pass through the defense to produce such unacceptable damage. While such a system is under construction, it would be a provocation for a preemptive first strike, making a less stable world. Nuclear weapons can be delivered on target in so many ways that closing off the ICBM route, or even the SLBM route, would not be an adequate defense. Air-launched missiles and bombs, cruise missiles, and tactical nuclear forces could still deliver an unacceptable number of nuclear weapons.

No perfect defenses against nuclear weaponry appear possible; it would thus seem that directed-energy weapons must be evaluated independently of such a dream. If they are to be developed, they ought to have other objectives. Defending ICBM silos may be a worthy goal of either missile-based BMD or directed-energy weapons. However, these would not seem an alternative to mutual assured destruction.

References

Bekefi, G., B. T. Feld, J. Parmentola, and K. Tsipis. "Particle-Beam Weapons—A Technical Assessment." *Nature,* Vol. 284, (1980), pp. 219–225.

Brennan, D. G., L. W. Johnson, J. B. Wiesner, and G. S. McGovern. *Antiballistic Missile: Yes or No?* New York: Hill and Wang, 1968.

Cahn, A. H. "American Scientists and the ABM: A Case Study in Controversy." In *Scientists and Public Affairs,* A. H. Teich, ed., pp. 41–120. Cambridge, Mass.: MIT Press, 1974. A review of the role of scientific experts in the ABM discussion.

Caywood, T. E., et al., "Guidelines for the Practice of Operations Research." *Operations Research,* Vol. 19, no. 5 (September 1971), pp. 1123–1257.

Chayes, A., and J. B. Wiesner, eds. *ABM: An Evaluation of the Decision to Deploy an Antiballistic Missile System.* New York: Harper & Row, 1969.

Garwin, L., and Hans A. Bethe. "Anti-Ballistic-Missile Systems." *Scientific American,* Vol. 218, no. 3 (March 1968), pp. 13–23. Contains good technical information, particularly about penetration aids. See also D. J. Fink, A. W. Betts, R. L. Garwin, and H. A. Bethe. "Letters to the Editor." *Scientific American,* Vol. 218 no. 5 (May 1968), pp. 6–8.

Hafemeister, D. H. "Science and Society Test for Physicists: The Arms Race." *American Journal of Physics,* Vol. 41, (1973), pp. 1191–1196.

Halstead, T. A. "Lobbying Against the ABM, 1967–1970." *Bulletin of the Atomic Scientists,* Vol. 27, no. 4 (April 1971), pp. 23–28. A review of scientific opposition to the ABM.

Parmentola, J., and K. Tsipis. "Particle-Beam Weapons." *Scientific American*, Vol. 240, no. 4 (April 1979), pp. 54–65.

Tsipis, K. "Laser Weapons." *Scientific American*, Vol. 245, no. 6 (December 1981), pp. 51–57.

Yanarella, E. J. *The Missile Defense Controversy: Strategy, Technology, and Politics, 1955–1972.* Lexington: University of Kentucky Press, 1977. An excellent review of the political development of the ABM.

CHAPTER
11

Chemical and Biological Warfare

Any use of gas by any Axis power, therefore will immediately be followed by the fullest possible retaliation [in kind] upon munition centers, seaports, and other military objectives throughout the whole extent of the territory of such Axis country.

President Franklin D. Roosevelt, 1943

Nuclear explosives are devastating strategic weapons. Chemical and biological warfare (CBW) agents are potentially equally terrifying. They are deadly; as little as 1 microgram is required to kill a person in some cases. Since fairly large quantities of CBW material can be produced at relatively low expense, the potential for inexpensive large-scale death dealing is obvious.

This chapter concerns CBW warfare. The underlying motivation for this discussion is to ask whether CBW might be an alternative option to the use of nuclear weapons to achieve deterrence by mutual assured destruction. CBW has never been used on the strategic level; in what ways does it differ from the nuclear option?

The chapter will summarize the history of CBW to learn how restraints were placed on this technology, that is, how deterrence worked for it. The use of defoliants by the United States in Vietnam illustrates the difficulties of applying chemical agents successfully in a tactically controlled and restrained way. Worries about the balance in CBW capabilities in Europe echo some of the concerns about nuclear escalation that will be discussed in Chapter 12. Most current issues about CBW, such as the deployment of binaries and its possible use in Afghanistan and Southeast Asia, relate to the desire to achieve arms **260** control of these weapons.

HISTORY OF CBW

Warfare with chemical agents was practiced on a large scale in World War I—about 125,000 tonnes (metric tons) of chemical agents were used. The use of chlorine gas in 1915 was followed by the use of mustard gas in 1917. The resulting casualties and fatalities from chemicals were 1,300,000 and 91,000, respectively, about half suffered by Russia.

While these chemicals had some military utility, the injuries to troops on both sides seemed to outweigh the military benefits. Consequently, efforts were made after the war to control such weapons. The Versailles Treaty of 1919 prohibited the use of poisonous gases. The 1925 Geneva Protocol, banning all chemical and biological warfare, by 1931 was signed by all the major powers except Japan and the United States.

Just before World War II, the nerve gases Tabun and Sarin were discovered; some 11,000 tonnes of Tabun were produced in Germany between 1942 and 1945. Biological weapons were also available during World War II; for example, botulinus toxin was developed and stocked. Yet chemicals and nerve gases were not used during that war. Various countries disavowed any first use. In 1943 President Roosevelt announced that

> I state categorically that we shall under no circumstances resort to the use of such weapons unless they are first used by our enemies. (As quoted in Primack and Von Hippel, 1974, p. 146)

As summarized by Richard H. Ichord,

> [D]uring World War II . . . the Allies sent word to the Nazis that such use [of poison gas] would result in overwhelming retaliation. . . . Although the Allies had nothing comparable to Tabun, the Germans did not know this, and the general threat of retaliation deterred them. (*Reader's Digest*, September 1979, p. 208)

Lord Ritchie-Calder reported how a deterrence threat was communicated:

> Supplies [of toxins] existed and might have been used, but only if the Germans had first used something of the same. . . . Certain Canadian servicemen were briefed that if taken prisoner they would . . . reluctantly disclose that they had been vaccinated against botulin. . . . It could have meant (as we intended it to) "Don't do anything rash, chum, or else". . . . Or it might have provoked a preemptive strike, and we would have been in a chemical and biological war. (As quoted in Hoeber, 1981, pp. 14–15)

CBW deterrence worked in World War II. Based on the experience of World War I, CBW may not have seemed to be a good technology as field commanders worried about the need for ideal weather and about the possibility of harming friendly troops. Perhaps CBW really was in a balance of terror with everyone afraid of retaliation by the other side.

By 1956 a new CBW policy was in force in the United States. That year the U.S. Army field manual stated that "the United States is not party to any treaty, now in force, that prohibits or restricts the use in warfare of toxic or nontoxic gases, or smoke or incendiary materials or of bacteriological warfare." The United States began to consider the use of CBW materials in guerilla warfare.

The Vietnam war provided the opportunity to develop and test CBW materials as tactical weapons. The use of chemical agents in that war triggered protests; in 1966 the first anti-CBW petitions were signed and investigative trips to Vietnam were begun. Then in 1968 some VX nerve gas was accidentally released in Utah, killing over 6000 sheep as far as 45 miles away.

Under pressure from the Congress and the United Nations, and under the cloud of some poorly planned poison gas shipment announcements by the U.S. Department of Defense, President Richard M. Nixon in November 1969 renounced CBW and proposed that the United States should sign the 1925 Geneva anti-CBW Protocol. In April 1972 the United States signed a convention on the "Prohibition of the Development, Production, and the Stockpiling of Bacteriological (Biological) and Toxin Weapons, and on Their Destruction." In December 1974 the U.S. Senate finally ratified the 1925 Geneva Protocol.

In recent years the Soviet Union has been accused of producing anthrax spores and employing chemical agents against guerillas in Afghanistan; and their North Vietnamese allies are suspected of using mycotoxins ("yellow rain") as weapons in Laos and Kampuchea. The United States is considering production of new binary chemical weapons to replace older weapons using single chemicals. Fear about the possible usage of CBW in a European confrontation continues as both the United States and the USSR have large stockpiles of chemical weapons. The United States holds 15,000 to 30,000 tonnes of nerve gas, the USSR possibly 300,000 tonnes of various chemical agents.

THE NATURE OF CBW MATERIALS

Chemical Agents

A variety of chemicals have detrimental effects on humans even in small doses. Table 11.1 summarizes some of these effects.

Table 11.1 Estimated potencies of selected toxins or chemical warfare agents.

ICt50 is the inhaled dose needed to incapacitate 50% of the exposed persons. LCt50 and LD50 are the inhaled and ingested doses that are lethal for 50% of the exposed population. The density of air is 1.3 kg/m³, or 1,300,000 mg/m³. A dose of 1 mg-min/m³ means an exposure for 1 min when the material has a concentration of 1 mg/m³. After Robinson, 1973, pp. 42–43.

Agent	Aerosol Agent Respiratory			Sprayed or Dusted Agent		Contact Agent	
	Incapacitate ICt50 (mg-min/m³)	Kill LCt50 (mg-min/m³)	Time to Effect	Needed for Military Effect (kg/km²)	Time to Effect	Skin Contact LD50 (mg/person)	Oral LD50 (mg/person)
2,4-D	NA	NA	NA	2,000	1–16 wk	NA	30,000[a]
Cacodylic acid	NA	NA	NA	400	2–4 days	NA	100,000[a]
Agent CS	20	61,000	delayed	25,000	seconds	NA	NA
Agent BZ	110	200,000	delayed	NA	NA	NA	NA
Phosgene	1600	3,200	3–24 hr	NA	NA	NA	NA
Cyanogen chloride	7000	11,000	1–15 min	NA	NA	NA	NA
Hydrogen cyanide	NA	5,000	½–15 min	NA	NA	NA	50
Mustard gas	200	1,500	4–24 hr	10,000	4–6 hr	4500	50
Tabun	100	400	10–15 min	2,000	1 hr	1000	40
Sarin	55	100	2–15 min	NA	NA	1700	10
Soman	25	70	1–15 min	2,000	½–1 hr	1000	10
Agent VX	5	36	4–10 min	100	½–1 hr	15	5
Botulinal toxin A	NA	0.1	12–24 hr	NA	NA	NA	0.07
Shellfish poison	NA	5	¼–1 hr	NA	NA	NA	0.5
Staphylococcal enterotoxin B	0.5	200	Delayed	NA	NA	NA	NA

NA – Not applicable.

[a] Not likely to be used deliberately as a water contaminant.

Irritating gases incapacitate rather than kill. They irritate the eyes, the skin—leading to itching, or the respiratory tract—leading to coughing, nausea and vomiting, and headaches. This category includes the phosgenes of World War I, as well as Agent CS which is classified as a riot-control agent.

Blood gases such as hydrogen cyanide destroy the ability of blood to remove CO_2 from body tissue.

Vesicant gases such as mustard gases and Q agents burn the skin, producing, for example, blindness.

Nerve gases can lead to difficulty in breathing, drooling, nausea, vomiting, convulsions, and sometimes dim vision. They include the earlier organophosporus G compounds such as Tabun, Sarin, and Soman as well as the newer V agents, such as Agent VX. The V agents are very deadly; Agent VX, for example, can incapacitate with an exposure for 1 min to a concentration of 5 mg/m^3 or kill with a dose of 36 mg-min/m^3 (equal to 0.4 mg) of inhalation. A concentration of 36 mg/m^3 represents a mixture with air of about 30 parts per million (ppm). Production cost in the 1960s was about $5/kg, where 1 kg contained on the order of 2.5 million lethal doses. The G agents can readily be vaporized into aerosols, whereas VX is more oily and has to be sprayed. About 300 kg/km^2 of VX creates a skin-contact hazard lasting for as long as weeks. Nerve gases would seem to be the choice for battlefield use with high toxicity, rapidity of action, easy dispersal, stability, and fairly low cost.

Incapacitants are compounds such as Agent BZ or LSD that might be used to take the enemy out of action by temporary physical and mental incapacitation.

Defoliants such as 2,4-D and 2,4,5-T, or arsenic and cyanide compounds, attack the hormone auxin in leaves, causing them to fall off. Typically 1 liter is spread over 1 acre. Such compounds may lead to death in humans if a dose of 20 gm is ingested. At smaller doses, more subtle long-term effects may occur, leading to genetic defects and other problems.

Biological Materials

Biological weapons harm either through toxins produced by some bacteria or through diseases induced by the bacteria. The United Nations classifies toxins as chemicals since they cannot reproduce, but they produce symptoms like those produced by infectious organisms.

Toxins produced by bacteria considered for CBW warfare include botulinal toxins, shellfish poison (saxitoxin), and staphylococcal enterotoxin. The first of these is the most toxic and is produced by

Clostridium botulinum bacteria; it causes the type of food poisoning known as "botulism." Botulinus Type A can be made for perhaps $400/kg. It can be readily dissolved in water and stored for days; it decays rapidly in the open air. It hinders the transmittal of nerve impulses to muscles; death generally follows from paralysis of respiratory muscles. It is estimated that 1 kg of Type A botulinal toxin would contain about 3 billion lethal doses for people. Its decay in air reduces its lethality to that of VX for large-area aerosol spraying; it is more suitable for covert operations such as the sabotage of food or water.

Infective agents are bacteria that cause various infectious diseases in humans. Diseases considered particularly suitable for biological warfare include tularemia (rabbit fever), anthrax, plague, Q fever, and encephalomyelitis (caused by VEE virus). These bacteria can be quite virulent and the diseases are very debilitating even when not fatal. The bacteria *Francisella tularensis* can infect individuals when as few as 25 cells are inhaled, although orally as many as 100 million bacteria may be needed. The disease is incubated in 3 to 5 days and produces chills, fever, and lung complications that may persist for several weeks. The normal strain of this disease ordinarily leads to a low fatality rate of perhaps 1%. In comparison, anthrax requires a considerably larger dose; perhaps 20,000 spores may be needed to infect a person through the lungs; but the disease is more frequently fatal through the toxins generated by the *Bacillus anthracis* bacterium. Table 11.2 shows the threats posed by other biological agents.

Distribution of CBW Materials

CBW materials can be used in a variety of ways. When sprayed as an aerosol, as a fine liquid mist of VX, or in a dust cloud of BZ, they take

Table 11.2 Estimated potencies of selected infectious biological warfare agents. ECt50 and ED50 are the inhalation doses that produce the disease in 50% of the exposed population. After Robinson, 1973, p. 42.

| | | Respiratory | | Time to |
| | | ED50 | ECt50 | Effect |
Disease	Species	(cells/person)	(mg-min/m²)	(days)
Tularemia	*Francisella tularensis*	25	0.001	2–5
Anthrax	*Bacillus anthracis*	20,000	0.01	1–4
Plague	*Pasteurella pestis*	3,000	NA	3–4
Q fever	*Coxiella burnetii*	10	0.001	18–21
VEE	VEE virus	25	0.001	2–5
Rice blast	*Pyricularia oryzae*	NA	NA	1–4

NA–Not applicable.

effect primarily by inhalation. To produce effects on the outer skin, they can be sprayed in the form of larger liquid drops (e.g., of phosgenes). To produce effects by ingestion, some materials such as botulinal toxin can be dissolved in liquid to contaminate water or food supplies. In each case, although the quantity required for a lethal dose may be very small, the distribution methods tend to be very wasteful, so that a considerable amount of CBW material must be used.

The two most likely used methods of large-scale distribution of CBW materials are aerial spraying from a helicopter or aircraft and delivery by an explosive artillery shell. A B-52 bomber could drop 20 tonnes of VX nerve gas, which could be fatal over a 200-km^2 area. In one experiment ½ tonne of a bacterial suspension was sprayed along a 240-km stretch. The suspension drifted, covering about 150,000 km^2, to such a level that a person standing anywhere in the area would inhale at least 15 bacilli.

Artillery shells may be used in a barrage. Figure 11.1 shows the cross section of a chemical warfare artillery shell. The shell is to explode over the target at the appropriate altitude and form a fine aerosol of the CBW agent. This particular shell employs the contemporary binary concept. It contains two "relatively safe" chemicals such as QL and NM. After the shell is fired, inertial forces push the liquid in the first container through the rupture disk into the second liquid. The shell spins at 15,000 revolutions per minute in flight; this spin mixes the two components of the binary. For VX, the chemical reaction is complete in about 5 sec.

Binary weapons are safer to store, since the two "safe" chemicals are mixed only in flight to produce the final dangerous agent. Hence the U.S. Department of Defense has repeatedly proposed the production of such binary artillery shells, and plants for this production program may yet be built.

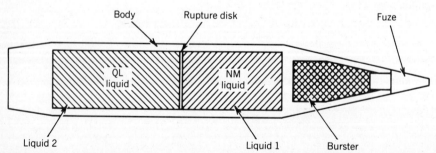

Figure 11.1 In binary chemical weapons, two nonlethal ingredients are mixed to form a lethal nerve gas such as VX.

CBW EFFECTIVENESS

Tactical Uses of CBW

Tactical usage of CBW has been of concern for years, not only in guerilla wars but in major nonnuclear wars as in a NATO-WPO confrontation in Europe. The Soviet Union has invested considerable effort into preparing the Warsaw Pact military for CBW usage, although much of the preparation is of a defensive nature. Tactical usage of CBW in direct confrontations of similar military forces in many ways does not seem very attractive. The effects on the enemy are uncertain if the dosage is to be kept low enough to avoid indiscriminate killing. Friendly troops can be protected; properly fitted gas masks can reduce the concentrations of chemical warfare agents in the air by a factor of 100,000, and chemicalproof protective clothing can be worn. But the gas masks and protective clothing hamper the performance of troops. The safe working time for soldiers wearing chemical protective clothing is displayed in Table 11.3. In hot temperatures the work periods may be quite limited because the chemicalproof clothing also prevents air circulation. This shows how difficult it would be to fight any kind of war in a CBW environment no matter which side first used the agents.

The largest experience with tactical chemical warfare agents since World War I has been during the Vietnam war. In that war the United States used about 110,000 tonnes of chemicals as defoliants. It also procured about 9000 tonnes of the CS harassing agent (the fraction actually used is not known). The objective in Vietnam was to use CW materials tactically to achieve specific military objectives such as removing protective tree cover over enemy troops with defoliants, destroying some of the food supplies for enemy soldiers, and using long-lasting irritants to keep the enemy out of certain areas for periods

Table 11.3 Work-pacing guide for personnel dressed in chemical protective clothing.
The times are sugggested maximum safe unit work times to minimize moderate risk of heat illness. From the U.S. Department of Defense, *Department of Army Field Manual FM 21–2* of August 1977, p. 148. Some newer suits may allow longer work times.

	Temperature Range					
	Cool: 50–70°F		Warm: 70–85°F		Hot: 85–100°F	
Work Rate	Open Suit	Closed Suit	Open Suit	Closed Suit	Open Suit	Closed Suit
Low	60 + min	40–60 min	45–60 min	25–40 min	30–45 min	15–25 min
Moderate	45–60 min	30–45 min	30–45 min	20–30 min	20–30 min	15–20 min
Heavy	20–30 min	15–20 min	15–20 min	10–15 min	10–15 min	5–10 min

as long as a month. The effectiveness of this use of CW agents gives some insight into the tactical usefulness of this alternative to nuclear weapons.

Between 1961 and 1973, the United States applied 54,000 tonnes of defoliant to forests and crop areas in South Vietnam. These agents also have been used as herbicides on U.S. croplands. The average level of application used in the military effort in Vietnam was an average of about 2 tonnes/km^2 (2 gm/m^2). About 10% of the 173,000 km^2 of South Vietnamese land was sprayed at least once, and about one-third of all sprayed areas were sprayed at least twice. Of all missions, 86% were directed at forests and other woody vegetation like mangroves, and the remaining 14% were aimed at crop plants. A single spraying would kill 10% of the trees, a double spraying 25%, a triple spraying 50%. The mangrove is particularly vulnerable to herbicides, a single spraying often destroying essentially the entire plant community. An estimated 1500 km^2 of mangroves have been destroyed, or 30% of all in South Vietnam; natural recovery is estimated to take more than a century.

This herbicide usage may have had an effect on the progress of the war, but it did not produce victory. Negative consequences from the use have gone beyond the direct ecological damage. The Agent Orange used in Indochina unfortunately contained parts per million of the exceedingly poisonous contaminant dioxin (or TCDD). The sprayed liquid may have contained an average of at least 2.5 gm/m^3 of dioxin; about 166 kilograms (kg) of dioxin is said to have been contained in the spray during the whole program. A dose of 0.2 mg of dioxin accumulated in a person over a nine-month period may be fatal. This dioxin contaminant is suspected of affecting the health of some Vietnam veterans who were exposed to Agent Orange during their tour of duty.

CBW Strategic Use

Chemical and biological weapons have many problems. They must be dispersed, and friendly troops and civilians must be protected without impairing their fighting efficiency. In the strategic context, the main question about the effectiveness of CBW is in comparison to nuclear weapons in large-area applications. Such a comparison is carried out in Table 11.4. The CBW agents seem at least as threatening as strategic nuclear explosions.

One might compare the lethality of CBW agents with that of nuclear materials. A lethal quality of ^{239}Pu when inhaled may be as little as $\frac{1}{2}$ mg. In comparison, as little as 0.4 mg of inhaled VX can be lethal, as is 0.4 micrograms (μg) of Type A botulinal toxin. Thus, CBW agents can be considerably more dangerous per unit mass than can ^{239}Pu. One might consider sabotage of water supplies; if $\frac{1}{2}$ kg of salmonella were

Table 11.4   The effects of various weapons.
The comparison is among a 1-Mt hydrogen bomb, 15 tonnes of a nerve agent, and 10 tonnes of a biological agent. Each weapon can be dropped by a single bomber on an unprepared population. After Meselson, 1970, p. 21.

Agents	Nuclear	Chemical	Biological
Area affected	About 75 km^2	Up to 60 km^2	Up to 100,000 km^2
Time to effect	Seconds	Minutes	Days
Structural damage	Widespread	None	None
Other effects	Fallout over 2000 km^2	Contamination; days or weeks	Possible epidemic; new disease foci
No normal use of area	3 to 6 months	Limited for days or weeks	Variable
Effect on humans	90% deaths	50% deaths	50% disease

introduced into a 1-million-gallon reservoir of water (4000 tonnes), drinking 0.1 liter (0.1 kg) of water from the mixed solution would lead to serious infection. This corresponds to a dilution factor of 1 part in 10 million. An equivalent threat from radioactive materials would be hard to achieve. In any number of strategic uses, CBW appears potentially more effective than nuclear warfare.

CBW ARMS CONTROL

The world's stockpile of chemical weapons is considerable. The United States is thought to have about 30,000 tonnes of mustard and nerve gases, including 10,000 tonnes of Sarin and 3500 to 5000 tonnes of VX. About half these agents are in munitions; most of those are kept in the continental United States. For the Soviet chemical stockpile, figures of 350,000 and 700,000 tonnes have been cited in the literature, but nothing definite is known. Much of it is said to be of World War I and II vintage, although Tabun is mentioned, and a version of Soman appears to be the standard nerve gas. Some Soviet CW agents may be stored in East Germany and could be made available to other Warsaw Pact Organization nations.

The signators of the 1925 Geneva Protocol agreed not to use asphyxiating or poisonous gases or bacteriological methods of warfare; both the Soviet Union (in 1928) and the United States (in 1975) have accepted this protocol. In 1972 a Biological Weapons Convention was accepted internationally; both the United States and the USSR agreed not to develop, produce, or stockpile biological weapons. These agreements might be thought of as comparable to freeze agreements about fissile material.

These CBW treaties have a variety of problems since unilateral exclusory riders have been attached to them. The United States, for example, considers itself bound by the 1925 Protocol only with respect to other states who obey these prohibitions; this makes the U.S. acceptance equivalent to a no-first-use declaration. The United States does not consider herbicides and riot-control agents (such as CS gases) to be covered by that protocol; this makes it difficult to decide what agents are forbidden. The accusation that the USSR has been engaged in chemical warfare in Afghanistan shows this to be a real problem since the Soviet Union may have been using incapacitating agents; it is very difficult to prove that the gases were more than riot-control agents.

Verification in general is a difficult problem in CBW treaties and agreements. There have been accusations that the Soviets have promoted the use of toxins ("yellow rain") in Laos and Kampuchea by their Vietnamese allies in recent years. Some think that the USSR has been working on anthrax in violation of the 1972 Biological Warfare Convention; an installation in Sverdlovsk has been suspected of being a biological warfare factory. It is difficult to resolve unequivocally whether violations have or have not taken place without on-site inspection. In the area of CBW, arms control has been seen as attractive and has been practiced for years. Yet, even in this favorable case, arms control has major difficulties, particularly in the conclusive verification of treaty violations.

CONCLUSIONS

Both similarities and major differences exist between CBW and nuclear weapons. CBW agents resemble nuclear weaponry: tactical use is difficult because of their indiscriminate and nonspecific effects. Strategic use of CBW may be easier because of their low cost, CBW agents may be useful as weapons of mass destruction when applied to populated areas. Table 11.4 has shown that similar areas could be affected by chemical agents in a retaliatory manner, whereas biological warfare could be even more effective, acting in the manner of a global doomsday machine spreading epidemics throughout the world. CBW may be cheap enough that it could provide an alternative form of MAD; that is, enough chemical or biological agents could be placed on targets to create assured destruction of the enemy.

The experiences of World War I did lead to the nonuse of chemical and biological agents in World War II, as the perceived mutual danger of the weapons caused CBW to be avoided by all sides. In that sense CBW had successful deterrence at that time.

Arms control of CBW seems to be at least as difficult as control of nuclear weapons. The research is closely related to medical work; the potential connection between progress in biological warfare agents and recombinant DNA research is not only obvious, but also ominous. The use of CBW is harder to prove, as nothing so detectable as radioactive materials will escape. It is not clear whether lack of a technological imperative or historical self-restraint is responsible for the present dominance of nuclear weapons over CBW. A deliberate policy of replacing nuclear MAD by CBW MAD seems feasible, but not particularly desirable.

References

Hoeber, A. M. *The Chemistry of Defeat: Asymmetries in U.S. and Soviet Chemical Warfare Postures*. Washington, D.C.: Institute for Foreign Policy Analysis, 1981.

Meselson, M. S. "Chemical and Biological Weapons," *Scientific American*, Vol. 222, no. 5 (May 1970), pp. 15–25.

————, and J. P. Robinson. "Chemical Warfare and Chemical Disarmament," *Scientific American*, Vol. 242, no. 4 (April 1980), pp. 38–47.

Primack, J., and F. von Hippel. "Studies as an Excuse for Inaction: The Saga of 2,4,5-T," Chapter 6 of *Advice and Dissent*. New York: Basic Books, 1974.

Robinson, J. P. *The Problem of Chemical and Biological Warfare*. Vol. II: *CB Weapons Today*. New York: Humanities Press for SIPRI, 1973.

Westing, A. H. *Ecological Consequences of the Second Indochina War*. Stockholm: Almquist and Wiksell for the Stockholm International Peace Research Institute, 1976.

Tactical
Nuclear War

Should a President, in the event of a nuclear attack, be left with the single option of ordering the mass destruction of civilians, in the face of the certainty that it would be followed by the mass slaughter of Americans? Should the concept of assured destruction be narrowly defined and should it be the only measure of our ability to deter the variety of threats we may face?

President Richard M. Nixon, 1972

In this chapter the focus will be on uses of nuclear weapons beyond mutual assured destruction, that is, uses in a counterforce or tactical mode as in a limited nuclear war. Tactical war requires the application of the right amount of military force, in the right place, to achieve some specific political objective. The question is how suitable nuclear weapons might be for achieving military objectives.

Two questions are of primary concern: Can nuclear weapons be used tactically without producing too much undesirable collateral damage? And can nuclear weapons be used without an escalation into a strategic nuclear exchange? To answer the first question, a specific war scenario will be considered, namely, the employment of tactical nuclear weapons in Europe as a defense against conventional weaponry. The second question about escalation will be addressed by reviewing the perceptions of various people concerning the likelihood of escalation and how their perceptions connect to such contemporary issues as the neutron bomb; the deployment of highly accurate intermediate-range nuclear missiles; improved command, control, communications, and **272** intelligence; and no-first-use policies.

THE TECHNOLOGY OF TACTICAL NUCLEAR WAR

In a tactical nuclear war, military commanders would want to deliver precisely controlled amounts of force on the right spot at the right time. The objective would be to minimize collateral damage while maximizing military effectiveness. Several contemporary technological developments are directed toward these goals. The neutron bomb is intended to minimize collateral damage to structures. With their great accuracy, the SS-20 and Pershing-II medium-range missiles, and the ground-launched cruise missile (GLCM), are intended to allow attacks on very hardened military targets. Improved capabilities in command, control, communication, and intelligence (C³I) systems are meant to decrease wasteful use of nuclear weapons in a limited war and to maintain control over nuclear weapons, thereby reducing the probability of escalation from limited to full-scale nuclear war.

Tactical Nuclear Weapons

Tactical nuclear weapons should be adjusted in size to the task, should have an accuracy commensurate with their explosive yield and the target size, and should have a range appropriate for local battlefield use or for interdiction behind the battle lines. Each of the current controversies about tactical nuclear weapons relates to one or more of these requirements.

The Neutron Bomb

The so-called "neutron bombs" for deployment in Europe are designed to maximize damage to enemy troops—specifically to enemy tank crews—yet minimize collateral damage to civilian and industrial installations. The neutron bomb differs from standard nuclear weapons insofar as its primary lethal effects come from the radiation damage caused by the neutrons it emits. Hence, it is also called an enhanced-radiation weapon (ERW). The augmented radiation effects mean that blast and heat are reduced so that physical structures, including houses and industrial installations, are less affected. Because neutron radiation effects drop off very rapidly with distance, there is a sharper distinction between areas with high lethality and areas with minimal radiation doses. These are the features desired by the forces of the North Atlantic Treaty Organization (NATO) for their tactical nuclear weapons. NATO forces have to be prepared to fight the next war on their home territory, particularly inside Germany. Western Europe is densely populated; any tactical nuclear explosion will endanger civilian lives and property.

Actually all small nuclear bombs are "neutron bombs." Consider the lethality radii for nuclear weapons listed in Tables 2.4 and 2.5 and shown in Fig. 2.19. For weapons with a yield below 1 kt, the primary lethal effects come from neutron and gamma-ray radiations. For such low yields, the dose due to neutrons exceeds that due to gamma rays for distances up to 1000 m. The design of the neutron bomb is intended to enhance this radiation effect further.

The neutron bomb is a very small fusion bomb triggered by a very small fission bomb in the manner described in Chapter 3. For each fission reaction the fissile material would be expected to release about 200 MeV of energy and allow about one neutron to escape the exploding mass. Table 12.1 shows the distribution of the energy released by such an explosion among the various weapons effects. For a fission bomb, most of the energy is carried away by the heavy fission fragments that quickly give up their energy to the fireball as they come to rest; that fireball energy ultimately is released as blast and heat. The one neutron per fission event that escapes the fireball carries away only about 2 MeV of energy. The fusion reaction in contrast gives 14.1 MeV of energy to the resulting neutron; the alpha particle carries away only the remaining 3.5 MeV of the 17.6 MeV available from one D + T reaction. Thus, a pure fusion bomb would give only 20% of its energy to the fireball since all the neutrons would escape from it. Only when these neutrons are captured in a tamper, as in some surrounding uranium shell, does a hydrogen bomb produce as much blast as an A-bomb. A 1-kt neutron bomb, producing 50% of its energy by fission and 50% by fusion, will have a blast equivalent to that of a 0.8-kt A-bomb, heat effects equivalent to a 0.5-kt A-bomb, fallout equivalent to a 0.5-kt A-bomb, and prompt radiation energy equivalent to a 6.5-kt A-bomb and will produce 6.5 times as many neutrons carrying 7 times the energy each, or 45 times the total neutron energy.

NATO forces would want to use the neutron bomb to offset the Warsaw Pact's superiority in tanks during a possible invasion of NATO territory. Neutron bombs would be exploded above a column of attack-

Table 12.1   The emissions from various nuclear devices with a yield of 1 kt, (i.e., each device releases 10^{12} cal).
Values are in percentages of the total energy yield for each bomb. After Glasstone and Dolan, 1977, p. 13, and Kaplan, 1978, pp. 46–47.

Bomb	Energy				Neutrons	
	Blast	Heat	Fallout	Prompt Rad.	Number	Energy
1-kt fission	50%	35%	10%	5%	$1.5 \cdot 10^{23}$	2 MeV
1-kt fusion	10%	10%	None	80%	$18 \cdot 10^{23}$	14.1 MeV
1-kt neutron bomb (fission = fusion)	40%	25%	5%	30%	$9 \cdot 10^{23}$ $0.7 \cdot 10^{23}$	14.1 MeV 2 MeV

ing tanks to disable the tank crews by radiation. To achieve this, the tank crew must be totally and promptly incapacitated. This requires large radiation doses. Figure 12.1 suggests that a dose of 8000 rem would be required, leading to nervous shock in minutes and to death within a day or two with no ability to do any work at all till death. A dose of 2000–4000 rem will lead to immediate incapacitance within 5 min of exposure; after 30 to 45 min, victims will recover somewhat, although they will remain functionally impaired until death 4 to 6 days later. An exposure of 500 to 2000 rem will lead to nausea within ½ to 1 hr; diarrhea may come thereafter, although the victim may feel reasonably well for some weeks. Two to 6 weeks after exposure these victims most likely will die of some infection. Below 450 rem the victim may feel nauseous, lose hair, and suffer from infection but will most likely survive. On the linear model of radiation damage, however, no radiation dose is harmless. Thus a 150-rem exposure will on the average have a 3% chance of causing death by cancer. For neutrons at low doses, the relative biological effectiveness may be high, so that the linear model may underestimate the effects of nonfatal neutron doses. Figure 12.1 leads to the conclusion that enemy troops must be exposed to 8000 rem to eliminate them as functioning soldiers. In contrast civil-

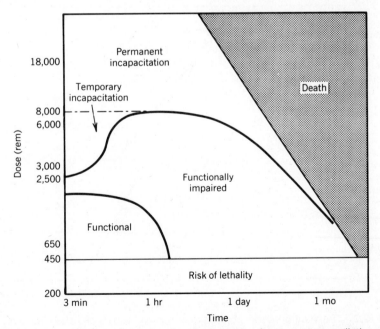

Figure 12.1 The effects on humans of various levels of exposure to radiation. These values are only approximate, depending on the physical conditions of the victims and on the tasks demanded of them. (After *Military Review*, Vol. 56, no. 5, May 1976, p. 3; see also Miettinen, 1977.)

ians should get as little radiation as possible, certainly less than the 450 rem that are likely to kill them.

Figure 12.2 shows the neutron radiation dose received from a 1-kt neutron bomb at various distances from the explosion. Tank crews inside a tank with a shielding factor of two will receive a neutron dose of 8000 rem at 650 m when the radiation dose outside the tank is 16,000 rem. A civilian inside a house with a shielding factor of three will receive a dose of 450 rem at 1130 m when the outside dosage is 1350 rem. Unprotected persons will receive a dose of 150 rem at 1700 m from the explosion center.

The neutron bomb has the other nuclear weapons effects of blast, heat, and fallout. But each of these is slightly less than those of an equivalent standard A-bomb. The 1-kt neutron bomb gives a 5 psi overpressure at about 465 m, 7% less than the 500 m of a 1-kt pure fission bomb; it gives a third-degree burn at 530 m, or 12% less than the 630 m of a 1-kt pure fission bomb. Such a small nuclear weapon will indeed produce less collateral blast and burn damage than radiation damage.

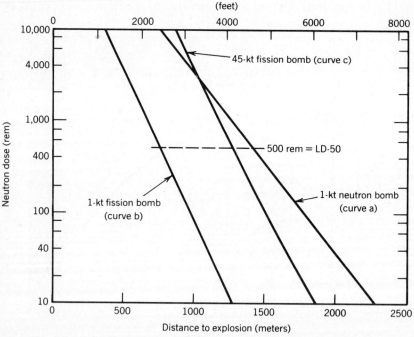

Figure 12.2 The neutron dose from various nuclear explosions as a function of the distance from the explosion. Curve (a) for the 1-kt neutron bomb is after Glasstone and Dolan, 1977, p. 47; curve (b) is based on Glasstone and Dolan, 1977, Figure 11.91; and curve (c) assumes that a 45-kt fission bomb has a neutron dose equivalent to 45 times that of a 1-kt fission bomb.

High-Accuracy Missiles

A tactical nuclear war would produce local collateral damage, would involve civilians, and would increase the chances of the local conflict escalating into a full-scale nuclear war. High accuracy is very desirable in tactical nuclear weapons to enhance the damage to hardened military targets and to minimize such collateral damage; much of the current technology is directed to improving such accuracy. Accuracy is involved in the current issues of new intermediate-range missiles and the proposed deployment of ground-launched cruise missiles.

Cruise missiles have already been discussed in Chapter 5. The high accuracy of the cruise missile would be useful in a tactical nuclear war. The various deployments of accurate intermediate-range ballistic missiles in Europe reflect not only a perceived need for longer-ranged missiles but also the usefulness of more accurate missiles. The deployment of the Soviet SS-20 and the American Pershing-II missiles is supposed to solve some problems presented in tactical nuclear wars.

Since 1977 the Soviet Union has been deploying an intermediate-range ballistic missile (IRBM) labeled the SS-20 by NATO. This missile is solid fueled, and essentially consists of the lower two stages of the SS-16 ICBM. The SS-20 can deliver 3 MIRVs of 150 kt each with an accuracy of about 400 m over a range of 5000 km. About 210 of the 315 presently deployed SS-20s are thought to be aimed at NATO targets. The good accuracy, MIRVing, and large range makes it a useful tactical weapon even when kept on Soviet soil west of the Ural mountains. It is mobile, although only in the limited sense shown in Fig. 12.3; it is

Figure 12.3 The SS-20 deployment mode. (Drawing courtesy U.S. Department of Defense.)

moved between pre-prepared sites with very large launchers and several support trucks to launch the missile.

The United States plans to deploy 108 Pershing-II IRBMs in Europe in response to the SS-20. Their accuracy is 40 m or better over their range of 1500 km; they deliver a single warhead of 250-kt yield. This relatively small size makes them mobile. The most impressive new feature of this missile will be its very high accuracy, achieved, as shown in Fig. 12.4, by terminal guidance (MARV) carried out through radar-scanning area correlations similar to the TERCOM system of the new U.S. cruise missiles. This missile can reach Moscow from NATO bases.

Command, Control, Communications, and Intelligence

If a limited nuclear war is to be kept limited, it requires excellent capabilities for command, control, communications, and intelligence (C^3I). Concern has recently been expressed about the survival of C^3I in a nuclear war environment, particularly through the effects of electromagnetic pulses generated by nuclear explosions. These concerns have led to some military changes, as through the development of AWACS aircraft shielded against these pulses.

Electromagnetic Pulse

A limited nuclear war requires good and survivable electronics communications. This includes ground and satellite observation and warning systems, communications links, and survivable command

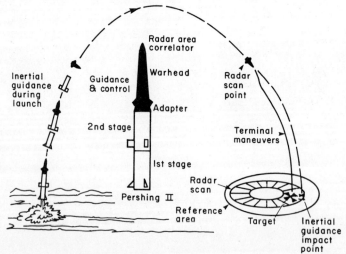

Figure 12.4 The trajectory and maneuvering capability of the Pershing-II IRBM mobile missile. (After drawing by U.S. Department of Defense.)

centers with the requisite linkages to the weapons and their guidance systems. Much of this C^{3}I is potentially vulnerable to electromagnetic pulses induced by nuclear explosions.

A nuclear weapons explosion emits copious quantities of gamma rays. When gamma rays collide with air molecules, they generate electrons and positive ions. If these charges move in a nonspherical pattern, they generate electromagnetic pulses (EMP) that contain for a short time very large electric and magnetic fields (Fig. 12.5). In an explosion near the earth's surface, the gamma rays travel only a few miles before generating such an EMP. The source of EMP for near-earth nuclear explosions is small, essentially coinciding with the region where direct blast effects occur. If a nuclear weapon is exploded at high altitudes, these gamma rays may travel hundreds of kilometers before reaching the atmosphere. In that case the gamma rays strike the atmosphere over a very large area and produce electrons that spiral in the earth's magnetic field to generate an EMP over a very large source region, far beyond the region of direct blast, heat, and radiation effects. A high-yield weapon exploded 300 km above the central United States could generate an electric field as much as 25,000 volts (V) per meter over the whole United States (Fig. 12.6).

This pulse can produce large effects in electronic circuitry; it could

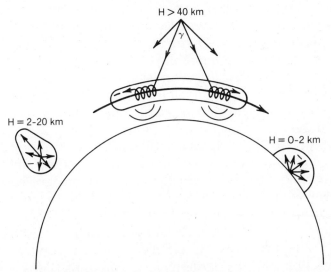

Figure 12.5 An electromagnetic pulse is generated by the movement of electrons produced in the atmosphere by the prompt gamma rays from the nuclear blast. For explosions in the earth's atmosphere, the asymmetric distribution of the scattered electrons produces the EMP. For high-altitude explosions, the movement of the generated electrons in the earth's magnetic field produces the EMP. (Hafemeister, 1983, Figure 1, p. 216, by permission of the American Institute of Physics.)

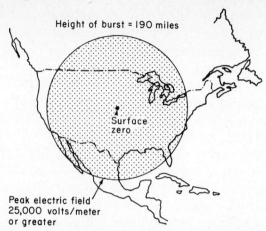

Height of burst = 190 miles

Surface zero

Peak electric field
25,000 volts/meter
or greater

Figure 12.6 A nuclear explosion 300 km high above the United States could blanket all of it with an electromagnetic pulse with electric fields as high as 25,000 volts per meter. (After Office of Technology Assessment, 1981, p. 297.)

induce in an exposed 2.5-cm long wire a pulse of 600 V that could easily burn out many modern solid-state components. A radar dish or an ICBM with a size of 10 m could experience a 250,000-V differential. If such large pulses are not filtered out by factors of thousands, sensitive circuits might be damaged.

The EMP signal resembles somewhat the electronic effects of lightning. However, its electromagnetic spectrum extends further into the communications frequencies, as an EMP delivers its energy in 10^{-8} sec, 100 times as fast as does lightning. In 1962 the EMP from a high-altitude nuclear blast near Johnston Island caused the failure of street lights, power-line circuits, and burglar alarms in Hawaii, 1300 km away. Modern solid-state electronics are much more sensitive to such electrical surges.

A single high-altitude explosion, therefore, might disable a significant fraction of all computers, communications systems, and satellites. This danger from EMP has gradually come to be recognized as critical, particularly if control over nuclear forces is desired. Because of the ban on above-ground nuclear tests, the effect of this phenomenon on contemporary circuits is not as well understood as would be desirable for assured survivability. Major efforts are now underway to improve the survivability of C^3I. Hardening of communications satellites is being carried out, redundant telephone lines are being installed, wire cables are being replaced by fiber-optical cables for laser light, and the Looking Glass airborne command centers are to be protected against EMP by improved metallic shielding.

TACTICAL NUCLEAR WAR

When speaking of a tactical nuclear war as an alternative to MAD, one generally thinks of a conventional war in which a limited number of tactical nuclear weapons are used. The consequences of such a war are very dependent on its particular scenario. But one can get an intuitive feeling for such a war by examining the possible consequences of another kind of limited nuclear war, namely, counterforce attacks.

Counterforce Attacks

To gauge the collateral damage from a counterforce strike, consider the attack on U.S. missile silos described in Fig. 9.2. In that attack, each ICBM silo is targeted with one ½-Mt air burst and one ½-Mt surface burst. The danger to civilians from the fallout resulting from such an attack would be considerable; the 1350-rem contours (450 rem inside houses that are above ground) cover more than 5% of the U.S. mainland. Assuming that about half the population were protected to a protection level of 3 against radiation inside a house, with the remainder protected by a factor of 14 to 100 (in a basement or a shelter), then around 5.6 million fatalities might result from the fallout. If two 1-Mt surface bursts were carried out on each silo, with 1-Mt air bursts over all 46 SAC bomber bases and the two SLBM submarine bases, then 16.3 million fatalities might result. The latter attack might destroy 57% of the ICBMs, 60% of the bomber force caught on the ground, and none of the submarines on patrol at the moment; a significant retaliatory force would survive. Such a counterforce attack would produce considerable civilian casualties through the local fallout. The explosions of 500 Mt of ground bursts might conceivably also cause some of the global effects described in Chapter 4.

Not only do the consequences of a counterforce war resemble those from a tactical nuclear war, but the control problems are likely to be similar. For a counterforce war, enough control over the weapons must be available to retaliate selectively on equivalent military targets of the enemy on a level of punishment appropriate for the initial first strike. In *The Third World War* (Hackett et al., 1979), a very limited nuclear exchange is postulated: Birmingham in England is destroyed, and in exchange Minsk in the Soviet Union is targeted. Under such very limited attacks, planning and control may be possible. A carefully controlled counterforce retaliation may be harder to carry out under the confusion of thousands of nuclear explosions. This is where the AWACS planes, the presidential chain of command, and the protection against EMP phenomena become very important; they preserve the ability to command. The contemporary concern with C³I is seen by some as demonstrating an interest in fighting a protracted, even if limited nuclear counterforce war.

Tactical Nuclear War in Europe

Many believe that a counterforce war between the United States and the Soviet Union is less likely than is a war in Europe involving the superpowers, a war that might go from the use of conventional weapons to the use of tactical nuclear weapons with subsequent possible escalation to a full-scale nuclear exchange. The confrontation would be between NATO and the Warsaw Pact Organization (WPO). From the NATO perspective, the confrontation in conventional weaponry has traditionally favored the WPO. NATO has therefore always reserved the right to use nuclear weapons if attacked. A review follows of the European situation and how nuclear weapons fit into it.

The balance in the conventional forces between these two forces facing each other across the German border (Fig. 12.7) is difficult to evaluate. Table 12.2 shows the balance for some force components. On a quantitative level NATO forces appear outnumbered in most categories. The major imbalance is in tanks, although the NATO forces negate some of that advantage with antitank weapons such as the TOW missile of Fig. 12.8.

The NATO partners want to limit their expenditures on conventional forces. They have tried to counter expensive tanks with less expensive high-technology defenses and have relied on tactical nuclear weapons to deter Soviet aggression. The difficulty lies in employing such tactical nuclear weapons without unduly damaging the NATO territories. The Soviet Union also has tactical nuclear weapons (many of them large and inaccurate) that it might use in response.

The balance of the tactical nuclear forces in Europe involves both quantitative and qualitative factors. One must consider the numbers of nuclear weapons deployed and their nature. When the balance between nuclear tactical weapons in Europe is discussed, the figures usually cited are 7000 versus 3500 tactical nuclear warheads for NATO versus WPO. The number for NATO has some basis in known fact—a recent confidential report by the U.S. Department of Defense (DOD) to Congress shows 5845 U.S. warheads in Europe. But the number for the WPO is based as much on the number of nuclear-capable delivery systems as on any warhead count. Since the Soviet Union likes to retain very strict centralized control over its nuclear forces, the numbers of Soviet tactical nuclear warheads actually located in Europe under normal conditions may be considerably less.

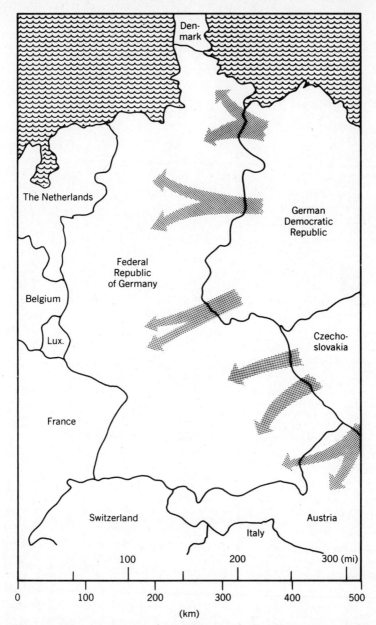

Figure 12.7 A WPO attack in Europe might involve six simultaneous breakthroughs into the Federal Republic of Germany. (After Hackett, 1979, p. 187.)

Table 12.2 The balance of conventional forces deployed in Europe.
Derived from the International Institute for Strategic Studies, 1983, pp. 138–139, and other sources as indicated.

	NATO (less U.S.)	U.S.	NATO Total	Ratio NATO:WPO	WPO (less USSR)	USSR	WPO Total
Personnel							
Total in uniform[a]	2,855	2,136	4,991	1.09:1	1,018	3,550	4,568
Reserves	4,390	955	5,345	1:1.26	1,718	5,000	6,718
Total ground forces	1,910	780	2,690	1.02:1	843	1,800	2,643
Total round forces in Europe (including trans-Caucasus)	1,764	222	1,986	1.16:1	843	871	1,714
Ground force equipment							
Main tanks	15,722	5,000	20,722	1:1.23	12,490	13,000[c]	25,490
Artillery	8,434	562	8,996	1:1.32	6,830	5,000[c]	11,830
Antitank guns	946	0	946	1:2.04	1,250	678[c]	1,928
A-T missile launchers[d]	1,380	700	2,080	1.16:1	1,500	287[c]	1,787
Antiaircraft guns	5,942	120	6,062	1.52:1	2,900	1,086[c]	3,986
SAM launchers	1,923	180	2,103	1:1.50	1,400	1,751[c]	3,151
Land-attack aircraft							
Bombers	34	0	34	1:13.4	0	455[c]	455
Ground-support planes	1,688	498	2,186	1.30:1	568	1,100[c]	1,668
Fighters	116	96	212	1:3.30	0	700[c]	700
Interceptors	647	0	647	1:6.8	1,506	2,880[c]	4,386
Armed helicopters	865	330	1,195	1:52:1	86	700	786

[a]Territorial defense forces are left out.

[b]Detailed comparisons of the forces in Central Europe generally show a ratio of about 1:1.1 favoring the WPO, depending on what French forces are counted and so on. See, for example, Fischer (1976) and Barnaby (1978); Barnaby has in the central region balances of NATO to WPO of 725,000:780,000 for ground forces, 6,090:14,800 for main tanks, and 2784:2800 for aircraft.

[c]Considerable reinforcements could be drawn from the western and southern European USSR, in many cases doubling the Soviet totals potentially available.

[d]Short range antitank missiles may be ten times this number.

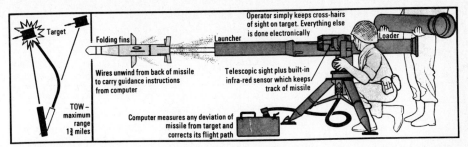

Figure 12.8 A TOW missile fired by infantry. (Illustration from The Insight Team of the London Sunday Times, *The Yom Kippur War*, New York: Doubleday, 1974; reprinted by permission of Doubleday & Co.)

As shown in Table 12.3, these warheads can be delivered by a variety of means. Some European tactical systems are really more strategic in character, for example, some Poseidon SLBMs that are allocated to the European theater. The intermediate-range Soviet SS-20 and (future) American Pershing II and ground-launched cruise missiles (GLCMs) can also be used in a strategic mode. Other nuclear warheads launched by artillery or short-range ground-support aircraft are closer to being tactical.

The warheads range enormously in yield. Some of the Poseidons carry 50-kt warheads; some Soviet SS-5 warheads have a yield of 5 Mt. These are hardly tactical weapons. On the other hand, the neutron bomb just described is specifically designed for tactical nuclear use as indicated by its small yield.

Nuclear war in Europe can best be considered by examining some scenarios as has been done in Barnaby (1978) and Calder (1979). A European war is usually seen as starting with a tank-led invasion from East Germany and Czechoslovakia into West Germany. As many as 600 tanks and 500 armored fighting vehicles might attempt a breakthrough in each of perhaps six locations simultaneously (Fig. 12.7), for a total of 3600 tanks plus 3000 armored vehicles. The breakthroughs are to be countered by defensive tank operations and antitank missiles such as the TOW shown in Fig. 12.8. The accuracy of this missile is quite good, as seen in Fig. 12.9; at a range of 1500 m, the TOW may have a probability as high as 90% of destroying an enemy tank. The TOW can be fired from armored vehicles, by four soldiers from a three-legged launch device or by helicopters. It is guided by a wire leading back to the launch site; the operator has to keep the target in his or her sights for 5 sec throughout the 1500-m flight of the missile traveling at 300 m/sec. In the ideal case, one TOW missile costing $7000 can destroy a $1 million tank.

The NATO fear is that the Soviet tank superiority might be so over-

Table 12.3   The balance of nuclear forces in Europe.
After International Institute for Strategic Studies, 1982, unless otherwise indicated.

	First Deployment	Range/ Combat Radius[a]	Warheads			Warheads Available[b]
			Inventory	Each	Yield	
North Atlantic Treaty Organization						
IRBM						
SSBS S-3 (FR)	1980	3000 km	18	1	1 Mt	16
SRBM						
Pershing IA	1962	160–720 km	180	1	400 kt	162
Pershing II	1983[c]	1500 km	108[c]	3	5–50 kt	108[c]
Gr.-Launch Cruise	1983[d]	2250 km	464[d]	1	50 kt[d]	464[d]
SLBM[e]						
Polaris A-3 (UK)	1967	4600 km	64	3[f]	200 kt	192
MSBS M-20 (FR)	1977	3000 km	80	1	1 Mt	80
Land-Based Aircraft						
F-111E/F	1967	1900 km	150	2	?	120
Mirage IVA (FR)	1964	1600 km	34	1	?	24
Bucaneer (UK)	1962	950 km	45	2	?	32
F-104 (common)	1958	800 km	261	1	?	55
F-4 (common)	1962	750 km	238	1	?	57
F-16 (US,BE)	1979	900 km	234	1	?	59
Jaguar (UK,FR)	1974	720 km	117	1	?	47
Mirage IIIE (FR)	1964	600 km	30	1	15kt	12
Carrier-Based Aircraft						
A-6E	1963	1000 km	60	2	?	48
A-7E	1966	900 km	144	2	?	114
Super Etendard (FR)	1980	560 km	36	2	15 kt	29
Warsaw Pact Organization						
IRBM						
SS-20	1977	5000 km	240[g]	3	150 kt	641
SS-5 Skean	1961	4100 km	16	1	1 Mt	12
MRBM						
SS-4 Sandal	1959	1900 km	223	1	1 Mt	157
SLBM[f]						
SS-N-5 Serb	1964	1400 km	48	1	Mt range	22
Battlefield						
SS-12 Scaleboard	1969	900 km	70	1	200 kt	56
Scud A/B	1965	300 km	440[g]	1	kt range	352
SS-22	1978	1000 km	100[h]	1	500 kt	80
SS-23	1980	350 km	10[h]	1	dual	8

Table 12.3   (continued)

	First Deployment	Range/ Combat Radius[a]	Warheads Inventory	Warheads Each	Warheads Yield	Warheads Available[b]
Land-Based Aircraft						
Tu-26 Backfire	1974	4025 km	100[i]	4	?	128[i]
Tu-16 Badger	1955	2800 km	310[i]	2	?	174
Tu-22 Blinder	1962	3100 km	125[i]	2	?	70
Su-24 (SU-19) Fencer	1974	1699 km	550[i]	2	?	176
MiG-27 Flogger D	1971	720 km	550[i]	1	?	176
Su-17 Fitter C/D	1974	600 km	688[i]	1	?	110
Su-7 Fitter A	1959	400 km	265[i]	1	?	37
MiG-21 Fishbed J-N	1970	400 km	100[i]	1	?	16

[a] Range applies for missiles; combat radius is for unrefueled aircraft assuming high-altitude approach, low-altitude penetration, and a normal payload.

[b] The number of available warheads is calculated taking into account the percentage of the weapon system likely to be used in a nuclear role and its servicability (see International Institute for Strategic Studies, 1982, pp. 129–139).

[c] The Pershing-II missile is being gradually deployed starting in 1983. Cochran et al. (1983) cite its yield as 5 to 50 kt.

[d] The ground-launched cruise missile with a 2400-km range is gradually being deployed in Europe starting in 1983. Cochran, et al. (1983) cite its yield as 50 kt.

[e] Only the SLBM of France and Great Britain are counted as theater nuclear weapons since only they are not counted in the SALT agreements.

[f] The British Polaris A-3 missiles carry three MRV warheads.

[g] Two-thirds of the 360 SS-20 missiles are thought to be targeted on Europe; the Scud A/B listed are those in Europe and the European USSR.

[h] These are the total nuclear-capable units available.

[i] This is the total thought at most to be assigned a nuclear strike role; only a fraction of these are likely to be used in that manner, hence, the low available warhead figure (see International Institute for Strategic Studies, 1982, pp. 129–139).

whelming that antitank defenses and missiles become insufficient to halt a Soviet advance. Then the tactical nuclear option might be exercised: nuclear demolition mines might block mountain passes or destroy bridges, and nuclear artillery and short-range missiles might directly attack Soviet troops and tank forces.

As an example of the possible consequences of such a limited war, consider the use of neutron bombs to attack Soviet tanks and armored vehicles. Figure 12.10 schematically shows a group of Soviet tanks advancing in a semirural area in West Germany in the expected manner, spaced about 100 m apart and in three rows for mutual support. A 1-kt neutron bomb is exploded 500 m above these tanks to disable the tank crews without destroying nearby villages and industry. Figure 12.2 shows the radiation effects from neutron bombs. Prompt radiation

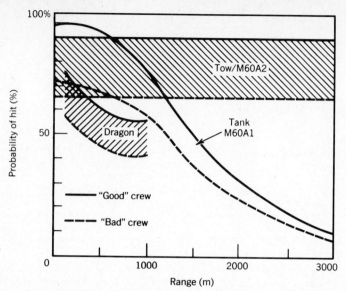

Figure 12.9 The probabilities of a hit at various distances for TOW and Dragon antitank missiles and for shells fired by a M60A1 tank. In each case the success of high-performance crews, indicated by the solid lines, exceeded that of low-performance crews, indicated by the dotted lines; that is, the success rate depends greatly on training.

doses of 16,000 rem, 1350 rem, and 150 rem extend to about 415 m, 1010 m, and 1625 m, respectively, out from the epicenter directly underneath the explosion. The tank crews will be immediately and permanently disabled within the circle with 415-m radius if the tanks have a protection factor of two—that is, over an area of 0.5 km². If all goes well, this one neutron bomb may therefore disable the crews of per-

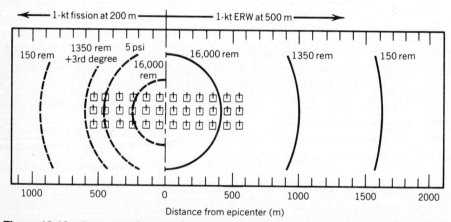

Figure 12.10 A group of Soviet tanks advancing in three rows with 100-m spacing. The solid and dotted lines indicate, respectively, the range of effects for a 1-kt neutron bomb exploded at 500 m and a 1-kt fission bomb exploded at 200 m, in both cases directly above the tanks.

haps 24 tanks. If the tanks were spaced farther apart, fewer would be disabled, but their mutual support would be decreased. The 1350-rem contour of 1010-m radius covers an area of 4 km^2 in which civilians in homes with protection factors of three will receive a median lethal dose of 450 rems. An additional area of 8.3 km^2 − 4.0 km^2 = 4.3 km^2 will be covered with 150 rem or more, sufficient to produce significant radiation sickness and cancer cases. There is here an important asymmetry in the dose required to disable soldiers and that which can accidentally injure or kill civilians.

The collateral blast and heat-damage effects are suppressed for this bomb. The blast effects would be equivalent to those from an 0.8-kt fission bomb; hence the 5 psi to destroy houses and light industry would reach out to 400 m from the center of the explosion; third-degree burns would be equivalent to those from a 0.5-kt fission bomb and, hence, would reach 445 m from the explosion. Neither effect would reach the ground. For this neutron bomb, the majority of the civilian casualties would come from the effects of the prompt neutron radiation.

The consequences to European civilians of a limited tactical nuclear strike on Soviet tanks using neutron bombs can now be estimated for the best possible case where no escalation takes place and the Soviets use none of their nuclear weapons. On a cost-benefit basis, it would seem profitable to destroy 24 $1-million tanks with a single $1-million missile carrying a neutron bomb. To incapacitate the crews of the 6600 vehicles postulated in the attack described would require 6600/24 = 275 neutron bombs. This would expose the civilian population in an area of 275 · 4 km^2 = 1100 km^2 to at least a median fatal dosage of 450 rem inside houses or an unprotected population in an additional area of 275 · 4.3 km^2 = 1183 km^2 to a dose of 150 rem. The population density in West Germany averages about 200/km^2. The spacing of villages in the northern German plain is such that there will be at least one population center in the 4 km^2 irradiated to 1350 rem by each neutron bomb; thus any neutron bomb is likely to affect one village. This is the inspiration for the statement that German villages are one kiloton apart. One can roughly estimate that each neutron bomb will kill everyone within 4 km^2, or 800 persons, while incapacitating three crew members in each of 24 tanks, or 72 tankers, and would injure an additional 860 people in 4.2 km^2. The 275 neutron bombs would then kill 220,000 persons and injure an additional 325,000 persons.

Peterson et al. (1983) do a similar calculation. They assume that radiation sickness will be produced in soldiers and civilians in an area of 5 km^2. But they analyze a somewhat larger war in which more than 1000 military targets would be struck by nuclear weapons. This scenario would lead to 1 million civilian fatalities. A past NATO exercise involving the hypothetical use of 500 to 1000 weapons against military targets produced at least 1½ million fatalities and serious injuries (Zuckerman, 1982). An actual nuclear war in Europe might well be considerably worse than that described here. Considering possible fall-out produced in a likely tactical nuclear war in Europe, fatality esti-mates range upward to 20 million (Peterson et al., 1983). If ground bursts were exploded in urban areas, the nuclear winter described in Chapter 4 could occur.

This calculation does not take into account several complicating fac-tors. As can be seen in Fig. 12.2, the neutron dose drops off very rapidly away from the blast because of the absorption of neutrons by the air. At the distance of 500 m that the tanks would be located from the ERW epicenter, the neutron dose continues to decrease by a factor of two in about 50 m. Thus the target location and the accuracy of delivery must be better than 50 m horizontally, vertically, and laterally combined to maximize the killing effect on tank crews. Generally, any inaccuracies most likely will reduce the number of tank crews incapac-itated by each neutron bomb without reducing proportionately the number of civilian casualties. Some of the warheads may miss the tank forces altogether; additional nuclear warheads would then have to be exploded. Fallout has not been taken into account in the calculation because the explosion fireballs would not touch the ground. If ground explosions were to take place, as for nuclear demolition weapons, fall-out might present a major problem.

Several military questions must be considered. A tank facing a neu-tron bomb barrage could protect itself against such radiation. Tanks already provide some shielding against neutrons. The half-thickness of iron for the absorption of neutrons is about 4 cm. However, the absorption thickness depends on the energy spectrum of the neutron flux, on scattering problems, and so on. The high-energy neutrons from a neutron bomb must first be slowed down before they can be absorbed; slow neutrons can cause more damage to humans than can fast neutrons, so that for some smaller thicknesses of iron, the absorber could actually increase the injury to tank crews. The shielding on modern tanks may be as much as 10 cm in front, but as little as 2.5 cm in other areas. The shielding factor thus depends on the direction of the incoming neutrons and on the positions of the tank crew members. Shielding factors of two are usually mentioned for typical modern tanks. This shielding factor might be increased. The best shield against fast neutrons is provided by hydrogen atoms. A shield of 7 cm of water (or its equivalent in paraffin) would reduce the neutron dose by a factor of two. A thin sheet of cadmium would absorb the slow neutrons exiting the hydrogen shield.

Neutron bombs can be really effective only if the friendly troops and civilians are well protected against neutrons (e.g., if bunkers are available). The provision of that protection to soldiers would, however, close off an option that is an alternative to the neutron bomb, namely, the use of antitank missiles. These missiles must be visually guided to the enemy tank. The infantry troops who operate these missiles must be both mobile and exposed; being unprotected makes them particularly vulnerable to neutron radiation. Enemy troops being transported in open trucks to the battlefield, or advancing with the tanks, are also exposed and vulnerable.

The usefulness of nuclear weapons in Europe depends on the answers to some questions: Which nuclear weapons are most useful in Europe? Are the consequences of a tactical nuclear war bearable? Can such a war be controlled? How much cheaper are nuclear weapons than equivalent conventional defenses?

Is the neutron bomb a useful weapon for halting an invading tank army; are there alternative methods for destroying tanks? Alternatives could include more NATO tanks and more antitank missiles (Walker, 1981). Assuming that NATO is committed to destroying WPO tanks by tactical nuclear weapons, are neutron bombs more effective than small pure fission bombs? A normal fission bomb indeed would have a larger area of physical destruction. Consider a 1-kt pure fission bomb exploded at an altitude of 200 m. Figure 12.2 suggests 313 m for the 16,000-rem distance and 500 m and 630 m, respectively, for the 5-psi and third-degree-burn contours; these distances from the epicenter would be, respectively, 240 m, 458 m, and 600 m. This bomb might incapacitate 15 tank crews, while killing civilians in homes over an area of 0.66 km², or 132 people. This bomb would disable more tank crew members per civilian fatality than would the neutron bomb. Indeed the neutron bomb kills people while destroying less property (Fig. 12.11).

ESCALATION

When dealing with tactical or limited nuclear war, important questions are those of control and escalation. An inevitable conflict arises between the desire to have centralized control to avoid the premature use of nuclear weapons on local initiative and the possible need to act promptly. The present line of request for permission to use nuclear

"--and the nifty thing is that it doesn't hurt the house!"

Figure 12.11 The moralist's view of the neutron bomb. (By permission of Douglas Borgstedt.)

weapons requires about one day to go from the request on the corps level up to the top level to obtain approval and then to return the permission to the field commander. A limited nuclear war would not be feasible if it were likely to escalate into a full-scale nuclear war with the traumatic consequences described in Chapters 3 and 4. The critics of counterforce weapons argue that the very act of developing the capability to fight a nuclear war increases the chances of having to fight one and thereby increases the chance of escalation to a full-scale nuclear war. Those in favor of a tactical nuclear capability argue that it makes the deterrence posture more realistic and believable and thereby reduces the probability of an all-out nuclear conflict.

U.S. Perceptions

This debate about tactical nuclear weapons cannot be resolved, although the probabilities of nuclear wars on various levels are discussed in Chapter 17. One can cite the statements of some who have roles to play in such decision making. President Richard M. Nixon in 1972 said: ". . . can full-scale nuclear war be the only alternative?" In 1974 Secretary of Defense James Schlesinger asked for the development of a capability for flexible response in which the level of retaliation could be adjusted to match appropriately the level of the attack. In 1979 President Jimmy Carter promulgated Presidential Directive 59, which gave targeting policies an increased orientation toward counterforce strikes. His press secretary said that the president "is prepared to use nuclear weapons to thwart a communistic attack on NATO members and would back efforts to regain any land lost through invasion" (Douglass, 1980, p. 272). In the early 1980s, the debate raged about the deployment of Pershing IIs and GLCMs in Europe not only to counter the existence of the Soviet SS-20s but also to preserve the credibility of the U.S. guarantee of a nuclear umbrella over Europe. The improved accuracy of these missiles makes nuclear warfighting seem more feasible, as does the improved accuracy of the future MX and the improved C^3I capabilities being developed.

The United States and NATO have always retained the option of using tactical nuclear weapons; the military structure of NATO is designed with this option in mind. The West has always argued that nuclear escalation is not inevitable. In recent years those who fear such escalation have suggested that the United States and NATO ought to establish instead a policy promising no first use of nuclear weapons. That policy could consist of a statement that the declaring nation would not be the first to use nuclear weapons. This would strengthen the firebreak between the use of conventional and nuclear weapons. This no-first-use policy would presumably apply to the European theater; it would then require adequate conventional defenses in Europe. However, NATO nations have been unwilling to spend the money that might be required to make NATO conventionally secure.

Actually the escalation from limited to full-scale nuclear war is already implied by the semantic difficulties of defining tactical versus strategic nuclear weapons. One might be able to picture a limited nuclear war fought with tactical nuclear weapons, but would expect strategic use of weapons to lead to a full-scale war. But which nuclear weapons are tactical, which are strategic? As Nigel Calder (1979, pp. 25–26) puts it,

> Distinguishing between "strategic" and "tactical" nuclear weapons is as tricky as differentiating in medieval theology between efficacious grace and sufficient grace. You might imagine that "tactical" nuclear weapons are all modest little battlefield bombs for strikes against tanks and airfields, but that is not the case. . . . Alternatively it might be supposed that the "tactical" bombs are for use against military targets only; wrong again, they can be used equally well against cities. Some writers prefer to call them "theater" nuclear weapons, meaning that they are stationed in regions away from the homelands of the superpowers . . . this is closer to the mark, although not as sharp as the cynic's version: "A tactical nuclear weapon is one that explodes in Germany."

In strategic arms negotiations the United States applies the word "strategic" to intercontinental ballistic missiles, SLBMs, long-range intercontinental heavy bombers, and probably ABMs. All others are presumed to be tactical nuclear weapons. The Soviet Union makes a distinction between weapons aimed at its homeland, and those aimed at battlefields outside the USSR itself. A distinction was drawn in Chapter 1 on the basis of use, whether the weapon is tactically aimed at precisely defined targets and objectives or is strategically aimed at populations and other soft countervalue targets. Others apply the term tactical to all battlefield (or theater) usage. Still others distinguish on the basis of yield, with kiloton weapons being tactical and megaton weapons being strategic. In all these criteria there is a continuous range between tactical and strategic nuclear weapons. As General Geller described it at a congressional hearing in 1973,

> the target system describes the purpose of the bombs perhaps better than the yield. I think it is the jargon of the trade, perhaps, that those bombs that are targeted through SAC (and which are in the Triad) are normally called strategic bombs whereas those that are assigned, with fighter bombers, are normally called tactical bombs. Quite a few of these delivery systems and bombs are capable of being employed in either tactical or strategic roles. . . . The Russians as I understand it define strategic as anything that can strike the homeland. Therefore, their argument is any system which can strike Russia is strategic. (As quoted in Barnaby, 1978, p. 5)

Soviet Perceptions

Since a war in Europe, or any tactical nuclear war anywhere else, would involve the Soviet Union, the Soviet view of tactical nuclear war is critical. That view is not clearly defined. Not only do some Soviet views seem internally inconsistent from a Western perspective, but there may be conflicts between material published for Western consumption and material aimed at internal consumption by the Soviet military.

There appears to be a Soviet consensus that any military confrontation between the superpowers may escalate to nuclear war, particularly in Europe if any nuclear weapons are used by either side:

> Soviet publications discussing a theater war in Europe warn that the use of tactical nuclear weapons or of "nuclear warning shots" will lead most likely to an escalation of the conflict and argue that any armed conflict in Europe . . . would inexorably involve all other states of the world in the orbit of a thermonuclear collision. (Gouré et al., 1974, p. 128)

From a Western perspective, the Soviets show some inconsistency in their views. They acknowledge the likelihood of nuclear escalation and the holocaustic devastation of a nuclear war, yet they equate deterrence with a warfighting capability:

Soviet military writings and military posture do not specifically distinguish between deterrence and war-fighting nuclear capabilities or postures, but appear to view them as one and the same. The Soviet assumption is that the better the Soviet Armed Forces are prepared to fight and, if possible, win a nuclear war, the more effective they will also be as a deterrent to an attack on the Soviet Union and as a support of Soviet foreign policy (Gouré et al., 1974, p. 47)

IS TACTICAL NUCLEAR WAR FEASIBLE?

The question addressed in this chapter has been whether nuclear weapons can be used other than to maintain mutual assured destruction. Two separate issues arose: Would the consequences of any conceivable limited nuclear war be so large as to make them unacceptable? And would a limited nuclear war stay limited? Neither of these questions can be answered definitively.

Various kinds of limited tactical nuclear wars have been examined here. A counterforce exchange involving intercontinental weapons to attack other strategic weapons of the Triad had consequences possibly smaller than those defined to be unacceptable in Chapter 4 but would still be quite large with many millions of civilian fatalities and large amounts of radioactive fallout. The use of nuclear weapons in Europe to halt tank attacks would likely produce somewhat fewer fatalities, but only if the usage of nuclear weapons were restricted to small nuclear warheads exploded on a very limited number of well-defined targets. If the nuclear weapons used would be controlled and if escalation of the limited wars could be avoided, some tactical nuclear wars might be feasible.

The problem of escalation is even more difficult to address. NATO believes it can be avoided; the Soviet Union believes escalation to be inevitable. The more inevitable the escalation from limited to full-scale nuclear war, the lower is the feasibility of a limited nuclear war.

No clear-cut answer can be given—it is unknown whether tactical nuclear war offers a alternative to mutual assured destruction. Arguments on both sides are equally unprovable.

References

Barnaby, F., ed. *Tactical Nuclear Weapons: European Perspectives.* New York: Crane, Russak, for SIPRI, 1978.

Calder, N. *Nuclear Nightmares: An Investigation into Possible Wars.* New York: Viking Press, 1979.

Cochran, T. B., W. M. Arkin, and M. M. Hoenig. *Nuclear Weapons Databook,* Vol. I, *U.S. Nuclear Forces and Capabilities.* Cambridge, Mass.: Ballinger, 1983.

Douglass, J. D., Jr. *Soviet Military Strategy in Europe.* New York: Pergamon Press, 1980.

Fischer, R. L. *Defending the Central Front: The Balance of Forces,* Adelphi Paper #127. London: International Institute for Strategic Studies, 1976.

Gouré, L., F. D. Koehler, and M. L. Harvey. *The Role of Nuclear Forces in Current Soviet Strategy.* Miami, Fla.: University of Miami Press, 1974.

Hackett, J., et al. *The Third World War: August 1985.* New York: Berkley, 1979.

Hafemeister, D. W. "Science and Society Test VIII: The Arms Race Revisited." *American Journal of Physics,* Vol. 51 (1983), pp. 215–225.

International Institute for Strategic Studies, *The Military Balance: 1982–1983.* London: IISS, 1982.

———— , *The Military Balance: 1983–1984.* London: IISS, 1983.

Kaplan, F. M. "Enhanced-Radiation Weapons." *Scientific American,* Vol. 238, no. 5 (May 1978), pp. 44–51.

Miettinen, J. K. "Enhanced Radiation Warfare." *Bulletin of the Atomic Scientists,* Vol. 33, no. 6 (June 1977), pp. 32–37.

Office of Technology Assessment. *MX Missile Basing.* Washington, D.C.: Government Printing Office, 1981.

Peterson, J., and the *Ambio* editorial staff of the Royal Swedish Academy of Sciences. *Nuclear War: The Aftermath.* New York: Pergamon Press, 1983.

Walker, P. F. "Precision-Guided Weapons." *Scientific American,* Vol. 245, no. 2 (August 1981), pp. 36–45.

Zuckerman, S. *Nuclear Illusions and Reality.* New York: Viking Press, 1982.

PART

4

ARMS CONTROL AND DISARMAMENT

The most obvious alternative to deterrence would seem to be disarmament. Disarmament could occur on several levels. One side could threaten to disarm the other by overwhelming power, as through a technological surprise; or it might partially disarm unilaterally, in the hope that the other side will respond in kind. Or both sides might mutually agree to gradual disarmament. Various experiences with arms control and institutional barriers to its success will be analyzed in this part of the text.

Chapter 13 will consider disarmament from a technological perspective, examining what features of science and technology influence arms control. Unfortunately, many technologies exert pressures that run counter to arms control, for example, many rapidly growing technologies that are fueled by progress in computers. Chapter 14 contains a consideration how the proliferation of nuclear weapons may be related to the growth of the nuclear electric power industry; in the past, nuclear weapon states have developed nuclear weapons largely independent of that industry, but that may not hold in the future.

Some limited success has been achieved in negotiating strategic arms control agreements since 1945. The partial test-ban treaty described in Chapter 15 forbids the above-ground testing of nuclear weapons. That is an achievement; it has at least reduced global nuclear fallout, although it has also reduced the political pressure on the nuclear weapons states to stop nuclear weapons **297** tests altogether. Chapter 16 describes strategic arms limitations. The SALT I agreement set some limits on the numbers of intercontinental nuclear weaponry. The limitation of weapons, however, has turned out to be insufficient to stop the nuclear arms race; control on weapons quality is needed if stability in the arms race is to be achieved. Unfortunately, the more qualitative the parameter to be controlled, the harder it is to find and agree upon a method of limiting it. SALT II illustrates this problem; it did not control the improving accuracy of weapons that can destabilize the strategic nuclear balance.

As discussed in Chapter 17, significant disarmament unfortunately is very difficult to achieve. The influence of economic and natural resource interests reduces the long-term stability of international relationships and creates international tensions that foster some arms races and could lead to war. International interests make it difficult to limit arms. It is even conceivable that human societies will always experience some psychological pressures toward war, making nuclear wars perhaps inevitable in the long run.

CHAPTER
13

Technological
Imperatives

*the technological side of the arms race has a life of its own, almost
independent of policy and politics.*

Herbert F. York, former director of the Livermore
Radiation Laboratory

To control the future, one must understand the forces likely to produce
it. This holds true for the nuclear arms race; knowledge of the causes
of war might help to reduce international tension and, thereby, to
prevent wars. Social events are driven by many forces. Some would
argue that international forces are so poorly understood and so unpredictable that it is not possible to anticipate and control the future in a
significant way. Others would list geophysical, biological, and socio-
logical factors as prime determinants of international actions. Factors
involved in international prediction and control from a technological
perspective will be considered in this chapter. Technology is one prime
mover of the nuclear arms race through technological imperatives.
Some technologies are so technically sweet and beautiful that they are
difficult to resist, and the resulting technological progress may force
some public policies that may not be desirable. Control of technological
imperatives may be of vital importance if arms control is to succeed.

This chapter will consider the relationship between technological
progress and the nuclear arms race. Some political events caused by
specific weapons technologies will be reviewed. Some examples will
be cited of weapons technologies that have been controlled more or
less successfully in the past, to ask why it was possible to limit the
nuclear airplane and the ABM but not the H-bomb and MIRVed
warheads. **299**

At the moment the most pressing technological imperatives seem to be those fueled by progress in computer technologies. The question of technological control can then be rephrased to ask whether nuclear weaponry can be controlled by guiding its technological base, such as computers. This would seem very difficult to achieve, since it is hard to anticipate the applications of a new technology. Perhaps one instead ought to control the resulting weapons systems before they are deployed. One needs perhaps to interfere not in the early weapons research but rather during the testing stage to ensure the deployment of only desirable technologies and rejection of the imperative pressures to deploy undesirable weapons.

TECHNOLOGY AND POLITICAL EVENTS

Sociopolitical events have many determinants. Technology plays a major role in the nuclear arms race. Historical examples of this connection come readily to mind.

The cold war characterized the world after World War II; it was circumscribed by the existence of the A-bomb. While the Soviet Union appeared to have enormous conventional war-making capacities, the United States could balance this threat with its nuclear monopoly. Nuclear weapons technology strongly influenced the international politics after 1945, perhaps stabilizing it.

The hydrogen bomb after 1952 established the political doctrine of massive retaliation, and later made MAD (mutual assured destruction) easy to achieve, producing the bipolarity of the two superpowers. Large-scale deployment of fission and fusion weapons technology so far appears to have removed full-scale war as a method of carrying on international politics.

Prior to 1960 one of the U.S. objectives had been the establishment of a series of forward bases from which the Soviet heartland could be bombarded. The development of intercontinental bombers such as the B-52, ICBMs, and SLBM submarines reduced the need for acquiescent allies; the United States relationship to Turkey, for example, could change without major negative consequences for the United States—even the need for NATO changed. Nuclear delivery technologies changed the framework of international alliances.

The launching of the first earth satellite started a space race but also made possible the stability of deterrence and strategic arms limitations, as orbital photography provided each of the superpowers knowledge about the other's strategic armaments. Monitoring of some arms limitation agreements became possible. Stability and arms control have at least a chance because of verification technologies.

The Vietnam war has affected U.S. military postures on both the conventional and the nuclear levels. The disaster in Vietnam has been changing perceptions on how far technology can fix political problems. At various stages of the war, the technologies of strategic bombings, defoliation, weather modification, smart bombs, and the electronic barrier between North and South Vietnam displayed a faith in superior U.S. technologies and represented an attempt to use it to overcome the ideological enthusiasms of guerilla warfare. The impact of the failure of these technologies on all future U.S. political and military conduct is not yet fully understood.

The United States and the world have made a commitment to a large civilian nuclear power industry. This peaceful nuclear technology has already had an enormous impact on political structures. Its one-time promise of energy "too cheap to meter" has been part of a spendthrift attitude toward energy consumption. The overreliance on cheap oil made the energy crisis of the 1970s possible, with its consequent political realignments in the Middle East vis-à-vis the oil producing Arab states. The use of nuclear electric power to solve energy problems conjures up the specter of nuclear proliferation as both technical knowledge and ^{239}Pu become available to more nations. These energy problems color all international political dealings; the technological need for energy complicates U.S. international politics.

CAN TECHNOLOGIES BE CONTROLLED?

If technology is such an important determinant of international security relationships, to what extent is it an uncontrollable factor in the nuclear arms race? Some technologies have been successfully controlled in the past; several appealing weapons systems have not been built, and certain technological improvements have not been made. Other high-technology weapons systems were built in spite of analyses suggesting they might not be desirable. What distinguishes these two catagories?

Some Controlled Technologies

The Nuclear Airplane

The best aircraft now are propelled by jet engines fueled by kerosene or other petroleum derivatives. In the 1950s an effort was made to develop nuclear reactor engines for aircraft. In an ordinary jet engine, air is taken in at the front end, compressed by a fan, mixed with the fuel, and then burned. The heated gases exit at the rear after turning the compressor fan; their reaction force pushes the engine and the attached aircraft forward. In a nuclear engine, air is heated by passing it around some nuclear fuel elements inside an operating nuclear reactor.

From 1946 to 1961, research work was performed on such nuclear engines with funding up to $100 million per year. The program faced great technical problems. It was difficult to find materials that would survive in the very high energy flux inside the reactor and that could contain the radioactive fission products in the fuel elements while enormous quantities of dirty air flowed through the reactor core. The crew and cargo had to be protected from the intense radiation in this reactor; the required massive shielding would reduce the plane's ability to carry a payload. The hazard of crashing the aircraft and spilling the radioactive fuel was an obvious major concern.

The impossibility of solving these problems finally caused President Kennedy to cancel this program, but the technological imperative was so strong that it had taken 15 years to achieve this cancellation. The technology seemed very desirable. A nuclear submarine could cruise submerged around the world, so why not build a nuclear-powered aircraft that could stay in flight indefinitely with an unlimited range requiring no refueling? The pressure to develop this plane had become so great that at various times in the 1950s plans were made to install a test reactor engine into a normally powered aircraft just to put it into the air. In 1958 the trade journal *Aviation Week* reported that

> A nuclear powered bomber is being flight tested in the Soviet Union . . . observed . . . by a wide variety of foreign observers . . . . Appearance of this nuclear powered military prototype comes as a sickening shock . . . for once again the Soviets have beaten us needlessly to a significant technical punch. (As quoted in York, 1970, pp. 71–72)

This technological imperative was ultimately overcome because the technology was too difficult. If it had been easier, the conceptual beauty of an aircraft with infinite range would have combined with the enthusiasm of the technological promoters in industry and in the bureaucracies to develop this weapons system in spite of its difficulties.

Follow-on Manned Bomber

The last B-52 bomber was built in 1962. Research and development of follow-on manned bombers have been going on ever since. The B-70 bomber reached the point where its deployment was proposed although ultimately it was not funded. Presently, it is proposed to build both B-1 and Stealth bombers.

As indicated in Chapter 5, all these follow-on models contain some interesting new technologies. The B-70 was to be a high-altitude supersonic bomber; the B-1 is to fly at very low levels and be partially supersonic; and the Stealth bomber is to be largely invisible. Yet these new technologies were not deployed, or will be deployed only with great reluctance.

The lack of enthusiasm for these weapons has been grounded in economics, politics, and technology. The B-70 was developed after 1957 at the same time as the ICBMs; hence, its deployment would have come at the expense of the other legs of the Triad. When the bomber and missile gaps disappeared, so did the primary military rationale for the B-70. Politically the employment created by building the B-70 bomber seemed important in 1960, but not later as the economy expanded without it. Mainly the high-altitude B-70 seemed unattractive after Soviet surface-to-air missiles shot down the high-altitude U-2 aircraft in 1962. The decision whether to deploy the B-1 bomber was first debated at a time when the military budget was not growing and when the Trident submarine consumed a great deal of the available strategic funding. At the same time, President Carter was trying to exercise political control over strategic weapons; canceling the B-1 bomber was symbolic of that control. The B-1 bomber was not technically sweet; detailed analyses generally show that a stand-off bombarding system using cruise missiles with the B-52 or a future bomber is cheaper and might be more survivable.

The new bomber models were and are technologically better than the B-52, but not enough superior to make it inevitable that they would be deployed. The bomber technological imperative has been weak. This weakness has allowed other factors to influence the deployment decisions; the B-1B bomber may be built as a symbol of the continuing military strength of the third leg of the Triad.

Missile Warheads

If one takes the concept of deterrence seriously, nuclear missiles ought to carry warheads of limited accuracy; if the warheads are too accurate, they threaten destruction of the opponent's retaliatory land-based ICBMS. However, warhead technologies have drifted toward improved accuracy. There have been occasional efforts to halt this drift.

Jane's Weapons Systems (Pretty, 1982) lists various U.S. warhead designs. It describes for example the Mk-12 design that placed three 200-kt MIRVs on the Minuteman III missile. Then it mentions some alternative warhead designs that were not pursued. It suggests that the Mk-17, an accurate multimegaton reentry vehicle, was canceled

> because of a funding clash with the Mk-12 but also because its evident first-strike potential was out of keeping with the U.S. strategic posture at the time and the Mk-19, another large and accurate reentry vehicle was first proposed in 1972 but rejected as inconsistent with the spirit of SALT as a result of public and Congressional pressure. (Pretty, 1982, p.5)

In this case, certain technologies were apparently delayed for strategic-political reasons. However, it also appears that the technology of highly accurate RVs in the long term has been too sweet to be suppressed. The accuracies of newer warheads has increased, such as that of the Mk-12A combined with the NS-20 guidance package for the Minuteman III. Even the yields of U.S. missiles have grown from 170 kt to 335 kt for the Minuteman III, although this growth seems not very necessary.

The ABM

The most impressive example of a controlled strategic technology is probably the ABM, as discussed in Chapter 10. The missile-based ABM of the late 1960s was a truly different technology designed to perform a function never before attempted—the interception of offensive missile warheads. The attempts to control this technology involved the usual elements of economics, politics, and technology as well as the desire to stabilize the arms race.

The ABM system proposed in 1969 to defend missile silos was not cheap; it also was perceived as a foot in the door for a much more expensive system aimed to defend cities against Soviet attacks. The escalating costs of the Vietnam war made the costs of the ABM appear dangerously large.

The ABM was not as good technologically as some thought it needed to be. In its Sentinel incarnation, it had promised to provide an adequate defense of cities against a very small attack by the Chinese. The Safeguard version was assigned a different task of protecting ICBM silos against Soviet attack; the ABM system was not designed for that job, its radar systems were vulnerable to attack by sophisticated Soviet missiles. Further development work was needed to overcome that vulnerability. The pressures on President Nixon to deploy the Safeguard in 1969 led to a premature commitment to an inadequate technology.

Politically, the ABM turned out to be surprisingly weak. The Vietnam war fueled antimilitary pressure groups. The deployment process was mishandled politically. And for the first time a major weapons system was discussed publicly, exposing all its weaknesses, including the ABM's destabilizing effects on the arms race. This combination of circumstances made it politically vulnerable; Congress approved it by the marginal vote of 51 to 50. This low level of approval made it easy to limit it under the SALT I Treaty. Its technical inadequacy led to the decommissioning of the single ABM deployment site. The ABM is perhaps the truest example of the deliberate rejection of a potentially promising new technology. The arousal of public debate may well have had a great deal to do with its ultimate control under SALT I.

Uncontrolled Technologies

Controlled technologies are rare compared with technologies for which the pressures of technological imperatives won out. A few examples will illustrate this point.

The Hydrogen Bomb

Chapter 3 told of the decision reached in 1950 to develop the hydrogen bomb. The economic argument then was against the H-bomb—the reactors required to build it could be used alternatively to build many more small A-bombs. Some political arguments spoke against it: the H-bomb would increase the U.S. commitment to the doctrine of massive nuclear retaliation against civilian populations. Teller's Super design for the H-bomb seemed technically flawed: the chances in 1950 were judged to be about 50% that an H-bomb might work, and then it seemingly would be clumsy to deliver. Some proposed to control this potential new technology by agreement with the Soviet Union. But, if only it could be invented, the H-bomb promised to be a truly revolutionary weapon. That made the technological imperative driving it too strong when combined with the political effect of the first Soviet fission bomb test.

Since at this time only five nations have the H-bomb, the technological imperative for the H-bomb has been contained since 1967, when China exploded its first fusion bomb. The control of this imperative has come primarily through controlling the first step toward fission bombs by nonnuclear states.

MIRV

Multiple, independently targetable, reentry vehicles are strongly dependent on computer technology mixed with inertial guidance technology. Over the last 20 years, computers have fueled some of the strongest military technological imperatives. Thus, the deployment of the MIRV technology has had a feeling of inevitability about it. Originally, MIRV was proposed in its MRV version to overcome

ABM defenses by providing multiple targets to saturate the ABM's capabilities.

Once begun, the MIRV technology took on a life of its own. Its development and deployment took place as the SALT I agreement limited the deployment of ABM systems. New justifications were developed for MIRV—it was to attack the large number of military targets that might still be useful to the enemy after a first nuclear exchange. Once MIRV was accepted as a component of strategic forces, its accuracy and yield seemed worthy of further improvements beyond the requirements of the anti-ABM mode.

These improvements in MIRV were technologically sweet; consequently, they met relatively little opposition on economic and political grounds—the military strategic bureaucracy was in favor of developing and deploying the MIRV.

> for the NS-20 guidance improvements, the Pentagon sought in the fiscal year 1977 budget to obtain funds to implement the programming change that would reduce the Minuteman CEP down to 750 feet. . . . funds requested for the NS-20 guidance system procurement were merely $4 million . . . perhaps the changes were too cheap to alarm those congressmen concerned with cutting defense spending. (Shapley, 1978, p. 1105)

Now MIRV has become a big threat to deterrence.

FUTURE TECHNOLOGICAL IMPERATIVES

Computers most likely will form the base for the greatest future technological imperatives, although laser-related (Chapter 10) and biological (Chapter 11) developments also have a great potential. The source of the computer-driven imperatives follows from the tremendous growth potential of the computer industry. This imperative is reflected in the almost inevitable improvement of any technology that is related to computers. Future improvements in missile accuracies as well as in the development of conventional smart bombs are prime examples of this interconnection.

Computer Growth

Computers consist of logic elements that can process and record digital numbers. They add, subtract, or compare numbers through various logic functions performed by semiconductor integrated circuits derived from transistors that were invented at Bell Laboratories in 1947. A useful computer must have many components to process information and store it; the processing must be done rapidly, and reliably. The circuit elements move electrical charges between defects that are deliberately introduced as impurity atoms into very pure germanium or silicon crystal lattices.

Transistors became possible only after crystals of the necessary purity could be made; transistor-derived electronics has improved as these materials have improved. The present fourth generation of semiconductor electronics has been created by the ability to engrave thousands of electronic components onto one chip of silicon to produce very-large-scale circuit integration (VLSI). The fifth generation is being planned; it most likely will not only increase the number of components per chip, but it will also perform calculations simultaneously (in parallel) in several circuits rather than sequentially. Processes similar to artificial intelligence will be used to help the separate circuits decide when to communicate with each other.

The miniaturization of semiconductor electronics has grown steadily (Fig. 13.1). The number of components that can be incorporated into a single chip has grown from 1 in 1960 to as many as 1 million in 1980; this corresponds to a doubling time of one year in the number of components per chip.

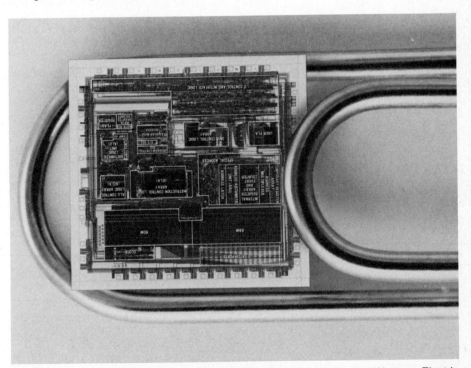

Figure 13.1 A BELLMAC-4 one-chip computer developed by the Western Electric Company in 1977. In the early 1950s an equivalent computer would have filled a 26 m² (400-ft²) room. (Photo courtesy Bell Laboratories.)

Part of this growth represents an increase in chip size; but most is due to a tighter packing of the circuit elements. Figure 13.2 shows that the number of components per cm² of chip has been doubling every three years. At the same time the speed of the computer's processing has been increasing enormously. The historical trends of Fig. 13.3 in the time various computers require to carry out one arithmetic operation (the add time) show a doubling in computer speed roughly every 2½ years. Computers are now being built that require the separate computer chips be moved close together because the travel time of the signals along the connecting wires is comparable to the computer processing times. Altogether computer capabilities (the number of components per cm² divided by the add time) have been growing since 1950 at a rate of a factor of two about every 1½ years.

The cost of semiconducter electronics has decreased dramatically, with a decrease of a factor of two about every 2 years over the last two decades for each electronic component, or for each unit of memory. At the same time the reliability of the circuitry has also been improving constantly; the breakdown rate per electronic component has been decreasing since 1960 by a factor of two about every 2 years.

Computer technology continues to grow rapidly; this growth will continue for some time to come. Ion implantation and nonphotographic methods for the etching masks are under development, so that computer components can be packed more tightly. The ultimate limit to computer technology will be imposed by the closest packing possible for the individual electronic components; that limit might be about

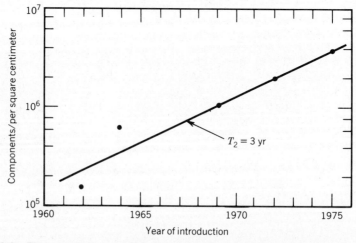

Figure 13.2 The growth of computer components per square centimeter of a chip over the last decades. The line is an approximate exponential fit to the data. (Derived from Keyes, 1977.)

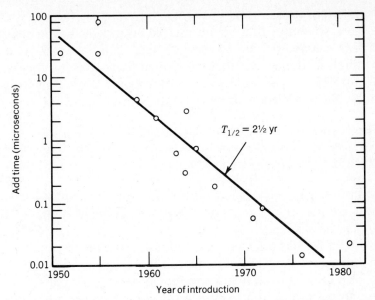

Figure 13.3 Historical data for the add time of various computers. The line is an approximate exponential fit to the data. (Derived mainly from Cave, 1977.)

10^{12} components per cm². This would be at least 10,000 times more tightly packed per cm² than the best present chips.

The Impact of Computers

If computers continue to improve dramatically, they will produce future advances in weapons technologies that are highly dependent upon them, including weapons guidance systems. Figure 6.8 showed the historical trends in the accuracy of U.S. and Soviet ICBMs. The CEPs for both nations have improved by a factor of two about every 7 years since 1960. Computers play a significant role in the guidance systems that have made these improved CEPs possible by translating the readings of the inertial guidance sensors into instructions for the rocket engines. The need for computers in missile guidance will be larger in future systems, such as the map comparison guidance on the cruise missile and the Pershing II, in the stellar navigation system of the Trident II, and in the use of the NAVSTAR satellite navigation systems. In each of these cases, a four-dimensional navigation has to be done (vertically, forward, laterally, and over time); a twofold improvement in missile accuracy might then demand a $2^4 = 16$-fold improvement in computers. Such a level of computer improvement may come about every 6 years. One ought not to be surprised if improvements in the CEP of missiles continue exponentially at the present 7-year doubling rate for another decade or two.

The Computer Race

Figure 6.8 also shows that Soviet missile accuracies have consistently lagged U.S. capabilities by a factor of two, or by about 7 years. This lead parallels a similar lead that the United States has in other relevant high technologies, particularly in computers. Many analysts tell the same tale. Nicolas Wade summarized the situation in 1974:

> Computers are a field in which the United States has a clear lead over the Soviet Union . . . reckoned as 2 to 3 years by Soviet sources, and 5 to 10 years by most American analysts. (Wade, 1974, p. 499)

This computer gap has existed for a long time: Figure 13.4 shows the historical trends in the lead in computer capabilities of the United States over the USSR.

This Soviet lag has affected views of trade relationships between the United States and the USSR. It is feared that computer technology sold to the USSR may be used to improve Soviet strategic capabilities. It was claimed, for example, that American-designed computers sold to the Soviet Union helped to develop Soviet MIRVs (Wade, 1974). Whether it is true or not that British scientific computers at the Soviet Serpukhov high-energy accelerator were used for MIRV calculations, it is true that the Soviet Union has uses for Western computers. Much of the controversy in the early 1980s about government-imposed secrecy in the

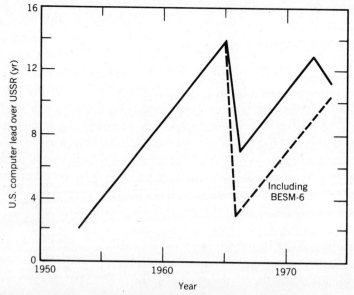

Figure 13.4 Historical trends in the computer lead of the United States over the Soviet Union. Only a small number of BESM-6 computers were available. (After Cave, 1977, Figure 8.3.)

computer industry relates to the fear that the Soviets might steal advanced Western computer technology. This may not be a major problem, however, since the Soviets can perhaps match the West in computer design on their own, but they lag in the production technology, which is difficult to steal.

There is an historical-philosophical reason for this Soviet lag. In the early days of computers until the middle of the 1950s, there was a philosophical hostility in the Soviet Union against computers. Cybernetics was a Western capitalistic science. It seemed to attack the importance of people, implying that limitations to their ability to cope with their environment existed (Graham, 1967). Computers became recognized as an absolute necessity only after Stalin's death.

This Soviet backwardness in computer technology has continued since then. It has had an impact on ICBM technologies. The Soviet Union was unable to miniaturize its nuclear warheads; hence, it developed large ICBMs. In turn, the large lifting capability put less pressure on the Russian computer industry to miniaturize, encouraging a continuing lag in computer technology.

The general feeling that there is a large U.S. computer lead continues; in 1979 the president of Texas Instruments, J. Fred Bucy, estimated that the Soviets were five to seven years behind (Shapley, 1979, p. 284). If these estimates of a continuing Soviet mass-production computer lag of five or more years indeed hold true, then one might expect also a continuing lag in the quality of Soviet strategic technology, including missile accuracy. Figure 6.8 shows this to be the case. It may be risky to make policy decisions based on estimates derived in a subjective manner, but this continuing U.S. computer lead should make one suspicious whenever the quality of Soviet weapons that are based on computers is claimed to be overtaking that of American systems.

CONTROL OF TECHNOLOGICAL IMPERATIVES

One may expect missile accuracies to be a weapon parameter where the technological imperative will exert great pressures. Due to the major role likely to be played by computers in future map-reading missile guidance systems, there is a great opportunity for continuing advances in missile accuracy. Any weapons system that can incorporate a terrain- or satellite-reading mechanism, and can have maneuverability along its path, could have virtually unlimited accuracy. The current revolution in precision-guided conventional arms is related to this computerization (Walker, 1981). Since the progress of computers is unlikely to be stopped, the question is how the technological imperative of computers is to be controlled. More generally, how can technically sweet advances in weapons technologies be guided into desirable channels?

To understand how one might control such technological imperatives, one must first understand how technological imperatives operate. In the past, it has often been argued that Soviet-U.S. reactions fueled the technological arms race. It is claimed by some that the Soviet Tallin antiaircraft system was built in reaction to the U.S. B-70 bomber development. In turn, the U.S. MIRV system supposedly was developed in reaction to the threat of this system which was perceived as a potential ABM system. In this cycle, the U.S. ABM was an offshoot of the antibomber defenses built when a bomber gap seemed to threaten the United States.

As Robert S. McNamara put it,

> what is essential to understand here is that the Soviet Union and the United States mutually influence one another's strategic plans. Whatever be their intentions, whatever be our intentions, actions—or even realistically potential actions—on either side relating to the build-up of nuclear forces, be they either offensive or defensive weapons, necessarily trigger reactions on the other side. It is precisely this action-reaction phenomenon that fuels our arms race. (As quoted in Allison and Morris, 1976, pp. 102–103.)

To a considerable extent, this is true; the two superpowers inspire each other—if for no other reason than that they desire a "mirror image" of each other's technologies. However, this international coupling cannot be so tight; for example, the U.S. MIRV development program really began before the Soviet ABM, and it was deployed after the ABM was banned. Thus, many ask for a broader view of arms race spirals, a view that should include the dynamics of technological development internal to each nation. Colin Gray made this point

> The newer proposition holds that the arms race behavior of the state-actors is determined not so much by the perception of threat, as by "the games that bureaucrats play." The range of models for the elucidation of this proposition is formidable indeed. At one extreme, analysts devise an action-reaction model wherein the principal actors are the U.S. Air Force, Navy and Army—competing with a somewhat astrategic budget ceiling, and with the Soviet Union performing an essential game legitimization function. (As quoted in Spielmann, 1978, pp. 2–3)

The technical bureaucracy seems to be driven by technological competition. Harvey Brooks argues that

> The principle of overaction or "worst case analysis" generally guarantees that the reaction to a revelation of technological innovation in weapons exceeds what was justified by the actual situation. (1976, p. 77)

These arguments make some sense—if the word "actual" is replaced by the word "perceived"; the perceived threat may sometimes be more and sometimes be less than the actual threat. Strategic weapons systems take 7 to 15 years to develop so that once an enemy system has made its appearance, it is too late to start a counterdevelopment. John Foster described such a situation in 1968 when he was director of Defense Research and Evaluation

> Our currrent effort to get a MIRV capability on our missiles is not reacting to a Soviet capability so much as it is moving ahead again to make sure that whatever they do of the possible things that we can imagine they might do, we will be prepared. (As quoted in Allison and Morris, 1976, p. 118)

The American MIRV may have been the result of a competition with the American ABM. Another way of putting it is to say

> The technical community seems to have been driven by the "sweetness" of the technology and the researchers' competitive instincts, which were aroused primarily by American ABM research, since so little was known about Soviet ABM activity. (Allison and Morris, 1976, p. 118)

Indeed technology at times drives itself; as Herbert F. York put it,

> these early developments of MIRV and ABM . . . were largely the result of a continuously reciprocating process consisting of a technological challenge put out by the designers of our defense and accepted by the designers of our offense, then followed by a similar challenge/response sequence in the reverse direction. (As quoted in Allison and Morris, 1976, p. 119)

In the scientific and technical communities this imperative has showed itself when

> official scientific advisors and some of the scientific community interested in such matters have advocated research and development to improve certain weapons technologies, even when they have strongly opposed the deployment of the corresponding specific weapons. (Brooks, 1976, p. 76)

This research was sometimes in the hope of showing the technology to be impossible. But once shown feasible, the technology often moved irresistibly on to deployment. More and better technical analyses might help to anticipate future applications, but such analyses are rare before the technology is developed.

Many factors combine to make technological imperatives work. International competition drives arms developments; the long incubation times of weapons systems force intramural competition; long-term and secretive uncertainties in weapons R&D encourage worst-case analyses; and technological sweetness makes some systems hard to resist. If efforts at arms control are to succeed, more early analyses of such technological imperatives are needed. Only an understanding of such processes may allow changes in institutions that would give control back to the body politic. Chapter 16 will ask how such technological spirals might be broken.

References

Allison, G. T., and F. A. Morris. "Armaments and Arms Control: Exploring the Determinants of Military Weapons." In *Arms, Defense Policy, and Arms Control*, F. A. Long and G. W. Rathjens, eds., pp. 99–129. New York: W. W. Norton, 1976.

Brooks, H. "The Military Innovation System and the Qualitative Arms Race." In *Arms, Defense Policy, and Arms Control*, F. A. Long and G. W. Rathjens, eds., pp. 75–97. New York: W. W. Norton, 1976.

Cave, M. "Computer Technology." In *The Technological Level of Soviet Industry*, R. Amann, T. M. Cooper, and R. W. Davies, eds., pp. 377–406. New Haven, Conn.: Yale University Press, 1977.

Graham, L. R. "Cybernetics." In *Science and Ideology in Soviet Society*, G. Fischer, ed., New York: Atherton Press, 1967.

Holloway, D. "Innovation in the Defense Sector" and "Innovation in the Defense Sector: Battle Tanks and ICBMs." In *Industrial Innovation in the Soviet Union*, R. Amann and T. M. Cooper, eds., pp. 276–367 and 368–414. New Haven, Conn.: Yale University Press, 1982.

Keyes, R. W. "Microstructure Fabrication." *Science*, Vol. 196 (1977), pp. 945–949; and the whole September 1977 issue of *Scientific American*, Vol. 237, no. 3.

Pretty, R. T. *Jane's Weapons Systems: 1982–83*. London: Jane's, 1982.

Shapley, D. "Technology Creep and the Arms Race: ICBM Problem a Sleeper." *Science*, Vol. 201 (1978), pp. 1102–1105.

———. "New Chips Shed Light on Soviet Electronics." *Science*, Vol. 204 (1979), pp. 283–284.

Spielmann, K. F. *Analyzing Soviet Strategic Arms Decisions*. Boulder, Colo.: Westview Press, 1978.

Wade, N. "Computer Sales to U.S.S.R.: Critics look for Quid Pro Quo." *Science*, Vol. 183 (1974), pp. 499–501.

———. "American-Soviet Relations: The Cancelled Computer," *Science*, Vol. 201 (1976), pp. 422–427.

Walker, P. F., "Precision-Guided Weapons." *Scientific American*, Vol. 245, no. 2 (August 1981), pp. 36–45.

York, H. F. *Race to Oblivion: A Participant's View of the Arms Race*. New York: Simon & Schuster, 1970.

Nuclear Proliferation: A Technological Imperative?

A minimal national *program [of nuclear weapons construction] would call for a group of more than a dozen well-trained and very competent persons . . . a staff of technicians, diverse laboratory facilities, and a field-test facility. . . . If . . . competently carried out, the objective could be attained approximately 2 years after the start of the program at a cost of a few tens of millions of dollars. This estimate does not include the time and money to obtain the fissile material.*

U.S. Congressional Office of Technology Assessment, 1977

On May 18, 1974 India exploded underground a plutonium nuclear device of 10 to 15 kt. The government of India argued that this device was developed entirely for peaceful purposes. Indeed a nuclear weapon has requirements on size, deliverability, and reliability that a peaceful nuclear explosive may not have; and India has exploded no further nuclear devices since then. Nonetheless, this explosion demonstrated the ability of India to produce an explosive chain reaction, an initial requirement for nuclear weapons production.

Six countries now overtly possess nuclear explosives: the United States, the Soviet Union, the United Kingdom, France, the People's Republic of China, and India. There is reason to believe that nuclear proliferation will extend further. In discussing nuclear weapons the focus so far has been on the balance between the United States and the Soviet Union. But that bipolar focus is inadequate; one should consider the other three proven nuclear weapons states, that first less developed nation with nuclear explosives, and other potential members of the nuclear weapons club. The essential armaments parity that exists between the two superpowers does not extend to the other nuclear weapons states. With that multiplicity of present nuclear weapons states, and with potential further proliferation in the future, can long-term nuclear stability exist?

This chapter begins by reviewing how the "other four" nations developed their nuclear capability. This history of nuclear proliferation examines efforts to resist the expansion of the nuclear club, e.g., by limiting the technological and political pressures toward proliferation through the nuclear Non-Proliferation Treaty (NPT) and the establishment of the International Atomic Energy Agency (IAEA).

A major nation can develop nuclear devices in a dedicated weapons program completely on its own, as did the United States and the USSR, and to a considerable extent the United Kingdom, France, and China. Future proliferators may connect their production of nuclear weapons to the nuclear electric power industry through technical expertise acquired in reactor development programs (as was the case for India) or through fissile material extracted from commercial electric power programs. A review of electrical power production using nuclear energy points out some of the weak links in this industry that might invite proliferation. These weak links will be illustrated by considering some candidates for potential nuclear proliferation.

Finally, an examination of the list of candidates and noncandidates for the nuclear club may help to answer that most important question: What can be done to prevent nuclear proliferation? Is nuclear proliferation one of those uncontrollable technological imperatives considered in Chapter 13?

HISTORY OF NUCLEAR PROLIFERATION

The history of the nuclear weapons development for the United States and the Soviet Union has already been discussed. The other four nations produced explosives by diverse routes. The United Kingdom became the third nuclear weapons state on October 3, 1952. Several factors influenced the British to "go nuclear" after World War II (Gowing, 1975), one being that the British had developed the scientific and technical knowledge during World War II as they cooperated extensively with the Manhattan project. The fact that an A-bomb project would tax their industrial resources at a critical time kept the British from developing the first nuclear weapons on their own during World War II. Throughout the war, the British considered themselves equal partners in the nuclear enterprise; the first large heavy-water nuclear reactor was built for the Manhattan project at Chalk River in Canada.

At the end of World War II, the United States reneged on the wartime promises of continuing nuclear cooperation. Since the British were not prepared to accept the status of an inferior world power, they resolved not to have to rely on other nations for protection against future enemies; hence, they tried to preserve their military status through nuclear weapons. The 1947 British decision to develop nuclear weapons was taken with a clear understanding of the consequences.

The British nuclear arsenal and delivery systems now consist of A-bombs and H-bombs deliverable by the bombers and nuclear submarines described in Chapters 5 and 7. If its survivability is credible, this arsenal would seem to be large enough to be considered sufficient for massive retaliation against the Soviet Union.

France became a nuclear weapons state on February 13, 1960. The French commitment to a nuclear weapons program was not made until 1954 (Weart, 1979); however, basic nuclear research had been pushed strongly after World War II, so that the technical capability for such a commitment existed by then. The French decision was to develop a wholly indigenous *force de frappe* (retaliatory force), to avoid being considered an inferior world power. This concern with inferiority was strengthened by the military humiliations in Indochina of the defeat at Dien Bien Phu in 1954, by being forced by the United States to end a war against Egypt in Suez in 1956, and by losing its Algerian colonial empire in 1958. France felt left out within the North Atlantic Treaty Organization (NATO) as the United States established a special nuclear relationship with Great Britain: Could the United States be relied upon to defend France by nuclear weapons? These self-doubts made it politically desirable to achieve nuclear independence.

The resulting commitment to nuclear development has extended to civilian nuclear power; the present French nuclear electric power program is one of the most advanced in the world; its breeder reactor program is superior to all others. Some believe that the French nuclear weapons program was inevitable in any case once technical feasibility was established. With the strong emphasis on experts in the French governmental bureaucracy, such a technical project was bound to be developed. French nuclear developments progressed in the typical way, graduating from ^{239}Pu implosion devices to H-bombs. The French nuclear weapons arsenal contains fighter bombers, intermediate-range ballistic missiles, and SLBMs. Like that of the United Kingdom, it seems large enough to act as a deterrent as long as the delivery vehicles are adequately safe from nuclear attack. The difference in the French arsenal compared with that of the United Kingdom is that all parts of the nuclear weapons systems were developed independently of U.S. programs.

The People's Republic of China (P.R.C.) became a nuclear weapons state on October 16, 1964. The Chinese nuclear weapons program had received some nuclear technology from the Soviet Union before these two nations had their falling out in 1960. China is the only nation whose first nuclear device used ^{235}U obtained from a gaseous diffusion plant; a ^{239}Pu implosion device came later. The P.R.C. developed hydrogen bombs by 1967. Its delivery systems are presently still restricted to medium ranges, usable in a war with its neighbors India, Japan, and the Soviet Union; however, a truly intercontinental ballistic missile is under development.

The most recent country to develop an overt nuclear weapons capability has been India. The plutonium device it exploded in 1974 appears to have been fueled with plutonium produced in a small research nuclear reactor that Canada helped to build in the late 1950s, a reactor moderated by heavy water supplied by the United States. That reactor is not under International Atomic Energy Agency (IAEA) nonproliferation safeguards; India did not sign the Non-Proliferation Treaty (NPT). India may have been able to separate as much as 100 kg of ^{239}Pu out of the spent fuel from that reactor. It is now designing and building its own copies of the Canadian 200-megawatt (electric) (MW(e)) CANDU (*Can*adian-*D*euterium-*U*ranium) reactor units, these will produce ^{239}Pu in much larger quantities. The short-range Indian weapons delivery systems are sufficient to carry into local conflicts nuclear bombs based on that peaceful nuclear device. However, there have been no further Indian nuclear explosions since that first one; no nuclear weapons have been tested in conjunction with any weapons delivery system.

THE NON-PROLIFERATION TREATY

The United States tried to control nuclear weapons after World War II ended. Under the Baruch plan placed before the United Nations in 1946, the United States might have been willing to give up its nuclear weapons if the Soviet Union would have relinquished its veto power in the U.N. Security Council. A U.N. nuclear energy agency would have been set up to supervise all nuclear research done in the world. But that proposal came to naught; internationalization of nuclear energy was an unrealistic expectation in a world where the United States was the only nation to have tested a nuclear weapon.

When international control of nuclear weapons failed, the next attempts were to limit the spread of nuclear weapons to other nations (the so-called "horizontal proliferation"). President Eisenhower in 1954 proposed the Atoms-for-Peace program; knowledge about nuclear fission was to be made available for nuclear energy development in exchange for renunciations of nuclear weapon development efforts.

Some political successes were achieved in controlling nuclear proliferation. For example, in 1954 West Germany renounced the development of nuclear weapons and has been willing to remain a full-fledged partner in the NATO military structure without having such weapons under its own control; it has been willing to stay under the American nuclear umbrella.

Unfortunately, the safeguards on the growing worldwide nuclear power industry began to seem inadequate, some saw this industry as a technological imperative toward nuclear weapons. The superpowers therefore looked toward tighter control over future nuclear proliferation. Finally, on March 5, 1970 the Treaty on the Non-Proliferation of Nuclear Weapons came into force. Nuclear weapons states (NWS) on signing this treaty agree not to release nuclear weapons or information on building them or in any way help any other nations to build nuclear weapons. Nonnuclear weapons states (NNWS) signatories agree not to develop "nuclear weapons or other nuclear explosive devices." In exchange for this self-denial, the NWS would help the NNWS with peaceful nuclear energy programs by providing, for example, low-level enriched uranium fuel for their reactors; but the NNWS nations must agree to allow verification of compliance. Further, the NWS promised to move toward some form of nuclear arms control and disarmament.

Verification of compliance with this treaty is carried out by the International Atomic Energy Agency; it presently has over 114 adherents. The NPT has not been signed by the P.R.C., France, and India. India argues that its underground nuclear device test was consistent with this treaty since it claims that device was designed for peaceful purposes as allowed under the phrase "the use of nuclear energy for peaceful purposes." While France has not signed the treaty, it has announced that it would behave as if it were a signatory. It has at times been rumored that the P.R.C. might sign this treaty, but this has not happened so far.

NUCLEAR POWER AND NUCLEAR PROLIFERATION

Political attempts to control horizontal nuclear proliferation have had some successes. West Germany and Japan have no nuclear weapons, and India is the only less developed country to have an overt nuclear explosive capability. But there are still no limits to the vertical proliferation of the nuclear arsenals of the major powers. Worst of all, large-scale horizontal nuclear proliferation could happen at any time. Because of the expanding nuclear science and technology, as in the nuclear power industry, the proliferation question has become "who wants nuclear weapons" rather than "who has the ability to make them." The science and technology related to nuclear weapons has been shown to be reasonably straightforward. The problem is the rising demand for energy coupled with the limited nonnuclear energy resources; this encourages the expansion of electricity production by nuclear reactors. That technology is also relevant to nuclear weapons production, where either ^{235}U or ^{239}Pu are required in kilogram quantities. Nuclear reactors use ^{235}U at 3% enrichment as their fuel and produce the latter as part of their waste products. A supplier of nuclear fuels must have the capability to separate ^{235}U; a user of nuclear fuels automatically produces enough ^{239}Pu to make nuclear weapons if a chemical separation plant for the reprocessing of reactor fuel elements is available. Any nuclear power reactor involves the owner not only in nuclear technology, but also implies an accumulation of fissile material that can be used for weapons if processed properly.

The world has a large nuclear power industry because of commitments made long ago to exploit nuclear fission for peaceful uses, particularly as a source of inexpensive energy. President Eisenhower's speech in 1954 on the peaceful uses of nuclear energy led to the release of much secret information and to a large economic investment in nuclear power plants. Now the existence of the nuclear power industry contributes to the potential for widespread proliferation in several ways (de Volpi, 1979; Greenwood, Feiveson, and Taylor, 1977).

^{239}Pu Proliferation

The example of India shows that ^{239}Pu obtained from a small, imported research-level nuclear reactor can be used in nuclear explosives. India was able to reprocess spent fuel, removing from it sufficient ^{239}Pu to fuel nuclear explosives. Any fission reactor containing natural uranium as part of its fuel produces such fissile ^{239}Pu. Kilogram quantities of ^{239}Pu are needed to make nuclear weapons; this preferably should have minimal contaminants of ^{240}Pu or ^{242}Pu. The amount of plutonium produced, and its weapons quality, depends on the design of the nuclear reactor as well as on its power level and operation time.

There are available commercially at present four basic types of nuclear power plants. The United States, France, West Germany, and Japan have concentrated on light-water reactors (LWR) of two types: pressurized-water reactors (PWR) and boiling-water reactors (BWR). Both the PWR and the BWR use ordinary water to slow down (moderate) the neutrons in the reactor and to remove the heat from the reactor core. Since ordinary water absorbs some neutrons, the core must be fueled with uranium enriched to about 3% in ^{235}U, to increase the fission probability.

Canada has developed the CANDU-type reactor. In this design, heavy water moderates the neutrons and cools the core. The low level of neutron absorption of the heavy water allows the fuel to consist of natural uranium, unenriched (0.7%) in ^{235}U.

Great Britain tried to commercialize reactors moderated by graphite, in which a gas such as helium cools the core. This type of reactor could be fueled by either natural or slightly enriched uranium and by thorium.

In addition to these three commercial reactor types, a current major development program aims to develop a commercially viable breeder reactor. Breeder reactors are designed to produce more fissile nuclei (such as ^{239}Pu) than are consumed in the steady-state chain reaction. The most likely model of this reactor will be a liquid-metal fast breeder reactor (LMFBR). In this reactor the core consists of uranium enriched in ^{235}U or mixed with ^{239}Pu. The moderating and cooling is done by molten sodium metal. A prototype of the LMFBR has been operating for almost a decade in France. The extent to which other countries will pursue breeder reactors depends on the future demand for nuclear electric power. PWR and breeder reactors will be discussed briefly, since the former are in most widespread use, and since the latter is most closely coupled to proliferation problems.

The Pressurized-Water Reactor

Anthony V. Nero, Jr., has reviewed various reactor designs (1979). The PWR is intended to produce electric power through the fissioning of ^{235}U nuclei. It is not specifically designed to produce excess fissile ^{239}Pu, but it does generate a significant amount during normal operations.

Figures 14.1 and 7.1 outline the design features of the PWR reactor. The core of the reactor is made up of a very large number of zircalloy tubes (cladding) filled with cylindrical UO_2 pellets. A large power reactor producing 1000 MW of electricity contains about 80 tonnes of UO_2 in its core. To maintain a steady chain reaction, the neutron multiplication factor is kept at 1 by injecting varying concentrations of boron into the light-water moderator and by inserting or withdrawing control rods containing boron or cadmium to absorb controllable amounts of neutrons. The uranium oxide has to be enriched in ^{235}U from 0.7% up to typically 3% to make up for the neutron absorption of the water. The water in the primary circuit also cools the core and carries the heat from the nuclear reactor to a heat exchanger. The heat energy there is transferred to a secondary loop, in which the steam generator converts the hot water to steam, which drives the turbines to produce electrical power. Since water tends to

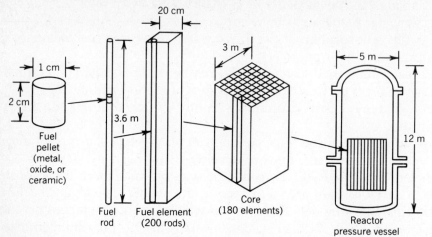

Figure 14.1 The components of the core of a typical electricity-generating nuclear power plant.

become steam at elevated temperatures, the reactor vessel must keep the water in the primary loop under pressures up to about 150 atmospheres (atm), and the highest reactor operating temperature is about 325°C.

In nuclear reactors the chain reaction drawn in Fig. 2.4 is kept under control with the neutrons from each fission reaction causing, on the average, one further fission reaction. Figure 14.2 illustrates the progress of that chain reaction. The neutrons released in the fission reaction are very energetic. Such neutrons can be absorbed in ^{238}U. Nuclear reactor cores usually contain many ^{238}U atoms; for example, the uranium in typical LWRs is 97% ^{238}U. Too many neutron absorptions by ^{238}U would halt the chain reaction. Low-energy neutrons, however, are not readily absorbed by light water. Therefore, LWR

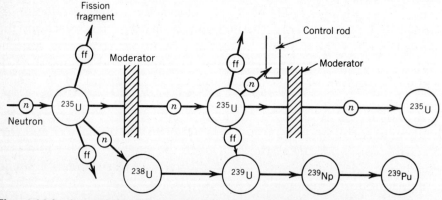

Figure 14.2 A sustained chain reaction in a nuclear reactor.

reactors have their cores permeated by a moderator that slows down the high-energy neutrons by repeated collisions. The moderator atoms must be light so that the neutron gives up its energy in a very few collisions. Normal light hydrogen is an excellent moderator except that it tends to absorb neutrons to become deuterium. Hence, reactors using normal light water as moderators must have more ^{235}U fissile atoms in their core to sustain the chain reaction. Heavy hydrogen (deuterium) is a good moderator for slowing down neutrons, and it absorbs very few neutrons. Therefore, reactors moderated by deuterated water can use natural unenriched uranium as fuel.

A commercial nuclear power reactor can be quite large. The energy production of a large reactor capable of producing 1000 MW of electric power [1000 MW(e)] is on the order of 3000 thermal megawatts [3000 MW(th)]. This reactor must fission about 1000 kg per year. Since the fuel in a U.S. LWR contains typically only 3% fissile ^{235}U, a 1000 MW(e) reactor operated continuously at full power fissions annually almost all the ^{235}U atoms contained in 38 tonnes of that enriched fuel (actually somewhat less because some of the ^{239}Pu produced in the core is also fissioned).

Table 14.1 shows the worldwide level of operation of the nuclear electricity producing industry. About 77% of the presently planned reactors are LWR type, 7% use heavy water, 15% are high-temperature graphite reactors, while only eight breeder reactors (Vendryes, 1977) are presently being built. The number of nuclear reactors is not as high as it once had been projected to be; the nuclear power industry faces many problems such as very rapidly escalating capital costs, limited long-term uranium fuel supplies, reactor safety, and waste disposal— as well as the proliferation question. Nonetheless, the level of operation is high enough to produce ^{239}Pu in amounts that are large compared with the amounts needed to produce nuclear weapons. A typical LWR will produce about 200 kg/yr of ^{239}Pu, sufficient for about 20 to 40 nuclear weapons.

The Breeder Reactor

Possible future shortages of uranium created the pressure to develop the breeder reactor, a reactor type that would threaten nuclear proliferation to a much greater degree mainly because of the reprocessng industry that would have to accompany its operations. The main differences between the breeder and nonbreeder reactors are caused by the desire to convert many ^{238}U nuclei into ^{239}Pu. While the breeder reactor provides electrical power, it must also produce its own future fuel plus some additional fuel for other nuclear reactors. The core of the breeder is similar to that of the nonbreeder reactors, but it is much

Table 14.1 World inventory of nuclear power plants of 30 MW(e) or over: operable, under construction, or just beginning (<10% complete), as of December 31, 1982.
After *Nuclear News* Feb. 1983, pp. 71–90.

Country	In Operation No.	In Operation MW(e)	10–90% Complete No.	10–90% Complete MW(e)	<10% Complete No.	<10% Complete MW(e)	Total No.	Total MW(e)
Argentina	1:	335	2:	1,292	—	—	3:	1,627
Austria	—	—	1:	692	—	—	1:	692
Belgium	4:	2,550	3:	2,900	—	—	7:	5,450
Brazil	—	—	2:	1,871	1:	1,245	3:	3,116
Bulgaria	4:	1,760	—	—	—	—	4:	1,760
Canada	10:	5,476	11:	7,213	3:	2,643	24:	15,332
P.R. of China	—	—	1:	300	—	—	1:	300
Czechoslovakia	2:	880	8:	3,520	—	—	10:	4,400
Egypt	—	—	—	—	2:	1,800	2:	1,800
Finland	4:	2,160	—	—	—	—	4:	2,160
France	32:	22,658	26:	28,535	4:	5,105	62:	56,298
East Germany (DDR)	5:	1,830	—	—	2:	880	7:	2,710
West Germany (BRD)	12:	9,801	8:	8,138	9:	11,305	29:	29,244
Hungary	1:	440	1:	440	2:	880	4:	1,760
India	4:	804	4:	880	2:	440	10:	2,124
Iraq	—	—	—	—	1:	900	1:	900
Italy	3:	1,285	3:	2,004	—	—	6:	3,289
Japan	25:	16,652	9:	8,120	4:	2,514	38:	27,286
Korea	1:	556	6:	4,824	2:	1,886	9:	7,266
Libya	—	—	—	—	1:	300	1:	300
Luxembourg	—	—	—	—	1:	2,250	1:	2,250
Mexico	—	—	2:	1,308	—	—	2:	1,308
Netherlands	2:	495	—	—	—	—	2:	495
Pakistan	1:	125	—	—	—	—	1:	125
Philippines	—	—	1:	620	—	—	1:	620
Poland	—	—	—	—	2:	880	2:	880
Rumania	—	—	1:	440	5:	4,400	6:	4,840
South Africa	—	—	2:	1,844	—	—	2:	1,844
Spain	4:	2,003	8:	7,399	6:	5,952	18:	15,354
Sweden	9:	6,400	3:	3,010	—	—	12:	9,410
Switzerland	4:	1,940	1:	942	2:	2,065	7:	4,947
Taiwan	4:	3,110	2:	1,814	—	—	6:	4,924
United Kingdom	33:	8,648	9:	5,740	—	—	42:	14,388
United States	77:	58,975	61:	67,361	9:	9,198	147:	135,534
USSR	32:	17,515	—	—	13:	11,280	45:	28,795
Yugoslavia	1:	615	—	—	—	—	1:	615
World Totals	275:	167,013	187:	161,207	71:	64,923	524:	393,143

smaller and more tightly packed to make more efficient use of the neutrons released in it. The resulting greater neutron economy uses many of these neutrons to produce ^{239}Pu by neutron capture (as in Fig. 14.2) inside a natural uranium blanket around the reactor core. This tighter packing means that more heat is released per unit volume in the reactor core. That heat must be carried away by a coolant. The pressure of steam would be too high to be contained at the resulting temperatures; hence, liquid sodium is employed both for this reason and because the neutrons do not need to be moderated in this design. The fuel in the core must be enriched to at least 15% in either ^{235}U or ^{239}Pu to ensure that enough fissions occur to maintain the chain reaction.

Many technical advantages and disadvantages arise in the breeder reactor as a consequence of its design for efficient production of fissile fuel. The sodium coolant is useful because the breeder reactor can then be operated at higher temperatures and hence with higher efficiency, while the pressures in the liquid sodium are much lower. However, the sodium coolant becomes intensely radioactive, is very corrosive, and is potentially explosive on contact with water, and the higher reactor operating temperature makes the technology more difficult. But the main additional problem may well be the increased potential for nuclear proliferation. The breeder produces ^{239}Pu; this is intended to be useful and commercially available. To be useful the ^{239}Pu must be extracted from the spent fuel elements and incorporated into new ones. This makes the Pu more accessible and, hence, increases the opportunities for interference since the fuel cycle contains a step in which the Pu is converted into a form more usable in weapons.

Figure 14.3 shows various stages in the fuel cycle; the breeder has more pathways for fuel diversions. The primary difference of the breeder reactor is the necessary parallel commitment to civilian reprocessing; up to now reprocessing in the United States has been carried out essentially only within the military weapons program.

Reprocessing

How might a nation obtain the ^{239}Pu for a nuclear explosive from its own nuclear power industry? If reprocessing is being done as part of the fuel cycle, ^{239}Pu could be diverted after it has been separated from spent fuel before it is incorporated into new fuel elements. A potentially proliferating nation that has only indigenous reactors would have to divert some of its spent fuel elements and develop a weapons-oriented reprocessing facility to remove the plutonium from them chemically. Chemical reprocessing is not a trivial job. The spent fuel is

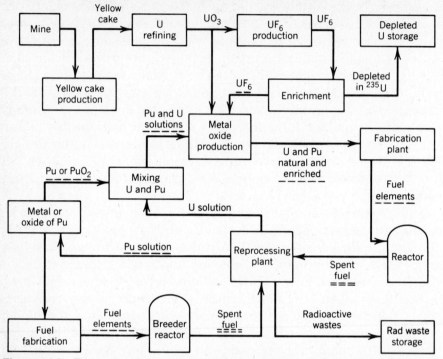

Figure 14.3 The nuclear fuel cycle, including reprocessing. Stages with a single underline would be tempting targets for nuclear proliferation if reprocessing is not available to the proliferator, whereas stages with a double underline would be tempting targets if reprocessing is available.

fiercely radioactive so that all the reprocessing must be done by remote control to shield workers from the material (Beddington, 1976).

Converting the plutonium to a metal requires great care to avoid fires since plutonium metal burns very readily. But the reprocessing technology is not secret. The process in India's plutonium chemical reprocessing plant was said to be based on published technological literature. The costs of the first Indian reprocessing plants have been estimated at about $30 million. William Epstein (1976) reports that

> It has been estimated that a [nuclear fuel reprocessing] plant capable of producing 15 to 20 kilograms of plutonium-239 a year could be built in a year or two by any reasonably advanced country at a cost of 1 to 3 million dollars. (p. 40).

The U.S. Office of Technology Assessment cites similar figures (1977, p. 36), although a sustained weapons program would run into the tens of millions of dollars. The reprocessing for a full-scale weapons program can be considerably more expensive, as suggested by the inside view of a huge U.S. reprocessing plant in Fig. 14.4.

Figure 14.4 The inside of a U.S. reprocessing plant at the Savannah River Plant near Aiken, S.C. Note the tracks for the overhead crane, which allows work by remote control on the radioactive plumbing below. (Photo courtesy U.S. Department of Energy.)

Design of a ^{239}Pu Bomb

After reprocessing, the design and fabrication of the bomb from the ^{239}Pu can be carried out by a group of reasonably competent scientists and technicians, as indicated by the introductory quotation for this chapter (Office of Technological Assessment, 1977). The technical information needed to design a reasonable nuclear fission device is publicly available. As long ago as 15 years, it could already be said that

> Basic problems connected with developing a nuclear device have been simplified in recent years. . . . Nuclear researchers have eliminated much of the expensive and time-consuming work. Aspiring nuclear scientists from all over the world can now find most of the information they need to build a bomb in their own public library. This fact, together with the great reduction of costs of equipment and raw materials, has taken away most of the difficulty of A-bomb construction. (Barnaby, 1979, p. 51)

Theodore Taylor, who at one time had designed both the smallest and the largest fission bombs, is one who believes that the construction of nuclear explosives is not so difficult. He argues that nations and even groups of terrorists could use either diverted ^{235}U or reactor-grade plutonium to fashion such devices. This argument can, however, be exaggerated. It has been reported that on several occasions undergraduate students have designed primitive nuclear weapons. These have often been found to be of poor design; actual construction would be a different matter, requiring some group effort and a certain amount of practical technical competence, for example, in the use of chemical high-energy explosives.

A major difficulty of building an A-bomb out of plutonium obtained from a power reactor stems from the contamination of the ^{239}Pu with other Pu isotopes. Such contaminated reactor-grade plutonium reduces the explosive power obtainable from a given fissioning mass. As shown in Fig. 14.2, during the operation of a fission reactor, some ^{238}U nuclei capture a neutron to become ^{239}Pu. As the reactor is operated further, some of these ^{239}Pu nuclei capture neutrons to become ^{240}Pu, and after even longer operating periods, considerable amounts of ^{241}Pu and ^{242}Pu can be built up, as shown in Fig. 14.5.

As explained in Chapter 2, this contamination of the ^{239}Pu with other plutonium isotopes makes it less suitable for weapons use, though still usable. In a typical critical mass of ^{239}Pu, only a hundred neutrons are released each second through spontaneous fission of that isotope; but an equivalent mass of ^{240}Pu may release several million neutrons per second. If the core of a nuclear device containing a mixture of ^{239}Pu and ^{240}Pu is imploded, the spontaneous fission neutrons may initiate a chain reaction before full compression is reached. Then the device may fizzle, and the explosive energy released may be only a fraction of the maximum possible. This preignition problem can greatly reduce the efficiency of a bomb containing ^{240}Pu, although it may not keep such a bomb from exploding. J. Carson Mark of Los Alamos has said

> I would like to warn people concerned with such problems that the old notion that reactor-grade plutonium is incapable of producing explosions—or that plutonium could easily be rendered harmless by the addition of modest amounts of the isotope Pu^{240}, or "denatured," as the phrase used to go—that these notions have been dangerously exaggerated. (In Feld et al., 1971, pp. 137–138)

If a purer weapons grade supply of ^{239}Pu is desired, the fuel elements must be exposed less inside the nuclear reactor prior to reprocessing. Consider the new Indian CANDU reactors that can produce 660 MW(*th*) (megawatts of thermal heat) for a core loading of 45 tonnes of uranium fuel. If these reactor cores were run continuously for two

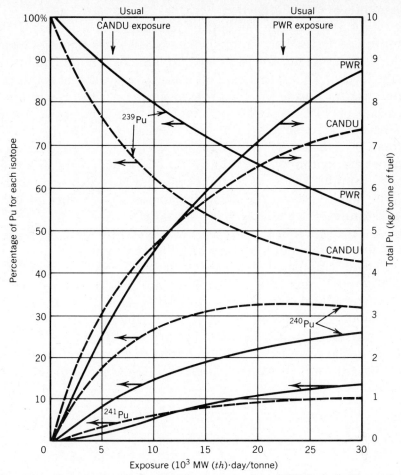

Figure 14.5 Growth of various plutonium isotopes in a PWR fueled with uranium enriched to 3% in ^{235}U and a CANDU reactor fueled with natural uranium. (After *Nucleonics*, Vol. 23, no. 8, August 1965, pp. 101–105.)

years before reloading, they would receive an exposure of 482,000 MW(th)·days, or 10,000 MW(th)·days per tonne. Assume that Fig. 14.5 holds for this reactor. This figure shows that at that point about 60% of the plutonium is ^{239}Pu. That is considerably less than weapons grade. If the reactor core were reprocessed every six months then the level of ^{240}Pu denaturing would be much less. For an exposure of $2.7 \cdot 10^3$ MW(th)·days/tonne, we see that ^{239}Pu makes up about 85% of the plutonium produced. The CANDU reactors are in fact ideally suited for such frequent core removal (McIntyre, 1975). For each day of operation typically 15 individual fuel elements are removed through sideways access tubes as in Fig. 14.6 while the reactor is operating.

Magnitude of ^{239}Pu Production

Figure 14.5 shows the buildup of plutonium in a standard PWR reactor of the design used in the United States. This figure points out that for large exposure levels, that is, for large burnup fractions of the ^{235}U, the level of ^{239}Pu saturates. This is due to the fact that at this point a significant fraction of the ^{239}Pu fissions in the reactor. For maximum production of ^{239}Pu, as well as for the least ^{240}Pu admixture, frequent reprocessing is desirable. The new Indian 660-MW(th) CANDU reactors, if refueled at two-year intervals, would produce about 45 tonnes·4.7 kg/tonne = 200 kg of Pu every two years. If refueled every six months, that is, if each fuel element were exposed to a level of 2.7·10^3 MW(th)-days, the same reactor would produce (4 refuelings)·(45 tonnes)·(2 kg/tonne) = 360 kg of Pu.

For Pu production at low exposures in enriched uranium reactors, such as the PWR, about 0.6 atoms of ^{239}Pu are produced for every ^{235}U nucleus that is fissioned. For natural uranium reactors, such as the CANDU model, about 0.85 ^{239}Pu atoms are produced for every ^{235}U nucleus that is fissioned. For the breeder reactor, this multiplication factor may be 1.2 or more (i.e., more fissionable material is produced than is consumed). But the exact value depends on the length of exposure of the core. Figure 14.5 indicates that these values decrease as the total exposure increases; higher exposures lead to the burnup of

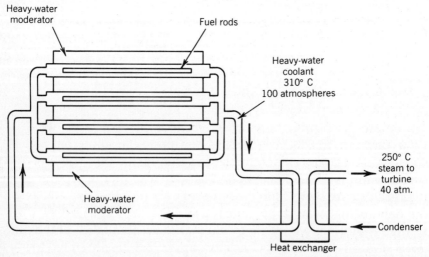

Figure 14.6 Sketch of a CANDU reactor moderated and cooled by heavy water. The fuel rods are independently accessible, so that the reactor does not have to be shut off to remove a small number of fuel rods.

some of the produced plutonium. For the typical reactor core exposures of 6000 MW(th)·days and 22,600 MW(th)·days per tonne for CANDU and PWR reactors, respectively, 1 MW(th)·day of electric energy produces 0.57 gm of Pu and 0.33 gm of Pu, respectively.

The old Indian CANDU reactor with a power output of 40 MW(th) then produces each year 8 kg of Pu. Small experimental reactors produce enough nuclear material to produce just a few critical masses of ^{239}Pu over several years. Reactors for electrical power generation are a different matter. As indicated, each of the new Indian power reactors will produce as much 100 kg of Pu each year, enough for perhaps 10 critical masses. When the production for the whole worldwide nuclear power industry is calculated, the amounts of Pu produced annually are staggering. Table 14.1 showed that the United States, Japan, and China (Taiwan) presently have maximum electrical capacities, respectively, of 59,000 MW(e), 17,600 MW(e), and 3100 MW(e). Since the average electric output is about two-thirds of capacity, the annual production of Pu in these plants is about 14, 4, and 0.7 tonnes (i.e., the United States produces annually enough Pu in its civilian nuclear power reactors to make 1400 critical masses of 10 kg each. This nuclear energy production level is only on the order of 10% of the present U.S. electrical power generation. If all the nuclear plants presently under construction in the world were built and in operation, a capacity of 393,000 MW(e) would exist. Operating at two-thirds of capacity, these plants would generate annually about 95 tonnes of Pu, enough for 9500 critical masses at 10 kg each, if the Pu were reprocessed and if the ^{240}Pu contamination would not make the bomb designs too difficult.

^{235}U Proliferation

Nuclear weapons can also be made from ^{235}U. The separation of ^{235}U from natural uranium presents the technological challenge of using purely physical means to separate isotopes. The gaseous diffusion method described in Chapter 2 (Villani, 1979) has so far dominated the separation industry. That method is not attractive for small-scale nuclear weapons programs; diffusion plants must be very large and technologically complex, are expensive to build and costly to operate, and consume large quantities of electrical energy.

By changing the interconnections between cascade units a diffusion plant can produce uranium with various levels of enrichment in ^{235}U, including 3% for reactors and 90% for weapons. The rejected uranium tailings can have various levels of ^{235}U left in them; typically they are depleted down to 0.2%. To produce 1 kg of uranium enriched to 90% in ^{235}U while producing tailings with 0.2% ^{235}U requires 64 times as much energy and plant capacity as producing 1 kg of 3% ^{235}U with 0.2% tailings. The present U.S. gaseous diffusion plants can process 17,000 tonnes of natural uranium each year into 4000 tonnes of uranium enriched to 3% in ^{235}U; at maximum capacity they consume 6000 MW of electricity (about 1.5% of the total U.S. electrical power capacity). That effort now produces typically 3000 tonnes of 3%-enriched fuel each year, of which about 1300 tonnes is used by the U.S. power industry, about 500 tonnes is sold to foreign customers, and the rest is added to a stockpile; the rest of the plant capacity is used to produce highly enriched ^{235}U to fuel naval propulsion reactors.

A developing nuclear power would probably prefer one of several alternative separation techniques that are now becoming available. Three primary alternatives use high-speed centrifuges, nozzles, and lasers.

Centrifuges. During World War II one attractive uranium separation method was not thoroughly developed, namely, that involving high-speed centrifuges (see Figs. 14.7 and 14.8). This technique has now been improved substantially (Olander, 1978). A German-built plant has been constructed in The Netherlands with the capacity to produce about 40 tonnes of 3% ^{235}U per year. A full-scale palnt with a capacity to produce 2000 tonnes of uranium enriched to 3% is planned for

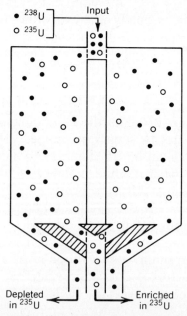

Figure 14.7 Sketch of a centrifuge for enriching uranium in ^{235}U. As the centrifuge spins around its vertical axis, the heavier ^{238}U tends to drift toward the outside.

Figure 14.8 Centrifuges in the Advanced Equipment Test Facility of the Oak Ridge National Laboratory. (Photo courtesy U.S. Department of Energy.)

completion by 1985. The advantages for the nuclear industry of this process are the much lower electricity costs shown in Table 14.2 as well as a much smaller minimum plant size. The latter advantage highlights the fact that a small plant could be suitable to produce enough weapons-grade ^{235}U for a reasonable number of nuclear explosives. If operating at weapons-grade enrichment levels, a 10-tonne-SWU plant could generate 36 kg of 90% ^{235}U product per year.

Nozzle enrichment. A possible separation process is the nozzle enrichment method. In this aerodynamic process, sketched in Fig. 14.9, uranium hexafluoride (mixed with hydrogen) is forced through a nozzle. It flows rapidly along the inside of a curved wall. In the process, centrifugal forces move the heavier ^{238}U to the outside of the curve, while the lighter ^{235}U tends toward the inside. A knife edge separates the stream into two segments: the inner part of the stream is enriched in ^{235}U, while the outer part is depleted in ^{235}U. The enrichment is slight; hundreds of enrichment stages are needed to reach a useful level of enrichment. A plant to produce perhaps 100 tonnes of 3% ^{235}U

Table 14.2. Costs and performance factors for four types of enrichment processes.
Estimates are derived from *Science,* Vol. 188 (1975), p. 912 and Vol. 191 (1976), p. 1163; also Barnaby, 1979.

	Diffusion	Centrifuge	Nozzle	Laser
Separation factor per stage	1.0043	~1.2	~1.015	10–1000
Stages for reactor grade	1200	~13	~450	1
Stages for weapons grade	4000			
Energy required (MWhr) per tonne-SWU[a]	2400	~250	3000	170
Economic size in tonnes-SWU[a]	7000	800	2000	3000
Process area (acres)	60	20	—	1–8

[a] 1-tonne separative work unit (tonne-SWU) can process 0.875 tonne of natural uranium to produce 210 kg of uranium enriched to 3% in ^{235}U plus 665 kg of 0.2% tailings.

a year is in operation in Germany. Plants 10 times this size are under construction or are planned for South Africa and Brazil. The biggest drawback of this enrichment technique is the large amount of electric energy demanded by it, as shown in Table 14.2. But Brazil, presently a nonnuclear nation, has large hydroelectric resources far in the interior, where there is little use for electricity; production of enriched reactor-grade ^{235}U might be a convenient way of exploiting that resource. Brazil has a nuclear agreement with West Germany that includes purchases of this enrichment technology along with several reactors.

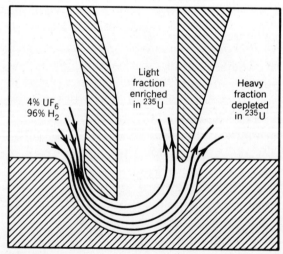

Figure 14.9 Sketch of the nozzle enrichment process. (After Barnaby, 1979, Figure 3.1, p. 63.)

Laser enrichment. An isotopic separation technique using laser light is being developed (Zare, 1977; Krass, 1977) to produce enriched [235]U or to remove [240]Pu from reactor-grade Pu. This technology is viewed with alarm by some arms control experts who think it potentially might "enable people to build bombs in their basement," by allowing them to bypass the nuclear fuel cycle with its NPT and IAEA safeguards. There are very slight differences in the orbits of electrons in [235]U and [238]U atoms due to the differences in the sizes of the nuclei. These orbital differences are reflected in very small binding-energy differences typically on the order of one part in 10^5. In this enrichment procedure, laser light is used to ionize selectively only one of the uranium isotopes; thereafter, standard electromagnetic techniques can be used to separate the two isotopes.

Figure 14.10 outlines one such process. Uranium is vaporized in an oven; the resulting uranium gas passes through one or more laser beams. These lasers may selectively excite the atoms of one of the two isotopes by moving an orbital electron into an excited state. Because of the slight orbital energy differences for the two isotopes caused by the different sizes of the [235]U and [238]U nuclei, a laser with photons of a precisely defined energy can do this.

If a first laser has not completely removed the electron from the atom, a second laser of another precisely defined frequency may be used to excite further the atoms of one of the uranium isotopes so that the electron is totally separated from the atoms. When the charged U^+ ions and the neutral U^0 atoms pass through an electric or magnetic field, the charged U^+ ions are deflected and the neutral U^0 atoms are not. This gives a separation of these two isotopes. The technical advantages are that little thermal energy is required to produce relatively

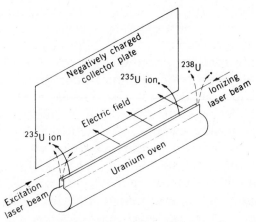

Figure 14.10 Sketch of an atomic laser enrichment apparatus. (After Krass, 1977, p. 90.)

large separation ratios and that only a few consecutive separation steps are required to achieve high levels of enrichment. However, lasers are generally inefficient in producing the photons, so that the energy required to make the lasers operate may be quite large. At present many technological problems suffice to make this an uncertain enrichment method, but isotopic separation by the laser method has been shown to be feasible. It might ultimately be suitable for producing small quantities of ^{235}U in a reasonably sized plant, making possible clandestine preparation of weapons-grade material for a small number of nuclear fission warheads. Pilot plants are in the planning stage in the United States, and other states are known to be pursuing this method actively.

CANDIDATES FOR NUCLEAR PROLIFERATION

It would appear that nuclear proliferation can be achieved by any country with reasonable nuclear technology that has the political desire to produce nuclear explosives. The technological capabilities may in part be related to the size and form of the nuclear power industry and perhaps to the uranium resources available. The desire for nuclear proliferation is affected by many political circumstances and may be reflected in an unwillingness to sign and ratify the nuclear nonproliferation treaty.

Technical Aspects

The discussions thus far suggest that nuclear proliferation does not require the possession of large resources of uranium. The fuel for nuclear power reactors can be bought from other nations. However, purchasing reactor fuel brings some restrictions and controls on the use of the resulting ^{239}Pu. The availability of indigenous uranium supplies makes the politics of proliferation less complicated. Any nation with large uranium resources would see these as valuable raw materials whose value would rise enormously if processed into nuclear fuel and would be interested in developing an enrichment capability. Once an enrichment capability exists, it would be easy to produce weapons-grade material. Therefore, the amount of uranium resources a nation possesses is one measure of the ease with which that nation could develop nuclear weapons. Uranium resources are not spread equally throughout the world, as Table 14.3 shows. The most striking concentrations of uranium resources are in the nonnuclear weapons states of Australia, South Africa, and Canada and in the United States and the USSR.

A certain technical sophistication is desirable for producing nuclear explosives. This may be acquired by concentrating research efforts specifically in the nuclear area; India did this in its sophisticated nuclear research center at Trombay. An overall general technical sophistication could also be a measure of the capability to "go nuclear." This may be measured by the overall level of research activity, for example, in terms of the total money invested in research and development (R&D) or by the quality of that R&D. For example, Israel does not have a particularly large R&D budget, but the quality of its science and engineering effort is very high. Such a commitment to high-

Table 14.3 Uranium resources and production.
Data derived from Greenwood, Feiveson, and Taylor, 1977, p. 8.

Country	Resource Estimates (kt uranium recoverable at specific U_3O_8 price per pound)				Production (tonnes uranium per yr)	
	Reasonably Assured		Estimated Additional		Annual Production	Production Capacity
	$15	$15–30	$15	$15–30	1974	1978 (est)
United States	230 kt	201 kt	655 kt	405 kt	8,800 t	19,000 t
Australia	243 kt	—	80 kt	—	—	760 t
South Africa	186 kt	90 kt	6 kt	68 kt	2,711 t	9,200 t
Canada	145 kt	28 kt	303 kt	302 kt	3,420 t	8,500 t
Algeria	28 kt	—	—	—	—	—
Argentina	9 kt	11 kt	15 kt	24 kt	50 t	120 t
Brazil	10 kt	1 kt	9 kt	—	—	—
Britain	—	2 kt	—	4 kt	—	—
Central Afr. Rep.	8 kt	—	8 kt	—	—	—
Denmark, Greenland	—	6 kt	—	10 kt	—	—
Finland	—	2 kt	—	—	—	—
France	87 kt	18 kt	25 kt	15 kt	1,610 t	2,200 t
Gabon	20 kt	—	5 kt	5 kt	436 t	120 t
Germany	1 kt	1 kt	1 kt	3 kt	26 t	250 t
India	3 kt	26 kt	1 kt	23 kt	—	—
Italy	—	1 kt	—	1 kt	—	—
Japan	1 kt	7 kt	—	—	9 t	30 t
Korea	—	2 kt	—	—	—	—
Mexico	5 kt	1 kt	—	—	—	210 t
Niger	40 kt	10 kt	20 kt	10 kt	1,250 t	2,200 t
Portugal	7 kt	—	—	—	89 t	130 t
Spain	10 kt	94 kt	9 kt	98 kt	60 t	340 t
Sweden	—	300 kt	—	—	—	—
Turkey	3 kt	1 kt	—	—	—	—
Yugoslavia	4 kt	2 kt	—	15 kt	—	—
Zaire	2 kt	—	2 kt	—	—	—
Total (rounded)	1190 kt	810 kt	1140 kt	980 kt	18,461 t	44,100 t

quality research may be seen in the fraction of Israel's gross national product invested in R&D.

The level of activity in the nuclear power industry provides one indication of the potential for nuclear proliferation, as indicated by the megawatts of electric power provided by nuclear power reactors. Projections of planned capacity look into the future; Table 14.2 suggests which nations might have the larger technological potential toward nuclear weapons.

The introductory quotation for this chapter from the Office of Technology Assessment (1977) indicates the size of the economic investment required to carry out a small nuclear weapons program. A 1968 study carried out by the United Nations had made the estimates listed in Table 14.4; while these assume a longer-term project, they are essentially in agreement with the figures from the Office of Technology Assessment. The costs given by either study are low enough to be within the reach of most nations.

Nuclear weapons also require delivery systems to make them useful as armaments for war. These delivery systems and their sophistication depend on the nature and proximity of the expected enemy. In the case of Israel, any fighter bomber could be used to deliver a nuclear warhead on enemy cities in Egypt, Syria, or Lebanon. In the case of India, a nuclear attack on Pakistan could be carried out by unsophisticated medium-range bombers. In the case of Japan, an attack on the Soviet Union would require sophisticated long-range bombers, missile-launching submarines or ICBMs.

Political Aspects

These discussions of technical competence are probably on the whole academic. As India demonstrated, a less developed nation can produce

Table 14.4. **The cost of nuclear weapons production, given in millions of 1968 U.S. dollars.**
These estimates were made by the United Nations. They assume a 10-year period for the program.

	Small Program 10 Weapons @ 20 kt (millions)	Moderate Program 100 Weapons @ 20 kt (millions)
Plutonium-239 metal	$70	$151
Design and fabrication	18	18
Testing	12	15
Total	$100	$184
Cost per nuclear weapon	$10	$1.9

nuclear explosives if it makes the necessary technological and economic commitment. In asking who are the most likely next nuclear nations, one really needs to ask who has the most pressing political reasons for desiring nuclear weapons. Some nations in the Middle East, Asia, and South America may have hostile neighbors against whom a small number of nuclear weapons might appear to provide a useful armament. For some other countries, such as the NATO nations, Japan, and Sweden, only a large-scale nuclear weapons capability would seem to make much sense, since any confrontation worthy of nuclear weapons would most likely involve a superpower.

The nuclear proliferation report of the OTA (1977) lists a variety of political incentives and disincentives for "going nuclear" (pp. 94–98).

General Incentives

(1.) *Deterrence*: "The primary incentive for many states to acquire nuclear weapons would be to deter external efforts to undermine or destroy the existing regime or governmental system." (2.) *Increased international status*: Nuclear weapons can give self-confidence, and respect of neighbors and superpowers. (3.) *Domestic political requirements*: ". . . international status can serve to bolster a government's domestic political standing." (4.) *Economic considerations*: Nuclear weapons programs might provide technological spinoff and expanding internal economic interests. (5.) *Increased strategic autonomy*. (6.) *Strategic hedge against military and political uncertainty*. (7.) *A weapon of last resort*. (8.) *As an instrument of the third world*. Nuclear weapons might be equalizers. (9.) *Peaceful nuclear explosives*.

General Disincentives

(1.) *Diversion of resources*. (2.) *Adverse public opinion*. (3.) *Disruption of assured security guarantees*. Nuclear weapons might remove the proliferator from under the protective umbrella of a superpower. (4.) *Infeasibility of a desired nuclear strategy*: A modest nuclear force might not be sufficient to deter a nuclear enemy, and hence might invite a preemptive attack. (5.) *Adverse international reaction*. (6.) *Adverse reactions by adversaries*: This reaction could be diplomatic, in the form of an arms race, or as a preemptive attack. (7.) *Advocacy of neutrality aims*: Some neutralist leaders see the possession of nuclear weapons as eroding their credibility on arms control issues.

It is difficult to measure the strengths and balance of these incentives and disincentives for any given nation. The most readily accessible measure of the political desires of a nation for "going nuclear" is whether it has signed and ratified the nuclear non-proliferation agreement. That treaty forbids all development of nuclear explosives. Signatory nations who have no nuclear weapons also have submitted all their nuclear facilities and fuel shipments to inspection by the International Atomic Energy Agency (IAEA). These actions signal an absence of nuclear intentions for the present, although they provide no firm assurances for the future since there is a three-month withdrawal clause. Table 14.5 indicates which nations have accepted the NPT treaty. More detailed political answers about historical perspectives, geographic situations, relationships with neighboring nations, historical perspectives, and alliances may give further indications of political will toward proliferation.

The Candidates

Among the most likely future nuclear nations, there is not necessarily a direct correspondence between technical possibilities and political likelihood. Several nations that are technically most capable are unlikely to "go nuclear."

The Federal Republic of Germany is technically able to produce nuclear explosives at any time (Kelleher, 1975). It not only designs and builds its own nuclear reactors, but it even exports them; it builds and sells enrichment plants for ^{235}U; and it has sold several PWR reactors plus enrichment, fuel fabrication, and chemical plutonium reprocessing plants to Brazil. But West Germany pledged itself in 1954 not to manufacture nuclear weapons on its territory, and it has signed the NPT; it has made a political decision not to exploit its nuclear capability for military purposes. It is an integral part of NATO and as such is under the U.S. nuclear umbrella. The Soviet Union would feel very threatened by German nuclear weapons; a small German nuclear capability would risk a Soviet preemptive first strike.

Canada has the nuclear technology for producing fission explosives. Its CANDU reactors are suitable for producing weapons-grade ^{239}Pu. It is building many nuclear power stations, and it is actively promoting foreign sales of such nuclear reactors. But Canada has signed the NPT, opting against nuclear proliferation. It has no nearby enemies and is relying on the U.S. nuclear umbrella. In its new sales of nuclear plants it tries to retain the reprocessing rights to the spent fuel elements.

Sweden does not have quite as much nuclear technology as Canada, but that technology certainly is sufficient to build nuclear weapons at any time. Sweden has demonstrated its commitment to and capability for military self-defense, for example, with its aircraft industry, but it has signed the NPT, disavowing the nuclear option.

Table 14.5 Nations that have signed, ratified, acceded or succeeded to the Treaty on the Non-Proliferation of Nuclear Weapons (NPT) as 31 December 1980.
(Stockholm International Peace Research Institute, 1981, p. 303.)

Afghanistan	Fiji	Liberia	Senegal
Australia	Finland	Libya	Sierra Leone
Austria	Gabon	Liechtenstein	Singapore
Bahamas	Gambia	Luxembourg	Somalia
Bangladesh	German Dem.	Madagascar	Sri Lanka
Barbados	Rep.	Malaysia	Sudan
Belgium	German Fed. Rep.	Maldives	Suriname
Benin	Ghana	Mali	Swaziland
Bolivia	Greece	Malta	Sweden
Botswana	Grenada	Mauritius	Switzerland
Bulgaria	Guatemala	Mexico	Syria
Burundi	Guinea-Bissau	Mongolia	Taiwan
Canada	Haiti	Morocco	Thailand
Cape Verde	Holy See (Vatican)	Nepal	Togo
Central African	Honduras	Netherlands	Tonga
Republic	Hungary	New Zealand	Trinidad &
Chad	Iceland	Nicaragua	Tobago[a]
Colombia[a]	Indonesia	Nigeria	Tunisia
Congo	Iran	Norway	Turkey
Costa Rica	Iraq	Panama	Tuvalu
Cyprus	Ireland	Papua New	USSR
Czechoslovakia	Italy	Guinea[c]	United Kingdom
Democratic	Ivory Coast	Paraguay	United Republic
Kampuchea	Jamaica	Peru	of Cameroon
Democratic (South)	Japan	Philippines	United States
Yemen	Jordan	Poland	Upper Volta
Denmark	Kenya	Portugal	Uruguay
Dominican Republic	South Korea	Romania	Venezuela
Ecuador	Kuwait[a]	Rwanda	Northern Yemen[a]
Egypt[b]	Laos	St. Lucia	Yugoslavia
El Salvador	Lebanon	Samoa	Zaire
Ethiopia	Lesoto	San Marino	

[a] Have signed but not ratified.
[b] Ratified in 1981.
[c] Acceded in 1982.

Italy does not appear to want nuclear weapons. But it is politically unstable: if its government were to become communist and leave NATO, then its nuclear motivation might change.

Japan has so far been uninterested in nuclear weapons (Endicott, 1975). In part this is due to its memories of Hiroshima and Nagasaki. Beyond that, Japan is somewhat like West Germany. It has no small local enemies to fear; any conflict in which it might become engaged would presumably involve at least the P.R.C., if not the Soviet Union. A small number of nuclear weapons might then be a danger; only a large-scale deterrent would be useful.

Argentina is symbolic of the tensions of the South American situation. It has several nuclear reactors (although these are under IAEA safeguards) plus a small plutonium reprocessing plant as well as a nuclear cooperation agreement with India. It has not signed the NPT. Thus, it has the potential for nuclear proliferation. If it were to do so, it might well trigger a local nuclear arms race with Brazil and Chile. There are political incentives for developing a nuclear capability, but such a capability might in the long run backfire.

South Africa has only a few nuclear reactors, and on technical grounds, it would not seem as likely a nuclear candidate as some other nations. But with German help, it appears to have developed a successful nozzle method of uranium enrichment. Once sufficiently-enriched ^{235}U is available, building a nuclear explosive becomes easy. The Union of South Africa has large uranium resources and exports natural uranium to France. It would be very desirable and profitable for South Africa to sell the uranium fuel already enriched; a nuclear explosion would be a good advertisement for the quality of its enrichment process. South Africa has not signed the NPT; however, so far it has not overtly gone nuclear. A few years ago a suspicious light flash was detected in the vicinity of South Africa by U.S. Vela satellites. This flash resembled the double peak from a nuclear explosion shown in Fig. 2.12, thereby arousing suspicion that it came from a South African nuclear explosion. Since then most experts have accepted that no nuclear explosion did take place. Nonetheless, South Africa would seem a likely candidate for developing nuclear weapons. Psychologically, it might find it desirable to have a small nuclear arsenal. Militarily such weapons might not be very useful in guerilla warfare, but as South Africa becomes politically more isolated from the rest of the world, such a symbol of military prowess might reestablish enough self-confidence to make such a development worthwhile.

Israel has only one 40-MW(*th*) nuclear research reactor. This can produce only enough plutonium for about one nuclear bomb a year. It does have the technology to reprocess the plutonium and fabricate the bombs; it may even be developing the laser uranium enrichment method. Because of its sophisticated technology base, if interested Israel could become a nuclear weapons state, even though it has no nuclear electric power stations and has repeatedly said it would "not be the first country to introduce nuclear weapons into the Middle East." Militarily it might be in Israel's interest to have some nuclear weapons available in case of an extreme national emergency. But it would also be undesirable to have this arsenal confirmed, because that would encourage and enable her neighbors like Egypt to ask for nuclear aid from the United States or the USSR. There are rumors that Israel indeed has a nuclear arsenal of possibly a dozen fission bombs. Perhaps such a rumor may provide the ideal deterrent for Israel vis-à-vis its neighbors.

Pakistan has for some years expressed its intention to develop an "Islamic" nuclear bomb. It has tried to acquire nuclear reprocessing technology from France and has started the construction of an uranium enrichment plant. The political motivation is its continuing confrontations with India. The United States has attempted to exert economic and political pressures to keep this proliferation from happening, but the invasion of Afghanistan by the Soviet Union has resulted in the removal of these sanctions.

THE FUTURE OF NUCLEAR PROLIFERATION

The knowledge of nuclear technology and practical experience is spreading via the expanding nuclear electric power industry. That nuclear expertise provides many nations with an increasing capability for the production of nuclear weapons. Whether nuclear proliferation is a true technological imperative depends on the extent to which these technological capabilities combine with the nontechnical incentives to pressure nations to build nuclear weapons. Steps can be and have been taken to slow the rate of proliferation.

Slowing down the breeder reactor development and large-scale plutonium reprocessing might reduce the technical part of the proliferation momentum; this is the theme of the cartoon in Fig. 14.11. Encouraging nations to submit to inspections by the IAEA might reduce the opportunities to divert fissile materials from that nuclear power industry. On the political side, persuading all nations to sign the nuclear non-proliferation treaty might decrease some local tensions that could otherwise lead to local nuclear arms races. Political pressures have worked surprisingly well so far. In the short run the vertical proliferation of the nuclear arsenal of the superpowers may well be the larger threat, and even in the long run the status of mutual stable nuclear deterrence between the superpowers may have to be rethought. Nonetheless, long-term resistance to the technological imperative of horizontal nuclear proliferation may be difficult. That will raise the question of what is to be done if there are many fingers on nuclear triggers.

'With the plutonium rings out it would look more like a halo'

Figure 14.11 Does the reprocessing of plutonium increase the probability of nuclear proliferation? (Reprinted by permission from *The Christian Science Monitor*. Copyright 1977, The Christian Science Publishing Company, all rights reserved.)

References

Barnaby, F., ed., *Nuclear Energy and Nuclear Weapons Proliferation*. New York: Crane, Russak for SIPRI, 1979.

Beddington, W. P. "The Reprocessing of Nuclear Fuels." *Scientific American*, Vol. 235, no. 6, (December 1976); pp. 30–41.

Endicott, J. E. *Japan's Nuclear Option: Political, Technical, and Strategic Facts*. New York: Praeger, 1975.

Epstein, W. *The Last Chance: Nuclear Proliferation and Arms Control*. New York: Free Press, 1976.

Feld, B. T., T. Greenwood, G. W. Rathjens, and S. Weinberg, eds. *Impact of New Technologies on the Arms Race*. Cambridge, Mass.: M.I.T. Press, 1971.

Gowing, M. *Independence and Deterrence: Britain and Atomic Energy, 1945–1952*. Vol. I: *Policy Making*. Vol. II: *Policy Execution*. New York: St. Martin's Press, 1975.

Greenwood, T., H. A. Feiveson, and T. B. Taylor. *Nuclear Proliferation: Motivations, Capabilities, and Strategies for Control*. New York: McGraw-Hill, 1977.

Kelleher, C. M. *Germany and the Politics of Nuclear Weapons*. New York: Columbia University Press, 1975.

Krass, A. S. "Laser Enrichment of Uranium: The Proliferation Connection." *Science*, Vol. 196 (1977), pp. 721–731.

McIntyre, H. C. "Natural-Uranium Heavy-Water Reactors." *Scientific American*, Vol. 233, no. 4, (October 1975), pp. 17–27.

Nero, A. V., Jr. *A Guidebook to Nuclear Reactors*. Berkeley: University of California Press, 1979.

Office of Technology Assessment. *Nuclear Proliferation and Safeguards*. New York: Praeger, 1977.

Olander, D. R. "The Gas Centrifuge." *Scientific American*, Vol. 239, no. 2 (August 1978), pp. 37–43.

Stockholm International Peace Research Institute. *World Armaments and Disarmament: SIPRI Yearbook 1981*. Cambridge, Mass.: Oelgeschlager, Gunn & Hain, 1981.

Vendryes, G. A. "Superphenix: A Full-Scale Breeder Reactor." *Scientific American*, Vol. 236, no. 3 (March 1977), pp. 26–35.

Villani, S., ed. *Uranium Enrichment*. New York: Springer, 1979. Very technical.

de Volpi, A. *Proliferation, Plutonium and Policy: Institutional and Technological Impediments to Nuclear Weapons Proliferation*. New York: Pergamon Press, 1979.

Weart, S. R. *Scientists in Power*. Cambridge, Mass.: Harvard University Press, 1979. History of French nuclear power programs.

Zare, R. N. "Laser Separation of Isotopes." *Scientific American*, Vol. 236, no. 2 (February 1977), pp. 86–98.

CHAPTER
15

Arms Control: Nuclear Test-Ban Treaties

"I Might Do A Little Experimenting With You, Too"

Figure 15.1 Herblock's cartoon of 1956 expresses the fear felt by many in the 1950s that global fallout from above-ground nuclear tests could cause considerable damage to human chromosomes. (From *Herblock's Special for Today* (Simon & Schuster, 1958), by permission of HERBLOCK CARTOONS.)

346

The dangers of nuclear weapons were recognized even before such weapons were known to be feasible. As soon as the first A-bombs were used in 1945, the first attempts at nuclear arms control were initiated. The Baruch plan of 1946 proposed total nuclear disarmament. Since that failure, the goals of arms control advocates have become more modest. Various arms control measures have sought to forbid those aspects of nuclear weaponry and their proliferation that were easily verifiable. Arms limitation agreements have limited the quantity, and to an extent the quality, of nuclear arms. Some treaties have included confidence-building measures. True disarmament has not been accomplished.

Tables 15.1 and 15.2 list a wide variety of treaties that have tried to control or limit arms. Some of these treaties will be considered in Chapters 16 and 17. This chapter will focus on measures that have tried to control nuclear weapons development by banning nuclear weapons tests. In 1958 the United States, the United Kingdom, and the Soviet Union took the first step toward such a ban when they established an informal moratorium on the testing of nuclear weapons. That informal agreement was based upon the apparent consensus among technical experts that violations of such a moratorium could be detected. When this scientific consensus collapsed, other political and military factors caused nuclear testing to be resumed in 1961. In 1963 a Limited Nuclear Test Ban Treaty (LTBT) was finally established; it has been signed by most nations. This treaty has banned all above-ground nuclear tests.

Since 1963 nuclear weapons deployment has been forbidden in outer space and on the sea bed, and some nuclear free zones have been established in the Antarctic and to some extent in South America. In July 1974 an agreement was reached between the United States and the USSR that after March 1976 neither side would conduct underground tests of nuclear weapons with a yield in excess of 150 kt. The United States has yet to ratify this treaty. Each treaty controlled the possible at minimum costs to the treaty partners. Thus, the limited test ban controlled the easily verifiable tests above ground that produced fallout, yet did not limit nuclear weapons technology. The space ban on nuclear weapons may have seemed somewhat harder to monitor; on the other hand, no one at that time really wanted to place nuclear weapons in orbit, or to build nuclear bases on the moon. Nuclear-free zones were established in areas where no nuclear weapons were contemplated.

The focus here will be on nuclear test-ban treaties for several reasons: (1.) Obviously test-ban treaties are major aspects of the arms race; how much they have accomplished? (2.) The test-ban treaties

Table 15.1 Multilateral arms control agreements signed since 1959
(After Stockholm International Peace Research Institute, 1981.)

Signed (In force)	Treaty[a]	Number of Parties	Important Nonsigners[b]
1959 (1959)	*Antarctic Treaty.* Prohibits military activity in the Antarctic area; a follow-up to the International Geophysical Year of 1958.	21	
1963 (1963)	*Limited Test Ban Treaty.* Prohibits nuclear explosions in the atmosphere, in outer space and under water.	112	Peoples Republic of China, France[c]
1967 (1967)	*Outer-Space Treaty.* Prohibits all military activity in outer space, including the moon. Military bases on the moon seem undesirable because of the transit time, and strategic weapons on satellites have a time window for launches that is too narrow.	82	
1967 (1968)	*Treaty of Tlatelolco.* Established Latin America as an area free of nuclear weapons.	22	Argentina, Brazil, Cuba
1968 (1970)	*Non-Proliferation Treaty.* Prohibits the acquisition of nuclear weapons by nonnuclear weapons states; the nuclear weapons states must help NNWS with peaceful uses of nuclear energy, and must work toward disarmament (see Chapter 14).	114	Argentina, Brazil, France, India, Israel, Pakistan, People's Republic of China, Saudi Arabia, South Africa, Spain
1971 (1972)	*Sea-Bed Treaty.* Prohibits placement of nuclear weapons and other weapons of mass destruction on or below the ocean floor. An extension of the international freedom of the seas. It does not forbid SLBM subs or ground-moored mines or submarine detection systems.	70	
1972 (1975)	*Biological Weapons Convention.* Prohibits the development, production and storing of bacteriological weapons (see Chapter 11).	91	
1977 (1978)	*Environmental Modification Convention.* Prohibits the hostile use of technologies to modify the environment.	31	

[a]Many of these treaties try to limit some regional nuclear proliferation.
[b]Important nonsignatories as of December 31, 1980.
[c]France has conducted no above-ground nuclear tests since 1974.

Table 15.2 Bilateral arms control agreements signed since 1963
Most of these agreements are to reduce tensions between the two superpowers. The SALT agreements attempt to go beyond arms control to arms limitation. (After Stockholm International Peace Research Institute, 1981.)

Signed	Agreement or Treaty
1963	*"Hot Line" Agreement.* Establishes emergency direct radio communications between the two superpowers during emergencies. In 1971 satellite circuits were added. A recognition of mutual assured destruction (MAD) and deterrence enhances strategic stability.
1971	*Nuclear Accidents Agreement.* Intends to reduce chance of accidental war.
1972	*High-Seas Agreement.* Together with a 1973 protocol this is designed to reduce confrontations on the oceans, as in the playing of the game of "chicken" between naval vessels. Designed to stabilize deterrence.
1972	*SALT I Treaty.* Prohibits the deployment of ABMs at more than two sites (reduced to one site in 1976); sets limits on the maximum allowed numbers of ICBMs and SLBMs for five years (see Chapter 16).
1973	*Nuclear War Prevention Agreement.* Various measures to avert nuclear war during tense situations. A symbol of deterrence and détente.
1974	*Threshold Nuclear Test-Ban Treaty.* Nuclear weapons tests with yields above 150 kt are prohibited even underground (has never gone in force because the U.S. Senate has not ratified it).
1976	*Vladivostok Statement.* New aggregate limits on the total strategic arsenal are set at 2400. Intended as a sketch of SALT II (see Chapter 16).
1979	*SALT II Treaty.* New aggregate totals and sublimits are set on strategic weapons, together with gross limits on some technologies such as MIRV. A true arms limitation agreement of usefulness in controlling some technologies. Has never gone in force because the U.S. Senate has not ratified it (see Chapter 16).

represent very important attempts to achieve arms control of the qualities of nuclear weapons. (3.) The technical aspects of test-ban treaty decisions show how technical improvements, as in seismology, can affect political situations and how in turn political requirements may modify the direction and rate of technological developments. (4.) The test-ban debates illustrate the very complex relationship among technical experts, the military, the government, and the general public. The first test moratorium was established on the basis of a scientific consensus and was abrogated after the consensus disintegrated; the 1963 LTBT came because of public pressure. The present debate contains a mix of opportunities provided by improved technological monitoring capabilities, political fears of proliferation, and a dream of totally controlling progress in nuclear weapons technology. (5.) The history of test-ban treaties symbolizes the pervasiveness in national security matters of the very conservative approach of worst-possible-case reasoning: arms control generally in the past has demanded almost total certainty in military security.

HISTORY OF NUCLEAR TEST-BAN TREATIES

At the end of World War II the United States was concerned with the implications of nuclear weapons for world stability. But after the failure of the Baruch plan of 1946, no further serious exploration of nuclear arms control was undertaken for the next decade. Up to 1955 technological breakthroughs in nuclear weaponry were coming so rapidly, everyone may have been too busy with arms developments to study the preconditions and possibilities of nuclear disarmament. In 1960, for example, Jerome B. Wiesner (1965), in suggesting an increase in arms control efforts, said that

> A major effort, compared to past efforts, would be twenty people working full-time, though a much bigger operation can easily be justified . . . why [was] this work not begun a long time ago? . . . Probably because sensitive seismic detectors are not needed in the development of nuclear weapons . . . (pp. 76–77)

In 1955 the views on nuclear testing began to change. In that year, several tests inside the continental United States produced considerable fallout on neighboring states and nearby Army units, with detectable fallout extending from New Mexico to Troy, New York. In admitting that the 1954 H-bomb had been of a fission-fusion-fission design, the AEC revealed that a 10-Mt blast had contaminated an area of 100,000 mi^2 with fallout (see Fig. 3.6). Also, fallout contamination was beginning to be considered·as more dangerous than previously expected; for example, the Nobel–prize winning geneticist Herman J. Mueller said that fallout radiation indeed could produce considerable genetic damage.

The USSR proposed that all nuclear tests should be stopped. In 1954 the U.S. physicist David R. Inglis proposed a nuclear test ban monitored from outside national boundaries. He felt this test ban would not only avoid fallout but also

> it would slow down the rate of development of new techniques of offense and allow the techniques of defense to come closer to catching up. (As quoted in Divine, 1978, p. 6)

The U.S. Department of Defense however saw nuclear testing as necessary for developing arms to keep the peace. Even as the public pressure to ban nuclear tests grew, some scientists such as Edward Teller wanted more tests to develop bombs free of fallout (neutron bombs) and argued that "The psychology of banning the discovery of new things is a dangerous road to take" (as quoted in Divine, 1976, p. 193).

President Eisenhower initially thought that a test ban was too little; he wanted comprehensive disarmament. But as the public alarm about fallout increased, he began to view the ban more favorably; maybe it could produce "disarmament by obsolescence."

In 1957 the fallout discussion in the United States was focused through the book *On the Beach* by Neville Shute, by the first Pugwash meeting bringing together Soviet and American scientists to discuss arms control issues, and by the launching in the fall of the Soviet *Sputnik* earth satellite. This led to the establishment of the Office of Presidential Science Advisor and the President's Science Advisory Committee (PSAC). "For the first time since the fallout debate began, the President had access to a broad spectrum of scientific opinion" (Divine, 1978, p. 171). James Killian, the presidential advisor brought in after *Sputnik*, favored a test-ban treaty. He was able to get agreement from the Bethe committee that

American nuclear weaponry was sufficient in terms of American military require-ments and Soviet nuclear capabilities to permit a nuclear test ban without prejudice to American security. (As quoted in Gilpin, 1962, p. 180)

On March 31, 1958 the Soviet Union announced a halt of its nuclear testing. In April, the PSAC recommended a similar test stop by the United States claiming that an "inspection system was feasible" (Divine, 1978, p. 209). A technical conference with the USSR on this issue was held. The scientific experts at this conference agreed that both above-ground and underwater nuclear tests were easily detect-able. The feasibility of detecting underground tests was not so clear-cut because of insufficient study of seismic detection systems. But in August 1958, this conference of experts agreed that a large seismic monitoring system plus some on-site inspections could detect all atmospheric explosions greater than 1 kt in yield and could detect with 90% certainty all underground explosions greater than 5 kt in yield. This technical consensus persuaded President Eisenhower in August 1958 to follow the example set by the USSR five months earlier; he stopped all U.S. nuclear tests.

Two things combined to ruin this voluntary informal test cessation. On the political side, the Soviet Union refused to accept such a large number of on-site inspections to investigate suspicious seismic events, while the United States insisted on virtually 100% certainty in the identification of suspicious events. On the technical side, considerable doubt was thrown on the ability to detect reliably even medium-level underground nuclear tests; the correctness of various seismic theories was challenged; the Air Force released data showing more earthquakes in the Soviet Union than previously believed; the concept of hiding nuclear explosions by setting them off inside caverns (muffling seismic effects by decoupling) was developed; even the ability to detect nuclear explosions in space was questioned.

After the collapse of the technical consensus, various political pressures caused the moratorium to break down in 1961. For example, the U-2 reconnaissance overflights and the Samos satellites embarrassed the Soviet Union by showing that its military strength was actually much less than generally believed (see Chapter 6). In 1961, first the Soviet Union and then the United States resumed nuclear tests.

The resumption of nuclear tests produced much radioactive and political fallout. The public concern about the fallout danger as exemplified by that Soviet 58-Mt explosion, and the brinkmanship of the Cuban missile crisis, finally produced enough renewed political pressure to force a reconsideration of a nuclear test ban. The United States, the United Kingdom, and the Soviet Union settled for a Limited Test Ban Treaty (LTBT) that banned all above-ground tests and all tests releasing radioactive materials beyond the boundaries of the testing state. Scientists could agree on the feasibility of detecting violations of this treaty and it could be monitored by national technical means without on-site inspections. The LTB Treaty became a reality in 1963.

FALLOUT FROM WEAPONS TESTS

Nuclear weapons explosions produce various radioactive isotopes as described in Chapter 3. The above-ground limited test ban treaty was forced on the United States and the USSR when nuclear fallout was widely detected globally and when radiological experts began to reach a consensus that damage to human beings could result from it.

The fallout products of concern are primarily ^{131}I, ^{90}Sr, and ^{137}Cs. The fallout from nuclear weapons test was observed globally. Figure 15.2 shows the concentration of the fission product ^{90}Sr in milk in Great Britain from 1958 to 1970. ^{90}Sr continued to reach the earth in measurable quantities long after the bomb testing had ceased. In a sense the above-ground testing program was a test of models of global air circulation. The fallout showed a consistently lower deposition rate during the winter and a higher one during the spring and summer. This is due to the fact that large nuclear weapons explosions inject radioactive

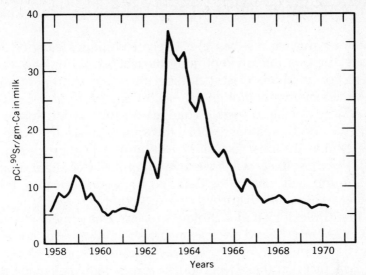

Figure 15.2 The ^{90}Sr concentration in milk in Great Britain after 1958. (After Bolt, 1976, Figure 5.1, p. 87.)

materials into the stratosphere; since the stratospheric air circulation is toward the poles, this leads to enhanced fallout in the spring shortly after the temperature in the Arctic has been coldest, producing large down drafts. The tests showed that there is little mixing of the stratospheric air between the southern and northern latitudes; the weapons tests took place mostly in the northern hemisphere and much less fallout was experienced in the southern hemisphere.

Chapter 3 deals with the effects from fallout. In retrospect, some of the concerns about the effects of the fallout may have been overstated at the time. It is estimated that the total dosage per person in the United States from fallout has been on the order of 3 to 4 millirem per year per person in the 1960s and 1970s (see, e.g., Bolt, 1976, p. 84). This compares with natural background exposures of about 150 mrem per year or to medical and dental x-ray exposures of about 90 mrem per year. If one were to accept the linear model of radiation damage and the estimate that 5000 person-rems causes 1 fatality, then 4 billion people exposed to 20 years of 3 mrem/year would experience 48,000 additional fatalities. In the 1950s and early 1960s, these dangers were not well understood and could easily have been overestimated, particularly when the Atomic Energy Commission continued to claim that there was no effect at all from the fallout. Whether justified or not, these concerns about fallout definitely had a political impact, making the banning of nuclear tests above ground politically acceptable.

THE DETECTION OF NUCLEAR EXPLOSIONS

To monitor a nuclear test ban effectively, techniques must be available to detect any possible surreptitious nuclear explosions. A variety of test-detection methods exist including the observation of atmospheric shock waves by microbarometers, electromagnetic pulses, radioactive debris, flashes of light, visible changes on the earth's surface, earth movements, and espionage. For atmospheric tests the first four of these methods are most useful. Detection of explosions far above the atmosphere most likely will have to monitor flashes of light. Explosions below ground will have to be detected by seismic means, unless the ground is accidentally disturbed or radioactivity escapes.

The first three detection techniques rely on phenomena discussed in Chapters 2, 3 and 12 and are reasonably straightforward. For example, the first Soviet nuclear test in 1949 was detected through its radioactive debris. The fact that these techniques work reliably has made the Limited Test Ban Treaty possible. Strictly speaking, espionage is not a technological method. The other methods, particularly detecting flashes of light and seismic disturbances, are more complex.

Light Flashes

The 1963 Limited Test Ban Treaty forbade all nuclear tests above ground, even those in outer space. To detect nuclear tests that leave no radioactive debris, and produce no blast waves, the United States developed a series of Vela satellites for optical detection of such explosions by their infrared and visible radiations. The Vela satellites of Fig. 15.3 "see" in all directions at the same time. Thus, they can detect light flashes both on the ground as well as above them in outer space. They rely on the characteristic double flash of a nuclear explosion, shown in Fig. 2.12, to differentiate a nuclear explosion from some other light source. Through 1979 these satellites had correctly detected 41 nuclear explosions. These satellites are not totally foolproof; in 1979 they interpreted a flash of light to be from nuclear explosion, even though no nuclear debris corresponding to such an explosion was ever found. Nonetheless, the technical ability to detect atmospheric and space nuclear tests appears quite good.

Detecting Underground Nuclear Explosions

Above-ground nuclear tests may be definitively detected through their radioactive fallout. For the case of underground explosions, if the blast does not leave a collapsed crater (Fig. 15.4) or accidentally vents some radioactive gases, or has some observable preparation activities associated with the test, then only seismic detection methods can be used.

Figure 15.3 A pair of Vela satellites ready for launching. They are designed to detect optical signals and other electromagnetic pulses from nuclear explosions. (Photo courtesy U.S. Department of Defense.)

Figure 15.4 Nuclear explosions too close to the earth's surface may leave a subsidence crater. The crater from this underground explosion is just forming. The 30-m tower has been rolled back from above the explosion center where it monitored the prompt radiation emissions. (Photo courtesy Los Alamos Scientific Laboratory.)

Underground nuclear explosions inject a significant fraction of their energy into ground motion. These fractions range from 0.01% for explosions in a large air-filled cavity through 0.1% for dry alluvium to 1% for granite. This energy produces seismic waves of different types. Part of the energy travels through the earth, either by longitudinal P-waves in which the earth alternately compresses and dilates or by transverse S-waves (or shear waves) in which the earth oscillates perpendicular to the direction of propagation of the wave. The speed of the P wave in hard rock of the earth's crust is faster than is that of the S-wave. At a distance of 10,000 km (the distance from the large NORSAR array in Norway to the USSR through the earth, or 65° along the earth's surface), these two waves will take about 645 sec and 1165 sec, respectively, to reach the detector so that there is a time lag of almost 9 min between the arrival of these two waves. Seismic signals traveling through the earth's core are more attenuated and refracted, so that the core essentially casts a shadow on the other side of the earth.

Besides the body waves, two types of surface waves travel from the seismic source along the earth's surface. The Love waves (L-waves) are transverse horizontal motions of the earth's surface, whereas the Raleigh waves (R-waves) are vertical waves traveling along the direction of motion. These waves travel more slowly than do the S- and P-waves. Figure 15.5 shows the P- and S-waves from an Arctic earthquake compared with those of a nuclear explosion of similar magnitude.

Seismic activity is described in terms of the magnitudes m_b of these body waves (actually the P-wave magnitude for a weapons test) and M_s

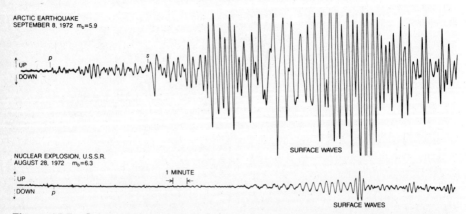

Figure 15.5 Seismometer tracings of an Arctic earthquake and a nuclear explosion of similar magnitude in the Soviet Union recorded in Israel. The body wave magnitudes are comparable, but the earthquake emits far more energy in surface waves. (Photo by permission of Lynn R. Sykes.)

of the surface waves. Figure 15.6 compares the theoretical relationship between yield and m_b with observations. These magnitudes are defined on the Richter scale as the response of a certain seismometer to seismic waves. The Richter magnitude basically represents the logarithm (to base 10) of the maximum seismic wave amplitude. An earthquake with a magnitude $m_b = 8$ releases 100 times as much energy as does one with an $m_b = 6$. A person jumping from a height of 2 m onto the ground releases a shock wave like that of an earthquake with magnitude zero. The 1906 San Francisco earthquake had a magnitude of 8.3 (according to Fig. 15.6, equivalent roughly to the effect of a 300-Mt nuclear blast in granite). Figure 15.7 shows the frequency of earthquakes each year throughout the world with a magnitude above the indicated value. A San Francisco–sized earthquake happens about once a year somewhere in the world.

There is a constant background of ground movement that hides seismic waves from earthquakes or nuclear explosions. Obviously, the detection limit for seismic signals varies not only with the location of the seismic detector, since there are some very earthquake-free areas, but also with the detection technology. Large seismic arrays combining many individual seismometers have much improved signal-to-noise ratios. The sensitivity of a seismometer array should increase as the

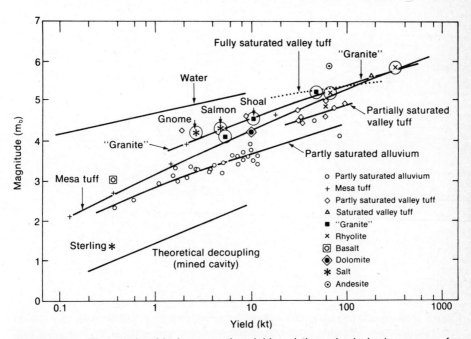

Figure 15.6 The relationship between the yield and the seismic body wave m_b for nuclear explosions in various materials. (Photo from U.S. Atomic Energy Commission.)

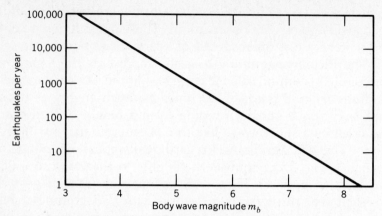

Figure 15.7 The average number of earthquakes with seismic magnitude in excess of the values of m_b. (After Bolt, 1976, Figure 4.7, p. 79.)

square root of the number of elements in it; hence, an array of 525 elements, such as the one near Billings, Montana, should have a sensitivity roughly 23-fold that of a single seismometer. Figure 15.8 shows how a seismic array may sum the seismic signals electronically to produce a large signal that can be electronically processed to extract correlated signals out of the noise and to determine the direction from which the signals arrived.

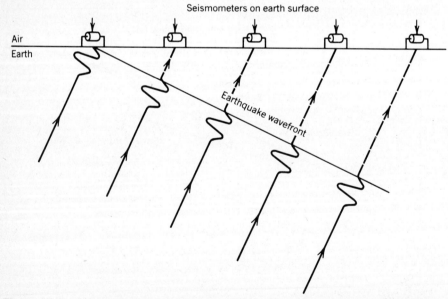

Figure 15.8 A seismic array can enhance the signal from a seismic event compared with seismic noise. A signal traveling upward arrives in sequence at the five detectors. By delaying the signal from each detector properly, the signal can be electronically added.

With these electronic capabilities, a proposed network of 15 seismic stations external to the Soviet Union could have the body-magnitude detection threshold for detection shown in Fig. 15.9; all earthquakes with $m_b \geq 3.8$ would be detectable at the 90% confidence level. For surface waves the detection limit would be $M_s \geq 2.6$.

Discriminating Underground Nuclear Explosions

Detecting underground nuclear explosions involves two problems: sensitivity of detection and discrimination. Once a seismic signal is detected, it is still necessary to decide whether it derives from an underground explosion or from an earthquake. Figure 15.10 points out that, as the seismic magnitude decreases, not only does the detection become harder in the face of seismic background, but so does discrimination between quakes and explosions. One discrimination technique relies on the fact that for underground explosions, all the earth initially moves outward. This leads to a spreading seismic wave that shows compression at the very beginning. In contrast, an earthquake shows both initial compression and dilation phenomena, since earthquakes result from slippage along a fault. This discrimination is unreliable if the earthquake is too small to give a clearly defined first motion.

An easier and more elegant discrimination technique consists of

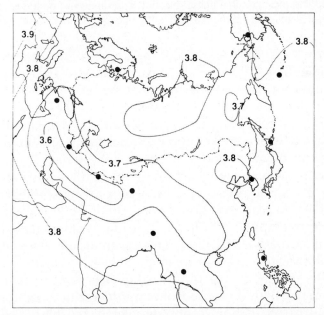

Figure 15.9 Thresholds of detection for body waves from seismic events in the Soviet Union using a proposed network of 15 seismic stations. The dots indicate the location of 12 of the stations. (Sykes and Evernden, 1982, p. 54, by permission of *Scientific American*.)

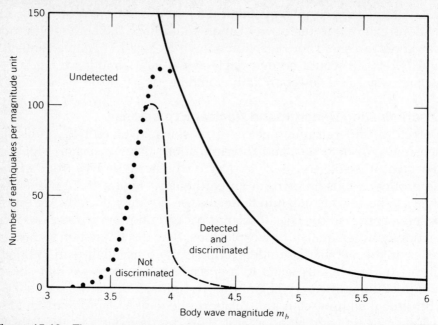

Figure 15.10 The average annual number of shallow earthquakes in the Soviet Union per magnitude unit is shown by the solid curve. The dotted line indicates the limit of detection above the seismic background by detectors outside the Soviet Union, whereas the dashed line indicates the limit of discrimination between earthquakes and nuclear explosions. These limits are themselves rather uncertain. (After Myers, 1972, p. 23.)

measuring the amplitude ratio of the body to the surface waves from the seismic disturbance. Shallow earthquakes usually send a considerably larger fraction of their energy along the earth's surface (magnitude M_s) than do nuclear explosions. Thus the ratio of M_s to the magnitude m_b of the energy transmitted directly through the earth can distinguish between quakes and explosions as is shown in Fig. 15.11.

For some low-magnitude earthquakes the surface wave may be hidden in the seismic background; thus, this technique will indicate some number of suspicious events rather than proving whether every event is or is not a nuclear explosion. For a limit on body wave magnitude of $m_b = 3.8$, perhaps two to four suspicious events might be recorded each year in the Soviet Union. This magnitude corresponds to about 1½ kt for hard-rock tests or to about 20 kt for partially saturated alluvium. The seismic waves from earthquakes tend to be considerably more complex than do those from an underground explosion. Unfortunately, this distinction is not completely reliable as some nuclear explosions have generated quite complex wave forms.

Most earthquakes can be identified as such because they occur under the oceans or because their focus is very deep in the earth. The

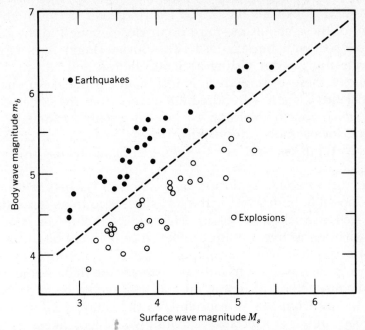

Figure 15.11 A plot of the observed body wave magnitude m_b versus the surface wave magnitude M_s of various earthquakes and underground nuclear explosions. (After Bolt, 1976, Figure 7.5, p. 153.)

remaining earthquakes of low magnitude present a discrimination problem. Improved seismic arrays in quieter locations combined with better electronic correlation capabilities are required to lower these limits beyond those shown in Fig. 15.9. The computer revolution presents the hope that better signal analyses will be coming. The ideal solution would come if the Soviet Union were to allow the use of some appropriate seismic stations (black boxes) in its territory, that might increase the sensitivity to 0.1 kt for explosions in hard rock or 1 kt if evasion ploys are used.

EVASION PLOYS

One reason the 1958 test moratorium broke down in 1961 was that several methods were proposed to evade the detection of underground nuclear explosions. These included hiding the test in earthquake-prone areas, setting the explosion off while an earthquake was in progress, exploding the device in soft soil, or decoupling the blast by setting it off in an underground cavity. The last of these was the most devastating argument in destroying the scientific consensus that seemed to have developed at that time.

About 1½% of all the world's earthquakes occur in the Soviet Union, of these about one-third occur close enough to the surface to be confused with nuclear tests. The Soviet Union does most of its underground nuclear testing at Semipalatinsk and Novaya Zemlaya. Neither of these testing areas is inside an earthquake-prone region; Semipalatinsk is a few hundred kilometers from the edge of a minor earthquake zone containing 6% of all Soviet earthquakes. Thus, present Soviet underground nuclear tests do not compete with very many earthquakes and are therefore difficult to disguise as earthquakes.

Hiding a nuclear explosion in the noise of a natural earthquake might possibly be feasible if the test sites were transferred to one of these active earthquake areas. This hiding technique would seem somewhat ineffective and unreliable, since it would be difficult to set up a nuclear test with all equipment ready to go on a few seconds notice and then wait for months or years for the right moment.

A better method of hiding nuclear tests would be to decouple the blast energy from the surrounding earth. Figure 15.6 shows that a 10-kt blast in partly saturated alluvium would look like a 1-kt blast in granite. Such a technique has restricted utility, since existing layers of soft dry soil are of limited thickness. If the layer is too thin, the chimney from the blast may cave in all the way in the surface; then the surface will reveal the effect of the blast, as in Fig. 15.4. This danger of

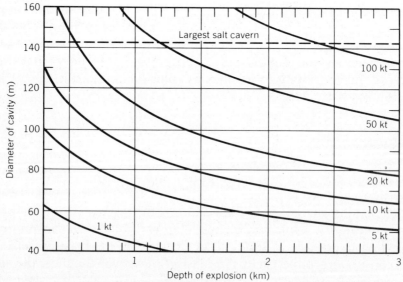

Figure 15.12 The diameter of cavities required to decouple underground explosions of various sizes. (After Bolt, 1976, Figure 8.3, p. 178.)

collapse limits the size of the explosions that could be hidden in this way. The United States has some alluvium deposits that might contain an explosion up to 20 kt; the USSR cannot hide explosions larger than a couple of kilotons.

The decoupling technique using a cavity is potentially better. If an explosion is set off inside a cavity in the ground, the seismic signal may be decreased as much as 100-fold compared with an explosion in hard rock (see Fig. 15.6). Cavities to contain significant explosions must be quite large. Figure 15.12 shows that decoupling a 20-kt explosion at a depth of 800 m requires a cavity with a diameter of 120 m. The volume of such a cavity is about 1 million m^3, roughly equivalent to the volume of the Empire State Building in New York City. The mass of soil of such a volume at 2 tonnes/m^3 (twice the density of water) is then 2 million tonnes, or the mass of 20 ocean liners. A more feasible method of decoupling explosions might be to use existing caverns from which salt has been extracted. The largest of these is 145 m in diameter. These caverns are limited in number and known in location so that an extensive undetected test program might be difficult.

TEST-BAN DISCUSSION

Two nuclear test bans currently apply: the LTBT of 1963 banning all above ground tests and the unratified 1974 agreement banning all underground tests in excess of 150 kt. These treaties have faced two difficulties. Some Soviet explosions may have exceeded the 150-kt limit, raising the question of verification. The treaties have also been condemned as not going far enough—the argument is that only a complete test-ban treaty would limit the further development of nuclear technology significantly.

Violations

The Limited Test Ban Treaty

The LTBT was signed in 1963. Since then, the United States and the Soviet Union have conducted all their nuclear tests underground. Both sides have violated the part of the treaty forbidding the release of any radioactive debris beyond the territorial limits of the nation conducting the test. A few U.S. tests, and more Soviet tests, have vented radioactive materials into the atmosphere to drift in detectable quantities beyond national borders. It is thought that these violations of the LTBT have been due to an unwillingness to undertake the effort to bury the explosions deep enough.

The 150-Kt Agreement

In 1974 the United States and the Soviet Union agreed not to test any nuclear devices in excess of 150 kt in yield. Some Soviet tests have yielded seismic waves with magnitudes in excess of what some believe a 150-kt blast generates. For example, in July and August 1976 three Soviet blasts were detected with m_b of 5.7 to 5.9. Figure 15.6 shows that these magnitudes would correspond in granite to yields well in excess of 150 kt. However, a large number of respected geophysicists argue that for the local geology, the observed m_b correspond to less than 150 kt.

This uncertainty in evaluating detected tests has discouraged some people from thinking about a total test-ban treaty. It has also led other experts to recommend that test-ban limits should be expressed in terms of seismic wave magnitudes rather than in terms of the yield of the explosion.

Comprehensive Test Ban Treaty

There are a variety of arguments against a threshold test ban treaty and in favor of a comprehensive one. One objection to a threshold treaty is that it gives the impression that something significant has been accomplished, thereby reducing the pressure toward a comprehensive test ban treaty (CTBT).

The second objection concerns a total test ban as a form of arms control to halt the development of new weapons technologies. To control advances in warhead technology, it is important to forbid as much testing as possible. A threshold should be as low as possible, as close to the current monitoring technology as possible. Presently, that could be less than 10 kt rather than 150 kt. The present test-ban treaties have hardly slowed the rate of testing. In the 18 years from 1945 to 1963, 488 nuclear tests took place, 80% above ground. In the 18 years from 1963 to 1981, 833 tests took place, 92% of them underground. Thus the LTBT has not decrease the rate of nuclear testing; only a comprehensive test ban treaty is likely to control the warhead arms race effectively.

Testing Nuclear Weapons Stockpiles

When bans on nuclear tests are discussed, a primary argument in favor of continuing testing is that existing nuclear stockpiles age and need to be checked regularly. Donald Kerr, as director of the Los Alamos Scientific Laboratory, felt that

a total cessation of testing in the long run would inevitably result in a steady decline of our confidence in the reliability of our nuclear deterrent. (As quoted in Stone, 1978, p. 4)

Some argue that there must be a constant testing of weapons designs.

> Thorn is concerned that he would lose his most valuable people if a comprehensive test ban made it impossible for them to test their designs. He agrees that a ban would freeze the Soviets into a position of inferiority in warhead sophistication, but only if the ban were observed. Thorn believes the Russians would be able to conduct clandestine tests, whether underground, escaping seismic detection, or in deep space, such as by missions to Mars. (Wade, 1978, p. 1106)

Other arms experts disagree. Richard Garwin, Norris Bradbury, J. Carson Mark, and Hans Bethe reject the notion that problems such as corrosion could limit reliability of weapons to lifetimes of 15 to 25 years; they argue that these problems can be detected by tests short of nuclear explosion and can be repaired by replacing the affected part by an identical replacement. They claim that

> the assurance of continued operability of stockpiled nuclear weapons has in the past been achieved almost exclusively by non-nuclear testing—by meticulous inspection and disassembly of the components of the nuclear weapons, including their firing and fuzing equipment. . . . This program is . . . supplemented by the instrumented firing of the entire nuclear weapon with inert material replacing the fissile materials, and the entire program thus far described would be unaffected by the requirements of a CTBT. (Stone, 1978, p. 5)

The real disagreement about this issue hinges on the definition of "correcting problems" and on "cheating." In the past, problems with nuclear weapons have often been fixed by redesigning the affected part. Such incremental improvements would often not be possible under a complete test ban, as cumulative changes sooner or later have to be tested if confidence in the weapons is not to become degraded. Of course, one objective of a CTBT might be to prevent improvements in weapons technology. If both the United States and the USSR cannot improve their technology, the CTBT might maintain the status quo.

Peaceful Nuclear Explosions
For many years various nuclear explosives experts such as Edward Teller, have hoped to turn nuclear weapons to peaceful uses, "beating swords into plowshares" (Weaver, 1970). Operation Plowshare concerned itself with civilian applications of nuclear explosives such as the excavation of harbors and canals, cracking rock for oil and gas production, creating underground storage cavities and dams for food control, capping oil and gas gushers, and producing energy via underground heat storage and shale oil ignition. Some engineers have had the long-standing dream of building a bigger Panama Canal using

nuclear explosions for excavations. Several such applications have been tried. The United States stimulated increased production for gas wells in 1967 and 1969. The Soviet Union has been more active in exploring such uses, particularly in oil research and excavation projects.

The desire to include a "loophole" for peaceful nuclear explosions (PNEs) in various treaties, such as the Nonproliferation Treaty, has so far on the whole led to poorer treaties without equivalent benefits from the peaceful uses. The first Indian nuclear explosion was justified as being a test of a nuclear device for future peaceful applications. With a rising antinuclear sentiment in the Western nations, Plowshare programs have not prospered.

DISCUSSION OF TEST-BAN TREATIES

The Limited Test Ban Treaty of 1963 has removed much radioactive fallout from the atmosphere; however, it has not dealt very satisfactorily with the broader arms control objective. It is also unsatisfactory because several important nuclear and potentially nuclear nations have not accepted it; these include France, the People's Republic of China, and Israel. The 150-kt threshold treaty is not particularly helpful either because its limit is set so high.

The technology of seismology has improved, particularly through computer analysis of seismic signals. If the present limit on reliably detectable underground nuclear explosions is much less than 10 kt, then it will be even lower in the future. In 1958 an underground ban may well have not been monitorable; presently, a test-ban agreement on all weapons above 10 kt seems technically very feasible; 10 years from now the lower limit on detectable weapons may well be below 1 kt. However, the decision to establish a more complete nuclear test ban is ultimately political. The Reagan administration has not been interested in participating in discussions of possible further test-ban treaties.

This example of arms control efforts shows how technological facts only set broad limits within which political purposes can determine the policies. The possibility of considering a test-ban treaty separately from a general disarmament package came from political events as a desire arose to control fallout and the expensive and dangerous arms race. There was a seeming technical consensus on the feasibility of test-ban verification. But it became clear that not enough was known at the time about seismology to contradict new theories and data without much further study.

The above-ground test ban was established in 1963 under the political pressures of heavy fallout from nuclear testing. This agreement was much more technically defensible, and internal politics demanded it. Here politics triumphed together with technology—those are the easy victories. But the effect of the treaty has not been true arms control. Global fallout has been decreased; that is clearly good. But the development of nuclear weapons has not been noticeably slowed.

The LTBT is characteristic of many of the arms control agreements listed in Tables 15.1 and 15.2. They forbid some actions that are potentially dangerous; they try to create an atmosphere of stability; or they keep weaponry out of some areas of the world. They have not significantly slowed the bilateral arms race, although they have somewhat slowed the proliferation of nuclear weapons. In fact the only weapons forbidden by these treaties are biological weapons and those excluded under the limits of SALT I and SALT II discussed in Chapter 16.

Generally treaties operate within areas of easy agreement (for example, it is not particularly worthwhile to place weapons in the Antarctic or on the moon), or if the limits on the number of weapons is about the same as the existing stockpile. Existing arms control agreements are generally easy to monitor. One can, therefore, evaluate these agreements negatively as achieving little, or one can be positive and point out that they ease tensions and admit that it is better at least to do the possible. But arms control has not gone far beyond the possible into the desirable.

References

Bolt, B. A. *Nuclear Explosions and Earthquakes: The Parted Veil.* San Francisco: W. H. Freeman, 1976. An excellent book on earthquakes and underground nuclear explosions, not only on the science but also on the history and politics of nuclear test-ban efforts.

Divine, R. A. *Blowing on the Wind: The Nuclear Test Ban Debate: 1954–1960.* New York: Oxford University Press, 1978. A very nice political history of the efforts through 1960 to reach a comprehensive test-ban treaty.

Gilpin, R. *American Scientists and Nuclear Weapons Policy.* Princeton, N.J.: Princeton University Press, 1962.

Myers, H. R. "Extending the Nuclear-Test Ban." *Scientific American,* Vol. 226, no. 1 (January 1972), pp. 13–23.

Stone, J. "Scientists Deny Stockpile Reliability Tests Needed." *F.A.S. Public Interest Report,* Vol. 31, no. 8 (October 1978), pp. 4–6.

Sykes, L. R., and J. F. Evernden. "The Verification of a Comprehensive Nuclear Test Ban Treaty." *Scientific American,* Vol. 247, no. 4 (October 1982), pp. 47–55.

Wade, N. "Defense Scientists Differ on Nuclear Stockpile Testing." *Science,* Vol. 201 (1978), pp. 1105–1106.

Weaver, L. E., ed. *Education for Peaceful Uses of Nuclear Explosives.* Tucson: University of Arizona Press, 1970.

Wiesner, J. B. *Where Science and Politics Meet.* New York: McGraw-Hill, 1965.

CHAPTER 16

Strategic Arms Limitation

"Gentlemen, the main course is getting hot!"

Figure 16.1   MIRV was foreseen as an arms control problem before its deployment (e.g., in this cartoon of 1969). Unfortunately it was not controlled in SALT I and, hence, could not be abolished in later agreements. This symbolizes the frustration of trying to control advances in arms before they are deployed. (By permission of R. Graysmith © Chronicle Publ. Co., 1969.)

The Antartic Treaty, the Sea-Bed Treaty, the Treaty of Tlatelolco, and the Outer-Space Treaty control to some extent the places where nuclear arms can be deployed. The Non-Proliferation Treaty (NPT) limits the possession of nuclear weapons to a few nations. These treaties do not limit directly either the quality or the quantity of nuclear weapons, and they have not led to disarmament.

Attempts to go beyond control to limitations became institutionalized in 1969 in the form of the Strategic Arms Limitations Talks (SALT). Among other motivations for SALT was Article VI of the NPT, in which all signatories promised to negotiate to halt the nuclear arms race and toward nuclear disarmament. Three agreements have so far derived from these talks: the SALT I, Vladivostok, and SALT II accords. These agreements not only place numerical limitations on the quantity of strategic weapons, but they also contain some qualitative restrictions.

The SALT II Treaty is not in force; while President Jimmy Carter signed it along with Premier Leonid Brezhnev, it has never been ratified by the U.S. Senate. This treaty illustrates the problems faced by such agreements. It is difficult to derive numerical limitations that seem exactly mutually equitable, since the technical, historical, and geopolitical circumstances of each superpower are so different that they have very different weapons configurations. Verification of weapons quantities by national technical means, such as satellites, can present some problems. Limiting the quality of weapons is more difficult, particularly once weapons have gone beyond testing into deployment.

Even if agreements can be negotiated, and verification is technically feasible, political disagreements can still remain. Any agreements are likely to be criticized both from the right and the left of the political spectrum. Those favoring more arms control will feel the agreements have become "a license to build," particularly when, as in SALT I and II, they basically accept the status quo as the limits. In contrast, there will be those who are unwilling to trust the opponent under any circumstances feeling that if he or she is willing to sign the agreements, they must be giving too much away.

SALT discussions are likely to become linked to superpower relations on other levels (e.g., to military adventurism on the nonnuclear level). As long as mutual assured destruction (MAD) is the basis for the policy of deterrence, it would seem reasonable to develop arms limitation agreements that maintain an assured destruction second-strike capability while avoiding a first-strike threat. Within the MAD picture, conventional weaponry and the lack of political rapprochement might be seen as irrelevant to SALT. Yet such linkages do exist in the mind of many. While the Soviet Union did not link United States involvement in Vietnam with SALT I in 1972, the United States did couple the Soviet invasion of Afghanistan in 1979 to SALT II.

SALT has not been spectacularly successful in producing arms reductions. Its single biggest technical success has been the prevention of large-scale ABM systems. Its single biggest failure has been its inability to control the spread of MIRV technology (Fig. 16.1). In general, SALT imposed status quo limits on some technologies and limited improvements in some strategic nuclear weaponry.

VERIFICATION

As discussed in the previous chapter, arms limitation treaties are easiest to establish when technical means exist to monitor them. Strategic arms limitations became feasible only after such arms could be counted by technical methods. Extraterritorial electronic listening posts have been in use since World War II. The significant new technologies making SALT treaties possible are what is known euphemistically as "national technical means," namely, the use of earth orbiting satellites and other devices to monitor strategic weapons and verify that arms limitations are obeyed.

The major provisions of the present SALT treaties that need to be monitored are the deployment of additional missiles and bombers, the testing of new strategic weapons, and the modification of existing versions into more advanced models. Some major components of strategic verification systems are shown in Fig. 16.2. The launch of a missile is seen by the Vela heat-sensing satellite (see Chapter 15). Ground-based electronic listening posts record electronic communications that flow between the weapons system and home base during tests. The flight-path of the missile, the MIRV bus, and the MIRV warheads are tracked by ground-based radar. Ferret satellites record the telemetry data sent back from the missile to the ground-control stations such as the burn times of the various stages, the maneuverings of the bus, and the launching of the MIRVs to obtain information about the size, throw weight, and number of MIRV warheads. Photographic reconnaissance satellites photograph all activity below them. Considerable duplication exists among these signals, so that each weapon parameter is over determined.

Satellite Reconnaissance
Orbital satellite reconnaissance has become one of the most stabilizing technologies for the arms race as it gives detailed information about the enemy's actual weapons inventory—not just uncertain information

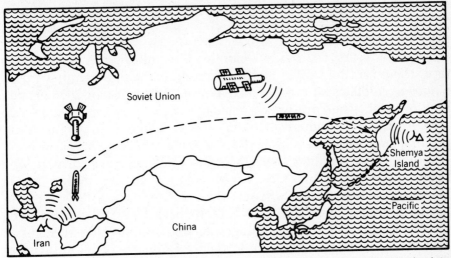

Figure 16.2 The U.S. verification system monitoring Soviet missile tests in the late 1970s included radar stations in Iran (now in Turkey and China), ferret satellites recording launch information, Big Bird satellites photographing the missiles in flight, and radar systems observing the reentry patterns of the multiple warheads. (After *Science*, vol. 216, 1982, p. 31.)

about possible capabilities. Satellites are a spinoff from ballistic rock-etry; they owe their existence to the same technological developments that made ICBMs possible except that the optical and radio-wave recording and transmitting equipment has replaced the nuclear war-head. Thus the simultaneity of ICBMs and satellites is not a surprise.

The idea of a satellite orbiting the earth is contained in Newton's laws from the end of the eighteenth century. The astronomer Johannes Kepler by then had already showed that a satellite in a circular orbit around the earth at a distance R_s from the center of the earth has a period of revolution T_s that is proportional to the ¾ th power of this distance: $T_s \propto R_s^{3/2}$. Thus a satellite near the earth's surface, 160 km up just above the atmosphere, will have a period of revolution of about 1½ hr (87.2 min). A satellite 35,000 km above the earth's surface will have a rotational period of one day; such orbits are called geosynchro-nous orbits: if a satellite is put in such an orbit above the equator and is launched into the orbit heading in an easterly direction, it will rotate around the earth's center in 24 hr, just as does the earth below it. Hence, it will hover permanently over the same spot on the earth's equator.

The U.S. satellite program was intimately coupled to the develop-ment of long-range military missiles. Not only was the missile devel-opment competition won by the Soviet Union as it launched both the first IRBM and ICBM, but it also won the publicity race on October 4,

1957 with the very visible launching of the first artificial earth satellite *Sputnik 1.* The early U.S. failures of the civilian Vanguard program were very embarrassing.

For many years, the Soviet Union led the United States in the space race. However, the United States seized upon the photographic possibilities of satellites. It quickly increased its rockets to lift 200-kg satellites into orbit. The Tiros weather satellites took TV pictures of the earth after April 1960 (although with very low resolution). In August 1960, the first payload from a photographic satellite (*Discoverer 13*) was recovered. These satellites took photographs of the Soviet Union. The much more powerful Atlas ICBM coupled to the Agena rocket launched the *Samos* satellite series; *Samos* 2 in January of 1961 transmitted more than a thousand photographs back to earth. After several months of analysis, these photographs allowed the United States in June 1961 to officially reduce intelligence estimates of the number of ICBMs deployed by the Soviet Union. These new estimates assured President Kennedy during the Cuban missile crisis that the USSR was unable to launch a missile first-strike attack; hence, he could impose a naval blockade without fear of nuclear retaliation.

The photographic ability of Soviet satellites was demonstrated when in October 1959 they transmitted to the earth photographs of the moon's hidden side. The Soviet Union also developed satellite recovery capabilities as demonstrated by their recovering of two dogs from orbit in August 1960.

Satellite Reconnaissance Techniques

Generally, the air space above a country is considered part of its sovereign territory; however, this is not the case for satellites. When the Soviet Union launched its *Sputnik 1,* it did not ask for overflight permission from other nations. This set an uncodified precedent that has stood up since then, making satellite overflights internationally acceptable and satellite photography a method used for international reconnaissance as one component of "national technical means."

In the orbital surveillance technique, an observation satellite such as the Big Bird of Fig. 16.3 is launched to pass over the area to be observed. By proper selection of orbital height, angle of the orbit with respect to the equator, and launch time, the target can be seen under the best lighting conditions. A TV camera in the satellite may transmit a picture directly back to the earth. Alternatively, a camera in the satellite can photograph the target, the film is developed on-board the satellite, and that developed film may then be scanned by a TV camera to transmit the image back to earth. These relatively low-resolution techniques are used for weather satellites and for low-resolution survey or monitoring

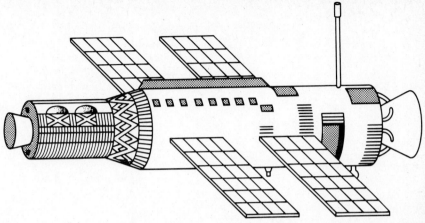

Figure 16.3 Artist's conception of a Big Bird photo and TV reconnaissance satellite. (See, for example, *The Christian Science Monitor* of September 23, 1980.)

work. For high-resolution surveillance, the film is ejected from the satellite toward the earth and is recovered in midair by an airplane.

Photographic satellites can be useful only as long as their film supply lasts. Some modern satellites, such as the Big Bird weighing more than 18 tonnes combine these two functions; when their TV cameras reveal an interesting object, high-resolution pictures can be taken and returned to earth.

Reconnaissance Resolution

The ability to distinguish objects on the surface of the earth is controlled by four factors (Greenwood, 1973). The ground resolution is determined by the focal length of the camera lens, the optical resolution of the camera film system, and the height of the orbit, where the optical resolution, in turn, depends on the lens size and the wavelength of light. The fourth factor is the optical refraction introduced by the thermal fluctuations in the density of the earth's atmosphere; the thermal vibrations of the atmosphere introduce a lower limit to the resolution of orbital photography of about 10 cm from an orbit 160 km above the earth.

This resolution means that a golf ball 10 cm from the hole on the course in Fig. 16.4 can be seen as an object separate from the hole, but it cannot be distinguished once inside the hole. An automobile license plate can be seen as a rectangle, but the license number cannot be read. A hot day will lead to greater density fluctuations of the atmosphere, resulting in a poorer resolution. A similar resolution problem is faced by earth-based astronomical telescopes that typically have better than an arc sec of resolution on a good day corresponding directly

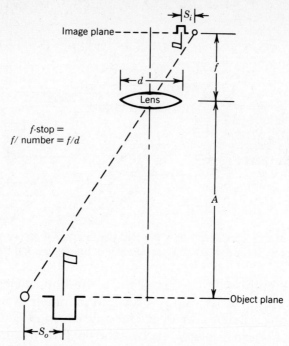

Figure 16.4 The resolution of a reconnaissance camera of focal length f in orbit at an altitude A. S_o and S_i are the object and image size.

to this 10 cm space-based resolution. Astronomers are trying to improve this resolution by computer analysis of the images and expect that this technique would be applied to satellite photography.

The atmospheric disturbances set only a lower limit to the resolution. The ground resolution is affected by the optical resolution R_{opt}. The ratio of the image size S_i to the object size S_o is equal to the ratio of the focal length f to the satellite altitude A. The minimum resolvable image size is equal to the optical resolution, which is a combination of the film resolution R_{film} and the lens resolution R_{lens}. The ground resolution G is equal to

$$G\ (\mathrm{m}) = \frac{A\ (\mathrm{km})}{f\ (\mathrm{m}) \times R_{opt}\ (\mathrm{lines\ per\ mm})} \tag{16.1}$$

Figure 16.5 shows that to obtain a ground resolution of 0.3 m (three times the atmospheric limit) for a satellite 160 km high ($A = 160,000$ m) and a camera focal length of $f = 2.5\ m$, an optical resolution of 200 lines per mm would be required. A 6-m focal length and an optical resolution of 300 lines per mm allows G to be comparable to the atmospheric limit. Such focal lengths can be achieved for example by using

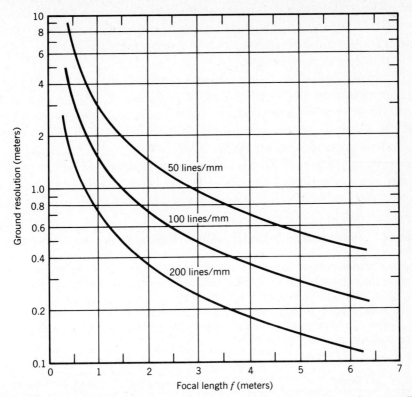

Figure 16.5 Ground resolution for various lens and film combinations for a satellite-based camera in orbit around the earth.

folded optical systems with mirrors to make light travel several times back and forth through a lens.

Films with a resolution of better than 200 lines per mm are available. However, the optical resolution also depends on the magnitude of diffraction effects produced by the limited size of the lens opening. This lens resolution R_{lens} can be calculated through

$$R_{lens} = \frac{0.82\,d}{\lambda f} \qquad (16.2)$$

where d is the aperture (opening) of the lens, λ is the wavelength of the light, and f is the focal length of the lens. For $f = 2.5$ m, for visible light with $\lambda = 0.55 \times 10^{-3}$ mm (0.55×10^{-6} m) and for a lens opening of 0.3 m (an f stop of 8), the best possible lens resolution would be 186 lines per mm. This lens resolution limits the sharpness of the image at the film plane. To calculate the overall optical resolution of the film-lens system R_{opt}, R_{lens}, and R_{film} must be combined through the equation $R_{opt} = 1/(1/R_{lens} + 1/R_{film})$. If R_{lens} is very poor, then even the best film cannot lead to a high ground resolution. To improve the lens resolution, either the ratio of the focal length to the lens opening f/d (i.e., the f stop) must be made smaller or the photograph must be taken with light of a shorter wavelength.

Ultraviolet light does have a shorter wavelength, but it cannot reach the camera from the earth's surface because it is absorbed by the earth's atmosphere. Infrared light has a longer wavelength and, hence, leads to a worse camera resolution. Not all verification efforts require equivalent ground resolution. To detect a surfaced submarine, a photographic resolution of 30 m is sufficient; to describe a bomber precisely demands a resolution of 1 m. Table 16.1 lists target resolutions required for a variety of verification tasks. These demands can be satisfied by

Table 16.1   Photographic ground resolution required for various interpretation tasks.

Detection means locating something; general identification means determining the general object type; precise identification means discrimination into known types; description means determination of the size of the object, its layout, construction components, count of equipment, etc. (From a NASA Authorization Hearing before the U.S. Senate Committee on Commerce, Science and Transportation, as quoted in Potter, 1980, p. 21.)

Target	Detection	Identification		Description
		General	Precise	
Bridge	6 m	4.5 m	1.5 m	0.9 m
Communications				
Radar	3 m	0.9 m	0.3 m	0.15 m
Radio	3 m	1.5 m	0.3 m	0.15 m
Supply dump	1.5 m	0.6 m	0.3 m	0.03 m
Troop units (bivouac, road)	20 m	2.1 m	1.2 m	0.3 m
Airfield facilities	6 m	4.5 m	3 m	0.3 m
Rockets and artillery	0.6 m	0.3 m	0.15 m	0.05 m
Aircraft	4.5 m	1.5 m	0.9 m	0.15 m
Command/control headquarters	3 m	1.5 m	0.9 m	0.15 m
Missile sites (SSM, SAM)	3 m	1.5 m	0.6 m	0.3 m
Surface ships	7.5 m	4.5 m	0.6 m	0.3 m
Nuclear weapons components	2.4 m	1.5 m	0.3 m	0.03 m
Vehicles	1.5 m	0.6 m	0.3 m	0.05 m
Land minefields	9 m	6 m	0.9 m	0.03 m
Ports and harbors	30 m	15 m	6 m	3 m
Coasts and landing beaches	30 m	4.5 m	3 m	1.5 m
Railroad yards and shops	30 m	15 m	6 m	1.5 m
Roads	9 m	6 m	1.8 m	0.6 m
Urban area	60 m	30 m	3 m	3 m
Terrain	—	90 m	4.5 m	1.5 m
Surfaced submarines	30 m	6 m	1.5 m	0.9 m

different satellites; Fig. 16.6 shows the ground resolution and orbital height of some U.S. satellite systems.

Satellite Coverage

If a satellite has a photographic ground resolution of 10 cm, this does not necessarily mean that all activities in the Soviet Union automatically can be monitored on that scale. To produce useful complete surveys, a large number of images must be recorded, and these must be scanned to extract information.

Consider some of the reconnaissance data given in the literature. Les Aspin (1979) suggests that the world could be covered by means of 3468 individual photographs taken by two shuttle-launched satellites. The photographs would be recorded on one mile of film, and they would supposedly have a ground resolution of about 20 m. Each photograph would cover an area of about 450 km by 1000 km.

The size of each negative along the mile of film would be about 0.5 m. The film would be exposed with the narrow side of the negative across the film, so that the film width will be about 0.2 m. If 1000 km is recorded in those 0.5 m with an object resolution of 20 m, then the image resolution must be about 0.01 mm, or 100 lines per mm. This resolution can readily be achieved; resolutions of 10 m (corresponding about 200 lines per mm) ought to be attainable for such a global scan.

If the film is perhaps 0.1 mm thick with a density slightly greater than that of water, its mass would be about 35 kg. Aspin (1979) states that a satellite film package (including the spools and containers) weighs a few hundred kilograms.

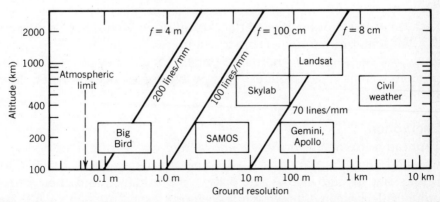

Figure 16.6 Ground resolution and orbit altitude of some U.S. satellite systems. *f* is the focal length, and the maximum line resolution is that of the optical system given in lines per millimeter. (After Klass, 1971, Figure 14.2, p. 330.)

TV transmissions of more detailed photographs present problems. Herbert F. York (1976) points out

> Let us suppose one wished to take a photograph of the Soviet Union or North America at a resolution of 10 centimeters. Given that both North America and the Soviet Union are about 20 million square kilometers and given that if the television system was continuously broadcasting the data down to earth, one would require more than a hundred mega-cycle band width to handle one picture per year. (p. 229)

A commercial TV channel has a bandwidth of perhaps 30 megahertz (MHz), much less than that required for transmitting one photographic survey per year. York (1976) also mentions that

> Another problem concerns data handling. To examine one complete picture of North America (or the U.S.S.R.) at a 10 cm resolution would take about 10,000 to 100,000 man years. (p. 229)

Some method must be used to eliminate uninteresting pictures. Displays with lower resolution can be used to select areas of interest, and comparisons with previous pictures can be used to detect unusual activities. Then the areas of interest could be looked at in more detail.

> There must be a major industry called photo interpretation, which must exist in both the Soviet and the United States, and probably tens of thousands of people in each country are employed to do nothing but look at satellite photographs of the other country. . . . So there are basically two kinds of reconnaissance satellites, those with poor resolution and those with high resolution: the former are poor not because they could not be made better but because one simply could not cope with the information that a high resolution system would produce. (York, 1976, p. 229)

Because of these difficulties of data handling, it would not be surprising that sometimes unusual construction activities in unexpected areas might not be "seen" by photo interpreters even if they are recorded by photoreconnaissance satellites. This problem goes beyond technological limitations.

Encryption

Verification demands not only knowledge of the numbers of weapons and their location but also some details of their quality. For ICBMs one would like to know their performance and their MIRV number. Technicians carrying out weapons tests also need such information. In developing a missile, its performance must be monitored from the ground whenever that missile is undergoing a test launch. On launch, information is needed about such things as fuel flow rates, rocket thrusts, the three-dimensional accelerations, missile stage separations, and so on. During the ballistic stage, information is needed about the maneuverings of the MIRV-carrying bus and the launchings of the separate warheads. A verifier is interested in these same flight details.

This information cannot be sent back to the ground station directly; rather, it must be transformed for transmission. Consider the fuel flow rate of one of the rocket engines. It is measured by a transducer that develops a voltage proportional to the flow rate. This voltage reading is to be transmitted. It could be sent as an analog signal (e.g., as an amplitude modulation (AM) or frequency modulation (FM) of a radio signal); the ground station must separate the information from the carrier. Alternatively, the analog voltage could be converted into digital form: the number 1000 might represent 10 volts and so on. These digital numbers can be transmitted in some standard way, as a burst of brief pulses within 1 sec of some radio signal. Each missile parameter that is to be monitored would have its own frequency channel. The separation of the second rocket stage from the first stage might be signaled by a brief burst of a radio signal at some other frequency. The missile launch and flight information is in a certain sense always encrypted, as it is never broadcast directly in its original form.

One important missile parameter is the number of MIRV warheads that a given missile could launch. In the spirit of the SALT II Treaty, a given MIRV bus may maneuver in flight only as often as the number of MIRVs it is allowed to carry. A violator of this rule would have to disguise some bus maneuverings that could potentially be used to launch excess MIRVs. Fuel flow rates in combination with acceleration data may be important to determine the launch weight of the missile. This launch weight is a parameter controlled under SALT II. These flow data, in their digital form, could be encrypted by scrambling the digits following some predetermined code unknown to foreign monitors. There is a distinction between encoding (translating) information for transmission purposes and encryption to keep the data secret; it is the latter that is forbidden by the SALT II Treaty for that information which is necessary to monitor the treaty.

HISTORY OF SALT

In 1963 the United States and the Soviet Union signed the Limited Test Ban Treaty (LTBT). It reduced the fallout problem, but it did not control arms as it just moved nuclear testing underground. Strategic Arms Limitation Treaties were subsequently established to try to remedy this failure. The photoreconnaissance and electronic-monitoring techniques described above made SALT treaties possible.

SALT I

In 1964 President Lyndon B. Johnson tried to open discussions of arms limitations by proposing a freeze on strategic weapons that would be monitored by on-site inspection. This proposal was rejected. In 1967 he threatened to deploy an ABM system if no discussions were begun. By 1968 the Soviet Union was prepared to start negotiations, as demanded by the NPT; unfortunately, the Soviet invasion of Czechoslovakia that August delayed the start until November 1969.

SALT began when it did because politically, technically, and militarily the time was right. On the political level, by then

> leaders in both countries had come to a general realization . . . that some form of mutual accommodation was mandated by the potential destructiveness of the strategic nuclear arsenals that were being created. (Talbot, 1979, p. 4)

National security within the two-power relationship seemed to require a change from cold war to détente at least at the nuclear strategic level; satellites promised the technological capability of monitoring such strategic agreements; and rough military parity was established in the strategic nuclear area as shown in Table 8.3. For financial reasons, both sides wanted to constrain their strategic forces and were worried particularly about the ABM systems—with MIRV on the horizon (see Fig. 16.1).

Descriptions of SALT negotiations as in Newhouse (1973), Smith (1980), Wolf (1979), and Talbot (1979) are not only fascinating but are also revealing about similarities and differences in national "character." In the negotiations both sides had similar problems with bureaucratic imperatives; advice from various departments and agencies was strongly colored by institutional perspectives. There were differences in negotiating style: the United States wanted functional and highly specific agreements as complete packages, whereas the Soviet Union was more interested in broad general restraints expressed first as agreements in principle. The USSR was secretive, denying even its own negotiators detailed technical information; the United States was open, providing information to everyone about the weapons systems of both sides. The USSR preferred to let the United States make the proposals and then reacted to them very cautiously and slowly.

In the SALT I negotiations, the Soviet Union had initially been interested in controlling both the existing ABM technology and the future MIRV capability. If the Soviet invasion of Czechoslovakia had not delayed the beginning of these discussions, perhaps MIRV might have been controlled before it had gone through its testing. But by 1972, the United States had the MIRV technology well developed and was unwilling to give it up. Thus only numerical limits on strategic rockets and restrictions on ABM systems could be agreed upon.

After many sessions by the official negotiator Gerard Smith (the "front channel") and the interjection of the "back channel" of President Richard Nixon and his advisor Henry Kissinger, the SALT I ABM and Interim Treaty on strategic offensive weapons were finally signed at a Nixon–Brezhnev summit meeting in May 1972. Congressional approval followed after some debate focusing on whether the treaty was truly symmetrical.

SALT II

The SALT II discussions considered the many uncertainties and asymmetries not addressed by the first agreement: U.S. forward-based systems (FBS) such as the FB-111, missile inequalities, and the new MIRV technology. The FBS question was never resolved, although it came up whenever the United States wanted to count intermediate-range weaponry such as the Soviet SS-20 or the Backfire bomber in the SALT totals. The other two problems were tackled in the Vladivostok agreement reached November 24, 1974 between President Ford and Secretary Brezhnev. The missile inequalities were addressed by establishing an overall ceiling of 2400 on the aggregate number of strategic launchers and by allowing some mixing within that aggregate. The technology of MIRV could be controlled only in the limited sense of allowing only about half the strategic weapons to contain multiple warheads.

After 1974 the major concern was no longer the size of the strategic arsenal; it was the potential vulnerability of the land-based ICBMs to a first strike by increasingly accurate MIRVed missiles (see Chapter 8). President Ford and Secretary of State Kissinger tried to attain a SALT II that would achieve some control over this vulnerability.

Before the end of the Ford presidency, a second SALT agreement had been nearly reached. It would have reduced the weapon totals slightly; it would have placed some further restrictions on the number of MIRVed missiles allowed, and it would have restricted modernization of the present missiles. The United States saw such MIRV limits as being so desirable that it was willing to give the Soviet Union something it wanted, namely, some restrictions on the newest U.S. technology of the cruise missile.

However, Jimmy Carter on becoming president in 1977 wanted to achieve significant arms reductions. He proposed a considerable cut—

on the order of 20%—in the number of allowed strategic weapons. Such drastic changes were rejected by the conservative leadership of the Soviet Union. It then took much bargaining to work back to an agreement that once more came close to the 1976 understanding. This SALT II agreement was signed by President Carter and Secretary Brezhnev on June 18, 1979. MIRV was indeed partially controlled by limiting the allowed fractionation of missile warheads and by defining the maximum number of warheads a given missile or bomber could carry. This, indirectly, put a ceiling on the total number of warheads; unfortunately, it was a very high upper limit.

In bargaining about the SALT II Treaty with the Russians, the U.S. negotiators were very mindful of the need to get the treaty approved by the Congress. Verification was expected to be much more than adequate. To get approval of the treaty by the military services, various technological options were kept open, such as improved missile accuracy, a new missile, and large cruise missile loads for bombers. The treaty did not significantly reduce the overall arms levels.

Under these circumstances many had only subdued enthusiasm for the agreement, and neither the hawks nor the doves were happy. The verification issue remained controversial. Then came the linkage problems as the Soviet "brigade" in Cuba and the Soviet invasion of Afghanistan turned the lukewarm support cold. SALT II has never been put to a vote by the U.S. Congress, in the expectation that it might well have been defeated. Although President Ronald Reagan has labeled the agreement "fatally flawed," he has agreed to do nothing to violate its essentials as long as the Soviet Union abides by it.

THE SALT AGREEMENTS

SALT I

The SALT I agreement of May 26, 1972 consists of three parts: an executive interim agreement to last five years, a protocol more precisely defining interpretations of the agreement, and a treaty of essentially unlimited duration restricting the deployment of ABM weaponry. The objectives of the agreement were to place a ceiling on strategic nuclear weapons and to control the ABM technology.

The Interim Agreement on "Certain Measures with Respect to the Limitation of Strategic Offensive Arms" froze the ICBM and SLBM levels at those existing at the time of the signing. The protocol listed these as shown in Table 16.2. Some interchanges between these categories were allowed; in particular, older Titan-II and SS-7 and SS-8 ICBMs could be converted into SLBM missiles. The limitations were not on the missiles themselves, but on the launcher systems (i.e., on the ICBM silos and on the SLBM tubes). Missile types were not defined, but there was an understanding that the dimensions of the launching silos were not to be increased by more than 10–15%. These limits were to be verified by "national technical means," and both sides agreed not to interfere with such verification methods.

The SALT I Interim Agreement did not provide any immediately significant arms limitations. Both sides could deploy all the weapons they were then planning; thus they were limited only in what they might someday have wished to deploy. The imbalance of 2358 to 1710 in allowed missile launchers made this agreement seem asymmetric, although intercontinental bombers that corrected some of this asymmetry were not included in these counts. Nor were forward-based systems counted or tactical nuclear weapons.

The greatest drawback of the SALT I agreement was that it placed no limits on the technology of the missiles. The size of missile silos was controlled, but the missiles could expand greatly to fill the holes, and they could be improved in quality. In particular, there were no limits placed on the upcoming MIRV deployments either in the size and number of warheads or in their accuracy.

The ABM Treaty set a meaningful limit on the deployment of anti-ballistic missile defense systems. The treaty allowed each nation the defense of only two locations, its capital and one ICBM deployment area; the United States then was preparing to defend one Minuteman silo complex, and the Soviet had an ABM system around Moscow. Within each defensive area 300 km in diameter, 100 ABM launchers and 100 ABM missiles can be deployed. The control radars also are limited in number; no other radar systems having ABM capabilities are allowed (i.e., any antiaircraft radar systems must be clearly distinguishable from ABM radars).

How much does this treaty limit the two sides? The U.S. Senate had approved the deployment of ABMs at two missile sites only with great reluctance. In 1974 a further protocol limited each side to only one ABM deployment site. The one U.S. ABM complex became obsolete so

Table 16.2 Limits on strategic missiles (ICBMs and SLBMs) and on nuclear missile submarines (SSBNs) imposed by the SALT I agreement. The old missiles could be replaced by SLBMs to add to the present number of SLBMs.

	ICBMs		SSBNs	SLBMs	
	Old	Modern	Modern	Present	Maximum
Soviet Union	210	1408	62	740	950
United States	54	1000	44	656	710

rapidly that it was soon disbanded. The technology controlled by the ABM treaty was apparently not very desirable; but if this treaty had not been established, the pressures on both sides to deploy newer ABMs might have been quite large.

The SALT I Treaty appears to recognize two facts of strategic life. It establishes rough equivalency in at least the number of strategic weapons; this was a step toward accepting the undesirability of numerical strategic superiority for either side. However, as discussed in Chapter 8, the possibility of qualitative strategic superiority was not addressed in SALT I. The ABM Treaty seems to acknowledge that strategic defense is potentially destabilizing as it threatens the second-strike capability. However, the control was placed on a system in which the United States had a lead. Similar controls were not placed on the bomber and civil defenses favored by the USSR or on the antisubmarine warfare technology favored by the United States SALT I was only a limited first step; SALT II was supposed to go further.

The Vladivostok Agreement

The 1974 Vladivostok agreement between President Ford and Secretary Brezhnev removed some of the numerical asymmetries of SALT I and made a small beginning toward a control of MIRV. Vladivostok set an aggregate limit of 2400 on the total of all strategic nuclear weapons launchers: ICBMs plus SLBMs plus intercontinental bombers. Within that limit the numbers of the separate components could be chosen without restraint; thus, the United States could have more bombers if it was willing to have fewer ICBMs. The agreement suggests a "freedom to mix," although light ICBMs could still not be converted to heavy ICBMs.

MIRV was considered in this treaty as it had not been in SALT I. By 1974 MIRV was an established fact. Hence, it could not be totally forbidden; rather, an upper limit of 1320 was placed on all ICBMs and SLBMs equipped with MIRV. Bombers were not included in this number. The accomplishments of the Vladivostok agreement were not very great. It allowed the United States an additional 258 launchers above the limit set in 1972, while the Soviet Union was allowed 99 fewer launchers than before. The MIRV controls did not prohibit any planned U.S. developments, and the USSR would not approach its limit before the 1980s.

The Vladivostok agreement was mostly a stopgap between SALT I and SALT II, indicating the outline of the projected next treaty. Hence, it left many unresolved matters such as the verification of the MIRV numbers. Nor was any attempt made to define the quality of allowed weaponry; that problem was to be addressed in SALT II.

The SALT II Treaty

The SALT II Treaty of 1979 is a much more carefully drawn and extensive document. The number of allowed strategic launchers is slightly lower than before. It goes considerably beyond SALT I in the number and types of limits set on launchers; a number of these limits address the quality of weaponry. SALT II defines its terms much more carefully than does SALT I.

Definitions

ICBMs are defined to be missiles with a range greater than 5500 km. Heavy ICBM are those whose launch weight or throw weight (payload weight) exceeds that of the Soviet SS-19. Each existing missile is defined in size, weight, propellant, and throw weight. If a missile has ever been tested with some observed maximum number of MIRV warheads, it is thereafter always defined to be a MIRVed missile, and the largest numbers of warheads it may carry is defined by that test. Each missile type is allowed a maximum number of MIRV warheads as indicated in Table 16.3. These limits restrict the possible proliferation of MIRV warheads.

Heavy bombers are defined to include the U.S. B-52 and B-1 bombers (but not the FB-111) and the Soviet Tu-95 Bear and Mya-4 Bison (but not the Backfire—which is limited in production by a separate agreement). Reconnaissance versions of any of these must be distinguishable by national technical means (i.e., they must not have a bomb bay, etc.). Bombers may carry cruise missiles or air-to-surface ballistic missiles, but these capabilities must be clearly distinguishable, and the cruise missile carriers are all counted as being MIRVed. Bombers may not carry more than an average of 28 cruise missiles.

Submarine-launched ballistic missiles are counted as SLBMs except those deployed by the USSR prior to 1965. If MIRVed, they may carry no more than 14 warheads (the maximum number that could be carried by U.S. Poseidon missiles, although they now carry only 10). Once a given missile has been tested in the MIRV mode, it is thereafter always counted in the MIRV category.

Cruise missiles are divided into two categories, short range and long range. These two must be clearly distinguishable on the basis of exter-

Table 16.3 The number of MIRVs allowed for various missiles under the SALT II agreement.

Missile	Titan II	MMII	MMIII	MX	SS-7/9	SS-17	SS-18	SS-19	SS-X	All SLBM
Number of MIRVs	1	1	3	10	1	4	10	6	10	14

nally observable design features; the short-range cruise missiles must never be flight tested beyond 600 km. According to the protocol lasting only until December 1981, longer-range cruise missiles may not be deployed on sea-based or land-based launchers. Any bomber carrying cruise missiles is considered to be a MIRVed launcher.

Air-to-surface ballistic missiles with a range in excess of 600 km are allowed to be carried by heavy bombers. Such bombers are counted as MIRVed launchers if these ASBMs are ever tested with MIRV warheads.

Some of these definitions are quite subtle. On the cruise missile range, for example, the United States wanted the 600-km limit to measure the shortest distance from launch point to impact point, whereas the Soviet Union wanted to measure the flight distance covered. Since a cruise missile does a considerable amount of in-flight maneuvering, this can be a significant difference; a 600-km cruise missile by U.S. (and SALT II) standards would have been a 900-km cruise missile in the opinion of the Soviet Union.

Limits on Strategic Weapons

SALT II set both quantitative and qualitative limits on strategic weapons. The Vladivostok limit of 2400 aggregate intercontinental launchers was to be reduced to 2250 on each side by the end of 1981. Within that limit there are various sublimits. Neither side can have more than 820 MIRVed ICBMs. For the United States this is sufficient to include the 550 Minuteman-III missiles plus the 200 projected MX missiles. The Soviet Union cannot MIRV all of its 1400 ICBMs. Neither side can have more than 1200 MIRVed SLBMs plus ICBMs; an emphasis on MIRVing submarine-launched missiles reduces the number of land-based ICBMs allowed to be MIRVed, and vice versa. If long-range bombers are equipped with air-launched cruise missiles, such bombers count toward the MIRV sublimit, but that sublimit is then raised to a total of 1320. This means that as long as the Soviet Union does not have cruise missiles or heavy bombers, it can have only 1200 MIRVed launchers; if the United States wants more than 120 cruise missile bombers, it must give up some MIRVed ICBMs or SLBMs.

SALT II sets various qualitative limits on missiles. Only one new type of (light) missile may be developed by each side, and it may carry no more than 10 warheads. In modernizing existing missiles, the size, launch weight, and throw weight may not be changed by more than 5%, the silo volume cannot be increased by more than 32%, and the number of stages, the number of MIRV warheads, and the type of propellant (liquid versus solid) may not be changed at all. The accuracy and yield of the warheads are not mentioned. Missile silos may not have a rapid reload capability. And the mobile Soviet SS-16 missile will not be deployed (although the SS-20 consisting of the bottom two stages of this missile may be deployed as an intermediate-range ballistic missile).

Several other limitations on missile technology are in the SALT II Treaty. Orbital nuclear weapons are forbidden, as are long-range underwater-launched cruise missiles and increases in the number of ICBM test launchers. Multiple launches of ICBMs or single-missile launches outside the normal test ranges and extending outside national territory must be preannounced. Missiles that go into fractional orbits (FOBS) are prohibited, and existing Soviet testing launch facilities for them are to be dismantled.

Various measures in the treaty are intended to aid verification. Interference with national technical means of verification is forbidden; deliberate concealment is not allowed. Thus, telemetric information that is important for monitoring missile launches may not be encrypted. Bombers that cannot carry cruise missiles must be clearly distinct from those that can, or else they would count as MIRV launchers. Short-range cruise missiles must be clearly distinct from long-range cruise missiles.

SALT II carries arms limitations a little farther by establishing counting rules that would reduce the total number of strategic weapons. By fixing the size of missiles and the number of MIRV warheads, it puts a lid on the number of targets that could be struck and to some extent on the yield of the explosions. Unfortunately, the reductions are not very significant. The aggregate equalities furthered the concept and acceptance of equality in the strategic area between the two superpowers. Table 8.2 confirms this equality in many of the important quantitative areas.

The SALT II Treaty goes farther than the previous agreements in dealing with some new technologies. The extent of MIRVing is limited. Several potentially destabilizing technologies, such as the mobile SS-16 and the FOBS, are banned, and some aspects of the cruise missile are temporarily controlled. Certain testing modes such as multiple launching are controlled. Unfortunately, the controls on some of these tests may be either too late or insufficient. At best SALT II is a start.

Openness in strategic matters has been significantly fostered. Uncertainty in verification is acknowledged to be destabilizing. Definitions of weapons parameters and their agreed upon constancy is a promising movement.

DISCUSSION

In spite of the progress in SALT, there is considerable pessimism about the process, and not just because of the failure to ratify the SALT II Treaty. For the little that the SALT agreements have achieved, the difficulties of reaching them to many seem to have been almost overwhelming. For all the care that has been taken in reaching the agreements, many people on both sides of the political spectrum do not accept the resulting treaties.

Difficulties of the SALT Process

The SALT process unfortunately must accommodate so many different perspectives that it is hard to achieve progress. The two superpowers have national interests and national security at stake. Each superpower experiences countervailing pressures from hawks and doves; from the branches of the military; from government agencies such as the Departments of State and Defense, the Arms Control and Disarmament Agency, and the National Security Council; and from economic, political, and social pressure groups. SALT is a complex mix in which technology and public policy at times are in opposition. Several negotiating issues at the SALT talks illustrate these conflicts.

Throughout the negotiations, the United States tried to move the Soviet Union out to sea. That is, the United States tried to set the limits on MIRVed ICBMs low to encourage more building of Soviet submarines. The United States sees the present lower accuracy of SLBMs as making them less useful as first-strike weapons. In contrast, the Soviet Union has had a traditional preference for weapons stationed in the Soviet heartland, since its access to the sea is restricted.

Throughout the negotiations, the military on both sides wanted their options left as open. The United States did not want to accept a limit of 20 air-launched cruise missiles per bomber because the Air Force was dreaming of future wide-bodied aircraft that could carry more. The Soviet Union was reluctant to accept a 5% limit even on the decrease allowed in a missile's weight, probably because some technologists dreamed of some tests they might want to make later on. The United States asked the Soviet Union not to develop depressed trajectory missiles since these might be useful in a surprise attack on bomber bases by offshore submarines and, hence, were potentially destabilizing. The Soviet Union countered by requesting a halt to U.S. antisubmarine warfare developments that endangered Soviet SLBMs and, hence, were also potentially destabilizing. Both requests were dropped. The largest difficulty in the SALT process was probably the informational asymmetry between the two countries. The United

States is a relatively open society. The number of missiles and their warheads are known; thus, the Soviet Union basically has a smaller verification problem. In contrast, the Soviet Union is a militarily secret society that has always been opposed to releasing any military information.

The SALT Debate in the United States

The debate in the United States about the ratification of SALT II has mirrored all these problems. The perceptions of SALT II ranged from positive to very negative. The pro-SALT forces generally saw SALT II as doing some things that are useful. And they saw it as keeping the process going; hoping that truly meaningful limits might be set in a future SALT agreement. The anti-SALT forces contained two very different groups.

Several liberal senators, such as William Proxmire, George McGovern, and Mark Hatfield, as well as some outsiders like Jeremy Stone, director of the Federation of American Scientists (FAS), were so unhappy with the SALT II agreement that they were uncertain whether to support it. They felt that it accomplished so little that it was hardly worthwhile. They saw this particularly in the case of the MX missile, which was developed in an effort to get SALT II passed to satisfy those critics who were disturbed by the asymmetry of the Soviet SS-18 heavy missiles. These critics ultimately did support SALT II as better than no treaty.

The major objections to SALT came from those who saw the treaty as "fatally flawed" because it is unequal, unverifiable, and improper in a time of a deteriorating relationship with the Soviet Union.

SALT II seemed inequitable to some. It limits U.S. land- and sea-based cruise missiles, the one technology in which the United States has a decisive lead. It allows the Soviets 308 heavy missiles (the SS-18), whereas the United States is allowed none. The Soviet Union is also allowed the intermediate-range SS-20 missile and Backfire bombers. In the complex negotiations the U.S. negotiators felt they got concessions for these, such as limits on the MIRV fractionation. In the SALT discussions U.S. negotiators were more concerned with the more accurate SS-19. The U.S. F-111 and the French and British nuclear forces are not counted in the treaty limitations. The mobile SS-16 is banned. The negotiators argued that some parameters in treaties that are unequal can always be found and that the treaty as a whole must be considered; one must compare it with the circumstances that would obtain if no treaty existed, and mainly one must ask whether there are net benefits from a treaty to both partners. SALT II does not prevent the ultimate future vulnerability of the ICBM forces of both sides through superaccurate MIRV warheads; short of forbidding MIRVs altogether, no treaty could completely remove that mutually shared danger.

SALT II has a variety of provisions that require verification. The number of submarines, bombers, and missiles and their sizes are verifiable by satellite photography. There was little challenge of this capability, except for claims that the Soviets had sometimes covered a few of their ICBM silos, as had the United States, to protect workers in the silos from cold weather. The largest concern has been monitoring the development of new missile types or the modification of old models, as described in Fig. 16.2.

Monitoring such missile flight raised the specter of encryption. As described, this encryption could be intended to enhance transmission, but it can make the information harder to read. The United States does listen to Soviet telemetry for purposes of

espionage as well as arms control. It monitors Soviet tests to collect information that is valuable as military intelligence but irrelevant to the verification of agreements. As the most secretive and paranoid sectors of a secretive and paranoid society, the Soviet military and intelligence establishments have, by all indications, found American prying well nigh intolerable, regardless of whether monitoring is carried out in the name of arms control. Therefore, the Soviets have, from time to time, scrambled or otherwise put into code their missile telemetry in order to inhibit remote eavesdropping by the U.S. It should be added that encryption also makes it harder for the Russians to read their own telemetry . . . How could the U.S. be confident that the Soviet Union is abiding by SALT if the Russians encrypt their telemetry? Officials have traditionally been reluctant to raise the issue at the negotiating table with the Russians for a number of reasons. For one, the more the U.S. remonstrates with the Soviets about their encryption practices, the more the Soviets will know about the American capability to intercept and decode their transmissions. Also, American officials knew that the ensuing conversation might not be entirely one-sided. The U.S., too, has used encryption and other methods of depriving foreign intelligence services of telemetric information about the testing of American systems. (Wolfe, 1979, p. 195)

In July 1978 the Soviets encrypted some information returned by the payload from an SS-18 missile. This was seen by SALT critics as a possible precedent endangering future monitoring to ensure that only one new type of missile would be developed. The monitoring of missile tests was further complicated when the Islamic revolution swept through Iran in 1978. The United States lost two radar and radio stations that had been monitoring Soviet test missile launches from Tyuratam in the South of the USSR. The subsequent degradation in verification capability was seen by some as being significant. This loss of information supposedly was to be regained soon by new radio and radar stations in Turkey and the P.R.C. and by new satellites. Nonetheless, these losses pointed out the critical importance and the uncertainties of monitoring the proposed SALT II agreement.

For those who accept the existence of mutual assured destruction (MAD), the SALT treaty should stand or fall on its own merits independent of other arms questions. But many asked how one can negotiate a strategic arms agreement with a nation that undertakes actions on the international scene that run counter to one's own interests. The concept of linkage says that international security on the strategic level is inevitably linked to confrontation on other international levels. SALT II became coupled to the deterioration of détente. The Soviet Union delayed SALT II discussions because of the U.S. stand on human rights with respect to Soviet citizens such as Andrei Sakharov. In the United States, the Senate approval of SALT II became slowed by Soviet adventurism in Ethiopia and Cuba and stopped altogether when the Soviet Union invaded Afghanistan in 1979. Critics of SALT II felt that dealing with the Russians while they were occupying a foreign nation is dangerous.

Strategic Arms Limitations

From a technical viewpoint, strategic arms limitations are difficult to achieve. The more rapidly a technology is progressing, the harder it is to control those arms that rely on this technology.

Technological fixes in arms limitations are not enough; a proper international climate and political will must also be there. If there is a perception that treaty partners will automatically cheat at the slightest opportunity, then treaties are impossible. If the strategic arena still contains a race for superiority, then arms limitations in fact make little sense and offer little benefit for a national security narrowly conceived in military terms only.

Unless a treaty is of benefit to both partners, it will be meaningless. Too often the usual vision of arms agreements has been that of a zero-sum game where one player improves his or her position at the expense of the other player. Acceptance of SALT-type treaties requires another approach. Strobe Talbott (1979) said

> In SALT . . . the object has not been for one player to beat the other. To play to win would be to seek "unilateral advantage" or "strategic superiority." It would be to violate the rules of parity and stability. In SALT, the object of the game is a draw. (p. 18)

The concept of a draw is difficult for policymakers to accept in matters of international security.

The Freeze

It appears that SALT II will never be ratified. Nonetheless, the need for some strategic arms limitations continues. President Ronald Reagan in the first part of his presidency has been retracing the path of the early Carter presidency. He renamed the "Strategic Arms Limitation Talks" the "Strategic Arms Reduction Talks" (START). His proposals, like the early Carter proposals, contain major cuts in the number of strategic arms. He too would propose particularly heavy reductions in the number of ICBMs in an effort to drive the Soviet warheads out to sea. He is, however, working in an atmosphere of worsening relations, and he appears to be more interested in the concept of arming in order to force the Soviets to negotiate. It is unclear whether this is likely to be a more successful approach.

An alternative arms limitation proposal has been the call for serious negotiations toward a bilateral nuclear weapons freeze. The freeze would stop the development, testing, and production of all nuclear weapons systems in the United States and the Soviet Union. If successful, such a freeze would stop not only the growth of strategic nuclear weapons, but also the development of counterforce and tactical nuclear weapons. A halt to the testing of nuclear weaponry, in the long run, would lead to disarmament by technological obsolescence. The freeze is arms limitation plus arms control taken to the limit.

The major objections to such a freeze are twofold. Some feel that it would freeze the United States into a position of quantitative inferiority, or they do not want to limit future U.S. technological advances. The more serious problem is that of verification; how can one monitor such a freeze? The freeze would require the verification not only of a halt in strategic weapons testing and deployment, but also of the production of both nuclear delivery systems and nuclear warheads. The originator of the freeze proposal, Randall Forsberg (1982), suggests the use of some nonintrusive on-site verification measures to supplement observations by satellites and other national technical means. The hope is that a freeze could lead to a build-down approach that would produce a more stable and smaller mix of nuclear weapons.

Summary

The hope in arms limitation and arms control agreements is not only to limit the number of arms but also to control technological imperatives such as those leading to more accurate ICBMs, SLBMs, and cruise missiles. One can think of attempting to control technological programs at the scientific level of discovery, at the applied science level of development, at the engineering level of weapons testing, at the industrial level of production, or at the military level of deployment.

Control of the science leading to the technology seems impossible, as the consequences of science often cannot be anticipated. The SALT discussions encouraged some enthusiasm for controlling the predeployment research stages of the R&D process. But on the whole, exploratory research into the technological possibilities probably cannot be halted either. For example, if computer guidance were not developed for missiles, it would probably come for commercial aircraft.

The most reasonable technical point for control of technological imperatives is most likely at the final testing stage of specific weapons systems. Before a new missile can be deployed with any degree of confidence, it must first be test fired 10 or more times. Before a TERCOM system in a cruise missile can be judged satisfactory, it must be test flown repeatedly in that particular missile configuration. A moratorium on testing a new weapons system might be a "technological fix" of the problem that would be posed by its deployment.

Political control by forbidding deployment is particularly difficult for the most destabilizing weapons systems. It is this past lack of political control that has given technological imperatives a chance to operate and has allowed the technological sweetness of some systems to make them inevitable. The long incubation times of weapons systems force intramural competition. Long-term and secretive uncertainties encourage worst-case analyses. Bureaucratic inertia tends to advance technologies once they have been invented. Once testing has taken place, the step to deployment usually becomes uncontrollable in the political arena. A bargain-chip weapon system that has been tested is unlikely to be controlled. The freeze is attempting to address the problem at an earlier stage. To slow the momentum of arms developments, it wants to control the earlier development and production stages.

References

Aspin, L. "The Verification of the SALT II Agreement." *Scientific American*, Vol. 240, no. 2 (February 1979), pp. 38–45.

Forsberg, R. "A Bilateral Nuclear-Weapon Freeze." *Scientific American*, Vol. 247, no. 5 (November 1982), pp. 52–61.

Greenwood, T., *Reconnaissance, Surveillance and Arms Control*, Adelphi Paper #88. London: International Institute for Strategic Studies, 1972.

_____ "Reconnaissance and Arms Control." *Scientific American*, Vol. 228, no. 2 (February 1973), pp. 14–25.

Klass, P. J. *Secret Sentries in Space*. New York: Random House, 1971.

Newhouse, J. *Cold Dawn: The Story of SALT*. New York: Holt, Rinehart and Winston, 1973.

Potter, W. C. ed., *Verification and SALT: The Challenge of Strategic Deception*. Boulder, Colo.: Westview Press, 1980; see particularly B. G. Blair and G. D. Brewer, "Verifying SALT Agreements," pp. 7–48.

Smith, G. C. *Doubletalk: The Story of the First Strategic Arms Limitation Talks.* Garden City, N.Y.: Doubleday, 1980.

Talbott, S. *End Game: The Inside Story of SALT II.* New York: Harper & Row, 1979.

Wolfe, T. W. *The SALT Experience.* Cambridge, Mass.: Ballinger, 1979.

York, H. F. "Reconnaissance Satellites and the Arms Race." In *Arms Control and Technological Innovation*, D. Carlton and C. Schaerf, eds., pp. 224–231. New York: John Wiley, 1976.

Disarmament

If you want peace, prepare for war.

Roman precept

This is absolute nuclear nonsense.

Lord Mountbatten

INTRODUCTION

The previous two chapters have described efforts at arms control and arms limitation in the nuclear strategic area, efforts that aim to limit the quantity and quality of some specific weapons systems. Measures for arms control and arms limitation can also include efforts to reduce by treaty the chances of war or the consequences of it. The consequences of a possible nuclear war might be reduced by large-scale nuclear disarmament. The probability of a nuclear war breaking out might be reduced by some of the measures discussed by James E. Dougherty (1973).

The chances of a nuclear war occurring can be reduced by measures that control provocative technologies, decrease the risk of accidents, or reduce international tensions. Such measures include the following, as listed by Dougherty (1973, pp. 32–33).

1. Administrative, technical, or political arrangements (for example, "failsafe," "two key" systems, the "permissive action link," and the "rules of nuclear engagement") calculated to minimize the risk of nuclear accident, unauthorized use of nuclear weapons, precipitate response to an ambiguous warning, or strategic miscalculation of the adversary's intentions.
2. A program of weapons research, development, and deployment, as well as a strategic doctrine, which stresses the nonprovocative and defensive aspects of national security postures, especially those associated with an "invulnerable second-strike capability."

3. Regional tension-reducing arrangements, such as disengagement, "thinning out" of forces, or the creation of demilitarized or nuclear-free zones.

4. Tension-reducing declarations such as a "no-first 'use' pledge" or a "nonaggression pact."

5. The improvement of facilities for emergency communications (for example, the "hot line").

6. Efforts to prevent or retard the proliferation of nuclear weapons to nations not already in possession of them.

The consequences of a nuclear war can be reduced by limiting its magnitude, or by preventing escalation from a regional to an international scale, from a conventional to a tactical nuclear war, or from a tactical nuclear to a full-scale nuclear war. Measures that might reduce such consequences include the following:

7. The prohibition of certain activities, such as the sale of conventional arms and delivery systems to countries in "tinderbox areas," nuclear weapons testing in proscribed environments . . .

8. The prudent management of crisis diplomacy and limited conflict strategy (including such concepts as "sanctuary," "flexible response," "city-avoidance strategies," and conflict de-escalation or termination strategies).

9. Efforts to separate nuclear forces and strategies from conventional forces and strategies through the utilization of various "firebreaks" (for example, time, geography, and command).

10. A formal, verified freeze on the production of specified items, such as fissionable materials for weapons purposes or strategic delivery vehicles.

The usefulness of measures that reduce the costs of armaments would seem obvious; these might include

11. Decisions to hold quantitative rates of weapons production below those levels which a nation is economically and technically capable of sustaining in an uninhibited "arms race".

All these measures are more likely to be undertaken if arms race discussions are institutionalized. Thus the final measures should include

12. The diplomatic institutionalization of arms control dialogues among governments and groups of experts. (Dougherty, 1973, pp. 32–33)

It must be remembered that these measures are not necessarily always mutually compatible. For example, the chance of having a direct conflict between the two superpowers is low, whereas the consequences of such a conflict would be high; the probabilities of a war between Third World nations might be much higher, but the consequences of such a war most likely also would be much smaller. (See Beer, 1981, and Falk and Kim, 1980, for reviews of some of the social science literature on international security, conflict resolution, and peace studies.) Some crisis-control measures such as improved command, control, communications, and intelligence (C^3I) and flexible response strategies might destabilize by weakening the opponent's retaliatory capabilities.

Disarmament refers to measures that attempt to reduce the consequences of the arms race by reductions in armaments. The range of disarmament could extend from some token amount that is almost a SALT-style limitation all the way to general and complete disarmament (GCD). Some of these measures may at times be seen as contradictory: arms control or limited disarmament may reduce the pressure toward more general or complete disarmament; sometimes they may be supplementary (i.e., arms control of technology may make disarmament less risky). Such contradictions are particularly likely to occur when GCD is on the agenda, as required, for example, of the nuclear weapons states in Article VI of the Non-Proliferation Treaty. Dougherty (1973) says that

> Some . . . arms controllers . . . do not wish to undermine these [rational] defense policies by embarking upon what they consider the utopian road to GCD—a road which in their estimate could lead to disaster . . . (p. 34)

The question is whether disarmament will be able to decrease at the same time both the chances of war and the consequences if one were to break out.

Disarmament would present the problem of verification and enforcement. The more comprehensive the disarmament, the more on-site inspection and international peacekeeping institutions would most likely be required. As indicated earlier, the Soviet Union is not likely to accept intrusive surveillance, and neither the United States nor the Soviet Union is likely to trust an international agency for protection in a disarmed world (although the IAEA has had some success in monitoring the NPT). The Soviet Union

> has never appeared to accept the proposition that radical disarmament, which it espouses, will necessitate many profound changes in the world, including a drastic reorientation of the techniques of Soviet rule affecting both domestic and foreign policy. (Dougherty, 1973, p. 68)

From a technological perspective there is general pessimism about the possibilities of a more generalized disarmament because of the inspection problem. The following sections explore this pessimism further. There may be somewhat more hope in considering larger-scale disarmament in the strategic nuclear arms outside of conventional arms. Some of the objections just raised ought not to hold so strongly for strategic arms (e.g., arming for strategic nuclear war beyond some minimal MAD level may not be very good at reducing either the probability or the consequences of a nuclear war). The following sections will focus on disarmament of strategic nuclear arms.

STRATEGIC NUCLEAR DISARMAMENT

Methods of Strategic Nuclear Disarmament

Rationally, disarmament of strategic nuclear weapons may not be as difficult as it seems. A way must be found to prevent instabilities in the disarmament process, and there must be verification on a safe level. The biggest problem probably would be to bypass the zero-sum syndrome, where the gains of one side are seen as the other side's loss. This zero-sum perspective is contained in the argument against the SALT II agreement that if the Soviet Union is willing to sign it, then it must be because they see profit from it at the expense of the United States.

If disarmament is to become an acceptable option, it would have to occur in such a way that all nations involved would benefit in security, economically and politically. If the United States agrees to disarm, but cheats successfully, it might achieve a considerable gain over the USSR, and vice versa. But if either side were caught cheating, the agreement would break down, and both the United States and the USSR would lose the benefit of the treaty. In such a situation, if any cheating is likely to be detected, both sides would win only if they both scrupulously honored the treaty commitment.

As long as strategic stability with mutually assured destruction is to be maintained, a disarmament process might have to look like that shown in Fig. 17.1. In a deterrence situation, disarmament would be stable as long as the number of arms stayed within the bounds of mutual deterrence. Such disarmament could be achieved by small alternating unilateral steps as shown in the solid line in Fig. 17.1 in going from P_1 to P_7. Or mutual disarmament could go gradually and mutually from P_1 by the dashed line in Fig. 17.1. In either case points of unilateral deterrence, such as 4' or 8, would have to be avoided. Greater disarmament steps could be taken by expanding the area of mutual deterrence, as by eliminating highly accurate MIRVed weapons first. The goal might be to reach the minimum level of nuclear arms

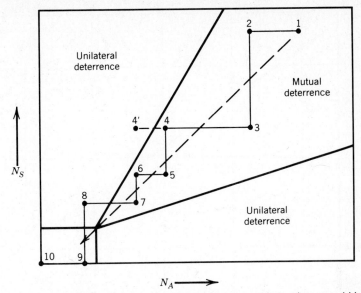

Figure 17.1 Disarmament by mutual or unilateral steps as shown here could be stable if it stayed in the bounds of mutual deterrence (e.g., in going from P_1 to P_7). Outside the bounds, at points $P_{4'}$ and P_8, the deterrence would be unilateral; at P_9, neither side would be deterred in spite of the imbalance; P_{10} represents general nuclear disarmament. (After Legault and Lindsey, 1976, p. 192.)

consistent with maintaining MAD. If it is desired to eliminate MAD altogether, strategic nuclear weapons could be reduced on both sides below the level of assured destruction. Thereafter, disarmament in the tactical nuclear and conventional weaponry would also be needed to discourage alternative nonstrategic wars.

The Frequency of Wars

Wars have been going on at least as long as humans have recorded these events. Studies by E. G. Richardson (1960) and Melvin Small and J. David Singer (1982) have suggested mathematical descriptions of the occurrences of wars. Figure 17.2 shows a mathematical record of the frequency of international wars of various sizes. The curve is based on data about wars between 1820 and 1946. During that period there were 102 wars with more than 3000 fatalities, but only 2 with more than 3 million dead. The frequency of wars appears to be inversely proportional to the square root of the number of fatalities. Figure 17.2 shows a curve following that mathematical relationship. Below 20 million fatalities the curve is a fit to observation; above that number it is an extrapolation. The agreement of this "theoretical" curve with the data

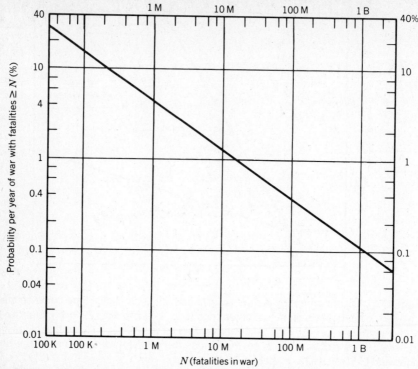

Figure 17.2 The frequency of deadly quarrels in which the number of fatalities, including civilians, exceed various sizes. This curve is based on actual wars between 1820 and 1946; beyond 30 million the curve is an extrapolation. (Based on Richardson, 1960. Small and Singer, 1982, has essentially the same numbers.)

is surprisingly good, although the idea that the frequency of wars drops off rapidly for large wars is intuitively reasonable.

It is a very dubious proposition to extrapolate from the past history of relatively small wars to the future probability of very large wars. It is hoped that technological and social changes will make the future unrecognizable from the past. But this mathematical formulation suggests that there seems to be a pattern to international wars. An extrapolation of Fig. 17.2 suggests a very crude guesstimate of the future likelihood of nuclear war. For a nuclear war that could be kept on the tactical level, say, at a level of 10 million fatalities or less, Fig. 17.2 suggests its probability might be on the order of 1% per year; over 35 years, there might be a 50% chance that such a war might have occurred. On the other hand, the chances of a full-scale nuclear war with a billion fatalities might be projected as 0.1% per year. The latter is a (mildly) comforting statement only if escalation from the tactical to the full-scale nuclear war is not likely to occur.

THE FUTURE OF DISARMAMENT

If strategic disarmament with continuing stability is as "easy" as has been described, why has it not been done before? It may be because strategic weapons are seen as increasing national security beyond the strategic deterrence through MAD. National security forces may ensure economic independence; the U.S. Navy protects the sea lanes, thereby assuring continuing resource supplies. This nonstrategic protection takes place under the MAD umbrella. National defense guaranteed by strategic arms may help maintain some desirable aspects of the present way of life.

The arms race has costs. Some of these are expressed in terms of economic expenditures. The burden of the arms race is often cited as a major reason why one ought to have arms control and disarmament; see, for example, Jolly (1978), J. S. Gansler (1980), R. L. Sivard (1982), J. H. Barton and L. D. Weiler (1976), and A. Myrdal (1976). These economic costs are hard to establish either absolutely, since the Soviet Union, for example, does not publish all of its defense expenditures, or even relatively, since it is difficult to measure what quality of equipment or personnel a given arms expenditure can buy. Figure 17.3 shows the annual total military world expenditures over the past two decades; they have been growing steadily in absolute terms, although relative to the total world gross national product, they have been decreasing or holding more or less steady in recent years.

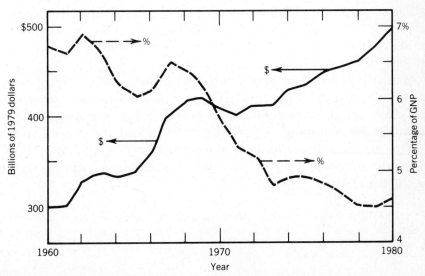

Figure 17.3 Total world annual military expenditures in constant 1979 dollars and as a percentage of the world's GNP. (Data from Sivard, 1982, p. 26.)

Are these military budgets dangerously large? Do they seriously interfere with other social efforts? In some underdeveloped countries, where military expenditures exceed those for health or for education, the expense may well be socially unacceptable. But for countries such as the United States, which have excess industrial capacity and work force, it is not so obvious that military costs are unacceptably high. Coral Bell suggests that

> When the U.S. economy falters, it tends to do so from deficiency of demand. A rapid rearmament programme, as from the outbreak of the Korean War, tends to produce economic boom, rather than hard times. America does not need to sacrifice butter for guns: on the contrary, the fact that the guns are being produced makes it more likely that practically everyone will be able to afford butter ("military Keynesianism," as Professor Galbraith calls it). The Soviet Union, in the contrary, is still an economy of comparative scarcity: if the steel has to go into making tanks, the waiting list for cars becomes even more hopelessly long. (Bell, 1977, pp. 58–59).

Some studies have tried to quantify the net economic costs of military expenditures (Beer, 1981). Studies by Emile Benoit in the early 1960s indicate that an increase in the defense budget equal to 1% of the GNP may lead to a ¼% decrease in the GNP. Bruce M. Russett found for the United States during the 1939–1968 period that each dollar of defense expenditure reduced personal consumption by 42 cents, whereas each dollar put into fixed civilian investment reduced personal consumption by only 29 cents.

Military expenditures create jobs, but these tend to be in the high-technology areas and hence are of little use to the unskilled sector of society. It has been estimated that $1 billion of military expenditures would create 76,000 jobs; however, an equivalent tax cut would create 112,000 jobs.

Almost half of all research and development expenditures in the world goes toward military R&D. A critical question is how much of that R&D produces technological spinoff that in the long run helps economic development. This issue arises about the role of military R&D in developing computers. Mary Kaldor (1976) sees computers as primarily military products in the United States, but as civilian products in Japan:

> in Great Britain and the United States resources (to electronics) are largely spent by the government for military purposes, while in Federal Germany and Japan they are largely spent by business enterprises for civilian purposes. (p. 327)

Kaldor believes that in spite of the fact that integrated circuits were developed first in the United States, they were standardized and widely commercialized by Japan while the United States kept building them for specialized military applications.

CONCLUSIONS

Disarmament is not primarily a technical matter; it deals with the sociology of personal perceptions and human institutions. Wars are inspired not only by rational cost-benefit analyses of preemptive first strikes versus mutually assured destruction but involve the desire to protect one's resources and one's way of life or may even be caused by religious fervor.

The prevention of many such wars fall under the injunction that "If you want peace, prepare for war." Unfortunately, the very act of preparing for war may precipitate it. In a world with MAD, preparation for war may be equivalent to preparing for a *Götterdämmerung*. This dictum no longer can be accepted simplistically.

Any disarmament programs must take into account facts about social behavior. This is particularly true for proposals that disarmament should come through subordination of nations to international authority. Alva Myrdal's pleas for disarmament (1976) hinge on the ability of some international body like the United Nations to exercise extended controls. Physical scientists for years have asked for international cooperation as an approach toward disarmament.

> A very strong conviction of the scientists is that science is a force for peace. . . . "Because of the similarity in outlook of scientists all over the world their increased influence on the national policies of the different countries should increase the ease of international communication."
> One senses in the case of many of these scientists a feeling that the internationalism of science itself would operate as a policing mechanism. (Gilpin, 1962, pp. 31 and 272)

Scientists have their norm of universalism that fosters such internationalism. It is not certain that most people would be willing to give up their nationalistic feeling of belonging to a group in exchange for such pannational unity.

It is time to return to the questions that inspired this text. How much impact do science and technology have on the nuclear arms race? Are arms the cause of conflict, or does the threat of conflict produce a demand for arms? From a technologist's perspective, technology does seem to have provided considerable impetus for the nuclear arms race. With technological imperatives like computer-assisted high accuracy

"Well! That concludes my statements about the kill capacity of the XL missile. Who would like some coffee and donuts?"

Richard Cline, United States

Figure 17.4 The arms race should not be dehumanized.

for missiles, this impetus is continuing. Arms alone may not cause war, but they do seem to increase the opportunities and incentives.

From a disarmament perspective, technological imperatives are unfortunate. They tend to run counter to disarmament as they offer opportunities for better weapons. They may create weapons that take on an uncontrollable life of their own. From that technological perspective, the most important arms control measures now would seem to be those that control future high technology that might destabilize the nuclear arms race.

Of course, one would expect such emphasis on technology from technologically oriented persons. Even if that technological emphasis should prove to be appropriate, it might be dangerous. It partially takes arms control out of the political sphere by encouraging an emphasis on numbers and shiny equipment rather than on people, thereby dehumanizing the arms race. The insensitivity of Fig. 17.4 is dangerous.

References

Barton, J. H., and L. D. Weiler, eds. *International Arms Control: Issues and Agreements.* Stanford, Calif.: Stanford University Press, 1976. See particularly Chapter 11 on "The Economics of Arms and Arms Control," p. 228–248, Chapter 12 on "Regional Arms Control: The European Example," pp. 249–270, and Chapter 13 on "Control of Conventional Arms," pp. 271–287.

Beer, F. A. *Peace Against War: The Ecology of International Violence.* San Francisco: W. H. Freeman, 1981. A textbook.

Bell, C. *The Diplomacy of Detente: The Kissinger Era.* New York: St. Martin's Press,

1977. See particularly Chapter 4 on "Strategic Doctrine and Arms Control: The Nature of Stability," pp. 54–79.

Dougherty, J. E. *How to Think About Arms Control and Disarmament*. New York: Crane, Russak, 1973.

Falk, R. A., and Kim, S. S., eds. *The War System: An Interdisciplinary Approach*. Boulder, Colo.: Westview Press, 1980. A collection of essays on peace, conflict, and conflict resolution.

Gansler, J. S. *The Defense Industry*. Cambridge, Mass.: MIT Press, 1980.

Gilpin, R. *American Scientists and Nuclear Weapons Policy*. Princeton, N.J.: Princeton University Press, 1962.

Jolly, R., ed. *Disarmament and World Development*. New York: Pergamon Press, 1978.

Kaldor, M. "The Role of Arms in Capitalist Economies: The Process of Overdevelopment and Underdevelopment." In *Arms Control and Technological Innovation*, D. Carlton and C. Schaerf, eds., pp. 322–341. New York: John Wiley, 1976.

Legault, A., and G. Lindsey. *The Dynamics of the Nuclear Balance*, rev. ed. Ithaca, N.Y.: Cornell University Press, 1976.

Myrdal, A. *The Game of Disarmament*. New York: Pantheon Books, 1976.

Richardson, L. F. *The Statistics of Deadly Quarrels*. Pittsburgh: Boxwood Press, 1960.

Sivard, R. L. *World Military and Social Expenditures: 1983*. Leesburg, Va.: World Priorities, 1983.

Small, M. and J. D. Singer. *Resort to Arms: International and Civil Wars, 1816–1980* (2d ed.). Beverly Hills, Calif.: Sage Publishers, 1982.

Index

When several references are cited, major discussions or the locations of definition are cited in *italic* type.

407